ROME AND RELIGION

Society of Biblical Literature

Writings from the Greco-Roman World Supplement Series

Ronald F. Hock
Series Editor

Number 5

ROME AND RELIGION:
A CROSS-DISCIPLINARY DIALOGUE ON THE IMPERIAL CULT

ROME AND RELIGION

A Cross-Disciplinary Dialogue on the Imperial Cult

Edited by

Jeffrey Brodd and Jonathan L. Reed

Society of Biblical Literature
Atlanta

ROME AND RELIGION

Copyright © 2011 by the Society of Biblical Literature

All rights reserved. No part of this work may be reproduced or transmitted in any form or by any means, electronic or mechanical, including photocopying and recording, or by means of any information storage or retrieval system, except as may be expressly permitted by the 1976 Copyright Act or in writing from the publisher. Requests for permission should be addressed in writing to the Rights and Permissions Office, Society of Biblical Literature, 825 Houston Mill Road, Atlanta, GA 30329 USA.

Library of Congress Cataloging-in-Publication Data

Rome and religion : a cross-disciplinary dialogue on the imperial cult / edited by Jeffrey Brodd and Jonathan L. Reed.
  p. cm. — (Society of Biblical Literature writings from the greco-roman world supplement series ; v. 5)
  Includes bibliographical references and index.
  ISBN 978-1-58983-612-9 (paper binding : alk. paper) — ISBN 978-1-58983-613-6 (electronic format)
  1. Rome—Religion. 2. Emperor worship—Rome. 3. Church history—Primitive and early church, ca. 30-600. I. Brodd, Jeffrey. II. Reed, Jonathan L.
  BL805.R66 2011
  292.1'721—dc23
                    2011034302

Printed on acid-free, recycled paper
conforming to ANSI/NISO Z39.48-1992 (R1997) and ISO 9706:1994
standards for paper permanence.

Contents

List of Figures ... vii

Foreword ... ix

Abbreviations ... xi

Part 1: Methodological and Theoretical Issues

1. The Cult of the Roman Emperor: Uniter or Divider?, *Karl Galinsky* ... 1

2. Normal Religion, or, Words Fail Us: A Response to Karl Galinsky's "The Cult of the Roman Emperor: Uniter or Divider?," *Steven J. Friesen* ... 23

3. To Complicate Encounters: A Response to Karl Galinsky's "The Cult of the Roman Emperor: Uniter or Divider?," *James Constantine Hanges* ... 27

4. Religion, Roman Religion, Emperor Worship, *Jeffrey Brodd* ... 35

5. Augustan Religion: From Locative to Utopian, *Eric M. Orlin* ... 49

Part 2: The Imperial Cult at Specific Sites

6. Imperial Cult in Roman Corinth: A Response to Karl Galinsky's "The Cult of the Roman Emperor: Uniter or Divider?," *Barbette Stanley Spaeth* ... 61

7. Embedding Rome in Athens, *Nancy Evans* ... 83

8. Honoring Trajan in Pergamum: Imperial Temples in the "Second City," *Daniel N. Schowalter* ... 99

9. Searching for Rome and the Imperial Cult in Galilee: Reassessing Galilee-Rome relations (63 B.C.E. to 70 C.E.), *James S. McLaren* ... 111

Part 3: Christian and Jewish Engagement

10. Roman Imperial Power: A Perspective from the New Testament, *Warren Carter* ... 137

11. The Emperor as Christ and Christian Iconography, *Robin M. Jensen*   153

12. Capitalizing on the Imperial Cult: Some Jewish Perspectives,
    L. Michael White   173

PART 4 : PROSPECTS AND RESPONSES

13. In the Shadow (or not) of the Imperial Cult: A Cooperative Agenda,
    Karl Galinsky   215

14. Response to Karl Galinsky, "In the Shadow (or Not) of the Imperial
    Cult: A Cooperative Agenda," *H. Gregory Snyder*   227

15. Response to Galinsky, White, and Carter, *Nancy Evans*   235

List of Contributors   241

Subject Index   243

Index of Ancient Sources   255

List of Figures

Chapter Six

6.1. Plan of Forum of Roman Corinth. *Courtesy of the American School of Classical Studies, Corinth Excavations, C. K. Williams II.*
6.2. Plan of Roman Corinth. *Courtesy of the American School of Classical Studies, Corinth Excavations, C. K. Williams II.*
6.3. Statue of Augustus from Julian Basilica: S-1116. *Courtesy of the American School of Classical Studies, Corinth Excavations, I. Ioannidou-L. Bartzioti.*
6.4. Statue of Gaius Caesar from Julian Basilica: S-1065. *Courtesy of the American School of Classical Studies, Corinth Excavations, I. Ioannidou-L. Bartzioti.*
6.5. Fragmentary Statue of Lucius Caesar from Julian Basilica: S-1080. *Courtesy of the American School of Classical Studies, Corinth Excavations, I. Ioannidou-L. Bartzioti.*
6.6. Base of the Monument of the Augustales in Forum. *Courtesy of Margaret Laird.*
6.7. Reconstruction of Monument of the Augustales in Forum. *Courtesy of Margaret Laird.*
6.8. Corinthian Coin with the Nero (obv.) and Genius Coloniae (rev). *Corinth* 6, nr. 57. *Courtesy of the American School of Classical Studies, Corinth Excavations, P. Dellatolas.*
6.9. Corinthian Coin with Fortuna Coloniae crowning Nero. *Corinth* 6, no. 54. *Courtesy of the American School of Classical Studies, Corinth Excavations, P. Dellatolas.*
6.10. Perspective Reconstruction of Scaenae Frons of Theater with Sculptural Assemblage. *Courtesy of the American School of Classical Studies, Corinth Excavations, J. A. Herbst.*
6.11. Head of Trajan from Theatre. S-364/3660/3700/unnumbered fragment. *Courtesy of the American School of Classical Studies, Corinth Excavations, I. Ioannidou-L. Bartzioti.*
6.12. Portrait Head of Faustina the Younger from Southwest Area of the Forum. S-2702. *Courtesy of the American School of Classical Studies, Corinth Excavations, I. Ioannidou-L. Bartzioti.*

6.13. Corinthian Coin with Livia as Ceres. *RPC* 1.2, nr. 1150. *Photo Credit: bpk, Berlin / Muenzkabinett, Staatliche Kunstsammlungen, Dresden, Germany / Art Resource, NY.*
6.14. Detail of Mosaic from Floor of Central Temple in Sanctuary of Demeter and Kore. *Courtesy of the American School of Classical Studies, Corinth Excavations, I. Ioannidou-L. Bartzioti..*

CHAPTER EIGHT

8.1. Acropolis of Pergamum from the southwest. *All photos courtesy of Daniel N. Schowalter (author).*
8.2. Vaulted chambers supporting the Trajaneum platform.
8.3. *Anastylosis* of the Trajaneum by the German Archaeological Institute.
8.4. Reconstructed entablature of the Trajaneum.

CHAPTER ELEVEN

11.1. The Good Shepherd, from the Catacomb of Callixtus, Crypt of Lucina, mid-third century C.E., Rome. *Photo credit: Estelle Brettman, copyright International Catacomb Society.*
11.2. Apse mosaic from the Mausoleum of Sta. Contanza, mid-fourth century C.E., Rome. *Photo credit: Robin M. Jensen (author).*
11.3. Passion sarcophagus, ca. 340 C.E., Rome. Now in the Museo Pio Cristiano, Vatican Museums. *Photo credit: Vanni/Art Resource, New York.*
11.4. Sarcophagus with central christogram mounted on a cross, ca. 340–350 C.E., Rome. Now in the Museo Pio Cristiano, Vatican Museums. *Photo credit: Alinari/Art Resource, New York.*
11.5. Coin (*nummus*) of Constantine I, 319–320 C.E. *Photo courtesy of the American Numismatic Society.*
11.6. Christian funerary epitaph, mid-fourth century C.E., Rome (Basilica of San Lorenzo fuori le mura). *Photo credit: Robin M. Jensen (author).*
11.7. Coin (*nummus*) of Constantine I, 327–328 C.E. *Photo courtesy of the American Numismatic Society.*
11.8. Prizes of the Pancratium, detail from a Roman mosaic of the spectacles from Batten Zamour, mid-fourth century C.E. Now in the Musée Archeologique, Gafsa, Tunisia. *Photo credit: Gilles Mermet/Art Resource, New York.*
11.9. Dome mosaic, Neonian (Orthodox) Baptistery, Ravenna, ca. mid-fifth century C.E. *Photo credit: Robin M. Jensen (author).*
11.10. Dome mosaic, baptistery of Sta. Restituta, Naples, early-fifth century C.E. *Photo credit: Robin M. Jensen (author).*
11.11. Sarcophagus with magi and Daniel, mid-fourth century C.E., Rome. Now in the Museo Pio Cristiano, Vatican Museums. *Photo credit: Vanni/Art Resource, New York.*

Foreword

Formally speaking, this *Cross-Disciplinary Dialogue on the Imperial Cult* is the print version of an actual dialogue that took place over the course of one year, during sessions at three meetings of the Society of Biblical Literature—the 2008 Annual Meeting in Boston, the 2009 International Meeting in Rome, and the 2009 Annual Meeting in New Orleans. These sessions were jointly sponsored by the Society for Ancient Mediterranean Religions and three SBL program units: Archaeology of Religion in the Roman World, Art and Religions of Antiquity, and Greco-Roman Religions. Beyond these formal settings, in a very real sense and in keeping with the vision of the various presenters, the dialogue continues and the number of participants increases.

The catalyst for the dialogue was Karl Galinsky, Floyd Cailloux Centennial Professor of Classics at the University of Texas and recipient of the Max Planck Research Award for studies of history and memory. He initiated the cross-disciplinary conversation in Boston with a paper titled *The Roman Cult of the Emperor: Uniter or Divider?* Respondents at that session and subsequently in Rome focused on theory, method, archaeology, epigraphy, and art as they relate to the study of the imperial cult. Finally, at New Orleans, most of the papers focused specifically on the relationship of early Christianity and Judaism to the imperial cult. Professor Galinsky's second paper, *In the Shadow (or not) of the Imperial Cult: A Cooperative Agenda*, together with responses, served to conclude the series.

Along with being both catalyst and closer, Karl Galinsky brought to the dialogue an extraordinary depth and breadth of learning with regard to the imperial cult. A leading authority on imperial Rome, he is author of Princeton University Press's *Augustan Culture*, a landmark synthesis and interpretation of Augustus's rule based on literary, artistic, and archaeological evidence; he edited *The Cambridge Companion to the Age of Augustus* (2005); and his biography of Augustus is about to be published by Cambridge University Press. A University Distinguished Teaching Professor, Professor Galinsky has directed several National Endowment for the Humanities Summer Seminars at the American Academy in Rome on the topic of Roman religion and culture, which have also included and profoundly influenced several SBL members over the years.

The goal of this project was to bring together classicists, biblical and religious scholars, historians, and archaeologists to discuss the study of religions in a Roman context, using as a focal point the imperial cult. This topic has been especially prominent of late in New Testament studies, fueled in large measure by the prolific writings of Richard Horsley and under the influence of John Dominic Crossan. Behind this intense interest in the Roman imperial cult are trends in both academia and realities in geopolitics. Among them are the impact of postcolonial studies, debates over the "new Paul," the recognition of the interconnectedness of religion and politics, and the serious treatment of archaeological and art historical evidence. Yet even as interest in the imperial cult is resurrected after Adolf Deissmann's *Licht vom Osten* from over a century ago, we wonder about excesses or mischaracterizations of the phenomenon among New Testament scholars, and more specifically about what happens when the imperial cult is examined not exclusively and over against the Pauline Christ cult, but within the broader context of Roman religion, the study of ancient Mediterranean culture and society generally, and the rise of Christianity in its Roman context over the long haul.

One of the main themes emerging from this dialogue involves the diversity of the imperial cult (prompting some participants to prefer the plural "imperial cults"). As Karl Galinsky points out in his opening paper, this diversity is easily—and too oftentimes—missed: "It is inevitable that in this nascent atmosphere of contextualizing the New Testament with the Roman Empire the latter in particular often comes across as more monolithic and undifferentiated than it was in actuality. This in part due to one impetus behind the new interpretive direction, that is to mark out the Gospels and Paul's letters as anti-imperial, if not anticolonial, because today 'empire' has the predominant connotations of oppression, injustice, and colonialism. Empire, *ipso facto*, is evil empire..." (p. 2).

This theme of diversity sets the stage for the volume's wide-ranging treatment of issues and interrelated themes. Attending to a variety of spatial locales (e.g. Corinth, Athens, Pergamum, Galilee), to a rich array of Jewish and Christian phenomena, and to pertinent theoretical and methodological concerns, the authors explore a spectrum of aspects radiating outward from the central connecting phenomenon of imperial cult, while looking across disciplines. Most of the papers in this volume interact with one another, and retain aspects of their presentation in oral form. In other words, this print rendition remains essentially a dialogue, a dialogue that the reader is invited to join.

Abbreviations

Ancient Authors and Texts

Appian, *Mith.*	*Mithridates*
Apuleius, *Metam.*	*Metamorphoses*
Arrian, *Anab.*	*Anabasis*
Athenaeus, *Deipn.*	*Deipnosophistae*
Athenagoras, *Leg.*	*Legatio pro Christianis*
Cod. theod.	*Codex Theodosianus*
Cyprian, *Laps.*	*De lapsis*
Dig.	*Digesta*
Eusebius, *Vit. Const.*	*Vita Constantini*
Herodotus, *Hist.*	*Historiae*
Horace, *Carm.*	*Carmena*
Jerome, *Epist.*	*Epistulae*
Josephus, *A.J.*	*Antiquitates judaicae*
Josephus, *B.J.*	*Bellum judaicum*
Josephus, *Vita*	*Vita*
Justin, *1 Apol.*	*Apologia 1*
Lactantius, *Mort.*	*De morte persecutorum*
Pausanias, *Descr.*	*Graeciae description*
Philo, *Legat.*	*Legatio ad Gaium*
Philo, *Mos.* 1, 2	*De vita Mosis* I, II
Plato, *Resp.*	*Respublica*
Pliny the Elder, *Nat.*	*Naturalis historia*
Pliny the Younger, *Ep.*	*Epistulae*
Plutarch, *Ant.*	*Antonius*
Plutarch, *Demetr.*	*Demetrius*
Plutarch, *Sull.*	*Sulla*
Prudentius, *Cath.*	*Cathemerinon*
Res gest. divi Aug.	(Augustus) *Res Gestae divi Augusti*
Strabo, *Geog.*	*Geographica*
Suetonius, *Aug.*	*Divus Augustus*
Tacitus, *Ann.*	*Annales*

Tertullian, *Apol.*   *Apologeticus*
Tertullian, *Cor.*   *De corona militis*

Periodicals, Series, and Collections

AB	Anchor Bible
ABull	*The Art Bulletin*
ACW	Ancient Christian Writers
AE	*L'année épigraphique*
Aeg	*Aegyptus*
AGJU	Arbeiten zur Geschichte des antiken Judentums und des Urchristentums
AHR	*American Historical Review*
AJA	*American Journal of Archaeology*
AJP	*American Journal of Philology*
ANRW	*Aufstieg und Niedergang der römischen Welt*
ANSMN	*American Numismatic Society Museum Notes*
ARIDSup	*Analecta Romana Instituti Danici Supplementum*
BCHSup	*Bulletin de correspondance hellénique. Supplement*
BibInt	*Biblical Interpretation*
BJS	Brown Judaic Studies
BMC	*British Museum Catalogue of Greek Coins*
BR	*Biblical Research*
CAH	*Cambridge Ancient History*
CBQ	*Catholic Biblical Quarterly*
CCSL	Corpus Christianorum: Series latina
CSEL	Corpus scriptorum ecclesiasticorum latinorum
CH	*Church History*
CIG	*Corpus inscriptionum graecarum*
CIJ	*Corpus inscriptionum judaicarum*
CIL	*Corpus inscriptionum latinarum*
CJ	*Classical Journal*
CSEL	Corpus scriptorum ecclesiasticorum latinorum
CSJH	Chicago Studies in the History of Judaism
GNS	Good News Studies
HDR	Harvard Dissertations in Religion
Hermeneia	Hermeneia: a critical and historical commentary on the Bible
HTR	*Harvard Theological Review*
HTS	Harvard Theological Studies
IBerenike	Joyce Reynolds, "Inscriptions," in *Excavations at Sidi Khrebish Benghazi (Berenice). Vol. 1: Buildings, Coins, Inscriptions, Architectural Decoration* (ed. J. A. Lloyd)

IEJ	*Israel Exploration Journal*
IG	*Inscriptiones graecae*
IGR	*Inscriptiones graecae ad res romanas pertinentes*
INJ	*Israel Numismatic Journal*
Int	*Interpretation*
IvE	*Die Inscriften von Ephesos*
IvP	*Die Inschriften von Pergamon*
JAAR	*Journal of the American Academy of Religion*
JAF	*Journal of American Folklore*
JBL	*Journal of Biblical Literature*
JEH	*Journal of Ecclesiastical History*
JMS	*Journal of Mithraic Studies*
JQR	*Jewish Quarterly Review*
JR	*Journal of Religion*
JRASup	Journal of Roman Archaeology Supplementary Series
JRS	*Journal of Roman Studies*
JRSM	Journal of Roman Studies Monographs
JSJ	*Journal for the Study of Judaism in the Persian, Hellenistic, and Roman Period*
JSNT	*Journal for the Study of the New Testament*
JSNTSup	Journal for the Study of the New Testament: Supplement Series
JTS	*Journal of Theological Studies*
LHBOTS	Library of Hebrew Bible/Old Testament Studies
LSTS	Library of Second Temple Studies
MAMA	*Monumenta Asiae Minoris Antiqua*
MH	*Museum helveticum*
NovT	*Novum Testamentum*
NovTSup	Supplements to *Novum Testamentum*
NTS	*New Testament Studies*
OGIS	*Orientis graeci inscriptiones selectae*
PCPhS	*Proceedings of the Cambridge Philological Society*
REL	*Revue des études latines*
SBLRBS	Society of Biblical Literature Resources for Biblical Study
SBLSymS	Society of Biblical Literature Symposium Series
ScAnt	*Scienze dell'Antichità*
SEG	*Supplementum epigraphicum graecum*
SemeiaSt	Semeia Studies
SIG	W. Dittenberger, ed., *Sylloge inscriptionum graecarum*. 4 vols. Chicago: Ares, 1999.
SJLA	Studies in Judaism in Late Antiquity
SNTSMS	Society for New Testament Studies Monograph Series
Spec	*Speculum*

TAPA	*Transactions of the American Philological Association*
TSAJ	Texte und Studien zum antiken Judentum
USQR	*Union Seminary Quarterly Review*
VCSup	Supplements to *Vigiliae Christianae*
WGRWSup	Writings from the Greco-Roman World Supplement Series
WUNT	Wissenschaftliche Untersuchungen zum Neuen Testament
ZAC	*Zeitschrift für Antikes Christentum*
ZPE	*Zeitschrift für Papyrologie und Epigraphik*

Chapter 1
The Cult of the Roman Emperor: Uniter or Divider?

Karl Galinsky

To an ancient historian the exceptional attention the cult of the Roman emperor has attracted of late—its current popularity seems second only to its standing at the height of the empire—may come as somewhat of a surprise. After all, it is only one of many phenomena, including religious phenomena, that were operative in the culture of that period. The reason for the current upswing is, of course, the Columbus-like discovery of the historical context of the New Testament by biblical scholars. As an inveterate historical contextualizer, who has seen the swing of the pendulum in literary interpretation between the historicizing approach and others that are blissfully unencumbered by such considerations,[1] I have to admit I was amazed to see that this orientation in New Testament studies, as evidenced especially by the use of the label "new" in Pauline studies, has been hailed as a genuinely new departure[2]—after some two thousand years. I should have it that easy as a classicist. The reasons for it, however, are timely, and I am delighted, therefore, to look at the imperial cult in this new interpretive context, to contribute some perspectives to this dialogue, and, since this is a continuing project, to point out some emphases and directions that we might usefully explore.

---

1. Cf. my introductory chapter to the collection of essays I edited in 1992: Karl Galinsky, ed., *The Interpretation of Roman Poetry: Empiricism or Hermeneutics?* (Studien zur klassischen Philologie 67; Frankfurt: Lang, 1992). The term "New Historicism" was used at the time to signal the return to a more historicizing orientation. Since the term "new" can be used meaningfully only so many times, trends after the New Historicism have had to employ different labels, the current emphasis on memory being a good example; see the Max Planck Research Award project I am directing (http://www.utexas.edu/research/memoria).

2. An acknowledged ancestor, of course, is Adolf Deissmann, *Licht vom Osten: Das Neue Testament und die neuentdeckten Texte der hellenistisch-römischen Welt* (4th ed.; 1908; repr., Tübingen: Mohr, 1923).

First, some basics. It is inevitable that in this nascent atmosphere of contextualizing the New Testament with the Roman Empire the latter in particular often comes across as more monolithic and undifferentiated than it was in actuality. This in part due to one impetus behind the new interpretive direction, that is to mark out the Gospels and Paul's letters as anti-imperial, if not anticolonial, because today "empire" has the predominant connotations of oppression, injustice, and colonialism.[3] Empire, *ipso facto*, is evil empire; the phrase, for instance, is quickly applied to Gal 1:4, where Paul speaks of deliverance from αἰῶνος τοῦ ἐνεστῶτος πονηροῦ—to a Greek audience, πονηροῦ might mean no more, or less, than "full of toils," which makes excellent sense in this context of deliverance. Add to this that for centuries the church, in various denominations, was a collaborator, whether active or tacit, with empires and you can see the desire to break free of all that and situate the Jesus movement firmly in an agenda of social justice and more. The resulting schema, therefore, tends to set up dichotomies and goes on to privilege them. Further, the search for coded evidence in the texts[4] often owes much, without overt admission and perhaps awareness, to some of the literary hermeneutics we have worked through in the past four decades and with which I am quite familiar especially from my own work on Vergil,[5] including the implied reader and the incessant search for subversiveness.[6] Now, I am not asserting that some of this does not have its place nor am I trying to be Pliny or Aristides reincarnate and sing *laudes imperii*.[7] I do recommend, however, Amy Chua's recent book because it has no axes to grind and singles out religious toleration and pluralism as a key reason for the rise of hyperpowers, including Rome,

---

3. Prominent examples are Richard A. Horsley, ed., *Paul and Empire: Religion and Power in Roman Imperial Society* (Harrisburg, Pa.: Trinity Press International, 1997); Richard A. Horsley, *Jesus and Empire: The Kingdom of God and the New World Disorder* (Philadelphia: Augsburg Fortress, 2003) and *In the Shadow of Empire: Reclaiming the Bible as a History of Faithful Resistance* (Louisville, Ky.: Westminster John Knox, 2008); the proceedings of the conference at Union Theological Seminary in Brigitte Kahl, Davina C. Lopez, and Hal Taussig, eds., "The New Testament and Roman Empire: Shifting Paradigms for Interpretation," *USQR* 59 (2005); and John Dominic Crossan, *God and Empire: Jesus Against Rome, Then and Now* (San Francisco: HarperSanFrancisco, 2007).

4. Esp. with reference to James C. Scott, *Weapons of the Weak: Everyday Forms of Peasant Resistance* (New Haven, Conn.: Yale University Press, 1985) and James C. Scott, *Domination and the Arts of Resistance: Hidden Transcripts* (New Haven, Conn.: Yale University Press, 1990).

5. Karl Galinsky, "Clothes for the Emperor," *Arion* 10 (2003): 143–69, a review article.

6. Implied reader: Wolfgang Iser, *The Implied Reader: Patterns of Communication in Prose Fiction from Bunyan to Beckett* (Baltimore: Johns Hopkins University Press, 1974); subversiveness *über alles*: Susan Rubin Suleiman, *Subversive Intent: Gender, Politics, and Avant-Garde* (Cambridge, Mass.: Harvard University Press, 1990).

7. Cf. the frequently cited chapter by P. A. Brunt, "*Laus Imperii*," in *Roman Imperial Themes* (ed. P. A. Brunt; New York: Oxford University Press, 1990), 288–323.

to global dominance.[8] What I am asserting is that all major subjects in this discussion, whether the administration of the Roman Empire, the living conditions under it, and even Paul's perspectives, cannot be reduced to a single, let alone simple, matrix. The imperial cult is a paradigm in this regard.

In the sensible words of Beard, North, and Price, whose authoritative and accessible work is not cited in these discussions as much as one might expect (nor is the *Cambridge Ancient History*, among others), there was "no such thing as '*the* imperial cult.'"[9] In other words, and to keep sticking to basics, it is important to remind ourselves of what the cult of the emperor is, and what it is not. Let me start with the latter. It was not a centrally steered phenomenon, with the exception of the four provincial cults, two in the east, two in the west, established under Augustus, with his permission, at the initiative of the provincials. They, and the additional cult for Tiberius at Smyrna (and the short-lived Caligulan experiment at Miletus), came without dogma. It is misplaced, certainly at this level, to superimpose an alien matrix and speak of concepts like "imperial theology" and "the gospel of Caesar." The policy of the emperors is spelled out, retrospectively, by Dio Cassius (52.35) in the advice he has Maecenas give to Augustus, and I can refer to Duncan Fishwick's excellent treatment of the issue.[10] The bottom line is that emperors should not get involved in setting up cult, especially to their living presences. The underlying reason is the tradition, well attested, even in its key phrases, both by literary (Plutarch, Tacitus) and epigraphical sources, that "the ruler really becomes a god in the minds [*animis*] and hearts of his subjects."[11] Or, to return to Dio, "if you are ἀγαθός as a man and rule καλῶς, the whole earth will be your hallowed precinct, all cities your temples, and all men your statues [ἀγάλματα] since within their thoughts you will ever be enshrined and glorified."

Now, this is certainly one aspect of the vast panorama of variegated local practices that comprise the umbrella phenomenon that we call "the imperial cult." Of course the locals did not simply leave things at carrying the emperor just within the hearts and minds, but, in the decentralized manner typical of the Roman Empire, they translated their attitudes into the material evidence we know, or know of, of cult places and images. None of them were imposed by the Romans, but they clearly were part of the environment for many inhabitants of

---

8. Amy Chua, *Day of Empire: How Hyperpowers Rise to Global Dominance and Why They Fall* (New York: Doubleday, 2007).

9. Mary Beard, John North, and Simon Price, *Religions of Rome*. Vol. 1: *A History* (Cambridge: Cambridge University Press, 1998), 348. S. R. R. Price, *Rituals and Power: The Roman Imperial Cult in Asia Minor* (Cambridge: Cambridge University Press, 1984) is another indispensable resource.

10. Duncan Fishwick, "Dio and Maecenas: The Emperor and the Ruler Cult," *Phoenix* 44 (1990): 267–75.

11. Ibid., 247.

the empire. "Negotiation" has become the term of choice here: Simon Price has famously argued that the imperial cult was a means, especially for the denizens of the east, of negotiating and constructing the reality of the Roman Empire.[12] The early Christians, who lived in these cities and towns, did of course the same; I can refer to the sensible formulations by Warren Carter whose central thesis is that John's Gospel is a work of imperial negotiation. He emphasizes that this requires "modifying a monolithic stance of opposition by attending to a whole span of practices and attitudes signified by the terms 'negotiation,' 'interaction,' and engagement.... The Gospel's encounter with Rome is much more multifaceted and complex than allowed by a limited and ahistorical binary construct of 'us against them' of opposition to Rome."[13] Conversely, that is also a salutary perspective for considering the imperial cult.

Besides its tremendous diversity, let me highlight some of its aspects that so far have not received much attention from New Testament scholars. One is, as Simon Price already documented at length,[14] that the cult of the emperor often was intertwined with that of other gods. There are, to be sure, freestanding examples, such as at Aphrodisias and Ephesus. As Steve Friesen has well pointed out, in this provincial capital "the municipal imperial cult dominated the upper agora, the sector where social organization was administered."[15] Next on the spectrum come temples like the *tholos* on the Athenian Acropolis—in a prominent location, to be sure, but much less intrusive than Agrippa's temple in the agora and clearly overshadowed by the Parthenon and its companions.[16] We can add to this category the small temple at Petra, which has been reasonably identified as an imperial cult temple and gleamed with "imperially associated luxury material,"[17] that is, white marble. But in many other sites the picture that emerges is far more varied,[18] involving dedications to Theoi Sebastoi in conjunction with others, such as Asclepius (Pergamum, Rhodiapolis; cf., in Spain, Aesculapius Augustus [*CIL* 2.2004] and Iuppiter Pantheus Augustus [*CIL* 2.2008]). Examples from Pisidia: Theoi Sebastoi, Zeus Megistos Sarapis and *patris* (Adada); Apollo Clarius, Theoi

---

12. Price, *Rituals and Power*.
13. Warren Carter, *John and Empire: Initial Explorations* (New York: T&T Clark, 2008), 13.
14. Price, *Rituals and Power*, 146–56.
15. Steven J. Friesen, *Imperial Cults and the Apocalypse of John: Reading Revelation in the Ruins* (New York: Oxford University Press, 2001), 102.
16. Concise description by Heidi Hänlein-Schäfer, Veneratio Augusti: *Eine Studie zu den Tempeln der ersten römischen Kaiser* (Rome: Bretschneider, 1985), 156–59.
17. Sara Karz Reid, *The Small Temple: A Roman Imperial Cult Building in Petra, Jordan* (Gorgias Dissertations in Near Eastern Studies 7; Piscataway, N.J.: Gorgias Press, 2005), 187.
18. See the compilation by Price, *Rituals and Power*, 249–74; also Steven J. Friesen, *Twice Neokoros: Ephesus, Asia, and the Cult of the Flavian Imperial Family* (Leiden: Brill, 1993), 169–208.

Sebastoi, *patris* (Sagalassus). Or, to change the scenery for a moment, at Thuburbo Maius in Africa Proconsularis the Capitolium was dedicated to its traditional deities and Marcus Aurelius and Commodus; another shading, for instance at Dougga, is the dedication of the Capitolium to the usual triad "for the well-being of Marcus Aurelius and Lucius Verus."[19] Or, in Egypt: joint oath to Augustus and Zeus Eleutherios;[20] in Macedonia: monthly sacrifices to Zeus and Augustus (*SEG* XXXV.44); in Eresos: honorific inscription for a man who was "priest and high priest for life of the Sebastoi and of all the other gods and goddesses" (*IGR* 4.18). And even in Ephesus: sacrifices to Asclepius and the Sebastoi (*IvE* 3.719), and to Demeter and the Sebastoi (*IvE* 2.213); the basilica on the upper agora was similarly dedicated to Ephesian Artemis, Divus Augustus, Tiberius, and the demos of the Ephesians. In other words, and this is one of the directions I suggest, we need to look yet more closely at instances of this kind of embedding of the "imperial cult"—it cannot be treated as an easily "isolable phenomenon, and hence potentially a more easily isolable competitor for Christianity."[21] After all, it is the cult of Artemis, and not the imperial cult, that is the issue during Paul's extended stay at Ephesus (Acts 19), even though there was a small Augusteum that was somehow connected with the Artemision. In short, it is an overstatement to label the cult of the emperor as "the dominant cult in a large part of the empire."[22] On the material level alone, the claim does not stand up in light of the evidence adduced by Price for temple building in general.[23]

The emperors clearly realized this when it came to approving requests for additional imperial cults. In connection with the cult at Smyrna,[24] one condition was that there should not be too much competition around for a new cult, and such places were hard to find. For the municipal cults, that was not a criterion and the cult of the emperor was simply added to those of the other divinities. Similarly, the Christian apologist Athenagoras (ca. 133–190) parallels this aspect of the material and cultic evidence when he places the imperial cult in the con-

---

19. Thuburbo Maius: Paul-Albert Février, "Religion et domination dans l'Afrique romaine," *Collection de l'École française de Rome* 225 (1996): 789–812; Dougga: Claude Poinssot, *Les ruines de Dougga* (Tunis: Secrétariat d'État à l'éducation nationale, Institut national d'archéologie et arts, 1983), 34–38.

20. Johanna Helena Maria de Jong, "Emperors in Egypt: The Representation and Perception of Roman Imperial Power in Greek Papyrus Texts from Egypt, AD 193–284" (Ph.D diss., Radboud Universiteit Nijmegen, 2006), 71.

21. Beard, North, and Price, *Religions of Rome 1*, 360. For a different perspective regarding Ephesus see Friesen, *Twice Neokoros*.

22. So, for instance, N. T. Wright, "Paul's Gospel and Caesar's Empire." Online: http://www.ntwrightpage.com/Wright_Paul_Caesar_Empire.pdf.

23. Price, *Rituals and Power*, 164–65.

24. Detailed discussion by Friesen, *Twice Neokoros*, 15–21.

text of a lengthy enumeration of Greek men, such as Heracles and Perseus, and Syrian women, such as Semiramis, that were deified (*Leg.* 30.1–2). His particular target, one that also figures in Justin (*1 Apol.* 29.4) and others, is Antinous. But Antinous is not isolated in an imperial context. Rather, he is part of a tradition of pagan deifications. Similarly, as Fergus Millar has noted, when provincial magistrates in later times questioned the Christians who were brought before them, they "applied the test of the recognition of the imperial cult, but along with that of the cults of the other gods."[25]

What I am cautioning against is looking at the imperial cult as if it were the overwhelming, let alone only, cult or religious phenomenon in town whose presence early Christianity had to negotiate. That presence extends to terminology like *sōtēr* and "son of god." These terms are anything but unique to the imperial cult. *Sōtēr* had been a cult appellation for centuries—Zeus Soter, Artemis Soteira, and so forth, and then of course we have Ptolemy Soter and the soteriology of other Hellenistic dynasts. These are, to use the basic formulation of J. M. Kitagawa, examples of this-worldly salvation, and not of other-worldly salvation.[26] They were civic cults and so was the imperial cult. The degree of effusiveness of the blessings attributed to the emperor would vary from individual cult to individual cult; in Egypt for instance, references to the emperor as *sōtēr* were not frequent.[27] The central point is that while the emperor could be praised for the blessings in this world he was not alone in this. Instead, he had plenty of divine (and human) predecessors and contemporaries.

This is another aspect, then, of the embedding. Due to the work of Simon Price in particular, we are well informed about the details of the setting of the imperial cult, especially in the cities of the Greek East and their cultural and social network. The significant corollary is, as he put it succinctly, that "the existence of Roman rule intensified this dominance of Greek culture."[28] In this context, resistance cannot be isolated as resistance to Rome or the imperial cult alone, but to a whole nexus of phenomena, and that is another, differentiated issue that needs, at least at times, to be more clearly addressed in the contextualization of the New Testament with its times. Obviously, Christian reaction or negotiation could cover a wide spectrum. For instance, the thrust of Warren Carter's most

---

25. Fergus Millar, "The Imperial Cult and the Persecutions," in *Le culte des souverains dans l'empire romain* (ed. Willem Den Boer; Entretiens sur l'Antiquité classique 19; Vandoeuvres/Geneva: Fondation Hardt, 1973), 164.

26. Joseph M. Kitagawa, "Primitive, Classical, and Modern Religions: A Perspective on Understanding the History of Religions," in *The History of Religions: Essays on the Problem of Understanding* (ed. Joseph M. Kitagawa; Chicago: University of Chicago Press, 1967), 39–65.

27. See Friederike Herklotz, *Prinzeps und Pharao: Der Kult des Augustus in Ägypten* (Oikumene 4; Frankfurt: Verlag Antike, 2007).

28. Price, *Rituals and Power*, 100.

recent book *John and Empire* is that this Gospel is aimed at Jesus believers in late first-century Ephesus who are perceived as having "overaccommodated" and being "without appropriate societal distance, no longer viewing active participation in imperial society as a troublesome act."[29] And, indeed, where should these individuals draw the line? Some may have continued their involvement in civic activities because they cared about the demos of the Ephesians, without necessarily being ardent patrons of the imperial cult. Were such degrees of separation possible? Are we imposing too monolithic a scheme by saying it was not? We will never have conclusive evidence, one way or the other. What is clear is that the Roman system, under which many cities of the Greek East flourished, was a comprehensive and, at the same time, elastic order of things that was based on such interdependences. If you were an enemy of the Roman order, to use the title of one of Ramsay MacMullen's books,[30] could you take on just one aspect of it, like the imperial cult, without rejecting the remaining network? What is imperial here and what is local? The overarching notion of resistance to Rome tends to blur such lines. Similarly, what was the real target—the imperial cult per se or the imperial cult as the representative of the cult of the traditional gods in which it was embedded?

A connected topic that I can only sketch here and recommend for further inquiry is that of religious pluralism. This goes beyond the multiplicity of civic cults I have just mentioned. Rather, the issue is to situate early Christianity more precisely within the broadening of religious life in the Roman Empire. As defined by scholars such as John North[31] and Richard Gordon,[32] the story here is "one of development from religion as embedded in the city-state to religion as a choice of differentiated groups offering different qualities of religious doctrine, different experiences, insights, or just different myths and stories to make sense of the absurdity of human experience."[33] For good reason North rejects the view that this development came about as a result of Christianity emerging from the projection of sharply differentiated, competing versions of Judaism into the Gentile world. Instead, he looks at the wider context of social changes and movements of population in the Mediterranean world—a topic that since then has been treated

---

29. Carter, *John and Empire*, 381.
30. Ramsey MacMullen, *Enemies of the Public Order* (Cambridge, Mass.: Harvard University Press, 1966). His discussion merrily lumps together all the usual troublemakers: brigands, highwaymen, pirates, and professors of philosophy.
31. John North, "The Development of Religious Pluralism," in *The Jews Among Christians and Pagans in the Roman Empire* (ed. Judith Lieu, John North, and Tessa Rajak; London: Routledge, 1992), 174–93.
32. Richard Gordon, "Reality, Evocation, and Boundaries in the Mysteries of Mithra," *JMS* 3 (1980): 19–99.
33. North, "Religious Pluralism," 178.

excellently by Nicholas Purcell.[34] Above all, North points to the striking growth of autonomous religious groups in the third and second centuries B.C.E. in Rome, especially in connection with the worship of Dionysus and the Roman state's reaction to it which amounted to saber rattling rather than relentless persecution. One consequence is that the Roman state, with its emphasis on "locative" religion by the first century C.E. had seen its share of "utopian" religions[35] and pursued its usual policy of laissez-faire; the reaction of the authorities in Thessalonica, after hearing the Jewish allegations against Paul and Jason that they had been acting "contrary to the decrees (*dogmata*) of Caesar, saying there is another king—Jesus" was simply to take a security bond and let them go (Acts 17:7-9). We are still far removed from the erratic, and mostly local, use of the imperial cult as a loyalty test in later times; compare Trajan's policy of don't ask, don't tell.[36] And even if Acts is not historical at this point, what might that say about its own level of accommodation? It surely is relevant to note here that, as David Balch has argued, the theme of "welcoming all nations" is borrowed from imperial rhetoric.[37]

Two tasks, then. One is to contextualize the place of the Jesus movement within this evolving pluralism of the creation of distinct religious identities, defined in part as "existence as autonomous groups with their own organization or authority structure."[38] The other is the interface of the imperial cult with this phenomenon. For even if that cult was never a "utopian," eschatological salvation cult that attempted to control morality and the like, it provided distinct identity, a great deal of autonomy—even if civic, there was no *Gleichschaltung*—and it had its own authority structure. I would put the impact of the cult mostly in terms of *resonance*—not hard power, but soft power. It tapped into many strands, making it a more complex item to negotiate for early Christianity, and for us to assess that negotiation. Besides the factors I have just mentioned, let me list three others:

(1) It was part of the wider Augustan phenomenon of broadening civic participation, including on the part of freedmen and slaves, via religious activities. The municipal imperial cults in the east and west and the Augustales are prime

---

34. Nicholas Purcell, "Romans in the Roman World," in *The Cambridge Companion to the Age of Augustus* (ed. Karl Galinsky; Cambridge: Cambridge University Press, 2005), 85–105.

35. I am using the distinctions refined by Jonathan Z. Smith, *Map is not Territory: Studies in the History of Religions* (Leiden: Brill, 1978).

36. In his famous rescript to Pliny; Pliny the Younger, *Ep.* 10.96–97. On the imperial cult and the persecutions see Millar, "Imperial Cult."

37. David Balch, "The Cultural Origin of 'Receiving All Nations' in Luke-Acts: Alexander the Great or Roman Social Policy?" in *Early Christianity and Classical Culture: Comparative Essays in Honor of Abraham J. Malherbe* (ed. John Fitzgerald, Thomas Olbricht, and L. Michael White; NovTSup 110. Leiden: Brill, 2003), 483–500.

38. North, "Religious Pluralism," 184.

examples.³⁹ And this participation could evidence another dimension of pluralism: at the time of Nero, for example, Julia Severa, descended from the royal line of Ankara, was priestess of the imperial cult in Akmoneia in western Phrygia and also gave the building for the local synagogue, "even though she clearly was not Jewish nor a Jewish 'sympathizer.'" ⁴⁰

2) While they were mostly municipal cults and, as emphasized earlier, not easily isolable, their numbers and spread also gave them a supra-local dimension, in addition to the figure of the emperor himself. Ambassadors from Mytilene, for example, went as far as Tarraco in Spain to let everyone know Mytilene now had a cult of the emperor.⁴¹

3) Their terminology could overlap with that of other-worldly salvation cults that were part of the spectrum of religious pluralism as we have just defined it. In Egypt, for instance, the appellation *theos ek theou* is paralleled mostly in inscriptions from the cult of Isis and Sarapis.⁴² Relevant in this context is the intriguing, though vague, evidence that H. W. Pleket collected some forty years ago about some imperial cult practices at Pergamum approximating those of mystery religions; inter alia, the priests are called Sebastophants.⁴³

Another important development at Augustus's time rounds out the picture. I am referring to the provincial coinage. Until 1992, there existed no systematic collection of the coinage issued by over two hundred cities around the Roman Empire; our perceptions were shaped mostly by the standard catalogues (British Museum etc.) with the issues of the imperial mints (and, incidentally, the emperors did not design the coins they issued).⁴⁴ Like the municipal cults, the local mints were autonomous and under no pressure from Rome. Yet they increasingly

---

39. Overview in Karl Galinsky, *Augustan Culture* (Princeton: Princeton University Press, 1996), 288–331; cf. Karl Galinsky, "Continuity and Change: Religion in the Augustan Semi-Century," in *A Companion to Roman Religion* (ed. Jörg Rüpke; Malden, Mass.: Blackwell, 2007), 71–82.

40. L. Michael White, "Counting the Cost of Nobility: The Social Economy of Roman Pergamon," in *Pergamon: Citadel of the Gods* (ed. Helmut Koester; Harrisburg, Pa.: Trinity Press International, 1998), 352; cf. L. Michael White, *Texts and Monuments for the Christian Domus Ecclesiae in Its Environment* (vol. 2 of *The Social Origins of Christian Architecture*; HTS 42; Valley Forge, Pa.: Trinity Press International, 1997), no. 65.

41. *OGIS* 456 = *IGR* 4.39.

42. Herklotz, *Prinzeps und Pharao*, 263 and PHI (=Packard Humanities Institute) database: http://epigraphy.packhum.org/inscriptions/

43. H. W. Pleket, "An Aspect of the Emperor Cult: Imperial Mysteries," *HTR* 58 (1965): 331–47.

44. Two volumes of *The Roman Provincial Coinage* have appeared so far, covering the period from 44 B.C.E. to 96 C.E.: Andrew Burnett, Michel Amandry, and Pere Pau Ripollès, *From the Death of Caesar to the Death of Vitellius (44 BC – AD 69)* (vol. 1 of *Roman Provincial Coinage*; London: British Museum Press, 1992); Andrew Burnett, Michel Amandry, and Ian

chose to put an image of Augustus on their coins. Andrew Wallace-Hadrill[45] has studied this phenomenon in detail and points out that coins literally have two sides to them. One is legalistic, official, and economic—in this case, the choice of the imperial head was economically advantageous because it literally gave a local coinage wider currency. The other is an appeal to values shared by the user; it is more emotive and the notion of "charisma" looms large in such discussions, including Clifford Ando's, of the imperial image.[46] This again is something we should look at more closely; I am more inclined to skepticism on this issue. Add to this the observations by Beard, North, and Price that Roman cults were mostly cults of place and, therefore, not movable,[47] and Ando's elaboration,[48] in my own words, that the Romans imported more gods than they exported, and you wind up with the image of the emperor, and its divine and perhaps charismatic aura, as the only major export to the provinces (at least in the east; the Capitoline cult was ubiquitously adopted in the west, albeit with a wide variety of local adaptations).

This allows for locating the imperial cults more precisely within the associative spectrum. Some would call the emperor *sōtēr* and the like, but they were not other-worldly salvation cults. Hence the emperor could be called a god or equal to a god (*isotheos*); I will return to this differentiation, and its impact, shortly. On the other hand, notwithstanding the mortality of the emperor, there is a charismatic element, which registered to different degrees with different audiences,[49] in the imperial cult that is distinct from many other civic cults. To repeat, this did not make the imperial into "the dominant cult in a large part of the Empire," but it constituted a dynamic of continuing negotiation all by itself.

No question, therefore, that early Christians had experience with the cult of the emperor and, on a far larger scale, the Roman system in general, and they engaged with it. I now want to turn to one aspect of this engagement, and the methodology that has been used for its interpretation, and suggest some refinements. The issue is the appropriation of concepts and phrases, especially by Paul,

---

Carradice, *From Vespasian to Domitian* (vol. 2 of *Roman Provincial Coinage*; London: British Museum Press, 1992).

45. Andrew Wallace-Hadrill, "Image and Authority in the Coinage of Augustus," *JRS* 76 (1986): 66–87.

46. Clifford Ando, *Imperial Ideology and Provincial Loyalty in the Roman Empire* (Berkeley and Los Angeles: University of California Press, 2000), 206–73.

47. Beard, North, and Price, *Religions of Rome 1*, 167–210; cf. S. R. F. Price, "The Place of Religion: Rome in the Early Empire," in *The Augustan Empire: 43 B.C.-A.D. 69* (vol. 10 of CAH, 2nd ed.; Cambridge: Cambridge University Press, 1996), 812–47.

48. Ando, *Imperial Ideology*, and Clifford Ando, *The Matter of the Gods: Religion and the Roman Empire* (Berkeley and Los Angeles: University of California Press, 2008), 95–148.

49. Cf. the extensive discussion by Jean-Pierre Martin, *Providentia deorum: Recherches sur certains aspects religieux du pouvoir impérial romain* (Rome: École française de Rome, 1982).

from the system of Roman rule for constructing the community of the Jesus followers. I would like to inject some additional perspectives into the interpretation of this phenomenon.

One is to enlarge the horizons. Appropriation of this sort is not restricted to Paul, or Matthew, or John, but is a standard feature in Greek and Roman texts. An outstanding paradigm is the very first sentence of a key document of the times—Augustus's *Res Gestae* (the preamble, incidentally, concisely states the two overriding achievements: Augustus's extending the *imperium Romanum* over the *orbis terrarum* and his expenditures—not a word here of salvation, etc.): "At the age of nineteen on my private initiative and at my private expense, I raised an army with which I redeemed into liberty the commonwealth when it was oppressed by the tyranny of a faction." Every phrase here is appropriated.[50] The reference to his age harks back to conquerors like Alexander the Great and his Roman emulator, Pompeius Magnus. More important, the terminology of delivering the state into freedom from oppression is almost formulaically the same as that used by diverse predecessors, such as Cicero, Pompey, Caesar, Marius, and the Gracchi. Is Augustus's appropriation here oppositional? Hardly. It is juxtaposition rather than opposition, but there is an element of competition as well: I, Augustus, am in this tradition, but I am the best at it yet. And, certainly, contestation is part of the spectrum: Brutus is not the true liberator, but I am—a few short sentences later, Augustus goes on to refer to the battle of Philippi (42 B.C.E.); Philippi subsequently was developed as a Roman colony.

Or, to cite some examples from Augustan poetry where such appropriations are the norm. The poetic achievement of which Horace was immensely proud was his *Odes* that came out as a collection of three books in 23 B.C.E. The concluding poem of the collection was traditionally meant to make a statement, to put a seal on the work, hence the name *sphragis* for such poems. And there, Horace unabashedly calls himself *princeps*. "I shall be spoken of," he proudly states, "as having been the outstanding leader (*princeps*) in bringing Aeolian poetry to Italian verse" (*Carm.* 3.30.13–14). A clear reference to Augustus: Horace in his realm is as much a *princeps* as Augustus is in his. Similarly, and I could extend the examples, poets like Vergil appropriate for themselves the role of triumphator;[51] Mary Beard's excellent recent book on the triumph illustrates how loaded that

---

50. Details in Karl Galinsky, *Augustan Culture*, 42–57; Augustus and Alison Cooley, *Res Gestae Divi Augusti: Text, Translation, and Commentary* (Cambridge: Cambridge University Press, 2009), 105–11.

51. On the triumphal imagery at the beginning of *Georgics* 3 see, e.g., R. D. Williams's commentary, *Virgil, the Eclogues and Georgics* (London: Macmillan, 1979), 177–79.

term was—militarily, socially, and politically.[52] Or, to return to Augustus himself, the beginning of the *Res Gestae* is emblematic of his appropriation of the slogans of others in general and making them into his own. *Pietas*, for instance, was the watchword of Caesar's opponents at the battle of Munda (45 B.C.E.) and then of Sextus Pompey,[53] and Apollo had had a long history of appropriation on coins, including those of Brutus and Cassius.[54] But even these appropriations cannot be flattened out into purely negative contestations. Rather, they are synthesized into a more perfect version of the same concept.

It is useful, therefore, to look at such references in Paul from the entire spectrum of meanings that appropriation can entail. Certainly, as Helmut Koester has argued,[55] εἰρήνη καὶ ἀσφάλεια at 1 Thess 5:3 picks up on an Augustan motto, but what is the implication? An outright rejection of Roman Empire? A call to oppose it? Or, in this eschatological context, a juxtaposition with a degree (you determine the percentage) of contestation: peace and security in or of this world will go only so far and will end with the apocalypse? Another example: various mentions of *dikaiosynē*. A different hermeneutic issue comes into play here—I am simply trying to point out that there are differentiations and gradations among these terms and that one size does not fit all; in this case, it is the ubiquity of *dikaiosynē*. Of course it figures in Roman imperial discourse, including Augustus's *Res Gestae* and Golden Shield, but its range is far more traditional and universal.[56] It was not a Roman imperial monopoly and Paul's audience would make a variety of associations with it, depending on their backgrounds. Therefore we need to proceed case by case. In the case of Gal 2, for instance, Dieter Georgi views the Pauline term *dikaiosynē* as "derived more from the Jewish Bible," denoting "first and foremost the solidarity of God with mortals."[57] Without losing these associations,

---

52. Mary Beard, *The Roman Triumph* (Cambridge, Mass.: Harvard University Press, 2007).

53. Anton Powell, "The *Aeneid* and the Embarrassments of Augustus," in *Roman Poetry and Propaganda in the Age of Augustus* (ed. Anton Powell; London: Bristol Classical Press, 1992), 141–74; and Anton Powell, *Virgil the Partisan: A Study in the Re-Integration of Classics* (Swansea: Classical Press of Wales, 2008), 31–85.

54. Anne Gosling, "Octavian, Brutus, and Apollo: A Note on Opportunist Propaganda," *AJP* 107 (1986): 586–89; Karl Galinsky, "Vergil's Uses of *Libertas*: Texts and Contexts," *Vergilius* 52 (2006): 17–18.

55. Helmut Koester, "Imperial Ideology and Paul's Eschatology in 1 Thessalonians," in *Paul and Empire: Religion and Power in Roman Imperial Society* (ed. Richard A. Horsley; Harrisburg, Pa.: Trinity Press International, 1997), 158–66.

56. Good survey and discussion by Andrew Wallace-Hadrill, "The Emperor and His Virtues," *Historia* 30 (1981): 298–323.

57. Dieter Georgi, "God Turned Upside Down. Romans: Missionary Theology and Roman Political Theology," in *Paul and Empire: Religion and Power in Roman Imperial Society* (ed. Richard A. Horsley; Harrisburg, Pa.: Trinity Press International, 1997), 149–50.

the use of the term in Romans may take on an additional dimension, given the location. Paul specifically cites Habakkuk (Rom 1:17): Ὁ δὲ δίκαιος ἐκ πίστεως ζήσεται, but both Iustitia and Fides had a strong and even architectural presence in Rome and some of Paul's addressees might well have made that association,[58] especially as he is using, throughout Romans, language that is familiar to his recipients.[59] Again, are we dealing with the rejection of Roman concepts here or their more perfect fashioning in the realm of God? Paul's reference is multilayered and demands a similarly nuanced interpretive response; here again is a continuing task for our dialogic project.

Among many other examples, I want to single out just one more and the perspectives suggested by it. That is Paul's use of *ekklēsia*. It is another appropriation from governmental officialdom and, like many other such appropriations in Paul, Matthew, and John, it suggests a parallel organization, if not a parallel universe, for the community, or communities, of Jesus believers. Imitation, of course, is the sincerest kind of flattery and the point has not been lost on Warren Carter, for instance, who aptly sums up the phenomenon in Matthew by saying that "the alternative to Rome's rule is framed in imperial terms"; he considers this an "irony."[60] It is useful to pursue this more fully in a larger context. Take the cult of Isis; Apuleius writes in one of his accounts of an Isiac procession—the locus is Cenchreae, the eastern port of Corinth—that it included someone "playing at being a magistrate, with rods and purple toga."[61] Isis, it should be noted, was much more than an escapist cult: many of her inscriptions link her with protecting the Roman Senate and People and the imperial house; this *panthea*, whose huge sanctuary stood a block away from the Pantheon, became the kinder, gentler companion to the imperial cult.[62] Similarly, the Mithraic grade system can be considered a mimicry of the rank system in the Roman army.[63] And back, or forward, to the Christian organization in the third century: the meetings of the synods of African bishops, to give a well-documented example, show that "they

---

58. Cf. the section "God's Justice Revealed in the Gospel: *Romans*" in Wright, "Paul's Gospel."

59. Cf. David R. Wallace, *The Gospel of God: Romans as Paul's* Aeneid (Eugene, Oreg.: Wipf and Stock, 2008).

60. Warren Carter, *Matthew and Empire: Initial Explorations* (Harrisburg, Penn.: Trinity Press International, 2001), 171.

61. *Metam.* 11.8; cf. Ando, *Imperial Ideology*, 382–83.

62. Superb documentation in Ermanno A. Arslan, *Iside: Il mito, il mistero, la magia* (Milan: Electa, 1997) and Sarolta A. Takacs, *Isis and Serapis in the Roman World* (Leiden: Brill, 1995); on a new inscription from Mainz (late first century C.E.): Marion Witteyer, *Göttlicher Baugrund* (Mainz am Rhein: Von Zabern, 2003), 6.

63. E. D. Francis, "Bull-Slaying at Manchester," *Contemporary Review* 221 (1972): 290–98.

observed precisely the protocol of the Roman Senate."[64] Hence Tertullian's insistence on the legality of Christian assemblies by reference to the Roman Senate (*Apol.* 39.20–21): "When decent people, when good men, gather, when the pious and chaste assemble, *non est factio dicenda, sed curia*"; it is possible, too, that there may be a deliberate echo here of Augustus's claim, which I cited earlier and which had many precedents, to have liberated the *res publica* from the oppression of a *factio*. The rest is history: as the Jesus movement developed into a larger entity, it successfully appropriated the organizational system of the Roman Empire and ultimately was better at it than the empire itself. So what happened to the anti-imperial message?[65] At the very least, we need to reevaluate such terms. Note in this context, too, that the first imperial edict ending the persecution of the Christians, that of Galerius in 311, does not consider the Christians as anti-imperial, but looks forward to the protection of the Christian god: "[the Christians] shall pray to their god for our well-being, that of the state, and theirs."[66]

Similarly, consider the following *elogium* of the emperor's virtues: "To you alone, Emperor, along with your companion deity, let that secret be revealed. I will say only what is right for a man to understand and speak: such ought to be the man who receives the reverence of nations, to whom private and public prayers are addressed throughout the world, from whom those setting sail seek a calm sea; those about to travel, a safe return; and those about to fight, the favor of the gods." A true paradigm, one might suspect, of the fulsome flourish of *testimonia* to the imperial cult. In fact, it was written by Pacatus, the panegyrist of Theodosius.[67] The appropriation is complete and, like the *ecclesiae*, takes place in *this* world and not the next. What these examples make clear, then, is that in the negotiation of early Christian identity the Roman Empire and cult of the emperor are not simply The Other—and I refer to Judith Lieu's insightful chapter on this concept[68]—but they resonate, are rejected,[69] and are assimilated in various ways that defy absolutizing interpretation. So, I would argue, does Paul's stance: even if you try to explain Rom 13:1–7 as not expressing "a univocally positive attitude toward 'the governing authorities'"[70] it does show that for Paul, too, there existed contingencies. And again we can turn to Tertullian (you can see my Cath-

---

64. Ando, *Imperial Ideology*, 383.
65. Cf. Crossan, *God and Empire*.
66. Lactantius, *Mort.* 34.
67. *Panegyrici Latini* XII[2].6.4. Cf. Ando, *Imperial Ideology*, 388.
68. Judith Lieu, John North, and Tessa Rajak, eds, *The Jews Among Christians and Pagans in the Roman Empire* (Abingdon, United Kingdom; New York: Routledge, 1992).
69. As in John's *Apocalypse*; see Friesen, *Imperial Cults*.
70. Neil Elliott, "*Romans* 13.1–7 in the Context of Imperial Propaganda," in *Paul and Empire: Religion and Power in Roman Imperial Society* (ed. Richard A. Horsley; Harrisburg, Pa.: Trinity Press International, 1997), 196.

olic upbringing: the Church Fathers matter, and not just the Scriptures): even this Christian "with an avowed hostility to *religio Romanorum*, conceded that all men owed the emperor 'their piety and religious devotion and loyalty'" (*pietas et religio et fides* [i.e., *pistis*; cf. above]).[71] We should also note that neither Tertullian nor Paul renounced their Roman citizenship and, of course, take cognizance of 1 Pet 2:13–15, with its unequivocal insistence on submission to the worldly ruler, whether βασιλεῖ ὡς ὑπερέχοντι or, simply, ἡγεμόσιν because οὕτως ἐστὶν τὸ θέλημα τοῦ θεοῦ. And he emphatically concludes (2:17) with: "Fear God, honor the king!"

The imperial cult is part of this panorama. As Momigliano has noted, "the Christian emperors were in no hurry to eliminate it."[72] Emperor worship by Christians continued. There were some modifications: sacrifices, for instance, were eliminated and the emperor was called *sanctus* rather than *divus*, but, especially in the figurative arts involving the representation of *adventus*, "his presence was still, or perhaps more so, a divine presence: the presence of a lonely superior being."[73] Again, this is a vital perspective to have on whatever attitudes to empire, or the Roman Empire, we are trying to discern in the Gospels and Paul. Was their resistance to empire so coded that successive generations didn't get it? Or did they mean to juxtapose rather than oppose and once the empire became increasingly Christian, empire, imperial cult, *ecclesiae*, and so forth ceased being an issue because they were appropriated in fact? Was takeover the final stage of negotiation? Was it a result of receding apocalyptic expectations? This is definitely another topic we need to explore.

Let me conclude with one final, perhaps more speculative example of where I see some resonance of the imperial cult in the identity formation of early Christianity. I am referring to the so-called hymn in Phil 2. Adela Collins has argued, convincingly to my mind, that Paul here "adapted the form of the Greek prose hymn in order to instruct the Philippians in cultural terms familiar to them."[74] To move from style to content: to some Greek contemporaries in the east, the phrase ἴσα θεῷ (2:6) might have sounded familiar, especially in a context dealing with the godhead of Christ. Testimonia, both literary and epigraphic, to the imperial cults, employ similar terminology for the godhead of the emperor: in many

---

71. *Apol.* 36.2; Ando, *Imperial Ideology*, 393.

72. Arnoldo Momigliano, "How Emperors Became Gods," *American Scholar* 55 (1986): 191.

73. Ibid., 193.

74. A. Y. Collins, "Psalms, *Phillipians* 2:6–11, and the Origins of Christology," *BibInt* 11 (2003): 372.

he is called θεός, but others speak of ἰσόθεοι τίμαι.⁷⁵ When he shared a temple with other gods, he was often represented as subordinate to them, whether by the architectural configuration or the statuary of the cult images; the phenomenon has received different interpretations.⁷⁶ There is a gamut of appellations: *theos, Sebastos*, son of the *theos*; there were also differentiations when it came to the choice of sacrificial animals, with the aim of not placing the emperor on the same level with the other gods. As usual, there was no uniformity in all of this and the issue was a work in progress: the Mytilene decree specifically speaks of "making a god" (θεοποιεῖν).⁷⁷ The emperors themselves speak clearly: Tiberius, Claudius, and Germanicus in their rescripts concerning cultic honors emphasize their mortality; Caligula is the usual aberration. Similar gradations are found in the responses of Greek intellectuals, such as Plutarch, Dio of Prusa, and Aristides; the bottom line, in the words of Glen Bowersock, is that none would ever "consider an imperial *theos* as 'one of the gods.'"⁷⁸

These parallels add another layer to those that have been discerned in this very complex passage in Philippians. Philippians 2:6–11 is generally recognized to be seminal for Christology;⁷⁹ the issues that are succinctly stated here are the very ones that were to lead to many schisms later. There is plenty to explore here in relation to the imperial cult,⁸⁰ including the limits of neatly separating ontological and soteriological aspects. Also, Paul's use of ὁμοίωμα (7), harking back to μορφὴν (6), and phrases such as Christ being εἰκὼν τοῦ θεοῦ (2 Cor 4:4) could be usefully looked at, beyond the perspective they have recently received,⁸¹ in light

---

75. For the documentation see Christian Habicht, "Die augusteische Zeit und das erste Jahrhundert nach Christi Geburt," in *Le culte des souverains dans l'empire romain* (ed. Willem Den Boer; Vandoeuvres/Geneva: Fondation Hardt, 1973), 41–88.

76. Price, *Rituals and Power*, 146–56 emphasizes the emperor's subordinate aspect; Friesen, *Twice Neokoros*, 73–75 argues for a higher profile.

77. *OGIS* 456.45; *IGR* 4.39b.15.

78. G. Bowersock, "Greek Intellectuals and the Imperial Cult in the Second Century A.D.," in *Le culte des souverains dans l'empire romain* (ed. W. Den Boer; Vandoeuvres/Geneva, 1973), 206.

79. See Ralph P. Martin, *Carmen Christi: Philippians Ii.5–11 in Recent Interpretation and in the Setting of Early Christian Worship* (SNTSMS 4; London: Cambridge University Press, 1967) and Ralph P. Martin and Brian J. Dodd, eds., *Where Christology Began: Essays on Philippians 2* (Louisville, Ky.: Westminster John Knox, 1998).

80. Cf. Andreas Bendlin, "Vergöttlichung," in *Der Neue Pauly. Enzyklopädie der Antike*, vol. 12 (Stuttgart: Metzler, 2003), 69 and Manfred Clauss, *Kaiser und Gott: Herrscherkult in Römischen Reich* (Stuttgart: Teubner, 1999), 497–98.

81. E.g., John Dominic Crossan and Jonathan L. Reed, *In Search of Paul: How Jesus's Apostle Opposed Rome's Empire with God's Kingdom* (San Francisco: HarperSanFrancisco, 2004), 288–90.

of the complex tradition, recently discussed by Clifford Ando,[82] of Greco-Roman points of view on the nature of icons of the gods. Further, later writers like Basil "compared the alleged identity of the Father and the Son to the identity of the emperor and his image."[83] One more suggestion: this differentiated terminology in Philippians may reflect the fact that its Roman colonists knew the Latin terminology of the imperial cult that was imperfectly translated into Greek: the emperor was not "the son of god," *theos ek theou*, but "the son of the deified," *divi filius* (and not *dei filius*).

This is only one of many examples where I see the opportunity, and need, for constructive further work. Early on in his book, Simon Price observed that "there is a deep-seated ... desire to play off Greek and Roman cults against Christianity so as to define its standing and the imperial cult is closely bound up in this debate."[84] We can and need to do better and we can be united in this effort even if we have divided opinions—so much for a last minute connection with the title of this talk, which now reflects its embeddedness in a recent political context. It only goes to show that, much as I have criticized it, the overlaying of contemporary and ancient matrices can be quite seductive after all.

BIBLIOGRAPHY

Ando, Clifford. *Imperial Ideology and Provincial Loyalty in the Roman Empire*. Berkeley and Los Angeles: University of California Press, 2000.
———. *The Matter of the Gods: Religion and the Roman Empire*. Berkeley and Los Angeles: University of California Press, 2008.
Arslan, Ermanno A. *Iside: Il mito, il mistero, la magia*. Milan: Electa, 1997.
Augustus, and Alison Cooley. *Res Gestae Divi Augusti: Text, Translation, and Commentary*. Cambridge: Cambridge University Press, 2009.
Balch, David. "The Cultural Origin of 'Receiving All Nations' in Luke-Acts: Alexander the Great or Roman Social Policy?" Pages 483–500 in *Early Christianity and Classical Culture: Comparative Essays in Honor of Abraham J. Malherbe*. Edited by John Fitzgerald, Thomas Olbricht, and L. Michael White. Supplements to Novum Testamentum 110. Leiden: Brill, 2003.
Beard, Mary. *The Roman Triumph*. Cambridge, Mass.: Harvard University Press, 2007.
———. *Religions of Rome*. Vol. 2: *A Sourcebook*. Cambridge: Cambridge University Press, 1998.
———, John North, and Simon Price. *Religions of Rome*. Vol. 1: *A History*. Cambridge: Cambridge University Press, 1998.
Bendlin, Andreas. "Vergöttlichung." Pages 68–69 in *Der Neue Pauly. Enzyklopädie der Antike*, vol. 12. Stuttgart: Metzler, 2003.

---

82. Ando, *Matter of the Gods*, 21–48.
83. Price, *Rituals and Power*, 203.
84. Ibid., 14.

Bowersock, G. "Greek Intellectuals and the Imperial Cult in the Second Century A.D." Pages 179–206 in *Le culte des souverains dans l'empire romain*. Edited by W. Den Boer. Vandoeuvres/Geneva, 1973.

———. *Augustus and the Greek World*. Westport, Conn.: Greenwood Press, 1965.

Brunt, P. A. "*Laus Imperii*." Pages 288–323 in *Roman Imperial Themes*. Edited by P. A. Brunt. New York: Oxford University Press, 1990.

———. *Roman Imperial Themes*. New York: Oxford University Press, 1990.

Burnett, Andrew, Michel Amandry, and Ian Carradice. *From Vespasian to Domitian*. Vol. 2 of *Roman Provincial Coinage*. London: British Museum Press, 1992.

———, Michel Amandry, and Pere Pau Ripollès. *From the Death of Caesar to the Death of Vitellius (44 BC - AD 69)*. Vol. 1 of *Roman Provincial Coinage*. London: British Museum Press, 1992.

Carter, Warren. *John and Empire: Initial Explorations*. New York: T&T Clark, 2008.

———. *Matthew and Empire: Initial Explorations*. Harrisburg, Penn.: Trinity Press International, 2001.

———. *The Roman Empire and the New Testament: An Essential Guide*. Nashville: Abingdon Press, 2006.

Chua, Amy. *Day of Empire: How Hyperpowers Rise to Global Dominance and Why They Fall*. New York: Doubleday, 2007.

Clauss, Manfred. *Kaiser und Gott: Herrscherkult in Römischen Reich*. Stuttgart: B. G. Teubner, 1999.

Collins, A. Y. "Psalms, *Phillipians* 2:6–11, and the Origins of Christology." *Biblical Interpretation* 11 (2003): 361–72.

Crossan, John Dominic. *God and Empire: Jesus Against Rome, Then and Now*. San Francisco: HarperSanFrancisco, 2007.

——— and Jonathan L. Reed. *In Search of Paul: How Jesus's Apostle Opposed Rome's Empire with God's Kingdom*. San Francisco: HarperSanFrancisco, 2004.

de Jong, Johanna Helena Maria. "Emperors in Egypt: The Representation and Perception of Roman Imperial Power in Greek Papyrus Texts from Egypt, AD 193–284." Ph.D. diss., Radboud Universiteit Nijmegen, 2006.

Deissmann, Adolf. *Licht vom Osten: Das Neue Testament und die neuentdeckten Texte der hellenistisch-römischen Welt*. 4th ed. 1908. Repr. Tübingen: Mohr, 1923.

———. *Paul: A Study in Social and Religious History*. Translated by William E. Wilson. 1912. Repr. New York: Harper & Row, 1957.

Elliott, Neil. "*Romans* 13.1–7 in the Context of Imperial Propaganda." Pages 184–204 in *Paul and Empire: Religion and Power in Roman Imperial Society*. Edited by Richard A. Horsley. Harrisburg, Pa.: Trinity Press International, 1997.

Février, Paul-Albert. "Religion et domination dans l'Afrique romaine." *Collection de l'École française de Rome* 225 (1996): 789–812.

Fishwick, Duncan. "Dio and Maecenas: The Emperor and the Ruler Cult." *Phoenix* 44 (1990): 267–75.

Fitzgerald, John T., Thomas H. Olbricht, and L. Michael White, eds. *Early Christianity and Classical Culture: Comparative Studies in Honor of Abraham J. Malherbe*. Supplements to Novum Testamentum 110. Leiden: Brill, 2003.

Francis, E. D. "Bull-Slaying at Manchester." *Contemporary Review* 221 (1972): 290–98.

Friesen, Steven J. *Imperial Cults and the Apocalypse of John: Reading Revelation in the Ruins*. New York: Oxford University Press, 2001.

———. *Twice Neokoros: Ephesus, Asia, and the Cult of the Flavian Imperial Family*. Leiden: Brill, 1993.
Galinsky, Karl, ed. *The Cambridge Companion to the Age of Augustus*. Cambridge: Cambridge University Press, 2005.
———, ed. *The Interpretation of Roman Poetry: Empiricism or Hermeneutics?* Studien zur klassischen Philologie 67. Frankfurt: Lang, 1992.
———. *Augustan Culture*. Princeton: Princeton University Press, 1996.
———. "Clothes for the Emperor." *Arion* 10 (2003): 143–69.
———. "Continuity and Change: Religion in the Augustan Semi-Century." Pages 71–82 in *A Companion to Roman Religion*. Edited by Jörg Rüpke. Malden, Mass.: Blackwell, 2007.
———. "Vergil's Uses of *Libertas*: Texts and Contexts." *Vergilius* 52 (2006): 1–19.
Georgi, Dieter. "God Turned Upside Down. Romans: Missionary Theology and Roman Political Theology." Pages 148–57 in *Paul and Empire: Religion and Power in Roman Imperial Society*. Edited by Richard A. Horsley. Harrisburg, Pa.: Trinity Press International, 1997.
Giovannini, Adalberto, ed. *Opposition et résistances à l'empire d'Auguste à Trajan*. Entretiens sur l'Antiquité classique. Geneva: Fondation Hardt, 1987.
Gordon, Richard. "Reality, Evocation, and Boundaries in the Mysteries of Mithra." *Journal of Mithraic Studies* 3 (1980): 19–99.
Gosling, Anne. "Octavian, Brutus, and Apollo: A Note on Opportunist Propaganda." *American Journal of Philology* 107 (1986): 586–89.
Habicht, Christian. "Die augusteische Zeit und das erste Jahrhundert nach Christi Geburt." Pages 41–88 in *Le culte des souverains dans l'empire romain*. Edited by Willem Den Boer. Vandoeuvres/Geneva: Fondation Hardt, 1973.
Hänlein-Schäfer, Heidi. Veneratio Augusti: *Eine Studie zu den Tempeln der ersten römischen Kaiser*. Rome: Bretschneider, 1985.
Herklotz, Friederike. *Prinzeps und Pharao: Der Kult des Augustus in Ägypten*. Oikumene 4. Frankfurt: Verlag Antike, 2007.
Horsley, Richard A., ed. *Paul and Empire: Religion and Power in Roman Imperial Society*. Harrisburg, Pa.: Trinity Press International, 1997.
———. *In the Shadow of Empire: Reclaiming the Bible as a History of Faithful Resistance*. Louisville, Ky.: Westminster John Knox, 2008.
———. *Jesus and Empire: The Kingdom of God and the New World Disorder*. Philadelphia: Augsburg Fortress, 2003.
Iser, Wolfgang. *The Implied Reader: Patterns of Communication in Prose Fiction from Bunyan to Beckett*. Baltimore: Johns Hopkins University Press, 1974.
Kahl, Brigitte, Davina C. Lopez, and Hal Taussig, eds. "The New Testament and Roman Empire: Shifting Paradigms for Interpretation." *Union Seminary Quarterly Review* 59 (2005).
Kitagawa, Joseph M. "Primitive, Classical, and Modern Religions: A Perspective on Understanding the History of Religions." Pages 39–65 in *The History of Religions: Essays on the Problem of Understanding*. Edited by Joseph M. Kitagawa. Chicago: University of Chicago Press, 1967.
Koester, Helmut, ed. *Pergamon: Citadel of the Gods: Archaeological Record, Literary Description, and Religious Development*. Harvard Theological Studies 46. Harrisburg, Pa.: Trinity Press International, 1998.

———. "Imperial Ideology and Paul's Eschatology in 1 Thessalonians." Pages 158–66 in *Paul and Empire: Religion and Power in Roman Imperial Society*. Edited by Richard A. Horsley. Harrisburg, Pa.: Trinity Press International, 1997.
Lieu, Judith, John North, and Tessa Rajak, eds. *The Jews Among Christians and Pagans in the Roman Empire*. Abingdon, United Kingdom; New York: Routledge, 1992.
Lieu, Judith M. *Christian Identity in the Jewish and Graeco-Roman World*. New York: Oxford University Press, 2004.
MacMullen, Ramsey. *Enemies of the Public Order*. Cambridge, Mass.: Harvard University Press, 1966.
Martin, Jean-Pierre. *Providentia deorum: Recherches sur certains aspects religieux du pouvoir impérial romain*. Rome: École française de Rome, 1982.
Martin, Ralph P. *Carmen Christi: Philippians ii.5–11 in Recent Interpretation and in the Setting of Early Christian Worship*. Society for New Testament Studies Monograph Series. 4. London: Cambridge University Press, 1967.
——— and Brian J. Dodd, eds. *Where Christology Began: Essays on Philippians 2*. Westminster John Knox Press, 1998.
Millar, Fergus. "The Imperial Cult and the Persecutions." Pages 145–65 in *Le culte des souverains dans l'empire romain*. Edited by Willem Den Boer. Entretiens sur l'Antiquité classique. 19. Vandoeuvres/Geneva: Fondation Hardt, 1973.
Momigliano, Arnoldo. "How Emperors Became Gods." *American Scholar* 55 (1986): 181–93.
North, John. "The Development of Religious Pluralism." Pages 174–93 in *The Jews Among Christians and Pagans in the Roman Empire*. Edited by Judith Lieu, John North, and Tessa Rajak. London: Routledge, 1992.
Pleket, H. W. "An Aspect of the Emperor Cult: Imperial Mysteries." *Harvard Theological Review* 58 (1965): 331–47.
Poinssot, Claude. *Les ruines de Dougga*. Tunis: Secrétariat d'État à l'éducation nationale, Institut national d'archéologie et arts, 1983.
Powell, Anton, ed. *Roman Poetry and Propaganda in the Age of Augustus*. London: Bristol Classical Press, 1992.
———. "The *Aeneid* and the Embarrassments of Augustus." Pages 141–74 in *Roman Poetry and Propaganda in the Age of Augustus*. Edited by Anton Powell. London: Bristol Classical Press, 1992.
———. *Virgil the Partisan: A Study in the Re-Integration of Classics*. Swansea: Classical Press of Wales, 2008.
Price, S. R. F. "The Place of Religion: Rome in the Early Empire." Pages 812–47 in *The Augustan Empire: 43 B.C.–A.D. 69*. Vol. 10 of *Cambridge Ancient History, 2nd Ed*. Cambridge: Cambridge University Press, 1996.
———. *Rituals and Power: The Roman Imperial Cult in Asia Minor*. Cambridge: Cambridge University Press, 1984.
Purcell, Nicholas. "Romans in the Roman World." Pages 85–105 in *The Cambridge Companion to the Age of Augustus*. Edited by Karl Galinsky. Cambridge: Cambridge University Press, 2005.
Reid, Sara Karz. *The Small Temple: A Roman Imperial Cult Building in Petra, Jordan*. Gorgias Dissertations in Near Eastern Studies 7. Piscatataway, N.J.: Gorgias Press, 2005.
Rüpke, Jörg, ed. *A Companion to Roman Religion*. Malden, Mass.: Blackwell, 2007.

Scheid, John. "Augustus and Roman Religion: Continuity, Conservatism, and Innovation." Pages 175-93 in *The Cambridge Companion to the Age of Augustus*. Edited by Karl Galinsky. Cambridge: Cambridge University Press, 2005.
Scott, James C. *Domination and the Arts of Resistance: Hidden Transcripts*. New Haven, Conn.: Yale University Press, 1990.
———. *Weapons of the Weak: Everyday Forms of Peasant Resistance*. New Haven, Conn.: Yale University Press, 1985.
Smith, Jonathan Z. *Map is not Territory: Studies in the History of Religions*. Leiden: Brill, 1978.
Suleiman, Susan Rubin. *Subversive Intent: Gender, Politics, and Avant-Garde*. Cambridge, Mass.: Harvard University Press, 1990.
Takacs, Sarolta A. *Isis and Serapis in the Roman World*. Leiden: Brill, 1995.
Wallace, David R. *The Gospel of God: Romans as Paul's Aeneid*. Eugene, Oreg.: Wipf & Stock, 2008.
Wallace-Hadrill, Andrew. "The Emperor and His Virtues." *Historia* 30 (1981): 298-323.
———. "Image and Authority in the Coinage of Augustus." *Journal of Roman Studies* 76 (1986): 66-87.
———. "*Mutatas Formas*: The Augustan Transformation of Roman Knowledge." Pages 55-84 in *The Cambridge Companion to the Age of Augustus*. Edited by Karl Galinsky. Cambridge: Cambridge University Press, 2005.
White, L. Michael. "Counting the Cost of Nobility: The Social Economy of Roman Pergamon." Pages 331-71 in *Pergamon: Citadel of the Gods*. Edited by Helmut Koester. Harrisburg, Pa.: Trinity Press International, 1998.
———. *Texts and Monuments for the Christian Domus Ecclesiae in Its Environment*. Vol. 2 of *The Social Origins of Christian Architecture*. Harvard Theological Studies 42. Valley Forge, Pa.: Trinity Press International, 1997.
Williams, R. D., trans. and ed. *Virgil, the Eclogues And Georgics*. London: Macmillan, 1979.
Witteyer, Marion. *Göttlicher Baugrund*. Mainz am Rhein: Von Zabern, 2003.
Wright, N. T. "Paul's Gospel and Caesar's Empire." Online: http://www.ntwrightpage.com/Wright_Paul_Caesar_Empire.pdf.

Chapter 2
Normal Religion, or, Words Fail Us
A Response to Karl Galinsky's "The Cult of the Roman Emperor: Uniter or Divider?"

Steven J. Friesen

I want to begin by thanking the organizers for making these discussions possible. I don't even want to think about the logistics of sponsoring a collaboration among at least three professional societies. We are all the beneficiaries of your diligent leadership. And I also thank Karl for taking his task so seriously. Since moving to the University of Texas, I have come to expect this from Karl. He is a generous colleague, and always brings his A-game. I am continually surprised and enlightened by his commentary on any topic. And no, in case you're wondering, he does not sit on any committees at UT that determine my salary. I praise him without ulterior motive or hope of financial gain.

I have come, however, not to praise Karl (nor to bury him), but rather to participate in the conversation he has ignited. His paper[1] raises all sorts of great questions about Roman imperial cults, more than I or we can address. So I will highlight one theme from Karl's paper, and then make three suggestions in relation to it.

The general theme I want to highlight is this: Karl has given us a challenge to treat imperial cults like normal religion. For too long, we have treated imperial cults as bad religion, perverted religion, religion run amok. I think the problem has been our parochial vision. We live at a time in history on a slice of the globe when we tend to define religion and politics as separate spheres of social life. Or at least, we academics tend to think that religion and politics *should* be separate. And so we barely have concepts or words for this fusion of political leaders and

---

1. Karl Galinsky, "The Cult of the Roman Emperor: Uniter or Divider?" paper presented at the Annual Meeting of the SBL, Boston, 2008, and ch. 1 in this volume.

cult. But I think the rest of history is right: politics and religion are inextricable. Our analyses should reflect that.

Now on to my first suggestion, which is brief. I want to underline—nay, underline, put in bold font, and change to all capital letters—Karl's argument that imperial cults were a multifarious phenomenon, woven into nearly every aspect of social life under the empire. We should take Karl's exhortation to heart—a simplistic rendering of these cults will not suffice, a dichotomizing approach will not satisfy.

A simple linguistic practice will help us with this. My suggestion is: Let us stop referring to the worship of the emperors with the singular "imperial cult" and insist on the plural "imperial cults." In other words, let us treat it like any other normal religious phenomenon. Who would talk about "the Dionysus cult" in the ancient world, or "the Artemis cult"? Words fail us when we call this phenomenon "imperial cult," because the singular undercuts our efforts to develop sophisticated, nuanced interpretations of imperial cults. The new vocabulary might lead to new insights.

My second suggestion builds on Karl's appreciation of the subtleties of responses to imperial cults. There is a long history of discussing the *production* of imperial cults, but Karl pushes us toward discussion of the *consumption* of imperial cults. Can we render the nuances of variegated responses—the appropriation, competition, and opposition?

Here my suggestion is that we pay more attention to the diversity of the audience in our analysis. But to make that point, let me attempt a modern analogy, because I do not think imperial cults are as foreign to us as we assume, and the modern analogy might clarify the varieties of ancient responses.

Consider two media events from recent American political life that strike me as religious. Most of you can probably visualize them immediately, because they were created specifically to leave a lasting impression on you. One of them is George W. Bush's Mission Accomplished moment on May 1, 2003, when he declared victory in Iraq. The other event is the epiphany of Barack Obama in Berlin during his presidential campaign (July 24, 2008), when he brought together the whole human race. Both of these events articulated modern imperial power and focused it in the particularity of an individual. In the one case, a son of the Bush dynasty was made manifest to us; in the other case we encountered the rising star of Chicago's Democratic political machine. But more importantly, both "Mission Accomplished" and "Obama in Berlin" focused selected aspirations of empire in a single individual with a transcendent message of salvation, allegedly for all humanity. Neither one of these two divine figures presented himself as a divider. Rather, each claimed to be a uniter, although each claimed to unite in a different mode. On the aircraft carrier USS Abraham Lincoln we beheld the warrior who brought us together through conquest and victory; an image of

Augustus wearing the cuirass and crowned by a Nike comes to mind. In Berlin, on the other hand, we gazed with wonder at the tall figure striding across a temporary stage. He was a more complex trope, a young leader, charismatic, uniting cultures and peoples, an evocation reminiscent more of Alexander iconography than Augustan.

In these two figures, seen together in binocular fashion, we can perhaps begin to imagine the consumption of Roman imperial cults. We could talk about the differences between Bush and Obama, and the differences are important. But ultimately, both Obama and Bush are part of one imperial process. It is the production of cosmology, the shaping of this world, the proclamation of structures that frame our lives whether we like it or not.

Such a cosmology of imperial power is consumed in countless ways. The soldiers and journalists on the flight deck of the USS Abraham Lincoln no doubt received the Bush event in many ways, and the millions of supporters in the streets of Berlin did the same with Obama. But what if the population had been different, drawn from those who dislike this American cosmology? What if the flight deck of the USS Abraham Lincoln had been filled instead with Iraqi widows, or the streets of Berlin had been filled instead with the orphaned sons and daughters of suicide bombers?

Likewise in our analysis of Roman imperial cults we must imagine this range of experiences and responses. Karl began to chart it out—appropriation, competition, opposition. We might add questions about social stratification. How would elites and subelites assess these institutions? Male and female? Old and young? Well-fed and hungry? Slave, freed, and freeborn? Healthy and disabled? The privileged and the exploited? There are many axes against which we can and should plot the consumption of imperial cults. Just as there was no single imperial cult, there was also no single audience, and no single response. More attention to gender, to economy, to ethnicity, and so forth, will help us plot the responses.

My third and last suggestion grows out of the second one: in our study of imperial cults, let us be more systematic in our use of theories about the character of religion. I want to make clear that I am *not* advocating a search for the right theory that will give us the right interpretation of imperial cults. On the contrary, I think we need a lot of disciplined analysis from many points of view. For example, one of the signal accomplishments of Simon Price's landmark book *Rituals and Power* was precisely this—he gave us an interpretation that was thoroughly grounded in data and framed by a coherent theory. The result was that we could begin to see imperial cults as normal religion rather than as religion gone bad. His theory was influenced by anthropologists like Victor Turner and Clifford Geertz, and it focused on religion as a way of conceptualizing the world. Such theories have fallen on hard times lately, but Price used it well and taught us a lot about imperial cults.

There are other theories that might teach us other things about our topic (and perhaps about ourselves). In my book *Imperial Cults and the Apocalypse of John* I employed a modified phenomenological definition of religion based on the work of Larry Sullivan. Full disclosure: I am not now nor have I ever been a phenomenologist of religion. But I think the theory helped me isolate more precisely the role imperial cults played as a part of normal urban polytheism in the eastern Mediterranean during the early empire. I still am waiting for someone to do a thorough feminist evaluation of imperial cults, perhaps along the theoretical lines laid out by Elisabeth Schüssler Fiorenza.[2] Or a deconstructive, materialist interpretation based in the work of Bruce Lincoln.[3] Or maybe even something that draws on theoretical proposals from work on modern diasporas in the Americas.[4]

For ultimately, imperial cults comprised a normal sector of a complex religious system. That religious system was far too variegated to be captured by our feeble efforts to theorize about it, and our words often fail us. But the theories force us to be systematic in our thinking, and to lay our cards on the table. That is the kind of discipline and intellectual transparency we should strive for in our conversations. And for starting us on those conversations in a disciplined and transparent fashion, I thank Karl, who has united us in this endeavor.

Bibliography

Friesen, Steven J. *Imperial Cults and the Apocalypse of John: Reading Revelation in the Ruins*. New York: Oxford University Press, 2001.

Galinsky, Karl. "The Cult of the Roman Emperor: Uniter or Divider?" Paper presented at the Annual Meeting of the SBL, Boston, 2008, and ch. 1 in this volume.

Lincoln, Bruce. *Holy Terrors: Thinking About Religion After September 11*. 2nd ed. Chicago: University of Chicago Press, 2006.

Price, S. R. F. *Rituals and Power: The Roman Imperial Cult in Asia Minor*. Cambridge: Cambridge University Press, 1984.

Schüssler Fiorenza, Elisabeth. *The Power of the Word: Scripture and the Rhetoric of Empire*. Minneapolis: Fortress, 2007.

Tweed, Thomas A. *Crossing and Dwelling: A Theory of Religion*. Cambridge, Mass.: Harvard University Press, 2006.

---

2. Elisabeth Schüssler Fiorenza, *The Power of the Word: Scripture and the Rhetoric of Empire* (Minneapolis: Fortress, 2007).

3. Bruce Lincoln, *Holy Terrors: Thinking About Religion After September 11* (2nd ed.; Chicago: University of Chicago Press, 2006).

4. For example, Thomas A. Tweed, *Crossing and Dwelling: A Theory of Religion* (Cambridge, Mass.: Harvard University Press, 2006).

Chapter 3
To Complicate Encounters:
A Response to Karl Galinsky's "The Cult of the Roman Emperor: Uniter or Divider?"

James Constantine Hanges

Jonathan Reed and the Society for Ancient Mediterranean Religions are owed a debt of gratitude for organizing the initial national meeting of this new scholarly organization. What follows is a small contribution to the panel featured in that meeting, intended as a response to Professor Galinsky's stimulating paper,[1] a contribution informed by my participation in the Society of Biblical Literature's Greco-Roman Religions Section, which has now begun its third year pursuing the redescription of the ancient Greco-Roman world in light of new theoretical constructs—especially the potential of postcolonial perspectives.[2] Obviously, issues presented by Professor Galinsky resonate with this ongoing project. I want to suggest that despite the absence of any explicit reliance on postcolonial theory, Professor Galinsky's work, as represented by his current essay, his sensitivities to the subtleties of the evidence, and his concern for understanding the complexities of social relations echo the concerns and priorities of recent postcolonial studies, and invite application of these perspectives to his future investigations.

My focus on some of these concerns will begin with Jás Elsner, who among others has recently confirmed the importance of reading eastern literature during the imperial period as colonial literature.[3] Recent studies like Elsner's imply the need to reframe the question of whether the divine Augustus is better described as

---

1. Karl Galinsky, "The Cult of the Roman Emperor: Uniter or Divider?" paper presented at the Annual Meeting of the SBL, Boston, 2008, and ch. 1 in this volume.

2. The redescribing project has proceeded under the leadership of Professor Gerhard van den Heever of the University of South Africa.

3. Jás Elsner, "Describing Self in the Language of Other: Pseudo (?) Lucian at the Temple of Hierapolis," in *Being Greek Under Rome: Cultural Identity, the Second Sophistic, and the Development of Empire* (ed. Simon Goldhill; Cambridge: Cambridge University Press, 2001), 123–39.

either a unifying or dividing figure by asking not so much how and in what ways he divided or unified his society, but rather by asking from whose perspective the emperor functions in the way he does—probably at once dividing and unifying. How are the image of the emperor and other symbols of Roman power used by, and how do they function within, communities entangled in the continual contestation of identity? Even more intriguing is the question of Augustus's own wrestling, his own negotiation of identity in a Roman world that has suffered a civil war shaped in part (if not the whole) by its would-be leaders' fascination with the colonized other, that is, Egypt. Regarding all these questions, I would take Professor Galinsky's thematic charge to avoid simplistic and monolithic explanatory models as a prerequisite to any redescribing effort, a charge that could easily be advanced by a careful look through a postcolonial theoretical lens.

To be sure, postcolonial perspectives have certainly suffered a range of criticisms, from the shallow rant of Jacoby to specific and justified criticisms such as Acheraiou's critique of postcolonial discourse analysis.[4] Nevertheless, a solid core of principles—what we might describe as essentially "common sense," empirically grounded predictions—remains. The most important of these predictions echoes Professor Galinsky in assuming that cultural encounters will always be complex moments of reciprocal projection, identity reinscription, and cultural creativity or hybridization. In other words, a postcolonial perspective warns us that power—culturally affective power—does not travel, or is not exercised, in one direction only, from the colonizer to the colonized. Both colonizer and colonized are reshaped or reinscribed in the encounter. The second resonating postcolonial assumption warns us against expecting to find anything resembling a "pure" culture in a complex world like the Hellenistic-Roman Mediterranean, a period and region awash in migrating colonizing and colonized communities. This prediction of broad cultural complexity renders little more than convenient all reifying social or ethnic categories such as Jew/Jewish, Hellene/Hellenistic, and the like.[5] I would suggest that this postcolonial assumption finds an important correlate in Professor Galinsky's warning to avoid "a single ... simple, matrix."[6] His reminder that we are dealing with complex local variation and the encounters these variations include allows the expansion of an old maxim—religion, like politics, is ultimately a local phenomenon.

---

4. Russell Jacoby, "Marginal Returns: The Trouble with Postcolonial Theory," *Lingua Franca* 5 (1995): 30–37; Amar Acheraïou, *Rethinking Postcolonialism: Colonialist Discourse in Modern Literatures and the Legacy of Classical Writers* (New York: Palgrave Macmillan, 2008).

5. This problem is already well-known among scholars of early Christianity in terms of the critique of the category Jewish-Christianity; see, e.g., Matt Jackson-McCab, ed., *Jewish Christianity Reconsidered: Rethinking Ancient Groups and Texts* (Minneapolis: Fortress, 2007).

6. Galinsky, "Cult of the Roman Emperor," 3.

Professor Galinsky offers what I take to be a related but additional correlate of a postcolonial perspective in his crucial observation that "it is an overstatement to label the cult of the emperor as 'the dominant cult in a large part of the empire' [using N. T. Wright's descriptive phrase]."[7] I note with approval here that Professor Galinsky brings together his caution against oversimplification with the idea of negotiation, an important postcolonial presupposition in the description of cultural encounter—identities in cultural encounters, whether group or individual, are never fixed but are always multivariable, fluid, and negotiated.

To pursue this, I take my cue from Professor Galinsky's allusion to Richard Horsley's framing opposition between the "gospel of Caesar" and the "gospel of Christ."[8] Postcolonial consciousness requires that we scan beyond the description of the social encounter with the divine emperor in terms of central action versus peripheral reaction. Instead, as Professor Galinsky's work suggests, we must complicate, or multiply, perspectives, recognizing that such encounters are processes of negotiation directed toward the task of identity construction on the part of both the colonizer and the colonized. For example, Elsner's comparative analysis of Lucian's *De Dea Syria* and Philostratus's *Vita Apollonii* produces the provocative and persuasive conclusion that such literature, and the general focus on religion at the periphery of the empire—including the Christ cult—might be better understood as the expression of the development of counteridentities against the background of the hegemony of the imperial center—reactionary literature to be sure, but profoundly creative and complex. Even so, we must not lose sight of the fact that what is seen as the hegemony of the imperial center is also the point of enunciation of Roman identity, an enunciation that itself—just as any enunciation of identity—does not remain stable in the encounter, but is negotiated and reinscribed.[9] In terms of the encounter between local communities and the imperial cult, postcolonial critique would demand that we ask in what ways the Roman projections of themselves on the non-Roman other express or reveal the "articulation of forms of difference" necessitated by the "ambivalence of the object," the other both desired and despised, a process that is simultaneously the reinscription of Romanness over against the created other.[10]

---

7. Galinsky, "Cult of the Roman Emperor," 5.

8. See Horsley's General Introduction in Richard A. Horsley, ed., *Paul and Empire: Religion and Power in Roman Imperial Society* (Harrisburg, Pa.: Trinity Press International, 1997), 1–8.

9. Jeffrey Weeks, "The Value of Difference," in *Identity: Community, Culture, Difference* (ed. Jonathan Rutherford; London: Lawrence & Wishart, 1990), 88–100.

10. Homi Bhabha, *The Location of Culture* (1994; repr., Routledge Classics; London: Routledge, 2007), 96.

Professor Galinsky's cautionary tone regarding the weight or impact of the imperial cult is also important, and I would add only that locality is actually more fluid than scholars usually imagine. One of the diagnostic elements of this complexity is the phenomenon of moving people and the immigrant cults they establish in new locations.[11] The records these communities leave behind often reveal a complicated social encounter; their founders "negotiated" not just imperial encounters but seem primarily concerned with negotiating local encounters. The detailed history of the migrant cult of Sarapis on Delos makes this abundantly clear.[12]

What we mean by "negotiate" should also be clarified from a postcolonial perspective. In addition to the primary assumption that a narrow conception of the social encounter as one between the so-called dominant and dominated cannot suffice, postcolonial studies introduce to the study of the ancient world and to our concept of identity negotiation suspicions of mimicry and mirroring, of the presence of the divided self projected in the construction of the other. We must stop using the term "negotiation" as if we were describing something analogous to climbing over barricades on an obstacle course. Such a view complements and even sustains the stereotype of the impotent colonial, and inhibits our ability to perceive the contestation and the exchanges of power that characterize negotiation.[13]

Postcolonial perspectives problematize such simple oppositions, and speak of "negotiation" in terms of the exercise of power by both the "dominant" and the "dominated," recognizing the complexity and reciprocity of their interaction. Failing to do this produces a search for subversive resistance alone and ignores or misses the creativity of the encounter. Or to defer to someone who puts it far more sharply, Bhabha describes the colonizer face to face with the colonized as "confronted by his dark reflection, the shadow of colonized man, that splits his presence, distorts his outline, breaches his boundaries, repeats his actions at a distance, disturbs and divides the very time of his being."[14] I would argue that within the context of moving people, that is, one of the more distinctive characteristics of the Roman Mediterranean embodied in the migrations of Egyptians, Syrians, Anatolians, Jews, and Christians from the periphery—from the conquered and colonized spaces of the Greco-Roman world—to the center, to the Greek and

---

11. See, e.g., Marie-Françoise Baslez, *Rechérches sur les conditions de pénétration et de diffusion des religions orientales à Délos (IIe-Ier s. avant notre ére)* (Collection de l'École Normale Supérieure de Jeunes Filles; Paris: École normale supérieure de jeunes filles, 1977).

12. See *IG* XI4 1299, esp. ll. 23–28 and 66–92.

13. See, e.g., Ashis Nandy, *The Intimate Enemy: Loss and Recovery of Self Under Colonialism* (Delhi: Oxford University Press, 1983), especially ch. 1.

14. Bhabha, *Location of Culture*, 62.

Roman homelands, such reactions can be identified among the colonizers and can help us understand more thickly the ancient cultural encounter.

Realizing this, we might complicate Horsley's simple opposition from the history of Christian origins; Paul's contingencies, like those of other migrating cult founders, are primarily localized (for example, as we see in 1 Thessalonians and in the Corinthian correspondence). The urgent problem in these situations is negotiating life with one's immediate neighbors, not primarily with the imperial house. This problem in the cultural encounters of migrating religious communities was there prior to Roman influence; it is present in Euripides's *Bakchai* (circa 406 B.C.E.), and continued during the imperial period, in a text like the "Delian Aretalogy of Sarapis" alluded to earlier (late second century B.C.E.). It is a consistent theme; migrating gods miraculously defend their worshipers against local opposition, silencing the rulers not so much of this world, but the rulers of this or that place—the opponents found in local space. This is, in fact, what actually crops up time and again in the eastern, largely Greek, *leges sacrae*. Local opposition, by local magistrates of one sort or another, or internal squabbling and competition, provoking the need to reconfigure the cult's relations to the broader community—this is the common narrative.[15]

Not to diminish the weight of the imperial "presence" in Paul's consciousness, I only suggest that we begin to speak of different levels in the immediacy of his concerns, levels that may vary from time to time and from place to place. These concerns are never matters of simple dualisms, either Christ or Caesar. Migrating cults faced with the dominant social group in their new homes certainly felt the pressure of exercised power, but they too found ways to exercise reciprocal power—often magical or otherworldly—over those they perceived as trying to impose a particular identity on them.

To be sure, a simplistic "push/push back," "punch/counter-punch" understanding of "negotiation" correlates quite well with a hermeneutic of resistance, but this is a hermeneutics that is not very subtle or supple. While Horsley's description of early Christianity as "an anti-imperial movement" represents a valuable course correction in recent New Testament scholarship,[16] his "resistance" model suffers from oversimplification to the point that for Horsley the early Pauline groups were not in any substantive sense cultic, despite the fact

---

15. E.g., the series of documents covering the history of the Thracian cult of Bendis at Athens: see *IG* II2 1283, cf. *IG* I3 136 and *IG* I3 383; Plato, *Resp.* 1.327a, 328a, 354a; Strabo, *Geog.* 10.3.16; *IG* II2 1361 for the Athenian adaptation; for the general movement of foreign cults into the Greek homeland, see: Martin Persson Nilsson, *Die hellenistische und römische Zeit* (vol. 2 of *Geschichte der griechischen Religion*; Handbuch der Altertumswissenschaft; Munich: Beck, 1974), 910–11 and 914.

16. Horsley, *Paul and Empire*, 1.

that membership was acquired and maintained by cultic ritual and consisted essentially in participating in spirit possession.[17] Our description of the Pauline groups must be more complicated than what can be distilled by simply boiling up a kind of "political reduction." The cultic groups we encounter in this period are largely polymorphic, "all of the above-yet none of the above" associations, not simply one thing or the other, but Bhabha's "third thing."

To take another view of Horsley's resistance model and its monolithic tendencies, his comment in *Paul and Empire*, contrasting the embrace of the imperial cult in Asia Minor as the embrace of a savior with Paul's rejection of that same savior, could be given more potency if it were to take fully into account the potential for the exercise of power in such appropriations by the colonized. Postcolonial studies routinely show that the embracing of symbols of power are strategies of control, not symptoms of submission.[18] Here one might point to the ongoing controversy over the confiscation of the so-called N-word by young African-American males who have wrestled the term away from the dominator, reclaiming it as the medium of a counter-claim to power, and forcing the dominator to abandon its use. In the Pauline churches, the notion of possessing and being possessed by the savior can thus be seen as an exercise of power. By this reading of Paul, Christ possession makes present what is otherwise distant, and functions simultaneously as the supreme act of identity declaration.

Finally, having suggested that Professor Galinsky's challenge could be usefully answered by increasing our application of postcolonial critique to our data, I would make an additional but complementary suggestion regarding, in particular, our approach to understanding the encounter between the imperial cult and the various communities of the empire. Whatever else we may say religion is, it certainly includes strategies for transforming irresistible and indifferent powers into entities with which negotiation and barter are possible. Such powers are transformed into "one of us," personalities with which we can deal. Can such transformations be reduced simply to political resistance as Horsley's model seems to do? Professor Galinsky's call for a more complex description of the ancient world would lead us to answer in the negative.

---

17. I agree with the description and terminology found in Christopher Mount, "1 Corinthians 11:3–16: Spirit Possession and Authority in a Non-Pauline Interpolation," *JBL* 124 (2005): 313–40; cf. also ch. 4 in James Constantine Hanges, *Christ, the Image of the Church: The Construction of a New Cosmology and the Rise of Christianity* (Contexts and Consequences: New Studies in Religion and History; Aurora, Col.: The Davies Group, 2006); for a more general discussion of Paul as an ecstatic, see John Ashton, *The Religion of Paul the Apostle* (New Haven, Conn.: Yale University Press, 2000).

18. Stuart Hall, "The After-Life of Frantz Fanon: Why Fanon? Why Now? Why *Black Skin, White Masks*?" in *The Fact of Blackness: Frantz Fanon and Visual Representation* (ed. Alan Read; London; Seattle: Institute of Contemporary Arts; Bay Press, 1996), 19–20.

Here we might beneficially return to some of the seminal thinkers in the study of religion—to a concept of myth and ritual that may offer us a challenging opportunity to redescribe our phenomena. Claude Lévi-Strauss tried to teach us at least this, that myth's fundamental purpose is to transform the absolutely opposed into manageable relationships.[19] More recently, Jonathan Z. Smith echoed this principle in his essay, "A Pearl of Great Price and a Cargo of Yams," with its crucial subtitle, "A Study in Situational Incongruity." By "situational incongruity" Smith refers to the conscious dissonance between what *is* and what *ought to be*. He shows that the myths he selects as examples are best understood as strategies designed to reimagine the world. Thus myths are not primarily reflections of historical cultic practice—they are not simply scripts for ritual.[20] Rather, myths are often exercises in world-transforming power. This, of course, reminds us of Neusner's description of the imagined world constructed by the early rabbis in the Mishnah.[21] But Smith goes further; it is not just myth that constructs ideal worlds but ritual serves a similar function. Myth and ritual often create a world that ought to be but is not, and most importantly, the participants, the users of myth and the practitioners of ritual, are aware of this discontinuity. As Smith tells us in "The Bare Facts of Ritual," the ritual enactment of the hunt resolves the incongruity between the imagination of the ideal hunt and the down and dirty way that the hunt actually takes place in reality.[22]

If we apply Smith's view to understanding the encounter between local communities and the empire, especially as this is expressed in their embrace of the divine emperor, perhaps we would see that the often described as spontaneous embrace of the divine emperor and the local manifestations of cult that are established in his honor are, at least in part, attempts to transform the world—ways of comprehending and reinscribing a seemingly immovable power as someone who cares about their concerns, as a power that is "one of us." Such a description will certainly complicate our picture, but it may also help us avoid facile interpretive models of the encounter between Rome, the center, and its periphery and move us a long way toward realizing Professor Galinsky's vision for the redescription of Mediterranean antiquity.

---

19. Claude Lévi-Strauss, "The Structural Study of Myth," *JAF* 67, no. 270, Myth: A Symposium (1955): 428–44.

20. Jonathan Z. Smith, *Imagining Religion: From Babylon to Jonestown* (CSJH; Chicago: Chicago University Press, 1982), 90–101.

21. What Neusner describes as "the Mishnah's own, inaccessible world," in Jacob Neusner, *The Mishnah: A New Translation* (New Haven, Conn.: Yale University Press, 1988), xiii, see esp. xvi–xviii.

22. Smith, *Imagining Religion*, 60–61.

Bibliography

Acheraïou, Amar. *Rethinking Postcolonialism: Colonialist Discourse in Modern Literatures and the Legacy of Classical Writers*. New York: Palgrave Macmillan, 2008.

Ashton, John. *The Religion of Paul the Apostle*. New Haven, Conn.: Yale University Press, 2000.

Baslez, Marie-Françoise. *Rechérches sur les conditions de pénétration et de diffusion des religions orientales à Délos (IIe-Ier s. avant notre ére)*. Collection de l'École Normale Supérieure de Jeunes Filles 9. Paris: École normale supérieure de jeunes filles, 1977.

Bhabha, Homi. *The Location of Culture*. 1994. Repr. Routledge Classics. London: Routledge, 2007.

Elsner, Jás. "Describing Self in the Language of Other: Pseudo (?) Lucian at the Temple of Hierapolis." Pages 123–53 in *Being Greek Under Rome: Cultural Identity, the Second Sophistic, and the Development of Empire*. Edited by Simon Goldhill. Cambridge: Cambridge University Press, 2001.

Galinsky, Karl. "The Cult of the Roman Emperor: Uniter or Divider?" Paper presented at the Annual Meeting of the SBL, Boston, 2008, and ch. 1 in this volume.

Hall, Stuart. "The After-Life of Frantz Fanon: Why Fanon? Why Now? Why *Black Skin, White Masks*?" Pages 12–37 in *The Fact of Blackness: Frantz Fanon and Visual Representation*. Edited by Alan Read. London; Seattle: Institute of Contemporary Arts; Bay Press, 1996.

Hanges, James Constantine. *Christ, the Image of the Church: The Construction of a New Cosmology and the Rise of Christianity*. Contexts and Consequences: New Studies in Religion and History. Aurora, Col.: The Davies Group, 2006.

Horsley, Richard A., ed. *Paul and Empire: Religion and Power in Roman Imperial Society*. Harrisburg, Pa.: Trinity Press International, 1997.

Jackson-McCab, Matt, ed. *Jewish Christianity Reconsidered: Rethinking Ancient Groups and Texts*. Minneapolis: Fortress, 2007.

Jacoby, Russell. "Marginal Returns: The Trouble with Postcolonial Theory." *Lingua Franca* 5 (1995): 30–37.

Lévi-Strauss, Claude. "The Structural Study of Myth." *Journal of American Folklore* 67, no. 270, Myth: A Symposium (1955): 428–44.

Mount, Christopher. "1 Corinthians 11:3–16: Spirit Possession and Authority in a Non-Pauline Interpolation." *Journal of Biblical Literature* 124 (2005): 313–40.

Nandy, Ashis. *The Intimate Enemy: Loss and Recovery of Self Under Colonialism*. Delhi: Oxford University Press, 1983.

Neusner, Jacob. *The Mishnah: A New Translation*. New Haven, Conn.: Yale University Press, 1988.

Nilsson, Martin Persson. *Die hellenistische und römische Zeit*. Vol. 2 of *Geschichte der griechischen Religion*. Handbuch der Altertumswissenschaft. Munich: Beck, 1974.

Smith, Jonathan Z. *Imagining Religion: From Babylon to Jonestown*. Chicago Studies in the History of Judaism. Chicago: Chicago University Press, 1982.

Weeks, Jeffrey. "The Value of Difference." Pages 88–100 in *Identity: Community, Culture, Difference*. Edited by Jonathan Rutherford. London: Lawrence & Wishart, 1990.

Chapter 4
Religion, Roman Religion, Emperor Worship

Jeffrey Brodd

This paper is based on one that I presented at the 2009 International Meeting of the Society of Biblical Literature in Rome, in the second of three SBL sequential sessions on "Rome and Religion: A Cross-Disciplinary Dialogue." It therefore looks back to the papers presented in the first session, at the 2008 Annual Meeting of the SBL in Boston. The third session was held at the 2009 Annual Meeting in New Orleans. I am grateful to Jonathan Reed for having organized the series, and to all presenters for providing an array of interrelated but wide-ranging ideas on the subject of emperor worship, from across a healthy expanse of disciplinary perspectives.

Karl Galinsky launched the sequence of sessions with his paper "The Cult of the Roman Emperor: Uniter or Divider?"[1] It provides a wealth of observations and ideas, and a road map for ongoing study of emperor worship. Here I wish to integrate ideas from his paper, and from the response papers that also were presented at the 2008 session, with an analysis of issues pertinent to defining "religion." Along with making a general plea for the efficacy of proceeding with conceptual clarity whenever studying Roman religion (or any other type of religion, and from any disciplinary perspective), I hope to suggest useful answers to some basic questions. What would a suitable definition of religion look like? What are the consequences and challenges of moving from "religion" in general to the more specific category Roman religion, and then to the even more specific category emperor worship? This article strives to illustrate means and benefits of moving from general to specific with the conceptual clarity afforded by suitable definitional constructs.

To begin with, we consider a potent example of what I've come to call "defying 'religion'"—potent in part due to its being drawn from a book that for good

---

1. Karl Galinsky, "The Cult of the Roman Emperor: Uniter or Divider?" paper presented at the Annual Meeting of the SBL, Boston, 2008, and ch. 1 in this volume.

reason is regarded as a standard authority. Mary Beard, John North, and Simon Price note in the Preface of their *Religions of Rome. Vol. 1: A History* that they have chosen "not to provide any formal definition of 'religion' ... in the book...." They go on to elaborate, "We have not worked with a single definition of religion in mind; we have worked rather to understand what might count as 'religion' in Rome and how that might make a difference to our own understanding of our own religious world."[2]

A few brave souls have provided potent counterexamples. This from the opening page of the "Religion" chapter in Karl Galinsky's *Augustan Culture*:

> Religion can be defined in various ways. In the Roman context, we have to be especially careful not to transpose later and Christian notions of what constitutes belief and faith to a system that was *sui generis*. But even when we use the most general definitions, it is clear that religion had to be an integral aspect of the restabilization of the Roman state and empire at the time. Fundamentally, religion is a response and alternative to chaos; it is an attempt to provide structure, order, and meaning, the very efforts that lay at the heart of the Augustan reconstitution of the *res publica*.[3]

Much is stated in this passage; to some extent, it provides its own kind of road map for this paper. To get right to the heart of the matter, though, we note that the closing sentence, which incorporates a bibliographic reference to Geertz's essay "Religion As a Cultural System," boldly asserts something about the function of religion. By comparison, Beard, North, and Price not only refrain from providing "any formal definition," but they also reveal that they "have not worked with a single definition of religion in mind...."

As the ensuing analysis will make clear, I urge a more assertive approach to definition, as offered in Galinsky's chapter. It is important, however, that we be realistic about context and purpose. *Religions of Rome* is a survey—albeit a very impressively thorough and detailed survey—that encompasses some one thousand years of cultural history. The "Religion" chapter in *Augustan Culture* is, naturally, confined mainly to the first half-century of the imperial period. Such a relatively specific time span accommodates greater conceptual specificity. Given the scope of *Religions of Rome*, Beard, North, and Price sensibly favor an "open textured" approach, a term they have drawn from a very helpful article by Fitz

---

2. Mary Beard, John North, and Simon Price, *Religions of Rome*. Vol. 1: *A History* (Cambridge: Cambridge University Press, 1998), x–xi.

3. Karl Galinsky, *Augustan Culture* (Princeton: Princeton University Press, 1996), 288.

John Porter Poole (more on this below).[4] This is not to say that I fully commend their act of "defying 'religion'"—as the ensuing analysis also should make clear.

In hopes of providing a useful framework for approaching the definitional question, I assert the following three points:

(1) A sound study of religion demands as much conceptual clarity as possible. The most effective means of achieving this is through definition, broadly understood. In the words of Melford Spiro, whose definition of religion we shall consider shortly, "It is obvious ... that while a definition cannot take the place of inquiry, in the absence of definitions there can be no inquiry—for it is the definition...which designates the phenomenon to be investigated."[5]

(2) A suitable definition of religion is a modern academic construct, not to be confused with ideas discerned in the cultures that we study. This implies that *we*, not—in our case—the ancient Romans, determine what is meant by and included within this category. Otherwise, we let the tail wag the dog. (This implies, among other things, that we ought not be overly influenced by the ancient concept *religio*, which is the etymological source of our modern word but is not necessarily semantically correlative.) In the words of Jonathan Z. Smith,

> "Religion" is not a native term; it is a term created by scholars for their intellectual purposes and therefore is theirs to define. It is a second-order, generic concept that plays the same role in establishing a disciplinary horizon that a concept such as "language" plays in linguistics or "culture" plays in anthropology. There can be no disciplined study of religion without such a horizon.[6]

(3) In dialectical fashion, the inquiry should continue to inform the pursuit of conceptual clarity. On this front, Beard, North, and Price are right to insist that we must strive to understand how "what might count as 'religion' in Rome" "might make a difference to our own understanding of our own religious world." Embarking upon a study with conceptual clarity should not be accompanied with resolve to maintain stubbornly any given conceptual perspective. Theory and data are inextricably linked.[7] Failure to acknowledge this can result in great damage, while great advantages can be gained through tending to the nature of their interplay.

---

4. Fitz John Porter Poole, "Metaphors and Maps: Towards Comparison in the Anthropology of Religion," *JAAR* 54 (1986): 428–432.

5. Melford E. Spiro, "Religion: Problems of Definition and Explanation," in *Anthropological Approaches to the Study of Religion* (ed. Michael Banton; London: Tavistock, 1966), 90.

6. Jonathan Z. Smith, "Religion, Religions, Religious," in *Critical Terms for Religious Studies* (ed. Mark C. Taylor; Chicago: University of Chicago Press, 1998), 281–82.

7. Poole, "Metaphors and Maps," 418, citing S. F. Nadel, *The Foundations of Social Anthropology* (Glencoe, Ill.: Free Press, 1951), 20–34.

Steve Friesen, in his response to Professor Galinsky's paper, on one hand sides with this call for conceptual assertiveness, while also offering important cautionary points:

> [I]n our study of imperial cults, let us be more systematic in our use of theories about the character of religion. I want to make clear that I am *not* advocating a search for the right theory that will give us the right interpretation of imperial cults. On the contrary, I think we need a lot of disciplined analysis from many points of view.[8]

These emphases on "disciplined analysis" and "many points of view" are highly apt. So too is the cautionary stance with regard to the intended effects of a "right theory."

This brings us to the important article by Fitz John Porter Poole, "Metaphors and Maps: Towards Comparison in the Anthropology of Religion," published in the *Journal of the American Academy of Religion* in 1986 (and declared by Jonathan Z. Smith fourteen years later to be "the most suggestive article on comparison of the past two decades").[9] Beard, North, and Price have done students of Roman religion a great service by referencing this article. In my opinion, however, their dismissal of the definitional task is not true to the gist of Poole's perspective, which amounts to an impassioned plea for rigorous and sophisticated theorizing. In his words, "I have implied all along that I am concerned to promote the position in the academic study of religion that both local understandings and broad abstractions must be anchored to matters of theory if they are to be meaningful, and that description and interpretation are necessary but not sufficient unless they are anchored to explanation, which implicates theory and method."[10]

I hasten to add that Poole does not insist on the employment of definition per se as the only means of such anchoring; he refers on occasion, for instance, to "definition *or classification*"[11] as sound means (italics mine). But he doesn't at all argue against the use of definition in general. His main complaint is leveled at "the monothetic, substantive, and phenomenal definition of religion"[12] as being too rigid to allow for effective interpretation of data, and as being too narrow

---

8. Steven J. Friesen, "Normal Religion, or, Words Fail Us: A Response to Karl Galinsky's 'The Cult of the Roman Emperor: Uniter or Divider?,'" paper presented at the Annual Meeting of the SBL, Boston, 2008 (and ch. 2 in this volume), 25.

9. Jonathan Z. Smith, "The 'End' of Comparison: Redescription and Rectification," in *A Magic Still Dwells: Comparative Religion in the Postmodern Age* (ed. Kimberley Patton; Berkeley and Los Angeles: University of California Press, 2000), 237.

10. Poole, "Metaphors and Maps," 439.

11. Ibid., 416, 438.

12. Ibid., 425.

to encompass adequately the variety of phenomena that ought to be included in the category. By way of describing healthy alternatives to monothetic definitions, Poole draws upon Ludwig Wittgenstein's notion of "family resemblance," and then proceeds to advocate various interrelated analytic tools: "polythetic categories, metaphoric constructions, and analogic mappings."[13] All of this for sake of facilitating comparison: "The metaphoric or analytic character of theoretical models is critically important for understanding key facets of comparative analysis." Poole at this point cites in a footnote thirty-two(!) works "on the complex role of metaphor and analogy in analysis." He then offers his own summary explanation: "Analytic models that exhibit metaphoric or analogic structure invoke a comparison by delimiting the focus of analysis to the comprehension of one entity in terms of another...."[14]

Poole devotes much of the article to identifying and summarizing various exemplars of such analytic models: Geertz's *Islam Observed* and other studies, E. E. Evans-Pritchard's "explication of the Nuer concept of *kwoth*," Smith's "Sacred Persistence: Toward a Redescription of Canon," to name just a few.[15] I suggest that we have closer to home some fine examples of "metaphoric constructions" and "analogic mappings"—or at least, of maps to mappings. I refer to various ideas brought forth in the papers of Karl Galinsky and his respondents. For example, he shows how the notion *sōtēr* affords a provocative centerpiece for isolating and comparing elements of the emperor worship and a range of other phenomena.[16] Elsewhere in his paper, the beginnings are in place for an interesting "analogic mapping" between pagan and Christian manifestations of the imperial cult; in one sentence alone he alludes to variations in sacrifices and *divus/sanctus* appellation, and to persistence in the artistic presentation of *adventus*.[17] All of this is very suggestive, and in keeping with the sort of comparative approach that Poole advocates.

---

13. Ibid., 441.
14. Ibid., 420. Jonathan Z. Smith offers a summary of resemblance theory that is helpful in this regard. Properly expressed comparative statements include "*x* resembles *y* more than *z* with respect to..." and "*x* resembles *y* more than *w* resembles *z* with respect to..." Smith continues, "That is to say, the statement of comparison is never dyadic, but always triadic; there is always an implicit 'more than,' and there is always a 'with respect to.' In the case of an academic comparison, the 'with respect to' is most frequently the scholar's interest, be this expressed in a question, a theory, or a model—recalling, in the case of the latter, that a model is useful precisely when it is different from that to which it is being applied." Jonathan Z. Smith, *Drudgery Divine: On the Comparison of Early Christianities and the Religions of Late Antiquity* (Chicago: University of Chicago Press, 1990), 51.
15. Poole, "Metaphors and Maps," 419–38.
16. Karl Galinsky, "The Cult of the Roman Emperor: Uniter or Divider?" paper presented at the Annual Meeting of the SBL, Boston, 2008 (and ch. 1 in this volume), 6.
17. Ibid., 15.

And the list goes on, in Galinsky's paper and in those of his respondents. Barbette Spaeth, in the course of her analysis of the imperial cult at Corinth, addresses the "role of women in the imperial cult" in a manner that exhibits an array of enticing points of comparison, especially vis-à-vis the role of the emperor.[18] Robin Jensen, through her astute analysis of a single group of fourth-century "Passion Sarcophagi," produces a fruitful comparison of Christ to the earthly emperor and illustrates widely divergent manifestations of victory and rule.[19] James Hanges, addressing the phenomenon of "negotiation" and in reference to evidence ranging from "Euripides's *Bakchai* (circa 406 B.C.E.)" to "the 'Delian Aretalogy of Sarapis'" finds "a consistent theme; migrating gods miraculously defend their worshipers against local opposition...."[20] This "consistent theme" is an inviting model for "analogic mapping." Steve Friesen draws up the vivid metaphor of "Mission Accomplished" George Bush and "Obama in Berlin," and ventures that in "these two figures, seen together in binocular fashion, we can perhaps begin to imagine the consumption of Roman imperial cults."[21] His book, *Imperial Cults and the Apocalypse of John: Reading Revelation in the Ruins*, effectively draws from Edward Said the musical metaphor of "counterpoint" (reminiscent of Claude Lévi-Strauss's "musical metaphors" that Poole enthusiastically endorses[22]), and incorporates a definitional approach adapted from Lawrence Sullivan's morphology of the mythic consciousness.[23]

Certain specific features of Roman culture typically deemed to be "religious" (e.g. by *Religions of Rome* and other such works)[24] also hold potential for helping to set up analytic models useful for the study of emperor worship. One is the concept *do ut des* ("I give in order that you might give"). Analogic mapping between this attitude as it is manifested in the worship of the traditional deities, on one hand, and of emperors and empresses, deceased and living, on the

---

18. Barbette Stanley Spaeth, "Imperial Cult in Roman Corinth: A Response to Karl Galinsky's 'The Cult of the Roman Emperor: Uniter or Divider?,'" paper presented at the Annual Meeting of the SBL, Boston, 2008 (and ch. 6 in this volume), 71–77. Points include general nomenclature, the figure of *sōtēr/sōteira*, and means of identification with deities.

19. Robin M. Jensen, "The Emperor Cult and Christian Iconography," paper presented at the Annual Meeting of the SBL, Boston, 2008 (as "The Emperor as Christ or Christ as Emperor? Response to Karl Galinsky," (and ch. 11 in this volume), 158–169.

20. James Constantine Hanges, "To Complicate Encounters: A Response to Karl Galinsky's 'The Cult of the Roman Emperor: Uniter or Divider?,'" paper presented at the Annual Meeting of the SBL, Boston, 2008 (and ch. 3 in this volume), esp. 31.

21. Friesen, "Normal Religion," 24–25.

22. Poole, "Metaphors and Maps," 435.

23. Steven J. Friesen, *Imperial Cults and the Apocalypse of John: Reading Revelation in the Ruins* (New York: Oxford University Press, 2001), esp. 12–15 and 19–21.

24. See for example Valerie M. Warrior, *Roman Religion: A Sourcebook*, Focus Classical Sources (Newburyport, Mass.: Focus, 2002), 7–13.

other, would assist in exploring such elements as "honorific" devotion and the charismatic aspect of the imperial cult. Another specific feature that provides an inviting model for analytic mapping is the interconnectedness between religion and politics. While in general we are ill served to insist on the separation of religion and politics, this is true only at the level of first-order analysis; that is, in our direct perception of Roman culture. As a second-order conceptual construct, "the political" has potential as a useful centerpiece for an analogic mapping between the imperial cult and other aspects of Roman religion. Isolating such specific functions facilitates a clearer approach to comparative study.

Turning now to the question of definition per se, how do definitions relate to the approach advocated by Poole, and what would a sound definition of religion look like? In answer to the second question, some "ground rules" based on principles of logic have helpfully been set forth. Hans Penner and Edward Yonan, for example, following Irving Copi, cite five main "purposes" of definitions: "(1) to increase vocabulary, (2) to eliminate ambiguity, (3) to clarify meaning, (4) to explain theoretically, and (5) to influence attitudes." Penner and Yonan then cite basic rules regarding the relation of the *definiens* to the *definiendum*.[25] Rather than getting too slowed down here with the specifics, however, it will be helpful to examine a definition that is looked upon favorably by Penner and Yonan and many other theorists; this from Melford Spiro:

> I shall define "religion" as an "institution consisting of culturally patterned interaction with culturally postulated superhuman beings."[26]

Poole praises Spiro's definition. Its relatively open-ended nature efficaciously facilitates rather than hinders Poole's "analytic metaphors and sophisticated analogic mappings."[27] In other words, he finds the definition *useful*, and this is a vital criterion by which to judge definitions of religion. In the words of Peter Berger, himself an extraordinary contributor to "disciplined analysis" and the pursuit of conceptual clarity, "a definition is not more or less true, only more or less useful."[28]

Spiro's definition would seem to be suitably broad in terms of encompassing a wide array of cultural phenomena, while at the same time restricting things to (for lack of a better term) "religion," with its reference to "superhuman beings."

---

25. Hans Penner and Edward Yonan, "Is a Science of Religion Possible?" *JR* 52 (1972): 115.
26. Spiro, "Religion," 96.
27. Poole, "Metaphors and Maps," 436.
28. Peter L. Berger, *The Sacred Canopy: Elements of a Sociological Theory of Religion*, reprint, 1967 (Garden City, N.Y.: Anchor, 1969), 175.

This is an especially intriguing element for studying the imperial cult. It is worth our while to consider Spiro's clarification of "superhuman beings":

> These refer to any beings believed to possess power greater than man, who can work good and/or evil on man, and whose relationships with man can, to some degree, be influenced by ... [this from an earlier section] activities which are believed to carry out, embody, or to be consistent with the will or desire of [the] superhuman beings ... [and] activities which are believed to influence [the superhuman beings] to satisfy the needs of the actors.[29]

For purposes of studying emperor worship, applying Spiro's category and definition to questions surrounding the nature of the emperors has potential for instilling conceptual clarity in a typically murky pool.

Of course, Spiro's definition can be criticized for being *too* restrictive, precisely due to its reference to "superhuman beings." He anticipates this very charge when discussing at some length the objection that Theravada Buddhism could be seen, through the lens of this definition, as not being a religion. His response is essentially, So what? In words that get at the heart of the notion of definitions as "useful," Spiro asks,

> Does the study of religion become any the less significant or fascinating—indeed, it would be even more fascinating—if in terms of a consensual ostensive definition it were discovered that one or seven or sixteen societies did not possess religion?[30]

This is not letting the tail wag the dog with a vengeance! This same sort of bold assertion of the priority of conceptual construct could be applied for any definition. But here again, the criterion of usefulness must prevail. If a certain definition of religion proves to be overly limiting or otherwise ineffectual, it needs to be revised or even abandoned.

We shall later take up Spiro's definition again when we hone in on *Roman* religion, and then on emperor worship. First, in part to avoid the misconception that Spiro's definition is somehow more "true" than others, it is worth our while to consider some alternatives. Karl Galinsky asserts in his "Religion" chapter that "religion is a response and alternative to chaos; it is an attempt to provide structure, order, and meaning ..." (for the full passage see above). Characterizing religion in this manner certainly serves to elucidate its function in "the Augustan reconstitution of the *res publica*."[31] It might not be true of *all* religions; then

---

29. Spiro, "Religion," 98, 97.
30. Ibid., 88.
31. Galinsky, *Augustan Culture*, 288.

again, it might be—it depends on how one chooses to fence in the category. Generally speaking, theorists today shy away from functionalist theories of religion, due in large part to their common tendency to lead to reductionism.[32] But I don't think their potential pitfalls should be overstated. Identifying such functional aspects of religion can be very *useful*—and so we're back on the firmer ground of this crucial criterion. Furthermore, calling attention to certain functional aspects of religion as they apply to a particular historical setting seems to me a legitimate approach, so long as these certain aspects are not imposed in a limiting way on a general definition of religion. Calling attention to the role of religion in providing "structure, order, and meaning" during the Augustan period is a help, not a hindrance, to facilitating our understanding of religion in this particular cultural setting.[33]

Galinsky's assertion that religion is "an attempt to provide structure, order, and meaning" recalls the well-known definition of Clifford Geertz (first set forth in 1964, in the same anthology in which Spiro's definition appears):

> Religion is (1) a system of symbols which acts to (2) establish powerful, pervasive, and long-lasting moods and motivations in men by (3) formulating conceptions of a general order of existence and (4) clothing these conceptions with such an aura of factuality that (5) the moods and motivations seem uniquely realistic.[34]

With Geertz's definition, we encounter what many have found over the decades to be an enticing descriptive statement that seems to say enough without getting bogged down in unwanted specificity. In keeping with Geertz's alleged antireductionist stance, the definition seems to be amenable to data derived through social

---

32. For example, Nancy Frankenberry and Hans Penner, "Geertz's Long-Lasting Moods, Motivations, and Metaphysical Conceptions," *JR* 79 (1999): 629. The authors assert that "functionalism, the very theory he most relies on in explicating a definition of religion, was bankrupt as a theory before Geertz's essay was even written." Melford Spiro, who insists on "nominal" or "ostensive" versus "real" definitions of religion, offers specific objections: "Most functionalist definitions of religion are essentially a subclass of real definitions in which functionalist variables (the promotion of solidarity, and the like) are stipulated as the essential nature of religion. But whether the essential nature consists of a qualitative variable (such as 'the sacred') or a functional variable (such as social solidarity), it is virtually impossible to set any substantive boundary to religion and, thus, to distinguish it from other sociocultural phenomena." Spiro, "Religion," 89–90.

33. For another good example of emphasizing a functionalist aspect of religion to good effect, consider Simon Price's assertion that "both [politics and religion] are ways of systematically constructing power." S. R. F. Price, *Rituals and Power: The Roman Imperial Cult in Asia Minor* (Cambridge: Cambridge University Press, 1984), 247.

34. Clifford Geertz, "Religion as a Cultural System," in *Anthropological Approaches to the Study of Religion* (ed. Michael Banton; London: Tavistock, 1966), 4.

scientific means, and yet not necessarily to preclude the reality of a superhuman something with which religion is engaged. According to Nancy Frankenberry and Hans Penner, the essay ["Religion as a Cultural System"] has cast its own "aura of factuality" in a way that manages to lull both believers and secularists into uncritical adoption of Geertz's definition of religion. Believers can see in it an affirmation of the intentional reference of their symbolic meanings, and secularists can still understand religion as an "as if" fictional affair whose aura of factuality is largely illusory or self-induced.[35]

Geertz's definition has indeed been popular and influential. Frankenberry and Penner note that their survey of journals of anthropology and religious studies from 1966 to 1996 found that the article ("Religion as a Cultural System") was cited at least five hundred times. These same authors, though, argue that the definition should be discarded, and they do so with rather harsh words of condemnation: "We find all five points in Geertz's definition problematic."[36] Talal Asad, in a thoroughgoing and highly influential critique, objects to, among other aspects, the definition's dependence on religious belief. He proceeds with his analysis of Geertz's definition in part to substantiate his own assertion "that there cannot be a universal definition of religion..."[37]

Bruce Lincoln defends Geertz's from some aspects of Asad's critique, but agrees regarding the problem of "belief." Lincoln's own definition, which is sure to be an enduringly important contribution, deserves to be included here if for no other reason than to encourage consideration of this provocative and useful approach to the definitional challenge. Lincoln asserts that a religion always consists of four "domains"—discourse, practice, community, and institution:

> (1) A discourse whose concerns transcend the human, temporal, and contingent, and that claims for itself a similarly transcendent status...
>
> (2) A set of practices whose purpose is to produce a proper world / or proper human subjects, as defined by a religious discourse to which these practices are connected...
>
> (3) A community whose members construct their identity with reference to a religious discourse and its attendant practices...
>
> (4) An institution that regulates religious discourse, practices, and community, reproducing them over time and modifying them as necessary, while asserting their eternal validity and transcendent value...[38]

---

35. Frankenberry and Penner, "Geertz's Long-Lasting Moods," 639.

36. Ibid., 618, 619.

37. Talal Asad, *Genealogies of Religion: Discipline and Reasons of Power in Christianity and Islam* (Baltimore: Johns Hopkins University Press, 1993), 29, 46.

38. Bruce Lincoln, *Holy Terrors: Thinking About Religion After September 11* (2nd ed.; Chicago: University of Chicago Press, 2006), 5–8.

Lincoln's definition is an extraordinarily inviting means of exploring religions for many reasons, not least of which is its facilitation of the sort of "analytic mapping" that Poole prescribes. For our purposes however, we return to Spiro's definition, as we proceed with moving from general to specific.

This article asked at the outset, What are the consequences and challenges of moving from "religion" in general to the more specific category Roman religion, and then to the even more specific category emperor worship? Of course, "Roman" itself is a descriptor that does not exactly suggest specificity; among other things, it refers to a very long span of cultural history. This challenge of specifying within a long span of history is by no means limited to the ancient Roman context, and it can be met without needing to step outside of the conceptual construct provided by a general definition of religion. Employing what Gerald Larson calls "diachronic-synchronic specification," we can demarcate "a religion" appropriately. Larson also contends that "religions" can simply and effectively be regarded as "the class of 'entities' to which the term Religion may be applied."[39] But questions persist. Where do we draw the lines? How specific, diachronically and synchronically, ought we to be? Larson offers as examples of legitimate entities "Hellenistic Jewish Religion" and "eighteenth-century Enlightenment Religion." But differences of opinions in such matters naturally abound. In any event, Larson ties categorization of "religions" to the general concept "religion," showing that a sound definition of the general concept helps to yield sound demarcation of the specific manifestations.

Because Spiro's definition asserts that "religion" is "an institution," it is already in line with this shift from "religion" to "religions," or to "a religion." Spiro's definition, moreover, quite easily facilitates the move from "a religion" in general to "Roman religion," since any given "institution" that is counted as a "religion" can be qualified as belonging to a particular culture. "Roman religion," in other words, can be said to be an "institution consisting of culturally patterned interaction with culturally postulated superhuman beings"—as manifested within Roman culture. This is an extremely helpful move toward enhancing the "theoretical utility" of a "category formation" (to recall Smith's terms), for now we are confining our considerations entirely to *Roman* "patterned interaction" with "superhuman beings" as the *Romans* "postulated" them.

Spiro's definition allows us to narrow further, provided we identify a specific "institution" within the general institution of Roman religion—for example, emperor worship—that is self-sufficient enough to warrant such focused categorizing. Ittai Gradel's *Emperor Worship and Roman Religion* (2002) offers useful examples. Gradel quite admirably begins his book with serious consideration of

---

39. Gerald James Larson, "Prolegomenon to a Theory of Religion," *JAAR* 46 (1978): 449.

conceptual constructs, leading to statements of definition. Along with defining religion, Gradel puts forth a definition of "emperor worship or 'the imperial cult' (a more flawed term, because more specific, giving the impression of a neat and independent category) will follow the ancient term of *divini* or *summii* or *caelestes honores*, the highest form of honours, with which gods were cultivated (but probably never gods *only*): sacrificial rites, whether blood sacrifice or bloodless (wine and incense) to the emperor, dead or alive."[40] Gradel's definition is helpfully specifying, yet it fits nevertheless within his more general definition of religion, and for that matter within Spiro's definition. Emperor worship consists of "sacrificial rites" ("culturally patterned interactions") to (or, with) "the emperor"—but as means of cultivating "gods" ("culturally postulated superhuman beings").

This same sort of moving from general to specific can be extended. Insofar as "Roman emperor worship" can be considered "an institution" (and thus, according to Spiro's definition, a religion), we could parse further, and categorize more specific manifestations of emperor worship as institutions in and of themselves. This, I think, offers a reasonable solution to the question over whether there was one "imperial cult" or a multiplicity of "cults." It is not necessary to opt for either, provided one is clear about categories. One could identify as an institution, for example, the imperial cult of the emperor Augustus in Athens—itself a subsidiary category of "emperor worship," which in turn is subsidiary to "Roman religion," and this to "religion" in general.

The pursuit of conceptual clarity leads to the enhancement of conceptual clarity, and therefore to more effective studies. Not to engage at all—to "defy 'religion'" entirely—is not efficacious. It is better to sin boldly in this regard, with an open attitude towards repentance of course, and, through attending to the ongoing interplay of theory and data (and now rather than quoting Professor Galinsky I quote *with* him), make haste slowly.

Bibliography

Asad, Talal. *Genealogies of Religion: Discipline and Reasons of Power in Christianity and Islam*. Baltimore: Johns Hopkins University Press, 1993.

Beard, Mary, John North, and Simon Price. *Religions of Rome*, Vol. 1: *A History*. Cambridge: Cambridge University Press, 1998.

Berger, Peter L. *The Sacred Canopy: Elements of a Sociological Theory of Religion*. 1967. Repr. Garden City, N.Y.: Anchor, 1969.

Frankenberry, Nancy, and Hans Penner. "Geertz's Long-Lasting Moods, Motivations, and Metaphysical Conceptions." *Journal of Religion* 79 (1999): 617–40.

Friesen, Steven J. *Imperial Cults and the Apocalypse of John: Reading Revelation in the*

---

40. Ittai Gradel, *Emperor Worship and Roman Religion* (New York: Oxford University Press, 2002), 6–7.

Ruins. New York: Oxford University Press, 2001.

———. "Normal Religion, or, Words Fail Us: A Response to Karl Galinsky's 'The Cult of the Roman Emperor: Uniter or Divider?'." Paper presented at the Annual Meeting of the SBL, Boston, 2008, and ch. 2 in this volume.

Galinsky, Karl. *Augustan Culture.* Princeton: Princeton University Press, 1996.

———. "The Cult of the Roman Emperor: Uniter or Divider?" Paper presented at the Annual Meeting of the SBL, Boston, 2008, and ch. 1 in this volume.

Geertz, Clifford. "Religion as a Cultural System." Pages 1–46 in *Anthropological Approaches to the Study of Religion.* Edited by Michael Banton. London: Tavistock, 1966.

Gradel, Ittai. *Emperor Worship and Roman Religion.* New York: Oxford University Press, 2002.

Hanges, James Constantine. "To Complicate Encounters: A Response to Karl Galinsky's 'The Cult of the Roman Emperor: Uniter or Divider?'." Paper presented at the Annual Meeting of the SBL, Boston, 2008, and ch. 3 in this volume.

Jensen, Robin M. "The Emperor Cult and Christian Iconography," paper presented at the Annual Meeting of the SBL, Boston, 2008 (as "The Emperor as Christ or Christ as Emperor? Response to Karl Galinsky"), and ch. 11 in this volume.

Larson, Gerald James. "Prolegomenon to a Theory of Religion." *Journal of the American Academy of Religion* 46 (1978): 443–63.

Lincoln, Bruce. *Holy Terrors: Thinking About Religion After September 11.* 2nd ed. Chicago: University of Chicago Press, 2006.

Nadel, S. F. *The Foundations of Social Anthropology.* Glencoe, Ill.: Free Press, 1951.

Penner, Hans, and Edward Yonan. "Is a Science of Religion Possible?" *Journal of Religion* 52 (1972): 107–33.

Poole, Fitz John Porter. "Metaphors and Maps: Towards Comparison in the Anthropology of Religion." *Journal of the American Academy of Religion* 54 (1986): 411–57.

Price, S. R. F. *Rituals and Power: The Roman Imperial Cult in Asia Minor.* Cambridge: Cambridge University Press, 1984.

Smith, Jonathan Z. *Drudgery Divine: On the Comparison of Early Christianities and the Religions of Late Antiquity.* Chicago: University of Chicago Press, 1990.

———. "The 'End' of Comparison: Redescription and Rectification." Pages 237–41 in *A Magic Still Dwells: Comparative Religion in the Postmodern Age.* Edited by Kimberley Patton. Berkeley and Los Angeles: University of California Press, 2000.

———. "Religion, Religions, Religious." Pages 269–84 in *Critical Terms for Religious Studies.* Edited by Mark C. Taylor. Chicago: University of Chicago Press, 1998.

Spaeth, Barbette Stanley. "Imperial Cult in Roman Corinth: A Response to Karl Galinsky's 'The Cult of the Roman Emperor: Uniter or Divider?'." Paper presented at the Annual Meeting of the SBL, Boston, 2008, and ch. 6 in this volume.

Spiro, Melford E. "Religion: Problems of Definition and Explanation.". In *Anthropological Approaches to the Study of Religion.* Edited by Michael Banton. London: Tavistock, 1966.

Warrior, Valerie M. *Roman Religion: A Sourcebook.* Focus Classical Sources. Newburyport, Mass.: Focus, 2002.

CHAPTER 5
AUGUSTAN RELIGION: FROM LOCATIVE TO UTOPIAN

Eric M. Orlin

In his wide-ranging and stimulating paper, Karl Galinsky noted, among many other developments, the religious pluralism of the Roman Empire.[1] Citing the work of John North and Richard Gordon, Galinsky described the story as "one of development from religion as embedded in the city-state to religion as a choice of differentiated groups offering different qualities of religious doctrine, different experiences, insights, or just different myths and stories to make sense of the absurdity of human experience."[2] He noted that the Roman state, with its emphasis on what Jonathan Z. Smith has labeled "locative" religion, or what Mary Beard, John North, and Simon Price refer to as a "religion of place," had by the first century C.E. seen its share of "utopian" religions; the usual Roman policy of laissez-faire had provided room for these religious groups to grow. Using Smith's observations as a starting point, this paper suggests that Roman religion had already begun to develop away from the locative model over the last centuries of the Republic, and its development of certain "utopian" qualities needs to be seen as a significant part of the background within which to examine the spread of the imperial cult(s) and the rise of Christianity and other "utopian" religions.

The distinction between locative and utopian religions has proved useful in analyzing the religions of the ancient world. The model of locative religions provides a broader perspective to understand the polis-religion model; as formulated by Smith, "the homeplace, the place to which one belongs, was the central reli-

---

1. Karl Galinsky, "The Cult of the Roman Emperor: Uniter or Divider?" paper presented at the Annual Meeting of the SBL, Boston, 2008 (and ch. 1 in this volume), 7–9.

2. John North, "The Development of Religious Pluralism," in *The Jews Among Christians and Pagans in the Roman Empire* (ed. Judith Lieu, John North, and Tessa Rajak; London: Routledge, 1992), 17. See also Richard Gordon, "Reality, Evocation, and Boundaries in the Mysteries of Mithra," *JMS* 3 (1980): 19–99.

gious category."[3] One's self-definition was tied to a specific place, understood as both geographical and social place. Smith uses "utopian" in the strictest sense of the word, a religion of "nowhere," with an interest in transcendence or a place beyond the ordinary world. Roman religion fits well into the locative model; it is widely agreed that Roman religion of the early and middle Republic was a religion of place, in both the geographical and social senses.[4] Rituals needed to be performed not only in the prescribed way and at the prescribed time, but in the prescribed place: the Lupercalia needed to be run around the Palatine Hill, sacrifices by the consuls on their first day in office made at the temple of Jupiter on the Capitoline Hill, auguries taken in specified places. The *pomerium*, the ritual boundary that demarcated the city of Rome, reminds us of the importance of religious space, for throughout much of Rome's history it did not run the same course as the political or military boundaries of the city, its walls.[5] Roman religion defined not only physical boundaries, but social boundaries as well. Religious practices acted not only as a means of demarcating members of the Roman community from nonmembers by their participation in the ritual, but also of demarcating hierarchical boundaries within that community; one need only think of the battles over the access of plebeians to priestly offices to recognize the importance of religion in defining social space for the Romans.[6]

The best encapsulation of the notion of the religion of place from a Roman literary source comes from a speech that Livy ascribes to the great Camillus after his rescue of Rome from the hands of the Gauls in 390 B.C.E. In response to suggestions that the Romans might simply pick up and move to Veii, Camillus declares:

> there is no spot in [our City] which is not full of *religio* and the gods; the festive sacrifices have appointed places no less than they have appointed days.... Perhaps someone might suggest that we can either perform these rites at Veii or send our priests to perform them here. But neither of these things can be done without a violation of the ceremony ... in the case of the feast of Jupiter, where else but on the Capitol can the couch of Jupiter be prepared? ... [Our ancestors]

---

3. Jonathan Z. Smith, *Map is not Territory: Studies in the History of Religions* (Leiden: Brill, 1978), xiv.

4. Mary Beard, John North, and Simon Price, *Religions of Rome*, Vol. 1: *A History* (Cambridge: Cambridge University Press, 1998), ch. 4, esp. pp. 167–68.

5. On the *pomerium*, see Maddalena Andreussi, "Roma: Il pomerio," *ScAnt* 2 (1988): 219–34, and Bernadette Liou-Gille, "Le pomerium," *MH* 50 (1993): 94–106.

6. For conflicts over the participation of plebeians in Roman religion, see Beard, North, and Price, *Religions of Rome 1*, 63–68. Other ways in which Roman religion reinforced the hierarchies of Roman society include gender divisions in the worship of different divinities (such as the all-female worship of the Bona Dea, or restricted seating at *ludi*, said to have begun at the games for the Magna Mater in the early second century B.C.E. [Livy 34.54]).

left to us certain rites which need to be performed on the Alban Mount or at Lavinium.[7]

While one should not put much historical weight on these specific words, they seem to reflect a genuinely Roman point of view, visible both in cult activity and other literary sources. The context in which this passage was written is noteworthy; Livy wrote his history during the age of Augustus, when the nature of Roman religion was very much open to question in the wake of the civil wars.[8] Throughout his history Livy seems at pains to emphasize the notion of a "religion of place," which suggests that perhaps the notion was not as strongly implanted as it had been at one point, or as Livy might have wanted. Indeed I suggest that by the time of Augustus Roman religion should not be viewed so easily as a religion of place.

From the third century B.C.E. onward, as the Romans developed their territorial empire, a number of signs emerged revealing that Roman religious activities were no longer tied so exclusively to the city of Rome and no longer served to put only Romans in their place.[9] As early as 269 B.C.E., the Roman Senate began to accept prodigies that occurred outside of the city of Rome as having implications for the Romans' relationship with their gods; lightning did not have to strike in Rome, or blood flow from a statue in Rome, for the Romans to believe that the gods were angry at them and that expiations needed to be performed.[10] Perhaps even more significantly, on a number of occasions the Romans directed that an expiation should be performed outside of the city of Rome, as in 217 when expiations were performed in the forum of Ardea as part of the response to the many prodigies that accompanied Hannibal's arrival in Italy, despite the fact that none

---

7. Livy 5.52: *Urbem auspicato inauguratoque conditam habemus; nullus locus in ea non religionum deorumque est plenus; sacrificiis sollemnibus non dies magis stati quam loca sunt in quibus fiant... Forsitan aliquis dicat aut Veiis ea nos facturos aut huc inde missuros sacerdotes nostros qui faciant; quorum neutrum fieri saluis caerimoniis potest. Et ne omnia generatim sacra omnesque percenseam deos, in Iouis epulo num alibi quam in Capitolio puluinar suscipi potest? Illi sacra quaedam in monte Albano Lauiniique nobis facienda tradiderunt.*

8. On the lack of definition in Roman religion and Roman society more generally during the late Republic, see especially Beard, North, and Price (ibid.), ch. 3.

9. For a fuller version of the arguments contained in this paragraph, see Eric M. Orlin, *Foreign Cults in Rome: Creating a Roman Empire* (Oxford: Oxford University Press, 2010), 111–36, 164–96, 176–80.

10. Bruce MacBain, *Prodigy and Expiation: A Study in Religion and Politics in Republican Rome* (Collection Latomus 177; Brussels: Latomus, 1982), 31–32. On public prodigies in Rome, see also Veit Rosenberger, *Gezähmte Götter: Das Prodigienwesen der römischen Republik* (Heidelberger althistorische Belträge und epigraphische Studien 27; Stuttgart: Steiner, 1998), and Susanne William Rasmussen, *Public Portents in Republican Rome* (ARIDSup 34; Rome: L'Erma di Bretschneider, 2003).

of these prodigies actually came from Ardea.[11] These religious actions can be seen as part of the Roman effort to unite her Italian allies more closely with her in the struggle against Hannibal, but they begin to reveal a sense that Roman religion no longer concerned only Rome, but other parts of Italy as well.[12] This sense can only have been reinforced following the war against Hannibal, when in response to a plague in 180, the Senate decreed that supplications be held in all the *fora et conciliabula* of Italy.[13] Here, a ritual that had become part of the repertoire of Roman religious rituals was performed all over Italy; whatever functions were served by this ritual were shared equally by Romans and the residents of those Italian towns. The famous incidents of the Bacchanalia and the sacrilege of the roof tiles at the temple of Hera Lacinia in Croton can also be seen in this light, as the extension of Roman religious concern to include Italy.[14] Rome was no longer the only place where Roman religious acts could be performed, and those living in Rome were no longer the only ones whom the rituals concerned. As a result, it was now possible to imagine a religious community that had a place for Italian cities as well as Rome.

Despite the fact that Beard, North, and Price label their section on the Augustan era "The Re-Placing of Roman Religion," I want to suggest that this era actually marks an important moment in the development of Roman religion *away* from a religion of place, a confirmation of the trends of the late Republic. For all the efforts placed by the Augustan "message makers" on restoration, a closer look reveals that Augustan actions did more to detach Roman religion from its emphasis on place than the slow organic developments of the previous two hundred years. For example, the temple of Jupiter Optimus Maximus on the Capitoline had stood as the central temple of the Roman state religion for nearly five hundred years, yet Augustus clearly, and no doubt intentionally, de-emphasized it. The emperor's new temple to Mars Ultor became the central focus of religious actions related to the military: commanders set off from the temple, the Senate met there to consider voting triumphs, and triumphal spoils were dedicated there. The Sibylline Books, which had been stored in the cella of Jupiter

---

11. Livy 22.1.
12. See Rasmussen, *Public Portents* 241–46 for a discussion of the prodigies and responses at the time of Hannibal's invasion.
13. Livy 40.37.
14. The bibliography on the Bacchanalia is vast; Jean-Marie Pailler, *Bacchanalia: La répression de 186 av. J.-C. à Rome et en Italie: vestiges, images, tradition* (Rome: École française de Rome, 1988), and Jean-Marie Pailler, "Les Bacchanales, dix ans après," *Pallas* 48 (1998): 67–86, are essential starting points. On the incident at Croton, see Bruno Poulle, "D'Héra Lacinia à Fortuna Equestris (Tite-Live 42,3): 'Emprunt' ou sacrilège?" *REL* 82 (2004): 76–88, and Mary Jaeger, "Livy, Hannibal's Monument, and the Temple of Juno at Croton," *TAPA* 136 (2006): 389–414.

since their acquisition, were moved to new temple of Apollo on the Palatine Hill. Augustus even built an elaborate temple to Jupiter Tonans on the slope of the Capitoline Hill; the temple detracted enough from the glory of the older temple that the emperor hung bells on the gables of the new temple to claim that it was merely the doorkeeper for the main temple on top of the hill.[15] It is clear that the chief deity of the Roman Republic was dislodged from his position theologically, ritually, and physically.

The treatment of the goddess Vesta by Augustus shows a similar move away from the notions of place articulated by Livy. Under the Republic, Vesta's temple in the forum had functioned as one of the centers of Roman state religion, and the *pontifex maximus*, who supervised the Vestal Virgins among his other duties, lived in the *domus publica* next door. By the time Augustus eventually became *pontifex maximus* in 12 B.C.E., he was already comfortably ensconced in his house on the Palatine Hill, with its adjacent temple of Apollo. The emperor had no intention of moving down into the forum, but at the same time after emphasizing his scrupulous observance in waiting for Lepidus to die before succeeding to the role, he could hardly ignore this particular requirement. His solution was to make part of his house on the Palatine the Regia and give over part of the house to Vesta, thus enabling the *pontifex maximus* to live where he should. While this action has often been noted among Augustus's religious activity, its implications for notions of space have seldom been properly appreciated. Augustus's conception of Roman religion must have been different from that of Livy: Vesta could have her shrine moved from the forum to the Palatine with no apparent violation of her rites. This kind of re-placement served to cut the original link between place and cult, and instead established a new series of associations for Vesta, this time between the cult and the figure of the emperor. I will return to this point below.

Thus far, my focus has been to demonstrate that Roman religion at the time of Augustus was much less locative than is commonly thought, but several elements also indicate moves towards a more utopian notion of religion, at least in the sense of a religion that was not tied to worship in a specific place, Rome. One clear indication is the appearance of inscribed stone calendars from many communities in Italy in this period. These calendars describe the Roman festival year, listing single day celebrations such as the Lupercalia, multiday festivals such as the *ludi Romani,* and the dedication days of specific temples located in Rome; some even marked the day on which Rome was said to be founded. The fact that local magistrates were listed on these *fasti* alongside Roman ones sug-

---

15. Suetonius, *Aug.* 91.2. See further Karl Galinsky, *Augustan Culture* (Princeton: Princeton University Press, 1996), 295–96.

gests that these calendars were commissioned locally, but the primary intent of these calendars was surely not for people to make a pilgrimage to Rome in order to participate in these festivals. Clearly it was important for the residents of Antium or Praeneste (or wherever) to know what festivals were being celebrated in Rome; even separated by a several days' journey from Rome, the locals in some measure were able to "participate" in the rituals through their knowledge of them. Rome was the center of activity, but no longer were people in Rome the only people concerned with the celebration of rituals there. As Andrew Wallace-Hadrill put it: "Roman time becomes the property of all Romans."[16] One could be in any place and still partake in the Roman festival calendar. It is noteworthy that the inscribed calendars date almost exclusively to the late Republic or Augustan period; even if not a deliberate policy of the emperors, this phenomenon highlights the changes that must have already taken place by this period.

The worship of the Capitoline Triad outside Rome offers an even clearer example of the spread of Roman religious practice and its separation from its locative space. From 509 B.C.E. the Romans had worshiped Jupiter, Juno, and Minerva on the Capitoline Hill, in a location that in their minds was imbued with sanctity; even before the temple was built, one of the gods who was at that time receiving worship on the spot, Terminus, refused to move, and so the temple had to be built to accommodate the previous cult on that spot. This legend of the temple's founding serves to highlight the importance of place: the connection of Terminus to the spot was so strong that even the temple of Jupiter, the most important temple in Rome, had to accommodate it rather than vice versa. But already in the late Republic, Capitolia, or temples to the Capitoline Triad began appearing in Italian communities, notably in Pompeii and Ostia, but also in a number of other places, and eventually outside Italy as well.[17] Here the link between Jupiter and his accustomed place is again re-imagined—it is the specifically Capitoline version of Jupiter that is being worshipped, but the rituals honoring him no longer have to be performed on the Capitoline Hill. As with the calendars, a number of these temples, such as at Cumae and Assisi, date to the Augustan era; again we can see emerging a community of worshippers centered on Rome but extending throughout Italy, and at the expense of the specially locative notion of Roman religion.

A further example of the appearance of locative cults outside Italy during the first century of the empire underscores the degree to which Roman religion had

---

16. Andrew Wallace-Hadrill, "*Mutatas Formas*: The Augustan Transformation of Roman Knowledge," in *The Cambridge Companion to the Age of Augustus* (ed. Karl Galinsky; Cambridge: Cambridge University Press, 2005), 61.

17. Ian M. Barton, "Capitoline Temples in Italy and the Provinces (Especially Africa)," *ANRW* 12.1:259–342.

become available anywhere. Magistrates in the Spanish town of Irni, according to an inscription found in the town, were to swear by the *dei Penates* (among other gods) that they would act in accordance with the law and in the best interests of the town, and a similar clause is found in the towns of Malaca and Salpensa.[18] The Penates were divinities central to the Roman imagination; in theory they had been brought by Aeneas from Troy to Lavinium and so physically represented an important element of Roman identity. More than that, they are deities intimately connected with a sense of place; the Penates were supposed to be worshipped at Lavinium, the city founded by Aeneas.[19] Valerius Maximus even tells the story of Ascanius founding Alba Longa and attempting to move the Penates to the new town, only to find that the images of the gods moved themselves back to Lavinium not once, but twice.[20] The story is a prime example of the locative nature of early Roman religion: the Penates themselves indicated that they had their home in Lavinium, and only in Lavinium. Despite the fact that the Romans did build a shrine to the *dei Penates* in Rome, they did not move the cult statues to Rome, and every year the consuls made a pilgrimage to Lavinium to make offerings to the Penates. The appearance of the Penates in Spain testifies to the fact that their power was no longer (if ever) believed to exist only in Lavinium or Rome, but anywhere that the Romans held sway. That the Penates were felt to have power to enforce oaths as far away as Spain indicates a conception of the Penates that is very different from the gods for whom the Roman magistrates needed to make a twenty-mile journey, not tied to a place but to whom Roman citizens living anywhere could make appeal.[21] And those making such appeals could imagine Romans, both those living in Rome and those living elsewhere, making similar appeals, and thus existing as part of the same community.

I cite these examples to offer a sense of the changes in Roman religious behavior, but not to claim that the locative model no longer applies to religion in the empire, for there is of course much continuity in this area. The importance of specific places continued to be an important concept in the empire; the existence of a special, and apparently artificial, priesthood at Lavinium, specifically charged with performing the rituals associated with the Roman magistrates, attests to the continued importance of that site, even while the Penates could now be invoked

---

18. Julián González, "The Lex Irnitana: A New Copy of the Flavian Municipal Law," *JRS* 76 (1986): 147–243.

19. Annie Dubourdieu, *Les origines et le développement du culte des pénates à Rome* (Collection de l'École française de Rome 118; Rome: École française de Rome, 1989), 219–229 and 319–361.

20. Valerius Maximus 1.8.7.

21. Cf. Clifford Ando, *The Matter of the Gods: Religion and the Roman Empire* (Berkeley and Los Angeles: University of California Press, 2008), 95–99.

empire-wide.[22] Roman religion under the empire can be also viewed as locative in the broader sense of defining geographical and social place. Not only were practices that can be defined as "Roman" performed throughout the empire, but their performance contributed to defining the community of Romans. Just as early Roman religion, tied to specific places in the city, helped one's self-definition through association with the "homeplace," so the practices of the early empire identified one as a member of "Rome," conceived as a broader community and not just a location. Roman religion might still be viewed as embedded within Roman society, but only if we acknowledge that this society has expanded to include the territorial confines of the empire and not simply the residents of a polis.

The appearance of a utopian element within Roman religion is, however, a development that should not be underestimated, particularly if we are to understand religious developments in the Roman Empire. Specific locations can still have an important place in utopian traditions; the importance of Jerusalem or Mecca within modern-day Christianity, Judaism, and Islam might be considered alongside that of Lavinium in the Roman Empire. The knowledge of the Roman festival calendar outside Rome and the appearance of once locative Roman cults outside Rome allowed residents of the empire to imagine themselves as part of a larger community. People living outside the city of Rome or even outside Italy could imagine others partaking in similar festivals or paying homage to the same divinities. Furthermore Andreas Bendlin has suggested that we should not overemphasize the differences between the state religious system and other forms of religious activity, but that instead we might envisage a "deregulated religious pluralism [of] worshippers with variable commitments."[23] Such a system, with cults ranging from Capitoline Jupiter to Aesculapius to sanctuaries even outside Rome, implies a religion no longer embedded into society, but "semi-detached from it": the homeplace was not the overriding religious consideration, but inhabitants of a town might have chosen which cults to worship, whether in their own town or more geographically distant. These developments, both in Bendlin's model and what I have discussed above, were underway well before the advent of the imperial political system; although attention tends to focus on the religious activity of the emperor Augustus, the turning point came much earlier with the growth of a hegemonic empire.

---

22. Yan Thomas, "L'institution de l'origine: *Sacra Principiorum Populi Romani*," in *Tracés de fondation* (ed. Marcel Detienne; Leuven, Belgium: Peeters, 1990), 143–70.

23. Andreas Bendlin, "Looking Beyond the Civic Compromise: Religious Pluralism in Late Republican Rome," in *Religion in Archaic and Republican Rome and Italy: Evidence and Experience* (ed. Edward Bispham and Christopher Smith; Chicago: Fitzroy Dearborn, 2000), 134.

Understanding this background is essential to understanding Roman religion in the first few centuries c.e., and especially the actions of the emperors, which now appear as a continued development of a trend rather than an innovation. The imperial cult, the focus of Karl Galinsky's paper, comes into clearer focus even with all of its local and idiosyncratic permutations. As the imperial cult grew, all Romans participated (or were supposed to participate) in this cult in some fashion, and could imagine other Romans participating in the same cult, even if there were local variations in ritual, location, or other details. Here the differences with the republican religion of place become quite evident: imperial cult practices focused around the person (or persons) of the emperor rather than a specific place. The intertwining of the cult of Vesta with the emperor mentioned above can be understood in this light: what is important under Augustus is less the *place* where Vesta had been worshipped than the *person* of the emperor with whom she is now associated. As emperors came to travel more and more around the empire, even his personage was not tied to one place; more significantly, his power was not limited but was felt to be everywhere throughout the empire. Thus it should not be surprising to find that magistrates in Irni, in addition to the *dei Penates,* also had to swear by "the divine Augustus, the divine Claudius, the divine Vespasian Augustus, the divine Titus Augustus, [and] the genius of Imperator Caesar Domitian Augustus."[24] The imperial cult, just like the previously locative cults of Rome, helped to bind the inhabitants of the empire together in a religious community that could be shared anywhere in the empire.

I am not suggesting that Roman religion became just like other utopian religions, or that the imperial cult, however constituted, should be seen in these terms. The ability of the imperial cult to "transcend" space, and even time—a feature associated with other utopian traditions—seems at first blush unlikely, but it is worthy of further consideration. More significantly, however, the religious developments of the early empire need to be understood in the context of the developments in traditional Roman practice. Locative and utopian elements of course exist in some balance within most religious systems, and that balance shifted significantly already in the late Republic toward the utopian side of the scale. While attention has tended to focus on the developments under Augustus, I would suggest that the trend was set in motion by the development of Rome's hegemonic empire, and that the emperor's actions and the imperial cult are further stages in that process. Utopian traditions had not merely been tolerated but accepted within Roman religion for several centuries, and their visibility in the empire should not be seen as a new development or one contrary to the spirit of Roman religious practice, but as a natural outgrowth of that system itself.

---

24. *Lex Irnitana* 26 (from González, "Lex Irnitana.").

Bibliography

Ando, Clifford. *The Matter of the Gods: Religion and the Roman Empire.* Berkeley and Los Angeles: University of California Press, 2008.

Andreussi, Maddalena. "Roma: Il pomerio." *Scienze dell'Antichità* 2 (1988): 219–34.

Barton, Ian M. "Capitoline Temples in Italy and the Provinces (Especially Africa)." *ANRW* 12.1:259–342. Part 2, Principat, 12.1. Edited by Hildegard Temporini. New York: de Gruyter, 1982.

Beard, Mary. "A Complex of Times: No More Sheep on Romulus' Birthday." *Proceedings of the Cambridge Philological Society* 33 (1987): 1–15.

———, John North, and Simon Price. *Religions of Rome.* Vol. 1: *A History.* Cambridge: Cambridge University Press, 1998.

Bendlin, Andreas. "Looking Beyond the Civic Compromise: Religious Pluralism in Late Republican Rome." Pages 115–35 in *Religion in Archaic and Republican Rome and Italy: Evidence and Experience.* Edited by Edward Bispham and Christopher Smith. Chicago: Fitzroy Dearborn, 2000.

Bispham, Edward. *From Asculum to Actium: The Municipalization of Italy from the Social War to Augustus.* New York: Oxford University Press, 2007.

De Cazanove, Olivier. "Some Thoughts on the 'Religious Romanisation' of Italy Before the Social War." Pages 71–76 in *Religion in Archaic and Republican Rome and Italy: Evidence and Experience.* Edited by Edward Bispham and Christopher Smith. Chicago: Fitzroy Dearborn, 2000.

Dubourdieu, Annie. *Les origines et le développement du culte des pénates à Rome.* Collection de l'École française de Rome 118. Rome: École française de Rome, 1989.

Eder, W. "Augustus and the Power of Tradition: The Augustan Principate as Binding Link Between Republic and Empire." Pages 71–122 in *Between Republic and Empire: Interpretations of Augustus and His Principate.* Kurt A. Raaflaub and Mark Toher. Berkeley and Los Angeles: University of California Press, 1990.

Fraschetti, Augusto. *Roma e il principe.* Rome: Editori Laterza, 1990.

Galinsky, Karl. *Augustan Culture.* Princeton: Princeton University Press, 1996.

———. "The Cult of the Roman Emperor: Uniter or Divider?" Paper presented at the Annual Meeting of the SBL, Boston, 2008, and ch. 1 in this volume.

Giardina, Andrea. *L'Italia romana: Storia di un'identità incompiuta.* Rome: Editori Laterza, 1997.

González, Julián. "The Lex Irnitana: A New Copy of the Flavian Municipal Law." *Journal of Roman Studies* 76 (1986): 147–243.

Gordon, Richard. "Reality, Evocation, and Boundaries in the Mysteries of Mithra." *Journal of Mithraic Studies* 3 (1980): 19–99.

Gros, Pierre. *Aurea templa: Recherches sur l'architecture religieuse de Rome à l'époque d'Auguste.* Bibliothèque des Écoles française d'Athènes et de Rome 231. Paris: École française de Rome.

Jaeger, Mary. "Livy, Hannibal's Monument, and the Temple of Juno at Croton." *Transactions of the American Philological Association* 136 (2006): 389–414.

Kienast, Dietmar. *Augustus: Prinzeps und Monarch.* Darmstadt, Germany: Wissenschaftliche Buchgesellschaft, 1982.

Liebeschuetz, J. H. W. G. *Continuity and Change in Roman Religion.* New York: Oxford

University Press, 1979.
Liou-Gille, Bernadette. "Le pomerium." *Museum helveticum* 50 (1993): 94–106.
MacBain, Bruce. *Prodigy and Expiation: A Study in Religion and Politics in Republican Rome*. Collection Latomus 177. Brussels: Latomus, 1982.
North, John. "The Development of Religious Pluralism." Pages 174–93 in *The Jews Among Christians and Pagans in the Roman Empire*. Edited by Judith Lieu, John North, and Tessa Rajak. London: Routledge, 1992.
———. "Diviners and Divination at Rome." Pages 49–71 in *Pagan Priests*. Edited by Mary Beard and John North. London: Duckworth, 1990.
Orlin, Eric M. *Foreign Cults in Rome: Creating a Roman Empire*. Oxford: Oxford University Press, 2010.
Pailler, Jean-Marie. *Bacchanalia: La répression de 186 av. J.-C. à Rome et en Italie: vestiges, images, tradition*. Rome: École française de Rome, 1988.
———. "Les Bacchanales, dix ans après." *Pallas* 48 (1998): 67–86.
Poulle, Bruno. "D'Héra Lacinia à Fortuna Equestris (Tite-Live 42,3): 'Emprunt' ou sacrilège?" *Revue des études latines* 82 (2004): 76–88.
Purcell, Nicholas. "Romans in the Roman World." Pages 85–105 in *The Cambridge Companion to the Age of Augustus*. Edited by Karl Galinsky. Cambridge: Cambridge University Press, 2005.
Rasmussen, Susanne William. *Public Portents in Republican Rome*. Analecta Romana Instituti Danici Supplementum 34. Rome: L'Erma di Bretschneider, 2003.
Rosenberger, Veit. *Gezähmte Götter: Das Prodigienwesen der römischen Republik*. Heidelberger althistorische Beiträge und epigraphische Studien 27. Stuttgart: Steiner, 1998.
Rüpke, Jörg. *Religion of the Romans*. Translated and edited by Richard Gordon. Cambridge: Polity, 2007.
Smith, Jonathan Z. *Map is not Territory: Studies in the History of Religions*. Leiden: Brill, 1978.
Syme, Ronald. *The Roman Revolution*. Oxford: Oxford University Press, 1939.
Thomas, Yan. "L'institution de l'origine: *Sacra Principiorum Populi Romani*." Pages 143–70 in *Tracés de fondation*. Edited by Marcel Detienne. Leuven, Belgium: Peeters, 1990.
Wallace-Hadrill, Andrew. "*Mutatas Formas*: The Augustan Transformation of Roman Knowledge." Pages 55–84 in *The Cambridge Companion to the Age of Augustus*. Edited by Karl Galinsky. Cambridge: Cambridge University Press, 2005.
———. "Time for Augustus: Ovid, Augustus, and the *Fasti*." Pages 221–30 in *Homo Viator: Classical Essays for John Bramble*. Edited by Michael Whitby, Philip Hardie, and Mary Whitby. Bristol: Bristol Classical Press, 1987.

Chapter 6
Imperial Cult in Roman Corinth: A Response to Karl Galinsky's "The Cult of the Roman Emperor: Uniter or Divider?"

Barbette Stanley Spaeth

In his keynote paper in this volume, "The Cult of the Roman Emperor: Uniter or Divider?," Karl Galinsky focuses on the macro level of the imperial cult and offers some broad issues to consider. As he points out, there was no such thing as "*the* imperial cult," but rather the cities of the Roman Empire had their own individual imperial cults, which differed from each other in significant ways.[1] In this paper, I would like to shift to the micro level and consider how some of the issues that Galinsky raises played out in one city of the Roman Empire: ancient Corinth. Roman Corinth is an interesting test case for the study of the imperial cult for a number of reasons. First, it was in origin a Greek city that was later refounded as a Roman colony. It therefore had a dual Greek and Roman cultural identity, which has important implications for our understanding of its religious system.[2] Second,

---

1. Karl Galinsky, "The Cult of the Roman Emperor: Uniter or Divider?" paper presented at the Annual Meeting of the SBL, Boston, 2008 (and ch. 1 in this volume), 3.

2. On cultural identity in the Roman Empire and the related issue of "Romanization," see Ray Laurence and Joanne Berry, eds., *Cultural Identity in the Roman Empire* (London: Routledge, 1998) and Jane Webster and Nicholas Cooper, eds., *Roman Imperialism: Post-Colonial Perspectives: Proceedings of a Symposium Held at Leicester University in November 1994* (Leicester Archaeology Monographs 3; Leicester: University of Leicester, 1996). On the cultural identity of Roman Corinth, see James C. Walters, "Civic Identity in Roman Corinth and Its Impact on Early Christians," in *Urban Religion in Roman Corinth* (ed. Daniel N. Schowalter and Steven J. Friesen; HTS 53; Cambridge, Mass.: Harvard University Press, 2005), 404–5. This article is part of a larger project that I am currently working on dealing with memory, cult, and cultural identity in Roman Corinth. For my work on this project, I would like to acknowledge with gratitude the support of a research grant from the Memoria Romana project associated with the Max-Planck International Research Award. In addition, I would like to thank the following people for their assistance with my research on the cults of Corinth: Nancy Bookidis, Ron Stroud, Charles

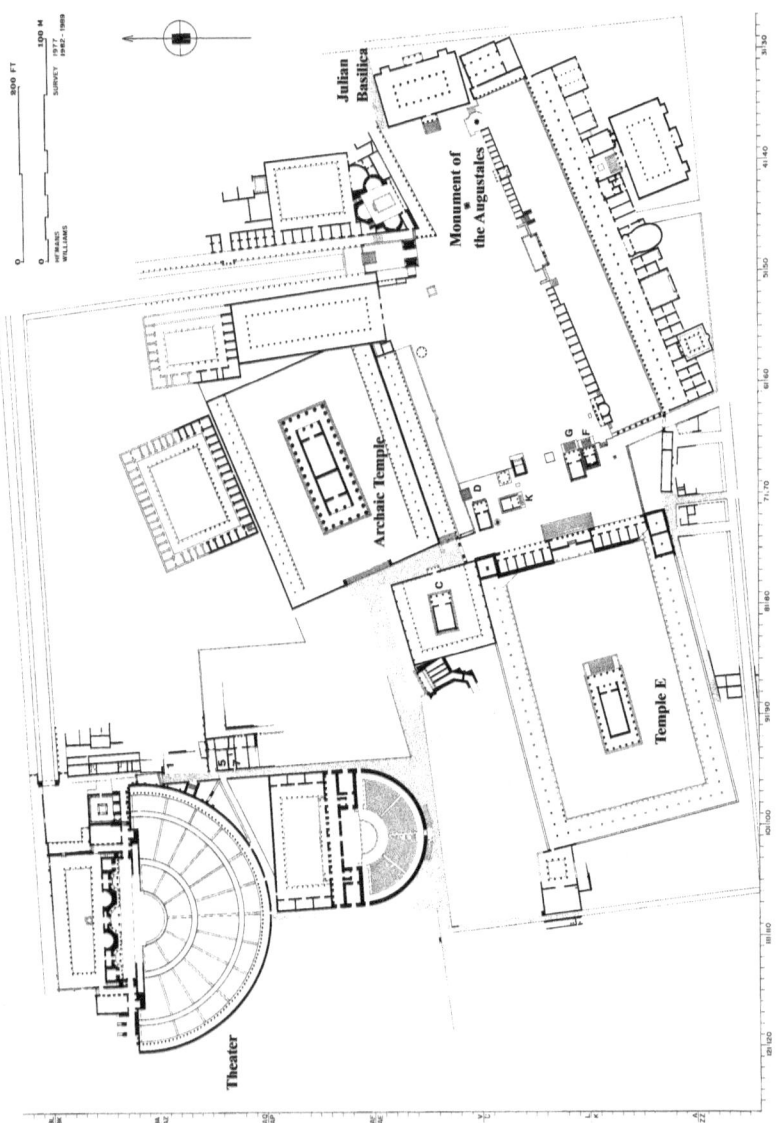

Fig. 6.1. Plan of Forum of Roman Corinth. *Courtesy of the American School of Classical Studies, Corinth Excavations, C. K. Williams II.*

Corinth had imperial cult both on the municipal and the provincial level, complicating our understanding of the role of this cult in the religious life of the city. Finally, of course, Corinth was the site of an early Christian community founded by Paul, whose letters to the Corinthians point to some of the problems that early Christians had in negotiating their relationship to the empire.

Let us begin with the issue that Galinsky raises regarding the "embeddedness" of the imperial cult. As he notes, this cult was not an isolated phenomenon: it was an integral part of the religious matrix of each individual city. In the Forum of Corinth (fig. 1), for example, temples to Fortuna, Clarian Apollo, and Venus have been identified on its western side, as well as the Archaic Temple on its northern edge, generally identified as that of Apollo.[3]

Other important cult sites in Corinth were the sanctuaries of Asclepius/Aesculapius, near the northern city wall; Aphrodite/Venus, atop Acrocorinth; and on its slopes the Sanctuary of Demeter and Kore or, in Roman terms, Ceres, Liber, and Libera (fig. 2).[4]

I give both the Greek and Roman names for these divinities, since the Greek names are more commonly used, but the Roman ones I believe reflect more accurately the change from Greek cults, practiced on these sites up until the destruction of Greek Corinth in 146 B.C.E., to Roman cults, practiced on these sites after the foundation of the Roman colony in 44 B.C.E.[5] In the Roman period,

---

Williams, Guy Sanders, Ioulia Tzounou-Herbst, James Herbst, Kathleen Slane, Mary Sturgeon, Betsey Robinson, Paul Scotton, Margaret Laird, Steven Friesen, James Walters, Dan Schowalter, John Lanci, Christine Thomas, Aileen Ajootian, Kevin Clinton, Jaquelyn Collins-Clinton, Mary Lee Coulson, Karl Galinsky, William Hutton, Michael Ierardi, Linda Reilly, Molly Richardson, Arthur Urbano, and Naama Zahavi-Ely.

3. On the identification of the Archaic Temple as the Temple of Apollo, see Pausanias, *Descr.* 2.3.6; Rufus B. Richardson, "The Excavations at Corinth in 1896," *AJA* 1 (1897): 479; Nancy Bookidis, "The Sanctuaries of Corinth," in *Corinth: The Centenary, 1896–1996* (ed. Charles K. Williams II and Nancy Bookidis; Corinth 20; Princeton, N.J.: American School of Classical Studies at Athens, 2003), 249–50. For other suggestions for the identification of this temple, see James Wiseman, "Corinth and Rome I: 228 B.C.–A.D. 267," *ANRW* 7.1:475, 530; Henry S. Robinson, "Excavations at Corinth: Temple Hill, 1968–1972," *Hesperia* 45 (1976): 235–36; and Richard Stillwell, "The Temple of Apollo," in *Introduction: Topography, Architecture* (Harold North Fowler and Richard Stillwell; Corinth 1; Cambridge, Mass.: Harvard University Press, 1932), 126–32.

4. I argued for the identification of the cult on the site of the Sanctuary of Demeter and Kore in the Roman period as that of Ceres, Liber, and Libera in a paper I gave in 2006 in the Greco-Roman Religions Section of the SBL with the title "Cultic Discontinuity in Roman Corinth: The Sanctuary of Demeter and Kore on Acrocorinth." This paper will be part of the larger study I am preparing on memory, cult, and cultural identity in Roman Corinth.

5. In contrast, scholars who write on the religion of Roman Corinth generally use exclusively Greek names for divinities in the Roman period, and they find the only truly Roman cults to be those dedicated to gods without Greek equivalents, such as Janus or the divin-

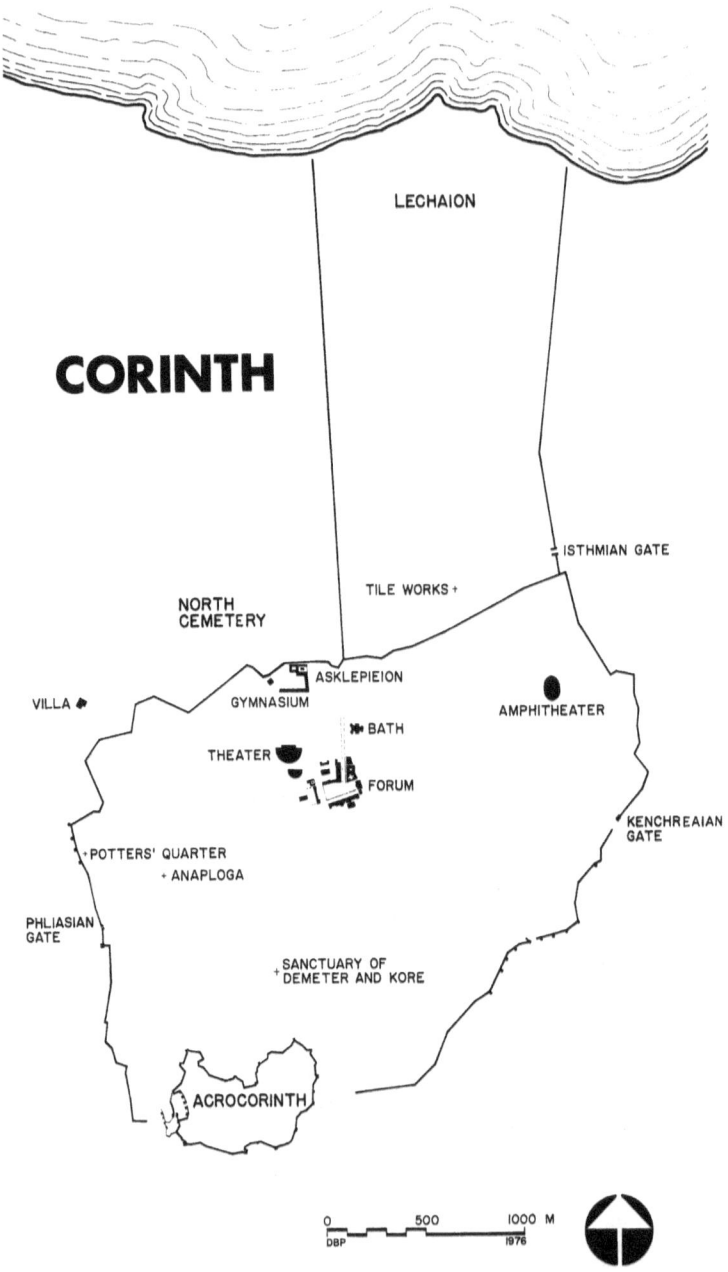

Fig. 2. Plan of Roman Corinth. *Courtesy of the American School of Classical Studies, Corinth Excavations, C. K. Williams II.*

there were also sites of several minor cults possibly of Greek origin in Corinth, such as that of Pegasus and Bellerophon, and others of foreign origin, such as those of Isis and Sarapis.[6] Inscriptions and coins multiply the evidence for divini-

---

ized emperor. See, e.g., Robert Lisle, "The Cults of Corinth" (Baltimore: The Johns Hopkins University, 1955), 2, 168; C. K. Williams II, "Laus Julia Corinthiensis et Diana Nemorensis," in *Philia Epe eis Georgion E. Mylonan: Dia ta 60 Ete tou Anaskaphikou tou Ergou* (Vivliotheke tes en Athenais Archaiologikes Hetaireias 103; Athens: En Athenais Archaiologike Hetaireia, 1986-, 1987), 384-85; Donald Engels, *Roman Corinth: An Alternative Model for the Classical City* (Chicago: University of Chicago Press, 1990), 93-95, 101-3; Petra Reichert-Südbeck, *Kulte von Korinth und Syrakus: Vergleich zwischen einer Metropolis und ihrer Apoikia* (Würzburger Studien zur Sprache & Kultur: Archäologie, Religionswissenschaft 4; Dettelbach, Germany: Röll, 2000), 21-22; Bookidis, "Sanctuaries of Corinth," 257. The Hellenocentric bias expressed in these practices is also seen in the notion that the Romans "revived" the Greek cults practiced on these sites. For example, the Sanctuary of Demeter and Kore on Acrocorinth has often been identified as a "revived" Greek cult in the Roman period: Lisle, "Cults of Corinth," 168; Wiseman, "Corinth and Rome," *ANRW* 7.1:509; Jerome Murphy-O'Connor, *St. Paul's Corinth: Texts and Archaeology* (Good News Studies 6; Wilmington, Del.: Michael Glazier, 1983), 38-39; Williams II, "Laus Julia Corinthiensis et Diana Nemorensis," 384-85; Mary E. Hoskins Walbank, "Pausanias, Octavia, and Temple E at Corinth," *Annual of the British School at Athens* 84 (1989): 383; Engels, *Roman Corinth*, 94-95; Nancy Bookidis and Ronald S. Stroud, *The Sanctuary of Demeter and Kore: Topography and Architecture* (Corinth 18.3; Princeton, N.J.: American School of Classical Studies at Athens, 1997), 434; Gloria S. Merker, *The Sanctuary of Demeter and Kore: Terracotta Figurines of the Classical, Hellenistic, and Roman Periods* (Corinth 18.4; Princeton, N.J.: American School of Classical Studies at Athens, 2000), 311-12; Reichert-Südbeck, *Kulte*, 21-22; Bookidis, "Sanctuaries of Corinth," 255-57. Cf. the argument of Charles Williams that "the Romans knew about and tried to revive the Greek sanctuaries of the city, if possible even on their original sites, but were not concerned to restore them to their original form or recreate their original Greek ritual with any great precision or accuracy." C. K. Williams II, "The Refounding of Corinth: Some Roman Religious Attitudes," in *Refounding of Corinth*, in *Roman Architecture in the Greek World* (ed. Sarah Macready and F. H. Thompson; Occasional Papers 2/10; London: Society of Antiquaries of London distributed by Thames & Hudson, 1987), 31-32. The distinction that Williams makes between the revival of a religious site versus that of a ritual is important, although I disagree with the implication that the Roman colonists of Corinth would necessarily have revived Greek ritual at all on these sites.

6. For the cult of Pegasus and Bellerophon, see Pausanias, *Descr.* 2.2.4, Betsey Ann Robinson, "Fountains and the Culture of Water at Roman Corinth" (Ph.D. diss., University of Pennsylvania, 2001), 159-60; Engels, *Roman Corinth*, 99-100; Domenico Musti and Mario Torelli, trans. and eds., *Pausania: Guida della Grecia*. Vol. 2: *La Corinzia e l'Argolide* (Milan: Fondazione Lorenzo Valla, Mondadori, 1986), 216; Charles Kaufman Williams, "Pre-Roman Cults in the Area of the Forum of Ancient Corinth" (Ph.D. diss., University of Pennsylvania, 1978), 167-69 with bibliography. On its possible connection with the spring of Upper Peirene, see: Engels, *Roman Corinth*, 99-100; Georges Roux, trans. and ed., *Pausanias en Corinthie (Livre II, 1 à 15)* (Annales de l'Université de Lyon 3.31; Paris: Les Belles Lettres, 1958), 129-30; Carl William Blegen, *Acrocorinth: Excavations in 1926* (Corinth 3.1; Cambridge, Mass.: Harvard University Press, 1930). For the cult of Isis and Sarapis, see Pausanias, *Descr.* 2.2.3 and 2.4.6; Bookidis, "Sanctuaries of Corinth," 254, 257-58; and Engels, *Roman Corinth*, 102-5.

ties worshipped in the city, including some Roman divinities that probably had a wide following, such as Victoria, Concordia, Janus, and Saturn, as well as others that seem highly individualized, such as the Greek *theoi en tē smēnē*, or "Gods in the Beehive."[7] The phenomenon of religious pluralism that Galinsky notes was thus clearly much in evidence in Roman Corinth.

The Roman imperial cult was an important part of that pluralism. Pausanias (2.3.1) mentions one significant imperial cult site in the city, which he calls the "Temple of Octavia." This building is often identified as Temple E, above the western end of the forum (fig. 1).[8] In addition, the Julian Basilica, on the eastern end of the forum, is also associated with the imperial cult (fig. 1).[9] This building has a set of sculptures of members of the imperial family, including Augustus (fig. 3) and Gaius (fig. 4) and Lucius Caesar (fig. 5), as well as a significant number of inscriptions and a shrine dedicated to the Lares Augusti.[10]

---

7. Victoria, Allen Brown West, *Latin Inscriptions 1896–1926* (Corinth 8.2; Cambridge, Mass.: Harvard University Press, 1931), no. 11; John Harvey Kent, *The Inscriptions 1926–1950* (Corinth 8.3; Princeton, N.J.: American School of Classical Studies at Athens, 1966), no. 199; Katharine M. Edwards, *Coins 1896–1929* (Corinth 6; Cambridge, Mass.: Harvard University Press, 1933), no. 333; Michel Amandry, *Le monnayage des duovirs corinthiens* (BCHSup 15; Athens: École française d'Athènes, 1988), nos. 126–127, 156–165, 232–234. Concordia: West, *Latin Inscriptions*, no. 9. Janus: Kent, *Inscriptions 1926–1950*, no. 195. Saturn, West, *Latin Inscriptions*, no. 104; Andrew Burnett, Michel Amandry, and Pere Pau Ripollès, *From the Death of Caesar to the Death of Vitellius (44 BC – AD 69)* (vol. 1 of *Roman Provincial Coinage*; London: British Museum Press, 1992), 250, no. 1122. *Theoi en tē smēnē*: Kent, *Inscriptions 1926–1950*, no. 68. The phrase may also be read as the "gods in the theater (building)" (i.e., *skēnē*), a less poetic but perhaps more probable reading.

8. Roux, *Pausanias*, 112–15; Williams II, "The Refounding of Corinth: Some Roman Religious Attitudes," 29–30; C. K. Williams II, "A Re-Evaluation of Temple E and the West End of the Forum," in *Temple E*, in *The Greek Renaissance in the Roman Empire: Papers from the Tenth British Museum Classical Colloquium* (ed. Susan Walker and Averil Cameron; Bulletin Supplement 55; London: University of London, Institute of Classical Studies, 1989), 156–62. Temple E has also been identified as the Capitolium of Corinth; see Sarah Elizabeth Freeman, "Temple E," in *Architecture* (Richard Stillwell, Robert L. Scranton, and Sarah Elizabeth Freeman; Corinth 1.2; Cambridge, Mass.: Harvard University Press, 1941), 232–36; Musti and Torelli, *Pausania*, 222; Walbank, "Temple E," 378–79; M. Osanna, "Tra monumenti, agalmata e mirabilia: Organizzazione del percorso urbano di Corinto nella Periegesi di Pausania," in *Éditer, Traduire, commenter Pausanias en l'an 2000: Actes du colloque de Neuchâtel et de Fribourg (18–22 Septembre 1998)* (ed. D. Knoepfler and M. Piérart; Geneva: Université de Neuchâtel, 2001), 193–94; Mario Torelli, "Pausania a Corinto," in ibid., 157–67.

9. Paul Douglas Scotton, "The Julian Basilica at Corinth: An Architectural Investigation" (Ph.D. diss., University of Pennsylvania, 1997), 263–66.

10. On the sculpture of the Julian Basilica, see Catherine de Grazia Vanderpool, "Roman Portraiture: The Many Faces of Corinth," in *Corinth: The Centenary, 1896–1996* (ed. Charles K. Williams II and Nancy Bookidis; Corinth 20; Princeton, N.J.: American School of Classical Studies at Athens, 2003), 375–77 and Scotton, "Julian Basilica," 255–61. On the inscriptions

The building seems to have been an important secondary site of the imperial cult in Corinth tied to the provincial administration.[11] Finally, a monumental statue base dedicated to the *divus* Augustus by the Augustales stood on the southeastern side of the forum as a highly visible sign of the imperial cult (figs. 1, 6, and 7).[12]

These monuments are in Galinsky's terms "free-standing examples" of imperial cult, and they dominated the open space of the forum.

Moreover, there is considerable evidence for what Galinsky calls the "intertwining" of the cult of the emperor with those of other gods in the city. In the numismatic evidence, this intertwining may be suggested by having the emperor's image on the obverse of a coin and that of a god on the reverse, such as a Roman Corinthian coin showing Nero on one side and the Genius of the Colony of Corinth on the other (fig. 8).[13]

Other examples indicate the direct connection of the emperor with the gods, such as the reverse of a Roman Corinthian coin showing the Fortuna of the colony crowning Nero (fig. 9).[14]

The "intertwining" of imperial cult with other civic cults is also shown by the numerous Roman Corinthian inscriptions giving gods or divine personifications the title "Augustus" or "Augusta," including Apollo, Diana, Mars, Saturn, Nemesis, Providentia, and Tutela.[15] Another significant example of intertwining at Corinth is the elaborate sculptural program of the backdrop of the theater (figs. 1 and 10), which had representations of deities in the first story and the three pediments, and an imperial group in the four niches, including a colossal image of the deified Trajan in the central position on the second story, of which the head survives (fig. 11).[16]

---

and shrine, see Saul S. Weinberg, *The Southeast Building: The Twin Basilicas, the Mosaic House* (Corinth 1.5; Princeton, N.J.: American School of Classical Studies at Athens, 1960), 35–57 and Scotton, "Julian Basilica," 191, 221–24, 244–54.

11. Ibid., 266–67.

12. On the Augustales base, see ibid. and Margaret L. Laird, "The Emperor in a Roman Town: The Base of the Augustales in the Forum at Corinth," in *Corinth in Context: Comparative Studies on Religion and Society* (ed. Steven J. Friesen, Daniel N. Schowalter, and James C. Walters; NovTSup 134; Leiden: Brill, 2010), 67–116.

13. Edwards, *Coins 1896–1929*, no. 57.

14. Ibid., no. 54.

15. Apollo Augustus: West, *Latin Inscriptions*, no. 120. Diana Pacilucifera Augusta: ibid., no. 15. Mars: Kent, *Inscriptions 1926–1950*, no. 212. Saturnus Augustus: West, *Latin Inscriptions*, no. 6. Nemesis Augusta: ibid., no. 10. Providentia Augusta: ibid., no. 110. Tutela Augusta: Kent, *Inscriptions 1926–1950*, nos. 193, 194.

16. Mary C. Sturgeon, *Sculpture: The Assemblage from the Theater* (Corinth 9.3; Princeton, N.J.: American School of Classical Studies at Athens, 2004), 9–16, 31–33, 57–60.

Fig. 3. Statue of Augustus from Julian Basilica: S-1116. *Courtesy of the American School of Classical Studies, Corinth Excavations, I. Ioannidou-L. Bartzioti.*

This example also illustrates how the cult of the emperor was embedded in other aspects of the daily life of the Corinthians besides religion.

As for the emperors who may have been worshipped in the imperial cult in the city, the Corinthian inscriptions name as *divi* or *theoi*, that is, deified humans, the following: Caesar, Augustus, Claudius, Vespasian, Nerva, Trajan, Hadrian, Marcus Aurelius, and Antoninus Pius.[17] More definitive evidence for cultic wor-

---

17. Caesar, West, *Latin Inscriptions*, no. 68; Kent, *Inscriptions 1926–1950*, no. 50. Augustus, ibid., nos. 51, 52, 53, 70, 72, 81; West, *Latin Inscriptions*, no. 50. Claudius, ibid., no. 68; Kent,

Fig. 4. Statue of Gaius Caesar from Julian Basilica: S-1065. *Courtesy of the American School of Classical Studies, Corinth Excavations, I. Ioannidou-L. Bartzioti.*

ship is provided by those inscriptions that name a priest attached to the cults of Caesar and Hadrian.[18] It is important to remember, however, that the emperors

---

Inscriptions 1926–1950, no. 81. Vespasian, ibid., nos. 84, 85, 86, 121. Nerva, ibid., nos. 58, 95, 102 (*theos*), 103 (*theos*), 111, 112. Trajan, ibid., nos. 111, 112; West, *Latin Inscriptions*, no. 21. Hadrian, Kent, *Inscriptions 1926–1950*, nos. 108, 111, 112. Marcus Aurelius, ibid., nos. 111, 112; Antoninus Pius, ibid., nos. 111, 112; Thomas R. Martin, "Inscriptions at Corinth," *Hesperia* 46 (1977), 178–98, no. 8.

18. *Flamen divi Iuli*, West, *Latin Inscriptions*, no. 68. *Hiereus* or *archiereus Hadrianou Panhelleniou*, Benjamin Dean Meritt, *Greek Inscriptions, 1896–1927* (Corinth 8.1; Cambridge,

Fig. 5. Fragmentary Statue of Lucius Caesar from Julian Basilica: S-1080. *Courtesy of the American School of Classical Studies, Corinth Excavations, I. Ioannidou-L. Bartzioti.*

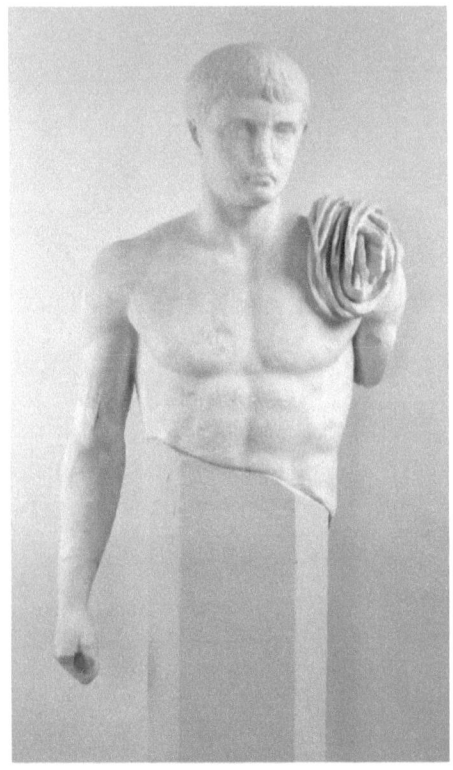

Fig. 6. Base of the Monument of the Augustales in Forum. *Courtesy of Margaret Laird.*

were not the only objects of imperial cult at Corinth. Other members of the imperial family, especially the wives of the emperors, also received worship. The inscriptions from Corinth name as *divae*, deified humans, both Livia, the wife of Augustus, and Faustina, that is, either Faustina the Elder, the wife of Antoninus Pius, or Faustina the Younger, the wife of Marcus Aurelius, and the latter is represented in a portrait head found in the southwest area of the Forum (fig. 12).[19]

The role of women in the imperial cult is an issue that is underemphasized in New Testament scholarship, leading to the creation of a misleading exclusive equation between the emperor and Christ as the Son(s) of God. This equation leaves out the question of the daughters, mothers, and wives of gods that the women of the imperial family represented. As the emperor was the *pater patriae*, or father of the fatherland, his wife was the *mater patriae*, or its mother.[20] The wife of the emperor is also given the title Mater Augusti or Mater Caesaris, to indicate her crucial role in producing the imperial heir, the next to become a god.[21] Her role as a mother figure is extended in other ways as well, for she is called *mater castrorum*, "mother of the (army) camp," *mater senatus*, "mother of the Senate," and even *genetrix orbis terrarum*, progenitress of the whole world.[22] This terminology, I suggest, may have influenced the development of the Marian cult in later Christianity. The titles attached to the wife of the emperor, however, even exceed those given to Mary, for like her husband, the empress could also be called "Savior," Soteira.[23] In Roman Corinthian coinage, the wives of the emperors are given divine attributes and thus identified with the gods. For example, a coin of the Tiberian age shows a seated female figure holding sheaves of wheat (fig. 13); from comparanda of other Roman coins that identify the figure either as

---

Mass.: Harvard University Press, 1931), nos. 80, 81; Kent, *Inscriptions 1926–1950*: nos. 139, 140.

19. Livia (Diva Augusta): ibid., no. 55. Faustina (Theia Fausteina Sebaste): Martin, "Inscriptions at Corinth," no. 7. Head of Faustina the Younger from the Forum Southwest: Vanderpool, "Roman Portraiture," 374, fig. 22.6.

20. On the title *pater patriae*, see: Andreas Alföldi, "Die Geburt der kaiserlichen Bildsymbolik," *MH* 9 (1952): 204–43; Leo Berlinger, *Beiträge zur inoffiziellen Titulatur der römischen Kaiser: Eine Untersuchung ihres Ideengeschichtlichen Gehaltes und ihrer Entwicklung* (Breslau: R. Nischkowsky, 1935); E. Skard, "Pater Patriae," in *Festskrift til Halvdan Koht på sekstiårsdagen 7de juli 1933* (Oslo: Aschehoug, 1933), 42–70. On the title *mater patriae*, see: Hildegard Temporini, *Die Frauen am Hofe Trajans: Ein Beitrage zur Stellung der Augustae im Principat* (Berlin: De Gruyter, 1978), 61–66.

21. Livia, Agrippina the Younger, Domitia Longina, Faustina the Younger, and Julia Domna all received these titles in inscriptions and on imperial coinage. See Barbette Stanley Spaeth, *The Roman Goddess Ceres* (Austin: University of Texas Press, 1996), 122 with note 79 for references.

22. See ibid., 122–23 with notes 83–86 for references.

23. E.g., Julia Domna as Savior of Athens: *IG* II2 1076. See Barbara Levick, *Julia Domna, Syrian Empress* (Women of the Ancient World; London: Routledge, 2007), 49.

Fig. 7. Reconstruction of Monument of the Augustales in Forum. *Courtesy of Margaret Laird.*

Fig. 8. Corinthian Coin with the Nero (obv.) and Genius Coloniae (rev). *Corinth* 6, nr. 57. *Courtesy of the American School of Classical Studies, Corinth Excavations, P. Dellatolas.*

Fig. 9. Corinthian Coin with Fortuna Coloniae crowning Nero. *Corinth* 6, no. 54. *Courtesy of the American School of Classical Studies, Corinth Excavations, P. Dellatolas.*

Fig. 10. Perspective Reconstruction of Scaenae Frons of Theater with Sculptural Assemblage. *Courtesy of the American School of Classical Studies, Corinth Excavations, J. A. Herbst.*

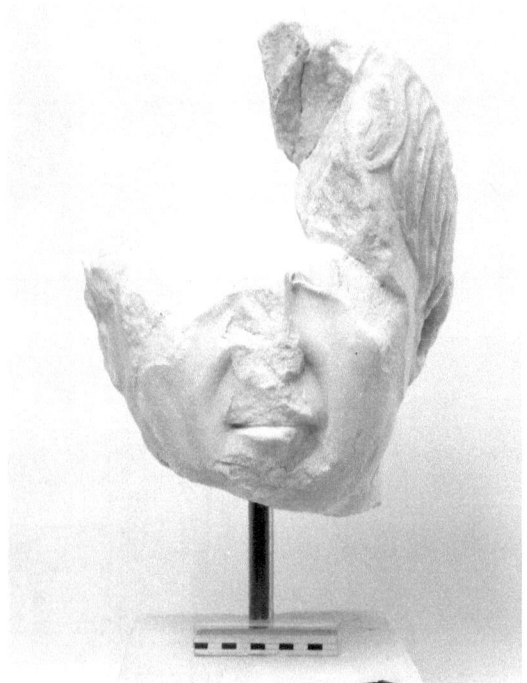

Fig. 11. Head of Trajan from Theatre. S-364/3660/3700/unnumbered fragment. *Courtesy of the American School of Classical Studies, Corinth Excavations, I. Ioannidou-L. Bartzioti.*

Fig. 12. Portrait Head of Faustina the Younger from Southwest Area of the Forum. S-2702. *Courtesy of the American School of Classical Studies, Corinth Excavations, I. Ioannidou-L. Bartzioti.*

Ceres Augusta or as Julia Augusta, it is clear that the figure is to be taken as Livia in the guise of Ceres.²⁴

Another example may be provided by a second-century mosaic inscription from the floor of the Central Temple of the Sanctuary of Ceres, Liber, and Libera on Acrocorinth (fig. 14), which reads "Octavius Agathopous, neokoros, had the mosaic made when Chara was priestess of Neotera."²⁵

As the excavators of the site, Nancy Bookidis and Ron Stroud, have pointed out, it is likely that the temple over which Chara presided and in which Neotera was worshipped is the one whose inscription recorded these facts.²⁶ It is further probable, then, that Neotera represents the name or at least the epithet of a divinity worshipped in the Central Temple. On the basis of comparanda from Eleusis, Bookidis and Stroud suggest that Neotera was another name for Persephone, who was called the "Younger (Goddess)" in contrast to Demeter, the "Elder (Goddess)."²⁷ As far as I know, however, these titles were not used for the goddesses anywhere besides Eleusis. Moreover, the identification as Neotera of the goddess of the Central Temple means that she would have been regarded as the main divinity in the cult, but we know that Greek Demeter was generally considered the more important of the pair, and the Roman Ceres was certainly more significant than her daughter Libera/Proserpina. I have proposed that the title of Neotera in the mosaic from the Sanctuary refers to a mortal woman who is being identified with a goddess, the "Newer" or "Younger" version of that divinity.²⁸ Other scholars have noted that in the Greek East the divinized wives of the emperor were frequently given the epithet of Nea or Neotera, to identify them with a goddess, such as Faustina the Elder identified with Isis at Gerasa, Plotina with Aphrodite at Dendera, and Faustina the Elder and Sabina with Demeter at Eleusis.²⁹ Perhaps the clearest parallel is the famous Egyptian queen, Cleopatra

---

24. Amandry, *Monnayage*, 58–59, 166–68 and pl. 15, no. 17; Burnett, Amandry, and Ripollès, *From the Death of Caesar to the Death of Vitellius (44 BC - AD 69)*, 46–47.

25. Bookidis and Stroud, *Sanctuary of Demeter and Kore*, 342–44, 362–66.

26. Ibid., 366.

27. Ibid., 365–66. The excavators also consider and ultimately reject (rightly, I believe) several other possibilities for Neotera which link her with a Near Eastern or Egyptian divinity. See ibid., 364–65.

28. I made this proposal in a paper with the title "Who Was Neotera? A Study of a Hybrid Romano-Egyptian Cult in Ancient Corinth," given in the Graeco-Roman Religion Section of the SBL in 2009.

29. Faustina the Elder at Gerasa: Carl H. Kraeling, ed., *Gerasa, City of the Decapolis* (New Haven, Conn.: American Schools of Oriental Research, 1938), 382, no. 15; Arthur Darby Nock, "Neotera, Queen or Goddess," *Aeg* 33 (1953): 294–95; Plotina at Dendera: *CIG* III, 4716c; Faustina the Elder or Sabina at Eleusis: Boekh, *CIG* 435 and Dittenberger, *IG* III 899. On this evidence, see also Luigi Moretti, "Note egittologiche: A proposito di Neotera," *Aeg* 38 (1958): 199–209.

Fig. 13. Corinthian Coin with Livia as Ceres. *RPC* 1.2, nr. 1150. Photo Credit: bpk, Berlin / Muenzkabinett, Staatliche Kunstsammlungen, Dresden, Germany / Art Resource, NY.

VII, who gave herself on her coinage the title Basilissa Kleopatra Thea Neotera, Queen Cleopatra the Younger Goddess, signaling her identification with a goddess, probably Isis, since she is connected with this goddess in other sources.[30] So, in the Central Temple of the Sanctuary of Demeter and Kore in Roman Corinth, I suggest that Neotera was one of the divinized empresses identified with the main goddess of the cult, Ceres/Demeter.

We have already noted another woman of the imperial family honored at Corinth in the imperial cult building that Pausanias (2.3.1) called the "Temple of Octavia," which may be identified with Temple E. Octavia was the sister of Augustus and the mother of Marcellus, his first chosen heir. Whether or not one accepts Pausanias's statement that an imperial cult building at Corinth was in fact dedicated to this woman, it is clear that it was not unreasonable for him to think so, for women of the imperial family had a major role in the imperial cult throughout the Roman Empire.

The evidence that I have surveyed points to the importance of the imperial cult in the religious life of the city. This cult was especially prominent here, I think, for two reasons. First, Corinth was the capital of the province of Achaea, and therefore presented the face of Roman power in Greece to its inhabitants.[31] The provincial cult helped to maintain that power by asserting the connections between the provincial administration and the central government in Rome.[32] The municipal cult, on the other hand, was more concerned with the needs of the inhabitants of Corinth itself. The city was founded as a colony by Julius Caesar, and the colonists maintained close connections with his imperial successors through the imperial cult, among other means. These connections were maintained in part to encourage the emperor to see himself as a patron of the city, and

---

30. The coins, dated to 35/34 and 32/31 B.C.E., are two bronzes, attributed respectively to Berytus and Cyrene, and a tetradrachm attributed to Antioch; see Theodore V. Buttrey, "Thea Neotera on Coins of Antony and Cleopatra," *ANSMN* 6 (1954): 98 with references. For Cleopatra's connection with Isis, see Plutarch, *Ant.* 54.6; Dio Cassius 50.5.3 and 50.25.3.

31. On Corinth as the capital of Achaea, see Wiseman, " Corinth and Rome," *ANRW* 7.1:501–2.

32. On the importance of the imperial cult in provincial capitals, see S. R. F. Price, *Rituals and Power: The Roman Imperial Cult in Asia Minor* (Cambridge: Cambridge University Press, 1984), 69–71 and Engels, *Roman Corinth*, 102.

Fig. 14. Detail of Mosaic from Floor of Central Temple in Sanctuary of Demeter and Kore. *Courtesy of the American School of Classical Studies, Corinth Excavations, I. Ioannidou-L. Bartzioti..*

indeed some emperors clearly fulfilled this role: Nero, Vespasian, and Hadrian, for example, all seem to have interested themselves directly in the affairs of the city.[33] Through the rituals associated with the imperial cult, the people of Corinth regularly reaffirmed their ties to the emperor as their patron and through him to Rome itself. The imperial cult thus formed part of the patronage system on which Roman society was based. It also provided an important means of social and political advancement for the elite inhabitants of the city. I have already shown how the woman Chara was marked out as a priestess of the imperial cult. The importance of her position is seen by the fact the mosaic inscription from the Central Temple in the sanctuary on the slopes of Acrocorinth is dated by the mention of her eponymous priesthood. More commonly, Corinthian inscriptions show men obtaining social position and political advantage through their offices

---

33. For Nero's interest in Corinth, see the two coins mentioned above, one with Nero on the obverse and the Genius of the Colony of Corinth on the reverse, and the other with a reverse of Nero and the Fortuna of the Colony of Corinth. In a paper with the title "The Cult of Ceres in Roman Corinth: Evidence from Two Archaistic Relief Bases" given in the Archaeology of Religion in the Roman World Section of the SBL in 2007, I suggested that these coins may reflect the reestablishment of the cult of the tutelary gods of the city in the Long Rectangular Building near the southwest area of the Forum under the sponsorship of Nero. For Vespasian's connection with Corinth, see David Romano's argument that Vespasian sponsored the recenturiation of Corinth and its renaming as Colonia Iulia Flavia Augusta Corinthiensis, as well as possibly assisting with the rebuilding of the city after the earthquake of the 70s: David Gilman Romano, "City Planning, Centuriation, and Land Division in Roman Corinth: Colonia Laus Iulia Corinthiensis & Colonia Iulia Flavia Corinthiensis," in *City Planning*, in *Corinth: The Centenary, 1896–1996* (ed. Charles K. Williams II and Nancy Bookidis; Corinth 20; Princeton, N.J.: American School of Classical Studies at Athens, 2003), 298–99. For Hadrian's connection with the city, see Pausanias, *Descr.* 2.3.5, which mentions both the bath that the emperor constructed in the city and the aqueduct that he built to bring water from Lake Stymphalus to Corinth.

in the imperial cult, and the city of Corinth recognizing them for their achievements in this area. For example, in an inscription dated to the first century C.E., Gaius Julius Spartiaticus is honored by the members of the *tribus*, or tribe, of Calpurnia, for, among other things, serving as "Flamen of the Deified Julius," and "High-Priest of the Domus Augusta forever."[34] The inscription also notes that the *tribus* is honoring him "because of his virtue and spirited and very expansive munificence toward the divine house and towards our colony," further indicating the close linkage between the imperial cult and municipal interests.[35] This evidence all shows how deeply embedded this cult was in the wider societal context of ancient Corinth and that embeddedness suggests some of the problems that the early Christian community may have had in negotiating that cult.

I have merely scratched the surface here in considering how the issues that Karl Galinsky raises in his paper regarding the imperial cult apply to Corinth. There is much more work that can be done on the extraordinarily rich material that this city offers for this topic. I hope that in showing some of the ways in which the imperial cult operated in a city of the empire that is highly significant for the study of early Christianity, I have opened a door to more dialogue with those whose knowledge of that topic is far greater than mine.

BIBLIOGRAPHY

Alföldi, Andreas. "Die Geburt der kaiserlichen Bildsymbolik." *Museum helveticum* 9 (1952): 204–43.
Amandry, Michel. *Le monnayage des duovirs corinthiens*. Bulletin de correspondance hellénique. Supplement 15. Athens: École française d'Athènes, 1988.
Berlinger, Leo. *Beiträge zur inoffiziellen Titulatur der römischen Kaiser: Eine Untersuchung ihres Ideengeschichtlichen Gehaltes und ihrer Entwicklung*. Breslau: R. Nischkowsky, 1935.
Blegen, Carl William. *Acrocorinth: Excavations in 1926*. Corinth 3.1. Cambridge, Mass.: Harvard University Press, 1930.
Bookidis, Nancy. "The Sanctuaries of Corinth." Pages 247–60 in *Corinth: The Centenary, 1896–1996*. Edited by Charles K. Williams II and Nancy Bookidis. Corinth 20. Princeton, N.J.: American School of Classical Studies at Athens, 2003.
―――― and Ronald S. Stroud. *The Sanctuary of Demeter and Kore: Topography and Architecture*. Corinth 18.3. Princeton, N.J.: American School of Classical Studies at Athens, 1997.
Burnett, Andrew, Michel Amandry, and Pere Pau Ripollès. *From the Death of Caesar to*

---

34. West, *Latin Inscriptions*, no. 68.
35. On this inscription, see further John K. Chow, "Patronage in Roman Corinth," in *Paul and Empire: Religion and Power in Roman Imperial Society* (ed. Richard A. Horsley; Harrisburg, Pa.: Trinity Press International, 1997), 104–25.

the Death of Vitellius (44 BC - AD 69). Vol. 1 of *Roman Provincial Coinage*. London: British Museum Press, 1992.

Buttrey, Theodore V. "Thea Neotera on Coins of Antony and Cleopatra." *American Numismatic Society Museum Notes* 6 (1954): 95–109.

Chow, John K. "Patronage in Roman Corinth." Pages 104–25 in *Paul and Empire: Religion and Power in Roman Imperial Society*. Edited by Richard A. Horsley. Harrisburg, Pa.: Trinity Press International, 1997.

Edwards, Katharine M. *Coins 1896–1929*. Corinth 6. Cambridge, Mass.: Harvard University Press, 1933.

Engels, Donald. *Roman Corinth: An Alternative Model for the Classical City*. Chicago: University of Chicago Press, 1990.

Freeman, Sarah Elizabeth. "Temple E." Pages 166–236 in *Architecture*. Richard Stillwell, Robert L. Scranton, and Sarah Elizabeth Freeman. Corinth 1.2. Cambridge, Mass.: Harvard University Press, 1941.

Galinsky, Karl. "The Cult of the Roman Emperor: Uniter or Divider?" Paper presented at the Annual Meeting of the SBL, Boston, 2008, and ch. 1 in this volume.

Kent, John Harvey. *The Inscriptions 1926–1950*. Corinth 8.3. Princeton, N.J.: American School of Classical Studies at Athens, 1966.

Kraeling, Carl H., ed. *Gerasa, City of the Decapolis*. New Haven, Conn.: American Schools of Oriental Research, 1938.

Laird, Margaret L. "The Emperor in a Roman Town: The Base of the Augustales in the Forum at Corinth." Pages 67–116 in *Corinth in Context: Comparative Studies on Religion and Society*. Edited by Steven J. Friesen, Daniel N. Schowalter, and James C. Walters. Novum Testamentum Supplements 134. Leiden: Brill, 2010.

Laurence, Ray, and Joanne Berry, eds. *Cultural Identity in the Roman Empire*. London: Routledge, 1998.

Levick, Barbara. *Julia Domna, Syrian Empress*. Women of the Ancient World. London: Routledge, 2007.

Lisle, Robert. "The Cults of Corinth." Baltimore: The Johns Hopkins University, 1955.

Martin, Thomas R. "Inscriptions at Corinth." *Hesperia* 46 (1977): 178–98.

Meritt, Benjamin Dean. *Greek Inscriptions, 1896–1927*. Corinth 8.1. Cambridge, Mass.: Harvard University Press, 1931.

Merker, Gloria S. *The Sanctuary of Demeter and Kore: Terracotta Figurines of the Classical, Hellenistic, and Roman Periods*. Corinth 18.4. Princeton, N.J.: American School of Classical Studies at Athens, 2000.

Moretti, Luigi. "Note egittologiche: A proposito di Neotera." *Aegyptus* 38 (1958): 199–209.

Murphy-O'Connor, Jerome. *St. Paul's Corinth: Texts and Archaeology*. Good News Studies 6. Wilmington, Del.: Michael Glazier, 1983.

Musti, Domenico, and Mario Torelli, trans. and eds. *Pausania: Guida della Grecia, Vol. 2: La Corinzia e l'Argolide*. Milan: Fondazione Lorenzo Valla, Mondadori, 1986.

Nock, Arthur Darby. "Neotera, Queen or Goddess." *Aegyptus* 33 (1953): 283–96.

Osanna, M. "Tra monumenti, agalmata e mirabilia: Organizzazione del percorso urbano di Corinto nella Periegesi di Pausania." Pages 185–202 in *Éditer, Traduire, commenter Pausanias en l'an 2000: Actes du colloque de Neuchâtel et de Fribourg (18–22 septembre 1998)*. Edited by D. Knoepfler and M. Piérart. Geneva: Université de Neuchâtel, 2001.

Price, S. R. F. *Rituals and Power: The Roman Imperial Cult in Asia Minor.* Cambridge: Cambridge University Press, 1984.

Reichert-Südbeck, Petra. *Kulte von Korinth und Syrakus: Vergleich zwischen einer Metropolis und ihrer Apoikia.* Würzburger Studien zur Sprache & Kultur: Archäologie, Religionswissenschaft 4. Dettelbach, Germany: Röll, 2000.

Richardson, Rufus B. "The Excavations at Corinth in 1896." *American Journal of Archaeology* 1 (1897): 455-80.

Robinson, Betsey Ann. "Fountains and the Culture of Water at Roman Corinth." Ph.D. diss., University of Pennsylvania, 2001.

Robinson, Henry S. "Excavations at Corinth: Temple Hill, 1968-1972." *Hesperia* 45 (1976): 203-39.

Romano, David Gilman. "City Planning, Centuriation, and Land Division in Roman Corinth: Colonia Laus Iulia Corinthiensis & Colonia Iulia Flavia Corinthiensis." Pages 279-302 in *City Planning. In Corinth: The Centenary, 1896-1996.* Edited by Charles K. Williams II and Nancy Bookidis. Corinth 20. Princeton, N.J.: American School of Classical Studies at Athens, 2003.

Roux, Georges, trans. and ed. *Pausanias en Corinthie (Livre II, 1 à 15).* Annales de l'Université de Lyon 3.31. Paris: Les Belles Lettres, 1958.

Scotton, Paul Douglas. "The Julian Basilica at Corinth: An Architectural Investigation." Ph.D. diss., University of Pennsylvania, 1997.

Scranton, Robert Lorentz. *Monuments in the Lower Agora and North of the Archaic Temple.* Corinth 1.3. Princeton, N.J.: American School of Classical Studies at Athens, 1951.

Skard, E. "Pater Patriae." Pages 42-70 in *Festskrift til Halvdan Koht på sekstiårsdagen 7de juli 1933.* Oslo: Aschehoug, 1933.

Spaeth, Barbette Stanley. *The Roman Goddess Ceres.* Austin: University of Texas Press, 1996.

Stillwell, Richard. "The Temple of Apollo." Pages 115-34 in *Introduction: Topography, Architecture.* Harold North Fowler and Richard Stillwell. Corinth 1. Cambridge, Mass.: Harvard University Press, 1932.

Sturgeon, Mary C. *Sculpture: The Assemblage from the Theater.* Corinth 9.3. Princeton, N.J.: American School of Classical Studies at Athens, 2004.

Temporini, Hildegard. *Die Frauen am Hofe Trajans: Ein Beitrage zur Stellung der Augustae im Principat.* Berlin: De Gruyter, 1978.

Torelli, Mario. "Pausania a Corinto." Pages 135-84 in *Éditer, Traduire, commenter Pausanias en l'an 2000: Actes du colloque de Neuchâtel et de Fribourg (18-22 septembre 1998).* Edited by D. Knoepfler and M. Piérart. Geneva: Université de Neuchâtel, 2001.

Vanderpool, Catherine de Grazia. "Roman Portraiture: The Many Faces of Corinth." Pages 369-84 in *Corinth: The Centenary, 1896-1996.* Edited by Charles K. Williams II and Nancy Bookidis. Corinth 20. Princeton, N.J.: American School of Classical Studies at Athens, 2003.

Walbank, Mary E. Hoskins. "Pausanias, Octavia, and Temple E at Corinth." *Annual of the British School at Athens* 84 (1989): 361-94.

Walters, James C. "Civic Identity in Roman Corinth and Its Impact on Early Christians." Pages 397-418 in *Urban Religion in Roman Corinth.* Edited by Daniel N. Schowalter and Steven J. Friesen. Harvard Theological Studies 53. Cambridge, Mass.: Harvard University Press, 2005.

Webster, Jane, and Nicholas Cooper, eds. *Roman Imperialism: Post-Colonial Perspectives: Proceedings of a Symposium Held at Leicester University in November 1994*. Leicester Archaeology Monographs 3. Leicester: University of Leicester, 1996.

Weinberg, Saul S. *The Southeast Building: The Twin Basilicas, the Mosaic House*. Corinth 1.5. Princeton, N.J.: American School of Classical Studies at Athens, 1960.

West, Allen Brown. *Latin Inscriptions 1896–1926*. Corinth 8.2. Cambirdge, Mass.: Harvard University Press, 1931.

Williams, Charles Kaufman. "A Re-Evaluation of Temple E and the West End of the Forum." Pages 156–62 in *Temple E*. In *The Greek Renaissance in the Roman Empire: Papers from the Tenth British Museum Classical Colloquium*. Edited by Susan Walker and Averil Cameron. Bulletin Supplement (University of London. Institute of Classical Studies) 55. London: University of London, Institute of Classical Studies, 1989.

———. "Laus Julia Corinthiensis et Diana Nemorensis." Pages 384–89 in *Philia Epe eis Georgion E. Mylonan: Dia ta 60 Ete tou Anaskaphikou tou Ergou*. Vivliotheke tes en Athenais Archaiologikes Hetaireias 103. Athens: En Athenais Archaiologike Hetaireia, 1986-, 1987.

———. "Pre-Roman Cults in the Area of the Forum of Ancient Corinth." Ph.D. diss., University of Pennsylvania, 1978.

———. "The Refounding of Corinth: Some Roman Religious Attitudes." Pages 26–37 in *Refounding of Corinth*. In *Roman Architecture in the Greek World*. Edited by Sarah Macready and F. H. Thompson. Occasional Papers (New Series) 10. London: Society of Antiquaries of London distributed by Thames & Hudson, 1987.

Wiseman, James. "Corinth and Rome I: 228 B.C.–A.D. 267." *ANRW* 7.1:438–548. Part 2, Principat, 7.1. Edited by Hildegard Temporini. New York: de Gruyter, 1979.

CHAPTER 7
EMBEDDING ROME IN ATHENS

Nancy Evans

The ongoing, cross-disciplinary project of understanding Christian origins within the religions of the Roman Empire brings us today to reexamine imperial cult. As Professor Galinsky sensibly reminded us at his initial address (November 2008, Boston), an historicizing approach that respects local interpretive contexts reveals that there was no single imperial cult.[1] Diverse institutions of emperor worship emerged organically from local environments, and allowed each people to negotiate their own particular relationship to imperial authority. Ritual was not imposed by Rome. Imperial cult was not the dominant mode of worship within the empire, but it fit alongside preexisting traditions. In the Greek East this meant, in part, that emperor worship was adapted to fit Hellenistic ruler cult, itself already intertwined with the traditional worship of local deities. In Athens it meant that very same thing, plus something more. Because of its history, cultural legacy, and iconic past, Athens presented Rome with a unique set of themes and symbols. These themes and symbols played differently in the hands of different actors. In this brief paper I will examine one pattern of these symbols that involve imperial cult, and then make a quick suggestion about how this pattern continued even beyond the reach of traditional Greek and Roman cult practice. I will analyze the archaeological evidence that links the physical realia of Roman imperial cult with centuries of earlier traditions—both Hellenistic ruler cult and the cult of the Olympian gods. This physical evidence points to a familiar narrative of freedom and victory that many generations of Greeks and Romans renewed, and then re-formed to fit their own purposes. At the close of the paper I will suggest that Christian leaders participated in a similar dynamic when they came to Athens.

---

1. Karl Galinsky, "The Cult of the Roman Emperor: Uniter or Divider?" paper presented at the Annual Meeting of the SBL, Boston, 2008 (and ch. 1 in this volume), 3, picking up an argument first made by Mary Beard, John North, and Simon Price, *Religions of Rome*. Vol. 1: *A History* (Cambridge: Cambridge University Press, 1998), 348.

When you visit Athens today and view the remains of the ancient city, three layers stand out: the fifth-century B.C.E. classical sanctuary high on the Acropolis and the lower city dominated by Roman ruins of the second century C.E., all with Hellenistic structures mixed in for good measure. Every age saw its own empires: the Persian Empire and the Athenian Empire, the short-lived empire of the short-lived Alexander the Great, and the long reach of the Roman Empire. Seven centuries, four empires, and a handful of foreign kingdoms unite the city that worshipped Athena, Zeus, and Dionysus, and the cities that worshipped Athena, Zeus, Dionysus, Alexander, Demetrius, Augustus, and Hadrian. Every postclassical kingdom and empire did its best to connect itself to the city that played an increasingly minor role politically and militarily, but exerted ever greater ideological influence over the men who ruled the eastern Mediterranean. Rome brought big changes when it embedded itself in Athens, but almost everything that happened under Roman domination had already happened before: the coming and going of empires; the stress of civil wars; the city under siege; episodic and extensive destruction followed by periods of growth and rebuilding; and the worship of nonnative rulers.

The most famous destruction was the sack of Athens in 480 B.C.E., when Xerxes led the armies of the Persian Empire across the Hellespont and into Hellas. Centuries later this narrative still held a firm grip on the Romans. The Persian army sacked Athens twice, breaching the city's defenses and destroying everything in its path, including the main agora and the entire sanctuary of Athena on the Acropolis. Some artwork was looted, and carried off to Sardis or Susa.[2] After the Greeks defeated Xerxes at Salamis and Plataea Athens was hailed as the savior of Greece (Herodotus, *Hist.* 7.139). A generation later Athens fully armed itself, created its own naval empire, and accumulated great wealth through warfare and taxation of allies. Revenue from the Athenian treasury was used to rebuild the city leveled by the Persians, including the agora and the Acropolis. The artistic theme that dominated throughout classical Athens was victory over the forces of chaos, whether that chaos be mythological characters or barbarians from the east.[3] Triumphant stories of Olympian gods had long been a part of

---

2. John M. Camp, *The Archaeology of Athens* (New Haven, Conn.: Yale University Press, 2001), 5. See below p. 92 on the return of some of this artwork in the time of Alexander.

3. Jeffrey Mark Hurwit, *The Acropolis in the Age of Pericles* (Cambridge: Cambridge University Press, 2004) is an extensive study of the iconography. Olympian gods battling the Giants were depicted on the Parthenon's east metopes, on the interior of Athena's shield, and were traditionally woven into the peplos given to the goddess at the Panathenaea. Lapiths battling drunken centaurs were visible on the Parthenon's south metopes, on the sandals of Athena Parthenos, and on the shield of the bronze Athena. The battle of the Greeks and Amazons was displayed on the west metopes, on the shield on Athena Parthenos, and in the pediment of the temple of Athena Nike. The north metopes depicted the sack of Troy.

the iconography surrounding Athena—especially the Gigantomachy and Amazonomachy—but victory over Persia inspired Athenians to expand on the theme. As victorious scenes from myth were enshrined on Athena's statues and on the Parthenon itself, so paintings of victorious battles against the Persians were on view in the porticoes of the city and chiseled into marble on the temple of Athena Nike.[4] The program of artwork in Athens points to an evolving narrative of freedom that positioned the Athenians as inevitable and eternal victors.

But history proved otherwise. Athens fell to the Macedonian king Philip, and foreign kingdoms remained in power from then on. The political mess created by the unexpected death of Alexander in 323 B.C.E. resulted in wars of succession among his generals, his advisors, and their children. The Ptolemies of Egypt, the Attalids of Pergamum, the Seleucids of Syria, and the princes of Macedon all left their mark on the city, and Athens experienced additional periods of destruction. During the wars of succession the city suffered not because it fell during a siege, but because Philip V of Macedon ravaged the towns and sanctuaries surrounding Athens.[5] When Philip was defeated by the Ptolemies and the Attalids, Athens benefited from an influx of cash that created a small building boom.[6] Athens rebounded and assumed its position as a city of philosophers and students until the Roman civil wars of the first century B.C.E. Especially significant was Sulla's siege of the city during Rome's war with Mithridates of Pontos in the early first century B.C.E. (Plutarch, *Sull.* 12–14; Appian, *Mith.* 30–41).[7] Sulla starved the city

---

4. The paintings described in Pausanias were on view in the Stoa Poikile (Painted Stoa) and the Stoa of Zeus Eleutherios. Among other things they depicted mythological scenes, scenes from the Trojan War, and the battle of Marathon. Camp, *Archaeology of Athens*, 67–69 and 104–5. On the iconography of the Nike temple see Jeffrey M. Hurwit, *The Athenian Acropolis: History, Mythology, and Archaeology from the Neolithic Era to the Present* (Cambridge: Cambridge University Press, 1999), 209–15, and Jeffrey Mark Hurwit, *Acropolis in the Age of Pericles*, 181–91. The north gallery of the Propylaia, or Pinakotheke, probably functioned as dining room for officials on festival days and it housed Athens's finest paintings, all of which were lost, but some reportedly depicted mythological scenes, portraits of leading Athenians, and scenes from Athens's wars. There is also evidence that the art program commemorated tales of another important Greek victory—the fall of Troy. Jeffrey M. Hurwit, *Athenian Acropolis*, 196, and Camp, *Archaeology of Athens*, 84.

5. Livy 31.23–26. For a full description of the archaeological evidence for the destruction in the countryside of Attica caused by Philip V of Macedon in 200 B.C.E. see Homer Thompson, "Athens Faces Adversity," *Hesperia* 50 (1981): 343–55.

6. E.g. the Stoa of Attalos in the agora, fully restored by the American School of Classical Studies in the 1950s, and the Stoa of Eumenes on the south slope of the Acropolis.

7. For a full description of the archaeological evidence for the destruction in Athens caused by Sulla during the wars between Rome and Mithradates of Pontos in 87/6 B.C.E. see Michael C. Hoff and Susan I. Rotroff, eds., *The Romanization of Athens: Proceedings of an International Conference Held at Lincoln, Nebraska (April 1996)* (Oxford: Oxbow Books, 1997).

until the citizens ate shoe leather and weeds (Plutarch, *Sull.* 13.2-3); then one night he entered Athens from the northwest and marched straight from the Kerameikos into the agora, where his army did great damage to the commercial and political heart of the city. Plutarch recorded that the streets of Athens flowed with blood (*Sull.* 14.3-4). Important public buildings were damaged or destroyed, but apparently the Acropolis itself remained untouched.[8] Still, Athens did not emerge unscathed. After defeating Mithridates in 84 Sulla returned to Athens and reportedly looted the Acropolis of gold, silver, statues, and paintings.[9]

In the decades following Sulla the generals of Rome fought their civil wars on Greek soil at Pharsalus, Philippi, and Actium just as the wars of succession had been fought in Athens and Attica among the heirs of Alexander.[10] Athenians in the first century developed the sad habit of consistently supporting the losing side in these struggles for power. They supported Mithridates (defeated by Sulla) and Pompey (defeated by Caesar). The assassination of Caesar occasioned another round of wars of succession, and this time Athens supported Brutus and Cassius (defeated by Octavian and Antony), and finally, Antony (defeated by Octavian). The city did not begin to recover until well into the reign of Augustus, and with the support of the emperors Trajan and Hadrian Athens was in full flower again by the second century C.E. This period of peace and stability lasted less than 150 years, until the city was sacked again by Herulians in the mid-third century.

Much of what the Athenians had experienced following Alexander they reexperienced with Rome, and this includes the worship of nonnative rulers. The veneration of Roman emperors that came with the reign of Augustus is closely related to Hellenistic ruler cult. The first instances of ruler cult in Greece date

---

Daniel Geagan, "Roman Athens: Some Aspects of Life and Culture. I. 86 B.C.-A.D. 267," *ANRW* 7.1:371-437 remains the best survey of the changes in Athens under Roman rule.

8. During this sack of the city the South Stoa, the Stoa Basileos and the *tholos* (all in the agora) were heavily damaged. Michael C. Hoff, "*Laceratae Athenae*: Sulla's Siege of Athens in 87/6 BC and Its Aftermath," in *The Romanization of Athens: Proceedings of an International Conference Held at Lincoln, Nebraska (April 1996)* (ed. Michael C. Hoff and Susan I. Rotroff; Oxford: Oxbow Books, 1997), 38-42 calls the damage in the agora "grievous" (p. 38) and he analyzes it in detail (pp. 38-42).

9. Sulla even dismantled some of the columns of an incomplete temple of Olympian Zeus in the lower city and shipped them to Rome where they were used in the temple of Jupiter Optimus Maximus on the Capitoline (Pliny the Elder, *Nat.* 36.6.45). The archaeological record hints that the city entered a period of steep economic decline following the siege of Sulla. The severity of this decline is still debated by scholars, as Hoff notes, ibid., 32. Hoff sides with those who conclude there was considerable destruction and a slower period of reconstruction. For a lengthy discussion of this "slow and painful recovery" see T. Leslie Shear, "Athens: From City-State to Provincial Town," *Hesperia* 50 (1981): 356-77.

10. Pharsalus 48 B.C.E. Caesar defeats Pompey; Philippi 44 B.C.E. Antony and Ovtavian defeat Brutus and Cassius; and Actium 31 B.C.E. Octavian defeats Antony.

back to the late fifth and fourth centuries B.C.E.[11] Alexander the Great was the first to whom the Athenian demos bestowed divine honors.[12] Hellenistic ruler cult constituted the Greeks' own response to a new type of authority, namely the power of kings whose base was not grounded in the local polis.[13] Modeled as it was on the traditional cult of the gods, ruler cult grafted itself onto ancient traditions of civic sacrifice and festivals as practiced in the autonomous poleis of mainland Greece, the Aegean, and Asia Minor.[14] Each city handled the worship of foreign kings in its own way.

Such honors were granted rarely in Hellenistic Athens, and with surprising results. In 307 the Athenian demos voted to extend divine honors to the Macedonian general Antigonos and his son Demetrius Poliorcertes after they intervened in a civil war and nominally restored democracy. Each became the eponymous patron of a new Athenian tribe.[15] Each was hailed as savior, and honored with processions, priests, altars, and sacrifices.[16] Athenians looked to their festival calendar and honored the foreign king Demetrius alongside Zeus, Athena, and Dionysus.[17] The demos even hailed Demetrius as the brother of Athena, but

---

11. The Spartan general Lysander is the first recorded example: Duris, frg. 26.71. He was worshipped as a god on the island of Samos at the very close of the Peloponnesian War.

12. S. R. F. Price, *Rituals and Power: The Roman Imperial Cult in Asia Minor* (Cambridge: Cambridge University Press, 1984), 23–47 discusses the origins of Hellenistic ruler cult in detail, including on p. 26 the evidence for granting divine honors to Alexander. Robert Parker, *Athenian Religion: A History* (Oxford: Clarendon, 1996), 256–58, with notes, covers similar ground in more detail.

13. Price, *Rituals and Power*, 28–40.

14. Ibid., 30. Price maintains that ruler cult was not fashioned after the cult of heroes. On the patterns of civic sacrifice in Athens before Alexander see N. A. Evans, "Feasts, Citizens and Cultic Democracy in Classical Athens," *Ancient Society* 34 (2004): 23: "Occasions of *thusia* and *heortai* [sacrifice and feasts] were occasions for traditional cultic activity that balanced the divine and human, and as such sacrifice and civic festivals were activities that the polis was very interested in."

15. Cleisthenes in the late sixth century B.C.E. created the ten tribes of Athens, and each tribe was assigned an eponymous hero. The tribes, along with the demes of Attica, became the building blocks for the new democracy. A statue group depicting each of the heroes was set up in the agora, and the base of the monument served as a public notice board. The base of the monument shows clear traces of having been expanded twice. Camp, *Archaeology of Athens*, 158–59 and 166, and Parker, *Athenian Religion*, 102–21.

16. Ibid., 258. The two new tribes were called Antigonis and Demetrius. Demetrius and Antigonos were honored as "Saviors" (*sōtēres*). Parker discusses Demetrius in great detail 258–264.

17. For Demetrius the traditional Dionysia was renamed "the Dionysia and Demetrieia"; ibid., 259. Demetrius received extraordinary honors during his lifetime, some of which were never repeated again. The Athenians even had Demetrius and Antigonos woven into the peplos of Athena at the Panathenaea in 306, fighting the Giants alongside Zeus: Plutarch, *Demetr.* 12.

Demetrius behaved badly. He not only failed to quell civil war, he reportedly even moved his household into a temple of Athena on the Acropolis, took objects from Athena's temple treasuries for his own personal use, and brought in prostitutes (Plutarch, *Demetr.* 23–26).[18] According to Plutarch, Demetrius and his Athenian supporters held orgies in the Parthenon. When Demetrius was challenged by another Macedonian general named Lachares, Lachares ascended the Acropolis to despoil it of gold and silver (Pausanias, *Descr.* 1.25.7; 1.29.16).[19]

From this low point Athenians granted few divine honors until they voted to make the Roman general Antony the "new Dionysus" during his struggle with Octavian in the 30s B.C.E. (Plutarch, *Ant.* 60).[20] Once Octavian defeated Antony at Actium, Athens signaled its allegiance to the victor by setting up cult. Shortly after Octavian assumed the name Augustus Athenian elites dedicated to him and to the city Rome a small, open *tholos* on the Acropolis.[21] This round temple built on the east side of the Parthenon was situated on the Parthenon's main axis. A dedicatory inscription was carved onto the curved architrave, and in this inscription Augustus was called "Savior," like Demetrius and Antigonos before him.[22]

We also have the text of a cult hymn dedicated to Demetrius Poliorcertes, discussed by Price, *Rituals and Power*, 38 and Parker, *Athenian Religion*, 259.

18. Jeffrey M. Hurwit, *Athenian Acropolis*, 261.

19. Lachares reportedly even stripped the golden ornaments from a statue of Athena. This account of the denuding of the Athena Parthenos is disputed by some, and the sources do not indicate exactly which of the many images of Athena was despoiled. Cf. Athenaeus, *Deipn.* 9.405 and Hurwit, *Athenian Acropolis*, 261–62.

20. In the intervening years they did give high honors to Rome by creating a festival called the Romaia in the mid-second century, and a festival for Sulla called the Sylleia. There is little evidence for full-blown ruler cult for Antony, but he did not rule very long and it is easy to speculate what might have happened had he lived and defeated Octavian at Actium. Hurwit, *Athenian Acropolis*, 263 relates a story of how the Athenians arranged for Antony the "new Dionysus" to "wed" Athena—behavior that resembles that of their treatment of Demetrius.

21. The temple itself was probably a small, cella-less ring of nine Ionic columns, perhaps framing statues of Augustus and personified Roma or a small sacrificial altar or both, though it would be a little unusual for an altar to be built underneath a roof. The nine columns were precise copies of the Ionic columns on the east porch of the Erechtheion. Camp, *Archaeology of Athens*, 187 notes that calling this structure "the temple of Rome and Augustus" is open to question. See also Hurwit, *Athenian Acropolis*, 279–80 and 317, plate X and figure 227. The structure was big enough to protect a statue but its profile was low enough so that it did not obstruct the sight lines, just as the earlier Attalid pillar did not get in the way of the temple. Professor Galinsky has suggested that this round building echoed the small round temple (commonly called the "temple of Vesta") in the Forum Boarium in Rome.

22. *IG* II² 3173: "The people to the goddess Roma and Caesar Augustus: Pammenes, the son of Zenon of Marathon, being hoplite general and priest of the goddess Roma and Augustus Savior on the Acropolis, when Megiste, daughter of Askepiades, of Halai, was priestess of Athena Polias. In the archonship of Areos, son of Dorion of Paiania."

Emperor cult was established in the lower city as well. No fewer than thirteen altars dedicated to Augustus have been found in the lower city.[23] A Roman-period annex built onto the back of the Stoa of Zeus Eleutherios in the agora was probably a site for worship of the emperor; the altar in front of that building was enlarged at the same time.[24] Augustus responded to Athens's devotion a few years later by completing construction of a whole new agora to the east of the old one, putting into practice new Roman ideas for urban design.[25] Having a new Roman market meant that the classical agora could be remodeled. Augustus's son-in-law and longtime friend Agrippa gave the Athenians a substantial new concert hall, the Odeion, which was sited in the center of the old agora's open square. To complete the makeover a temple to Ares was placed opposite the Odeion. An inscription honoring Gaius Caesar as the "new Ares" hints that the temple could have served the needs of imperial cult.[26] The renovated agora with its prominent Ares temple echoed the forum of Augustus completed in 2 B.C.E. with its new temple of Mars Ultor. By Hadrian's reign a century later the number of imperial altars increased—so far ninety-four have been found.[27] Meanwhile, Athenians

---

23. Anna Benjamin and Antony E. Raubitschek, "Arae Augusti," *Hesperia* 28 (1959): 65–85. These altars have the name of Augustus in the genitive or dative case, as with inscriptions on altars for traditional deities.

24. Both sites discussed by Homer Thompson, "The Annex to the Stoa of Zeus in the Athenian Agora," *Hesperia* 35 (1966): 171–87, and Susan Walker, "Athens Under Augustus," in *The Romanization of Athens: Proceedings of an International Conference Held at Lincoln, Nebraska (April 1996)* (ed. Michael C. Hoff and Susan I. Rotroff; Oxford: Oxbow Books, 1997), 69. The temple of Apollo Patroos next door to the Stoa of Zeus Eleuthereus could have housed an imperial cult as well. Apollo was a god favored by Augustus in Rome and Nicopolis (near Actium). Apollo Patroos—the cult of "ancestral Apollo"—may well have served as a native Athenian translation of a Roman cult. The Athenian temple of Apollo Patroos and original cult date to the early Hellenistic period, ca. 330 B.C.E. Camp, *Archaeology of Athens*, 156–57, and Charles W. Hedrick Jr., "The Temple and Cult of Apollo Patroos," *AJA* 92 (1988): 185–210.

25. Discussed by Shear, "Athens," 359, and Walker, "Athens."

26. It doesn't seem sensible to me that all these places in such close proximity—the Stoa of Zeus, the temple of Apollo, and the temple of Ares—were all sites of emperor cult, at least not at the same time. This Gaius Caesar honored as Ares was the son of Agrippa and the adopted son of Augustus. After this child's death Drusus Caesar, son of the emperor Tiberius, was honored with the epithet "new god Ares": *IG* II² 3257. The transformation of the agora, the temple of Ares, and the placement of the Odeion is analyzed in length by Shear, "Athens," 359–63. Under Augustus the cult of Mars became increasingly important in Rome, and the centrality of the temple of Ares in Athens reflects this. At the same time the Augustan art program was mindful of the importance of fifth-century Athenian art. The forum of Augustus completed in 2 B.C.E. included carefully worked copies of the Caryatids from the Erechtheion porch, and likewise the Panathenaic procession on the interior portico frieze of the Parthenon was echoed in the procession depicted on Augustus's Ara Pacis in the Campus Martius.

27. Anna S. Benjamin, "The Altars of Hadrian in Athens and Hadrian's Panhellenic Program," *Hesperia* 32 (1963): 57–86. Other Roman emperors between Augustus and Hadrian were

continued to look to their festival calendar to honor emperors. They named a new tribe for Hadrian, and put into place three new international festivals in his honor, following the model of the Demetrieia, Ptolemaia, Romaia, and Sylleia, all festivals instituted during the Hellenistic and republican Roman periods.[28] Instituting festivals reveals another way imperial cult was grafted onto preexisting modes of communal worship. Athenians came to worship Roman emperors by following age-old patterns.[29] As the traditional cult of the gods helped negotiate power relationships within the classical polis, and as Hellenistic ruler cult was an authentic reaction to foreign monarchs, so worship of Roman emperors allowed Athenians as a community to experience external authority.[30]

In the language of the archaic poet Homer, the Olympian gods were immortal and ageless, but this quality did not carry over to Hellenistic kings or Roman emperors. One notable aspect of ruler cult as practiced by Athenians was their willingness to revoke it. The Macedonian king Demetrius Poliorcertes is the first we know to receive this treatment in Athens. After being honored with ruler cult and civic festivals during his own lifetime, he lost it two generations later. Demetrius's grandson Philip V was also honored with ruler cult, but when his abuse of the Attic countryside became too much the Athenians voted to abolish and destroy his festivals, sanctuaries, priests, statues, and inscriptions.[31] Philip's

---

also worshiped, e.g., Claudius was honored with portraits and altars on the Acropolis: *IG* II² 3272 and 3276. Hadrian favored Athens and his plans included a modern Roman bath complex next to the completed temple to Olympian Zeus in the lower city just east of the Acropolis. That sanctuary had remained unfinished since the sixth century B.C.E. and the time of the tyrant Peisistratus. A Hellenistic Seleucid king, Antiochus IV of Syria (175–164 B.C.E.), had resumed construction of the temple of Zeus but construction apparently stopped with his death. Antiochus's architectural plan was significantly more grandiose than the original, and was carried to fruition by Hadrian. Camp, *Archaeology of Athens*, 173–76. Elsewhere in the city Hadrian rebuilt the theater of Dionysus, built libraries, aqueducts, basilicas, and a monumental arch that still stands, dividing the new Roman Athens from the old one. Inscriptions on the arch read (on the west side toward the Acropolis): "This is Athens, the former city of Theseus"; and on the east side (toward the temple of Zeus): "This is the city of Hadrian and not of Theseus." Camp (ibid., 201) discusses Hadrian's significant contributions to the city of Athens 193–208 C.E.

28. Demetrius the Macedonian king had first been honored with a festival, as discussed in n. 17 above. Later the Ptolemies were honored with a festival called the Ptolemaia and this festival likely superceded that honoring Demetrius and the Antigonid kings: Price, *Rituals and Power*, 40. The goddess Roma was first worshiped in Athens sometime after the fading of the Ptolemies and before 153, and Rome was honored with the festival of the Romaia: *IG* II² 1938. This was followed by the Sylleia in the 80s B.C.E., a festival in honor of the general Sulla. See also Shear, "Athens."

29. Price, *Rituals and Power*, 25.

30. Ibid., 52.

31. Philip's deceased Macedonian ancestors suffered the same fate. Livy 44.4–8 (as quoted by Camp, *Archaeology of Athens*, 170): "All statues and pictures of Philip as well as of all his

ancestors received the same treatment, and at that same time Demetrius lost his cult status, was stripped of his tribes and holidays, and had his name erased from inscriptions. Sometimes the erasing of memory was more subtle—not the result of citizen rage but a form of recycling common in the long annals of foreign powers honored and worshiped in Athens. Monumental pillars honoring the Pergamene kings Eumenes and Attalos on the Acropolis were recycled more than once. Antony had his name and image as the new Dionysus mounted on one of the pillars, and during the early empire both pillars were rededicated yet again, one in honor of Agrippa, and the other for Augustus.[32] Memory was molded and recycled on a larger scale also, as evidenced by the Roman practice of modifying and moving existing architecture. The temple of Ares in Athens was actually a composite of recycled fifth-century temples from rural Attica that were damaged during the wars of succession and then later dismantled and reengineered in the agora.[33] By reusing existing monuments and structures Rome laid claim to the urban cityscape and its local traditions.

Another Athenian tradition that Rome picked up on was the narrative of freedom dating back to the fifth century B.C.E. Even before the Persian invasion Harmodios and Aristogeiton achieved fame for "freeing" Athens from tyranny.[34] Heroic bronzes of these tyrant-slayers were dedicated in the agora. After the originals were taken by Xerxes in 480 new bronzes were cast (Arrian, *Anab.* 3.16.8).

---

ancestors in both the male and female line should be taken and destroyed; all holidays, rites, and priesthoods instituted in his honor or that of his forefathers should be disestablished; the places in which a dedication or an inscription of this import stood should be accursed." At this time pieces of an equestrian bronze depicting Demetrius may have been thrown down a well, as discussed by Camp (ibid.).

32. Hurwit, *Athenian Acropolis*, 278.

33. Susan Alcock, *Archaeologies of the Greek Past: Landscape, Monuments, and Memories* (Cambridge: Cambridge University Press, 2002), 51–73 has an extensive discussion of the Athenian agora as a memorial space that held simultaneously different meanings for ruling Romans and subject Athenians. Alcock (ibid., 54–58), Camp, *Archaeology of Athens*, 189–92, and Shear, "Athens," 364 on the "wandering" temples that were put to new uses in the early empire, including those remade into the agora Ares temple. This wandering temple had components from fifth-century temples to Athena (at Pallene) and to Poseidon (at Sounion), temples that had probably been heavily damaged by rampaging Macedonian princes in the early second century B.C.E. A temple of Nemesis at Rhamnous was recycled (but not moved) and transformed into a temple for the deified Livia probably in the 40s following her death, according to Shear (ibid.). Susan Alcock, *Graecia Capta: The Landscapes of Roman Greece* (Cambridge: Cambridge University Press, 1993) is a larger study of the rural, urban and civic landscapes of Greece, specifically using archaeology as evidence for how Greeks actively responded to imperial Roman rule.

34. Themes of victory and freedom are apparent already in Herodotus and Thucydides. For fifth-century historical perspectives on the tyrant-slayers see Herodotus, *Hist.* 5.55, 6.109 and 121, and Thucydides 1.20, 6.54–59. In actuality it was not Harmodios and Aristogeiton who freed Athens, but Sparta.

When Alexander took the Persian capital of Susa 150 years later he shipped the originals back to Athens where they were mounted alongside the replacements. Demetrius next fit himself into this freedom narrative. Heroic bronzes memorializing his restoration of democracy stood in the agora alongside the tyrant-slayers—until the Athenians voted to revoke his honors. They pulled the statues down and threw the pieces into an abandoned well. Under Roman domination Athenians for a short while celebrated two more tyrant-slayers with heroic bronzes of Brutus and Cassius, Julius Caesar's assassins, prominently displayed in the agora.[35]

A second narrative of freedom dating to the fifth century positioned Athens as the savior of Greece and vanquisher of eastern barbarians, and this narrative was used to great effect by subsequent foreign kings and emperors. Alexander the Great was the first foreign ruler to reference the Athenian victory theme. After he defeated the Persians at Granicus in 334 Alexander dedicated three hundred suits of Persian armor to Athena Parthenos and set up an inscription honoring the Greeks' victory over "the barbarians of Asia" (Arrian, *Anab.* 1.16). He had fourteen Persian shields mounted on the east architrave of the Parthenon; their position below the Gigantomachy metopes explicitly linked Alexander's campaigns with the mythological and historical freedom narratives dear to the Athenians. Later Hellenistic kings strengthened that link. Following a victory over the Gauls in the late third century Attalos of Pergamum dedicated a series of bronzes on the Acropolis in front of the Parthenon near the south citadel wall.[36] The so-called smaller Attalid group depicted defeated Giants, Amazons, Persians, and Gauls lying dead or wounded. Again these bronzes picked up on the victory

---

35. On the parade of heroic bronze tyrannicides see Camp, *Archaeology of Athens*, 55, 57, and 170, and Jeffrey M. Hurwit, *Athenian Acropolis*, 254, 261, and 263.

36. Roman copies of these statues remain. The "smaller Attalid group" was itself a copy of the more monumental bronzes that had been dedicated on the acropolis in Pergamum; ibid., 269–70. This same Attalos and his brother Eumenes also enshrined themselves on the Acropolis by placing heroic bronzes on monumental pillars commemorating their victories in athletic games. One pillar still stands on the northwest corner of the Acropolis, just to the left as you ascend towards the Propylaia. The other pillar (now gone) was built at the northeast corner of the Parthenon: Camp, *Archaeology of Athens*, 172 and Hurwit, *Athenian Acropolis*, 272–73. The pillar at the corner of the Parthenon was dedicated to Attalos II, and that next to the Propylaia was dedicated to Eumenes II. The tapering pillars served as bases for bronze sculptures recognizing their victory in chariot races at the Panathenaea of 186 B.C.E. (or 182). The Attalids were kings of Pergamum and received ruler cult in that city, but neither was worshipped at Athens. Still the Athenians knew they received cult in Pergamum, and the honors bestowed upon them followed some of the patterns already established, e.g., they named a new tribe after him, as they did earlier for Demetrius and Antigonos. Consider also the Seleucid *gorgoneia*, located on the south citadel wall of the Acropolis. The gorgon head was a clear reference to the gorgon on depictions of Athena's shield on the Acropolis; ibid., 273.

narrative, but developed it further by depicting the vanquished fully defeated and prostrate on the ground.

By the first century B.C.E. the evolving narrative of freedom transformed Persians into Parthians, and the Parthians remained a threat on the eastern frontier of the Roman Empire for many generations. Antony, Augustus, and others appropriated this narrative in Athens and Rome both. Before departing on a campaign to Parthia in 36 Antony took tokens of Athena with him from the Acropolis as good luck charms (Plutarch, *Ant.* 34).[37] Augustus exploited the link between Athens/Rome and Persia/Parthia to new heights.[38] At the dedication of the Forum of Augustus in Rome Augustus staged a reenactment of the battle of Salamis. Augustus's connection to the struggle against Persia was evident in Athens, too. One of Athens's probable sites for emperor worship was the Stoa of Zeus Eleutherios, which celebrated freedom (*eleutheria*) from Persian domination. Subsequent members of the Julio-Claudian dynasty continued the tradition of linking Persia and Parthia, and in 57 Nero staged another mock Salamis sea battle in Rome. A few years later as Nero was launching a new campaign against Parthia the Athenians dedicated to him a gilded inscription on the east architrave of the Parthenon, next to where Alexander had earlier mounted his shields commemorating victory over Persia.[39] In the victorious repetition of western triumph over eastern barbarism each generation reinforced the centuries-old Athenian theme. Rome slid into the pattern; Rome made itself the logical heir of the freedom narrative.

An evolving narrative of freedom offers a consistent and coherent way to view continuities over time. While early emperors renewed this narrative, another important figure is said to have journeyed to Athens, namely the early Christian leader Paul. According to Acts Paul visited Athens and gave a speech

---

37. Plutarch reports that Antony took an olive garland and water from the Klepsydra, a spring on the Acropolis.

38. Anthony Spawforth, "Symbol of Unity? The Persian-Wars Tradition in the Roman Empire," in *Greek Historiography* (ed. Simon Hornblower; Oxford: Clarendon, 1994), 233–47 on the so-called Persian War "mania" that overtook Greece in the early centuries of the Common Era. He sees this as the Persian Wars carrying a multivalent message during this time, depending on who was identifying with it.

39. "The Council of the Areopagus, the Council of the Six Hundred, and the Athenian people [honor] the Greatest Emperor Nero Caesar Claudius Augustus Germanicus, son of a God, when Tiberius Claudius Novius, son of Philinos, was Hoplite General for the eighth time, as well as Epimelete and Nomothete, and the priestess of Athena was Paulina, daughter of Kapito." *IG* II² 3277, dated to 61 C.E. The inscription mounted in gilt bronze letters was over 25 meters long; ibid., 234–37 is the best discussion of the Neronian inscription and complicity of the Athenian elite in Roman imperial structures. The Athenians also refurbished the theater of Dionysus and rededicated it to Nero. Jeffrey M. Hurwit, *Athenian Acropolis*, 280–81.

at the Areopagus (Acts 17:15–34).[40] Judging from this account of Paul's visit, the author of Acts pictured a city resembling that known by the emperors where Paul could wonder at Athens's shrines, altars, temples, and statues.[41] He found Athenians surrounded by idols; doubtless these idols of gold, silver, and stone included traditional Olympian deities as well as members of the Roman imperial family. The Athens of Acts also valued freedom—namely the free exchange of ideas. Athenians were eager to hear any new idea that reached their ears (Acts 17:19–20).[42] Paul is depicted preaching to Athenian Jews in the local synagogue, and to Stoic and Epicurean philosophers who taught in Athens's porticoes. Whoever happened to be in the agora was also a captive audience. The author of Acts understood that his first-century Greek-speaking audience saw Athens as the city that nourished new ideas and educated the Mediterranean ruling class as it had for centuries.[43]

Among the many idols and altars he saw in Athens Paul is said to have focused on an altar to "the unknown God" (Acts 17:23); as the character Paul explained it in Acts, Athenians were unknowingly worshiping the God of Jesus.[44] For the author of Acts Athenian polytheism and traditional piety anticipated the redemption possible in Christ. This dynamic mirrors that of the Romans, for whom Athens-triumphant-over-Persia anticipated Rome-triumphant-over-Parthia. Like the real emperors, this literary version of Paul had a desire to see in Athens a reflection of his own world. Each constructed the Athenian past so that

---

40. I take no stand on the historicity of this visit, but will for now leave all discussion to colleagues in early Christianity. If it took place, it would have been late in the reign of the emperor Claudius—probably in the early 50s. What I am interested in is the rhetorical function that Athens would have played for a Greek-speaking audience in the first-century Mediterranean.

41. Altars mentioned at Acts 17: 23, and idols at 17:16, 23, and 29. Joseph A. Fitzmyer, *The Acts of the Apostles* (AB; New York: Doubleday, 1998), 603–4 discusses other ancient literary evidence for the plethora of idols in Athens.

42. A similar comment about the Athenians' love for new sights and religious festivals can be found as far back as Plato's *Republic* 5.475d.

43. The intellectual freedom that valued ethical inquiry likewise dated back to the Athenian empire and the decades immediately following the war with Xerxes. David Balch, "The Cultural Origin of 'Receiving All Nations' in Luke-Acts: Alexander the Great or Roman Social Policy?" in *Early Christianity and Classical Culture: Comparative Essays in Honor of Abraham J. Malherbe* (ed. John Fitzgerald, Thomas Olbricht, and L. Michael White; NovTSup 110; Leiden: Brill, 2003), 483–500 convincingly argues that the Christian notion of "receiving all nations" was an aspect of Roman imperial social policy after Claudius, and not a value native to the Athenians or to the Hellenistic world of Alexander.

44. Acts 17:23 contains the reference to the altar to the "unknown god." There is no archaeological or epigraphical evidence for such a cult. Perhaps that reference served a more rhetorical purpose for the author of Acts. See Fitzmyer, *Acts of the Apostles*, 607–8 for more complete bibliography and discussion of "altars of gods called unknown."

the past predicted the new order, and each looked to the stones of Athens—the monuments, temples, and altars—to appeal to the Athenians' sense of traditional piety and free inquiry. But unlike generations of Greeks and Romans who mindfully referenced Athenian traditions, Paul claimed that Athenians lacked awareness of the true "Lord of heaven and earth" (Acts 17:24).

Another side to the Athenian freedom narrative tells the story of those who opposed changes to the traditional worship of the gods. Time constraints do not allow me to discuss resistance to ruler cult and emperor cult. Demosthenes sounded the first alarm about Philip and Alexander centuries before Augustus, and evidence for opposition can be found in every period. Even Augustus early in his reign faced resistance when a statue of Athena on the Acropolis was turned from the east, the traditional direction, to face the west. While facing west—that is facing towards Rome—the statue spat blood (Dio Cassius 54.7.2–3).[45] Paul visited Athens just three decades later. Perhaps from an early Christian perspective the need for redemption and the resistance to the status quo both responded to the entire nexus of traditional Greek and Roman practices that imperial cult existed within. It has been said that Roman deities never stand on their own, and this observation extends to imperial cult.[46] So in Athens we can imagine an image of a blood-spitting Athena standing near the Parthenon, alongside the *tholos* and an image of Augustus. And we can imagine Paul seeing altars for native gods alongside altars for Roman emperors and a putative unknown god. Emperor cult was grafted onto prior local traditions, and in Athens Romans and Christians alike fit themselves into an old ideology of freedom and triumph. One significant difference between the Romans and their emperors, and Christians and their new god, was this: the reach of the new Christian god was depicted extending beyond the familiar legacy of Greece and Rome, and it triumphed not

---

45. This curious episode and the Athenians' own caution in accepting Augustus is analyzed at length in Michael C. Hoff, "Civil Disobedience and Unrest in Augustan Athens," *Hesperia* 58 (1989): 267–76. It happened in the winter of 22/21 B.C.E., probably after the Athenians had already dedicated the *tholos* to Augustus and Rome. See also, on Athenian resistance to Augustus, Anthony Spawforth, "The Early Reception of the Imperial Cult in Athens: Problems and Ambiguities," in *The Romanization of Athens: Proceedings of an International Conference Held at Lincoln, Nebraska (April 1996)* (ed. Michael C. Hoff and Susan I. Rotroff; Oxford: Oxbow Books, 1997), 183–201.

46. John Scheid, *An Introduction to Roman Religion* (trans. Janet Lloyd; Bloomington, Ind.: Indiana University Press, 2003), 158–59: "Very rarely does one come across a ritual or a sanctuary in which a deity is invoked in isolation." "In the functional polytheism of the Romans the gods stand side by side and collaborate with one another.... Under the empire the situation became even clearer when ... the deified emperors were honored at the same time as the patron deities of other temples: such associations were expressed by the construction of secondary shrines and altars in most cult sites."

over eastern barbarians, but over perceived Greek ignorance of the true god who should be worshiped in Athens.

Bibliography

Alcock, Susan. *Archaeologies of the Greek Past: Landscape, Monuments, and Memories.* Cambridge: Cambridge University Press, 2002.

———. *Graecia Capta: The Landscapes of Roman Greece.* Cambridge: Cambridge University Press, 1993.

———. "The Reconfiguration of Memory in the Eastern Roman Empire." Susan Alcock. Pages 323–50 in *Empires: Perspectives from Archaeology and History.* Edited by Susan E. Alcock, Terence N. D'Altroy, Kathleen D. Morrison, and Carla M. Sinopoli. Cambridge: Cambridge University Press, 2001.

Balch, David. "The Cultural Origin of 'Receiving All Nations' in Luke-Acts: Alexander the Great or Roman Social Policy?" Pages 483–500 in *Early Christianity and Classical Culture: Comparative Essays in Honor of Abraham J. Malherbe.* Edited by John Fitzgerald, Thomas Olbricht, and L. Michael White. Supplements to Novum Testamentum 110. Leiden: Brill, 2003.

Beard, Mary. *The Roman Triumph.* Cambridge, Mass.: Harvard University Press, 2007.

———, John North, and Simon Price. *Religions of Rome.* Vol. 1: *A History.* Cambridge: Cambridge University Press, 1998.

Benjamin, Anna S. "The Altars of Hadrian in Athens and Hadrian's Panhellenic Program." *Hesperia* 32 (1963): 57–86.

Benjamin, Anna, and Antony E. Raubitschek. "Arae Augusti." *Hesperia* 28 (1959): 65–85.

Camp, John M. *The Archaeology of Athens.* New Haven, Conn.: Yale University Press, 2001.

Evans, N. A. "Feasts, Citizens and Cultic Democracy in Classical Athens." *Ancient Society* 34 (2004): 1–25.

Fitzmyer, Joseph A. *The Acts of the Apostles.* Anchor Bible. New York: Doubleday, 1998.

Galinsky, Karl, ed. *The Cambridge Companion to the Age of Augustus.* Cambridge: Cambridge University Press, 2005.

———. "The Cult of the Roman Emperor: Uniter or Divider?" Paper presented at the Annual Meeting of the SBL, Boston, 2008, and ch. 1 in this volume.

Geagan, Daniel. "The Athenian Elite: Romanization, Resistance, and the Exercise of Power." Pages 19–32 in *The Romanization of Athens: Proceedings of an International Conference Held at Lincoln, Nebraska (April 1996).* Edited by Michael C. Hoff and Susan I. Rotroff. Oxford: Oxbow Books, 1997.

———. "Roman Athens: Some Aspects of Life and Culture. I. 86 B.C.–A.D. 267." *ANRW* 7.1:371–437. Part 2, Principat, 12.1. Edited by Hildegard Temporini. New York: de Gruyter, 1980.

Hedrick, Charles W. Jr. "The Temple and Cult of Apollo Patroos." *American Journal of Archaeology* 92 (1988): 185–210.

Hoff, Michael C. "Civil Disobedience and Unrest in Augustan Athens." *Hesperia* 58 (1989): 267–76.

———. "*Laceratae Athenae*: Sulla's Siege of Athens in 87/6 BC and Its Aftermath." Pages 33–51 in *The Romanization of Athens: Proceedings of an International Conference Held at Lincoln, Nebraska (April 1996).* Edited by Michael C. Hoff and Susan I.

Rotroff. Oxford: Oxbow Books, 1997.
Hoff, Michael C., and Susan I. Rotroff, eds. *The Romanization of Athens: Proceedings of an International Conference Held at Lincoln, Nebraska (April 1996).* Oxford: Oxbow Books, 1997.
Hurwit, Jeffrey M. *The Athenian Acropolis: History, Mythology, and Archaeology from the Neolithic Era to the Present.* Cambridge: Cambridge University Press, 1999.
Hurwit, Jeffrey Mark. *The Acropolis in the Age of Pericles.* Cambridge: Cambridge University Press, 2004.
Parker, Robert. *Athenian Religion: A History.* Oxford: Clarendon, 1996.
Price, S. R. F. *Rituals and Power: The Roman Imperial Cult in Asia Minor.* Cambridge: Cambridge University Press, 1984.
Scheid, John. "Augustus and Roman Religion: Continuity, Conservatism, and Innovation." Pages 175–93 in *The Cambridge Companion to the Age of Augustus.* Edited by Karl Galinsky. Cambridge: Cambridge University Press, 2005.
———. *An Introduction to Roman Religion.* Translated by Janet Lloyd. Bloomington, Ind.: Indiana University Press, 2003.
Shear, T. Leslie. "Athens: From City-State to Provincial Town." *Hesperia* 50 (1981): 356–77.
Spawforth, Anthony. "The Early Reception of the Imperial Cult in Athens: Problems and Ambiguities." Pages 183–201 in *The Romanization of Athens: Proceedings of an International Conference Held at Lincoln, Nebraska (April 1996).* Edited by Michael C. Hoff and Susan I. Rotroff. Oxford: Oxbow Books, 1997.
———. "Symbol of Unity? The Persian-Wars Tradition in the Roman Empire." Pages 233–47 in *Greek Historiography.* Edited by Simon Hornblower. Oxford: Clarendon, 1994.
Thompson, Homer. "The Annex to the Stoa of Zeus in the Athenian Agora." *Hesperia* 35 (1966): 171–87.
———. "Athens Faces Adversity." *Hesperia* 50 (1981): 343–55.
Walker, Susan. "Athens Under Augustus." Pages 67–80 in *The Romanization of Athens: Proceedings of an International Conference Held at Lincoln, Nebraska (April 1996).* Edited by Michael C. Hoff and Susan I. Rotroff. Oxford: Oxbow Books, 1997.
Woolf, Greg. "Inventing Empire in Ancient Rome." Pages 311–22 in *Empires: Perspectives from Archaeology and History.* Edited by Susan E. Alcock, Terence N. D'Altroy, Kathleen D. Morrison, and Carla M. Sinopoli. Cambridge: Cambridge University Press, 2001.

Chapter 8
Honoring Trajan in Pergamum:
Imperial Temples in the "Second City"

Daniel N. Schowalter

It is my pleasure to join in on this discussion of the "imperial cult" and especially to participate in this follow-up to the presentation of Karl Galinsky at the SBL meeting in Boston (November, 2008). I am very much convinced by the argument cited by Galinsky, from Beard, North, and Price, that there is "no such thing as '*the* imperial cult'."[1] In fact, I made a similar argument in my dissertation in 1989. "This attempt to create a neat package of 'imperial theology' reflects more about a modern fascination with ideology than it does about the different ways in which the gods were portrayed throughout the Roman world."[2] All the evidence I have encountered over the course of the last twenty years has provided further confirmation of this point. The diversity of examples available for honors offered to the Roman emperor—even to a single emperor in a single location—make it impossible and, I think, inadvisable to think of an "imperial cult" in an artificially synthetic way. One of the dangers of using an oversimplified imperial theology is seen in the dualistic juxtaposition of the impossibly coherent "imperial cult" with supposedly anti-imperial voices within early Christianity.[3] Again, Galinsky has helped us by pointing out this problem, and in the interest of more specific and more helpfully focused research in the future, we might do well to abandon the

---

1. Karl Galinsky, "The Cult of the Roman Emperor: Uniter or Divider?" paper presented at the Annual Meeting of the SBL, Boston, 2008 (ch. 1 in this volume), 3, citing Mary Beard, John North, and Simon Price, *Religions of Rome*. Vol. 1: *A History* (Cambridge: Cambridge University Press, 1998), 348.
2. Daniel N. Schowalter, *The Emperor and the Gods: Images from the Time of Trajan* (HDR 28; Minneapolis: Fortress, 1993) 20.
3. John Dominic Crossan and Jonathan L. Reed foreground this explicit purpose in *In Search of Paul: How Jesus's Apostle Opposed Rome's Empire with God's Kingdom* (San Francisco: HarperSanFrancisco, 2004).

use of the phrase "imperial cult" altogether. I will return to this question at the end of the paper.[4]

In today's presentation, I would like to consider some of the evidence for honors offered to the emperor Trajan in the city of Pergamum, during the early second century C.E. This is a place and a time period on which I have focused research before,[5] and it highlights an important point for both the Roman Empire and the nascent communities of believers in Jesus. These developments come together in very interesting ways in the famous letter of Pliny to Trajan discussing problems with Christians in Pontus and Bithynia, and in the emperor's response to that letter.[6] This correspondence provides a glimpse of what it meant to be an elite administrator in provincial Roman society during the early second century, what it meant to exist as part of a distinct minority group within that society, and how honors offered to the emperor (along with honors to the traditional gods) were a natural part of that existence. Pliny's procedure of compelling suspected Christians to invoke a formula to the gods and offer incense and wine before Trajan's image underlines the fact that honors to the emperor were both related to and different from traditional worship of the gods. In this case, Pliny's pairing of these practices as a test of loyalty indicates an amazing confluence of political, social, and religious meaning.

Pergamum, of course, is not far from Bithynia, and in fact, Pliny traveled through Pergamum on the way to his provincial assignment.[7] In order to highlight what Galinsky calls "the vast panorama of variegated local practices that comprise the umbrella phenomenon that we call 'the imperial cult,'" I will examine architectural, epigraphical, numismatic, and literary evidence for how the Zeus Philios and Trajan temple (the Trajaneum) affected the social, religious, and political atmosphere of Pergamum and the whole province of Asia. In the process, we can also see how the practices for honoring the emperor in the early

---

4. Steven J. Friesen, "Normal Religion, or, Words Fail Us: A Response to Karl Galinsky's 'The Cult of the Roman Emperor: Uniter or Divider?,'" paper presented at the Annual Meeting of the SBL, Boston, 2008 (and ch. 2 in this volume), 24.

5. Schowalter, *The Emperor and the Gods*, and Daniel N. Schowalter, "The Zeus Philios and Trajan Temple: A Context for Imperial Honors," in *Pergamon: Citadel of the Gods: Archaeological Record, Literary Description, and Religious Development* (ed. Helmut Koester; Harrisburg, Pa.: Trinity Press International, 1998), 233–50.

6. Pliny the Younger, *Ep.* 10.96–97.

7. Pliny the Younger, *Ep.* 10.17a. Daniel N. Schowalter, "Honoring the Emperor: The Ephesians Respond to Trajan," in *100 Jahre österreichische Forschungen in Ephesos: Akten des Symposions, Wien 1995* (ed. Herwig Friesinger et al.; Denkschriften / Österreichische Akademie der Wissenschaften, Philosophisch-Historische Klasse 260.3; Archäologische Forschungen 1.3; Vienna: Verlag der Oesterreichischen Akademie der Wissenschaften, 1999), 121–26.

Fig. 1. Acropolis of Pergamum from the southwest. *All photos courtesy of Daniel N. Schowalter (author).*

second century were still connected to precedents that dated from over 130 years earlier.

In many ways, the Trajaneum is a perfect illustration of the way in which "rituals and power," to use Simon Price's terminology,[8] interacted as part of honors offered to the emperor. The actual temple was an incredibly impressive monument, sited in an unbelievably favorable location. The *anastylosis* done by Klaus Nohlen and the German Archaeological Institute provides modern visitors with a sense of how the building would have dominated the acropolis at Pergamum and served as both a landmark and potentially a source of pride for the community and the province of Asia.[9]

The tall Corinthian podium temple is located on a prominent platform constructed on the west side of the acropolis. The platform itself is a major accomplishment of engineering, with high vaulted chambers serving to extend

---

8. S. R. F. Price, *Rituals and Power: The Roman Imperial Cult in Asia Minor* (Cambridge: Cambridge University Press, 1984).

9. Klaus Nohlen, "Die Wiederaufrichtung des Traian-Heiligtums in Pergamon," *Mannheimer Forum* 82/83 (1983): 163–230; idem, "Planung und Planänderung am Bau zum Gewinnen räumlicher Vorstellung in Bauverlauf des Traianeum in Pergamon," in *Bauplanung und Bautheorie der Antike* (Diskussion zur archäologischen Bauforschung 4; Berlin: Deutsches Archäologisches Institut, 1983), 238–49; idem, "Restaurierungen am Traianeum in Pergamon," *Architectura* 15 (1985): 140–68; idem, "La conception d'un projet et son evolution: L'exemple du Trajaneum de Pergame," in *Le dessin d'architecture dans les sociétés antiques: Actes du colloque de Strasbourg, 26–28 janvier 1984* (Travaux du Centre de recherche sur le Proche-Orient et la Grèce antique 8; Leiden: Brill, 1985), 269–76; Klaus Nohlen, "Ästhetik der Ruine: Zur Präsentation antiker Baukomplexe am Beispiel des Traian-Heiligtums zu Pergamon," *Antike Welt* 28 (1997): 185–99; Wolfgang Radt, *Pergamon: Geschichte und Bauten, Funde und Erforschung einer antiken Metropole* (DuMont Dokumente; Cologne: DuMont, 1988).

Fig. 2. Vaulted chambers supporting the Trajaneum platform.

the hillside and provide a suitable *temenos* for the imperial temple among the Classical and Hellenistic monuments of the acropolis.

The temple was eventually surrounded by a colonnade, probably during the reign of Hadrian, giving the entire complex a look of appropriate grandeur. Even before the addition of the colonnade, however, the temple standing out from the hillside would have made a clear statement about imperial power and control.

This architectural statement of tribute and loyalty was made possible by the political intervention and probably the financial contributions of one of the richest residents of Pergamum, Aulus Iulius Quadratus.

"After his proconsulship in AD 109–110, he persuaded the emperor to agree to the proposal of the *Koinon of Asia* to grant Pergamum a second *neocorate* temple."[10] The persuasiveness of Quadratus meant that Pergamum was the first city in the Greek east to house two provincial imperial temples. The work of Steve Friesen and the more recent study by Barbara Burrell on the details of the *neoco-*

---

10. Bernhardt Weisser, "Pergamum as Paradigm," in *Coinage and Identity in the Roman Provinces* (ed. Christopher Howgego, Volker Heuchert, and Andrew Burnett; Oxford: Oxford University Press, 2008), 140.

Fig. 3. *Anastylosis* of the Trajaneum by the German Archaeological Institute.

rate status is very instructive here.[11] While Ephesus and other cities would soon follow suit, for a short time this must have given the Pergamenes bragging rights over their neighboring cities. Dietrich Klose describes the competition between the cities of Asia for "pompous honorary titles and the rank of 'first city'" as "a matter for vehement quarrel."[12] In this context of regional competition, the epithet of Zeus as Philios on the temple is especially poignant. Further reflection on this title (and on Quadratus) is enhanced by an inscription from Pergamum.

This inscription informs us that in addition to his role in obtaining the second *neocorate*, Quadratus also endowed a festival to be celebrated in honor of the new temple and its occupants. *IvP* II 269 includes a Greek address to the Pergamenes (probably the boule and the demos), the Latin text of a *senatus consultum* regarding the establishment of the games, and a Greek letter from Trajan

---

11. Steven J. Friesen, *Twice Neokoros: Ephesus, Asia, and the Cult of the Flavian Imperial Family* (Leiden: Brill, 1993). Barbara Burrell, *Neokoroi: Greek Cities and Roman Emperors* (Cincinnati Classical Studies [New Series] 9; Leiden: Brill, 2004).

12. Dietrich O. A. Klose, "Festivals and Games in the Cities of the East During the Roman Empire," in *Coinage and Identity in the Roman Provinces* (ed. Christopher Howgego, Volker Heuchert, and Andrew Burnett; Oxford: Oxford University Press, 2005), 126.

Fig. 4. Reconstructed entablature of the Trajaneum.

endorsing this action. In the *senatus consultum*, Quadratus is twice referred to as *vir clarrisimus* including once as *amicus vir clarrisimus*. Commentators have suggested that the most excellent friendship between Quadratus and Rome, and especially his close relationship with the emperor, is cast into high relief by the dedication of the temple to Zeus as Philios. For instance, Weisser reports that

> Anthony Birley expressed the idea that Zeus's epithet *Philios* (*Jupiter Amicalis*) was chosen to symbolize the close relationship between Trajan and his *amicus clarissimus*, Aulus Iulius Quadratus. Some contemporary observers might also have noted this association. We have to ask whether Pergamum's second *neocorate* temple should not be interpreted also as a personal architectural monument to the friendship between the city's most distinguished citizen and Trajan.[13]

Barbara Burrell offers an alternative understanding of the title for Zeus, pointing out that "in the Hellenistic period, Zeus Philios had joined the personifications of Concord and Rome in presiding over loyalty oaths among Asian cities and

---

13. Weisser, "Pergamum as Paradigm," 140.

between them and Rome."[14] In a way then, the association with Zeus Philios can be seen as a Pergamene statement of unity within the province of Asia, of course with Pergamum as the leading member.

In Burrell's view, the institution of this temple becomes a way in which the city, the province, and the empire are bound together in a relationship that goes beyond simple military and political domination. While not everyone in Pergamum would have counted Rome as a friend, the dedication of this temple reflects an attempt to portray the relationship in terms of mutuality. The question remains, of course, how this portrayal would have been perceived by the vast majority of the population of the city who were not part of this immediate circle of friends.

Certainly, this was primarily a friendly relationship between superelites like Quadratus, and most likely was a neutral factor in the lives of most people. On the other hand, one cannot discount the impact on the economy and society of building and maintaining the temple, as well as conducting the games and festivals associated with it. It is, of course, speculation to posit the reactions of any individual or group of people in an ancient city, but for even the poorest resident of Pergamum, the presence of the temple meant a regular calendar of events that often included festive distributions of food, and maybe even a break from daily toil.[15] For those on the bottom of the socioeconomic scale the oppressive nature of Roman rule was probably not that different from the oppressive and often unstable nature of local authorities. If the Roman emperor could settle political squabbles and ensure the city's grain supply, then perhaps he was worthy of honor.

Although fragmentary, the senatorial decree provides more information on the status of the Zeus Philios and Trajan games, declaring that they will be "triumphal games" (*eiselastikon*). This designation meant that winners were entitled

---

14. Burrell, *Neokoroi*, 23, citing Joyce Marie Reynolds and Kenan T. Erim, *Aphrodisias and Rome: Documents from the Excavation of the Theatre at Aphrodisias Conducted by Professor Kenan T. Erim, Together with Some Related Texts* (JRSM 1; London: Society for the Promotion of Roman Studies, 1982).

15. A recent stay in Archaia Corinth coincided with the annual Paniyiri Festival. Even in its modern, Christianized form, this occasion provided a glimpse of how an ancient festival could transform village life. Abundant food and drink, along with "exotic" merchants and merchandise filled the streets. Music rang out and processions wound through the city, while ongoing ritual took place at the churches. Of course, in antiquity the food and ritual would have been more directly connected, but otherwise the only thing missing was the athletic activities. Although any modern comparison comes with difficulties, the Paniyiri festival in Corinth gives one a distinct impression of how different life could be during a celebration. Of course this change meant more work for some people, but for a substantial portion of the population, it must have been a positive experience.

to receive special prizes, and also to have the right to a triumphal procession when they return to their hometown. This *eiselastikon* status is mentioned twice in the *senatus consultum* (once reconstructed), underlining the importance of this specific detail. Once again the competition between cities is instructive here. Klose remarks that "the more a festival surpassed those of other cities, the better it was for the economy of the city."[16] If a city wanted to attract the top athletes and thereby the greatest reputation for its games, it would be important to offer the top prizes. The opportunity to win special honors in the games associated with a provincial temple for the emperor would have offered plenty of incentive to participate and win.

The *senatus consultum* also stipulated that the contests in association with the new temple should be held on an equal basis with those connected to the temple of Roma and Augustus in Pergamum. This reference raises several interesting points about the realities of honors offered to the emperors. The first thing to note is the clear indication that almost 140 years after the Roma and Augustus temple in Pergamum was constructed, and one hundred years after the death of Augustus, celebrations in his honor were still a part of the religious calendar of the city, to the extent that they could be used as a reference point for the new celebrations. Given the amazing impact of Augustus on the development of the empire, and the desire of later emperors to promote their own reign in the image of Augustus, it is not surprising to see the longevity of the celebration. On the other hand, it is striking that the celebrations for the new temple honoring Zeus and the current emperor are expected to follow the standards set by the long-standing event. The inscribed *senatus consultum* is a clear indication that officials in Rome were cognizant of the significance of celebrations associated with *neocorate* temples, and took steps to establish and control them.

This connection between the Roma and Augustus temple and the Zeus Philios and Trajan temple takes on additional significance in light of Dio Cassius's later report on the circumstances around the original construction of the former building. According to Dio, Caesar (soon to be Augustus)

> gave permission that there be established sacred areas to Rome and his father Caesar, whom he named the hero Julius, in Ephesos and in Nikaia; for these were at that time the preeminent cities in Asia and Bithynia respectively. He commanded that the Romans resident there honor those divinities, but he permitted the foreigners, whom he called Hellenes, to consecrate precincts to himself, the Asians' in Pergamum and the Bithynians' in Nikomedia. (Dio Cassius 51.20.6–9)

---

16. Klose, "Festivals, and Games" 126–27.

Of course, Dio is writing from a much later perspective, but Burrell suggests that the language of the passage "seems to be quoting from an actual document or at least using the same terminology as such a document, at certain specific points."[17] She concludes that "it is likely that Dio was taking his account directly from a Latin source," and that parts "of the account may represent Augustus's response to the embassies of Asia and Bithynia closely."[18]

If the passage does preserve the policy if not the words of Augustus, this Dio quote is an important source for early understandings of honors offered to the emperors. If it is not, then it provides an interesting perspective on the topic from a late second-century viewpoint. In either case, the Hellenes of Pergamum are portrayed as receiving permission to honor Augustus with a sacred precinct, and by implication are perceived to have requested it. As Nicholas Purcell points out, Dio's description highlights the "second city" status of Pergamum (at that time) and also conforms to cultural stereotypes concerning easterners who would be willing to offer divine honors to the living ruler.[19] The irony is that by Dio's time, Pergamum, Ephesus, and a number of other cities had dedicated multiple temples to the living emperor usually with a divine counterpart, without much regard for who should or should not participate in the rituals therein. Meanwhile, worship of Julius Caesar had naturally taken a back seat to honors offered to Augustus, and Roma had become the standard counterpart of Augustus rather than Caesar.[20] Since Dio must have known that this was the way things developed, it seems unlikely that he would have included counterfactual material if he didn't have some sense that it was authentic.

The parallels between the Zeus Philios temple and the earlier one dedicated to Roma and Augustus do not end with the inscription and games. In fact, numismatic evidence from the reign of Trajan elaborates on the comparison. In addition to issuing coins that featured the laureate head of the long dead Augustus, one coin type from late in the reign features the new temple of Zeus Philios and Trajan on the obverse, and the first *neocorate* temple of Roma and Augustus on the reverse.[21] This issue allows the Pergamenes to highlight their position as first and twice *neocorate*, although this terminology does not appear on the coins until after the reign of Trajan.[22]

---

17. Burrell, *Neokoroi*, 17.
18. Ibid., 18.
19. Nicholas Purcell, "Romans in the Roman World," in *The Cambridge Companion to the Age of Augustus* (ed. Karl Galinsky; Cambridge: Cambridge University Press, 2005), 102.
20. Suetonius, *Aug.* 52. Burrell, *Neokoroi*, 18–19.
21. Ibid., 24–25 (Coin Type 13)
22. Ibid., 37.

According to Weisser, this juxtaposition of the two temples also allows the die cutter to draw attention to "a key difference between Pergamum's first *neocorate* temple and the *Trajaneum:* the latter stood on a podium, which was a feature of a Roman-style temple, and was surmounted by a figure of Victoria Romana, the symbol of Roman power."[23] The more Greek appearance of the Roma and Augustus temple on some of the coinage may reflect both the "ancient" nature of the building, then nearly 140 years old, as well as the location of the building in the Greek East. This perceived contrast between Greek and Roman architectural style also provides an interesting connection back to Dio's assertion that honors to Augustus were first intended specifically for the Hellenes in the community. Since the Roma and Augustus temple in Pergamum has never been located, it is impossible to determine the degree to which the image on the coin reflects the actual design.

This broad collection of evidence revolving around a single imperial temple in one city reveals the complexity of the various honors offered to the Roman emperor. The complexity is only increased when we realize that the evidence here is mostly official and monumental. Discussion of the various celebratory activities surrounding the festivals gives only a taste of how real people would have participated and made the honors an even more complicated process.

As I complete this paper, I am participating in an academic conference on Galilee in the Roman period at Tel Hai College in upper Galilee. During a discussion of imperial cult buildings at this meeting, the problem with using the phrase "imperial cult" was once again made abundantly clear. Even people who understood that there was a diversity of ritual, social, and political experience that made up the various honors offered to Roman emperors could not help but to lump together a huge variety of approaches under the same, vague terminology. It was interesting to hear some participants argue that Roman Judea would not allow for any manifestation of the imperial cult, only to be reminded that each day in the Jerusalem temple, sacrifice was supposedly offered on behalf of the health and well-being of the emperor. As Steve Friesen noted, this is not imperial cult as it is usually construed, but it does represent an attempt by Judeans to negotiate their power relationship with the emperor in light of their own local traditions. They may not have been willing to offer sacrifice to the emperor, but at least they were willing to do so on his behalf. This certainly qualifies as honoring the emperor, with special consideration, in one's own context.

The material from the *neocorate* temples of Pergamum offers us the opportunity to glimpse how another community attempted to negotiate this complicated but essential relationship.

---

23. Weisser, "Pergamum as Paradigm," 140.

Bibliography

Beard, Mary, John North, and Simon Price. *Religions of Rome*. Vol. 1: *A History*. Cambridge: Cambridge University Press, 1998.
Burrell, Barbara. *Neokoroi: Greek Cities and Roman Emperors*. Cincinnati Classical Studies (New Series) 9. Leiden: Brill, 2004.
Crossan, John Dominic, and Jonathan L. Reed. *In Search of Paul: How Jesus's Apostle Opposed Rome's Empire with God's Kingdom*. San Francisco: HarperSanFrancisco, 2004.
Friesen, Steven J. "Normal Religion, or, Words Fail Us: A Response to Karl Galinsky's 'The Cult of the Roman Emperor: Uniter or Divider?'" Paper presented at the Annual Meeting of the SBL, Boston, 2008, and ch. 2 in this volume.
———. *Twice Neokoros: Ephesus, Asia, and the Cult of the Flavian Imperial Family*. Leiden: Brill, 1993.
Galinsky, Karl. "The Cult of the Roman Emperor: Uniter or Divider?" Paper presented at the Annual Meeting of the SBL, Boston, 2008, and ch. 1 in this volume.
Klose, Dietrich O. A. "Festivals and Games in the Cities of the East During the Roman Empire." Pages 124–33 in *Coinage and Identity in the Roman Provinces*. Edited by Christopher Howgego, Volker Heuchert, and Andrew Burnett. Oxford: Oxford University Press, 2005.
Nohlen, Klaus. "Ästhetik der Ruine: Zur Präsentation antiker Baukomplexe am Beispiel des Traian-Heiligtums zu Pergamon." *Antike Welt* 28 (1997): 185–99.
———. "La conception d'un projet et son evolution: L'exemple du Trajaneum de Pergame." Pages 269–76 in *Le dessin d'architecture dans les sociétés antiques: Actes du colloque de Strasbourg, 26–28 janvier 1984*. Travaux Du Centre de recherche sur le Proche-Orient et la Grèce antique 8. Leiden: Brill, 1985.
———. "Planung und Planänderung am Bau zum Gewinnen räumlicher Vorstellung in Bauverlauf des Traianeum in Pergamon." Pages 238–49 in *Bauplanung und Bautheorie der Antike*. Diskussion zur archäologischen Bauforschung 4. Berlin: Deutsches Archäologisches Institut, 1983.
———. "Restaurierungen am Traianeum in Pergamon." *Architectura* 15 (1985): 140–68.
———. "Die Wiederaufrichtung des Traian-Heiligtums in Pergamon." *Mannheimer Forum* 82/83 (1983): 163–230.
Price, S. R. F. *Rituals and Power: The Roman Imperial Cult in Asia Minor*. Cambridge: Cambridge University Press, 1984.
Purcell, Nicholas. "Romans in the Roman World." Pages 85–105 in *The Cambridge Companion to the Age of Augustus*. Edited by Karl Galinsky. Cambridge: Cambridge University Press, 2005.
Radt, Wolfgang. *Pergamon: Geschichte und Bauten, Funde und Erforschung einer antiken Metropole*. DuMont Dokumente. Cologne: DuMont, 1988.
Reynolds, Joyce Marie, and Kenan T. Erim. *Aphrodisias and Rome: Documents from the Excavation of the Theatre at Aphrodisias Conducted by Professor Kenan T. Erim, Together with Some Related Texts*. Journal of Roman Studies Monographs 1. London: Society for the Promotion of Roman Studies, 1982.
Schowalter, Daniel N. *The Emperor and the Gods: Images from the Time of Trajan*. Harvard Dissertations in Religion 28. Minneapolis: Fortress, 1993.

———. "Honoring the Emperor: The Ephesians Respond to Trajan." Pages 121–26 in *100 Jahre österreichische Forschungen in Ephesos: Akten des Symposions, Wien 1995*. Edited by Herwig et al. Friesinger. Denkschriften / Österreichische Akademie der Wissenschaften, Philosophisch-Historische Klasse 260.3; Archäologische Forschungen 1.3. Vienna: Verlag der Oesterreichischen Akademie der Wissenschaften, 1999.

———. "The Zeus Philios and Trajan Temple: A Context for Imperial Honors." Pages 233–50 in *Pergamon: Citadel of the Gods: Archaeological Record, Literary Description, and Religious Development*. Edited by Helmut Koester. Harrisburg, Pa.: Trinity Press International, 1998.

Weisser, Bernhardt. "Pergamum as Paradigm." Pages 134–42 in *Coinage and Identity in the Roman Provinces*. Edited by Christopher Howgego, Volker Heuchert, and Andrew Burnett. Oxford: Oxford University Press, 2008.

CHAPTER 9
SEARCHING FOR ROME AND THE IMPERIAL CULT IN
GALILEE: REASSESSING GALILEE–ROME RELATIONS
(63 B.C.E. TO 70 C.E.)

James S. McLaren

Karl Galinsky notes the enthusiasm with which the imperial cult has been welcomed in recent New Testament scholarship as though it is a newly found context in which to explain and understand the emerging movement. In response Galinsky clearly highlights the need for caution and nuance when discussing the possible role of *the* imperial cult in the Roman Empire and, therefore, for the followers of Jesus as they staked their place within the empire.[1] It is not a simple case of being able to depict the imperial cult as representing all things evil and bad, in which a central authority tried to impose its will on its subjects, with the early Christians leading an ideological war of resistance and opposition in which its champion, Jesus, was the real deity. Galinsky explains that the imperial cult was one part of a larger process of constructing the reality of the Roman Empire in the east. The cult was shaped and formed by the local population; it constituted one of the mechanisms by which the empire was negotiated in a given location.[2]

The need to recognize the local dimension of giving practical expression to the imperial cult has two important implications. One is generic in nature to any discussion of the imperial cult, the other specific to the circumstances of early

---

1. Karl Galinsky, "The Cult of the Roman Emperor: Uniter or Divider?" paper presented at the Annual Meeting of the SBL, Boston, 2008, and ch. 1 in this volume. For recent examples of New Testament scholarship see John Dominic Crossan, *God and Empire: Jesus Against Rome, Then and Now* (San Francisco: HarperSanFrancisco, 2007) and Richard A. Horsley, ed., *Paul and Empire: Religion and Power in Roman Imperial Society* (Harrisburg, Pa.: Trinity Press International, 1997).

2. As noted by Galinsky, the work of S. R. F. Price, *Rituals and Power: The Roman Imperial Cult in Asia Minor* (Cambridge: Cambridge University Press, 1984), remains a key text for our understanding of the cult in the eastern part of the Roman Empire.

Christianity. The generic issue is how we are to decide whether certain information pertains to the imperial cult, especially on the basis that what constitutes the "cult" is negotiated in any given location. Galinsky rightly observes that any discussion of the imperial cult needs to recognize that it was not simply a stand-alone entity. As well as being integrated with other cults, it was embedded within the larger cultural and social network of Roman rule in a given location. It means we are compelled always to ask if it is possible, let alone appropriate, to distinguish between evidence of a Roman presence and specific evidence of the imperial cult in practice. The other implication relates to the nature of early Christianity. On the basis that the origins of the movement are to be found within the Jewish way of life, specifically as lived within the Jewish homeland, it means that any discussion of interaction between the early Christians and the imperial cult should be also situated within the context of existing Jewish-Roman interaction regarding the cult. The following discussion will address these two issues in combination.

I have previously argued that Herod the Great was very successful at performing the necessary negotiation to integrate the imperial cult. He instituted a means of ensuring that the visual public claims of Rome and Jerusalem could be accommodated in the Jewish homeland. The ground rules were straightforward; the imperial cult was assigned its own space at strategic locations in his kingdom while the Jewish cult avoided any risk of being integrated and merged by the decision to offer daily sacrifices at the Jerusalem temple to the God of the Jews for the well-being of Rome and the emperor.[3] In general, this two-pronged approach of providing separate but parallel sacred space proved to be a satisfactory solution for all parties. Jews continued to frequent the Jerusalem temple in large numbers in order to participate in the annual pilgrimage festivals. Even when the temple became part of the territory brought under direct Roman rule in 6 C.E., there was no attempt to alter Herod's negotiated settlement.

The success of what Herod instituted did not mean the imperial cult became a nonissue in Jewish-Roman relations. On at least four occasions testing allegiance to Rome through the imperial cult was used as a tactic in a larger dispute as a way of undermining the status of the Jews. In Alexandria, Jamnia, and Dora statues of the emperor were placed inside synagogues. Although isolated incidents, they all show a willingness of the local residents who were in dispute with the Jews to use the imperial cult as a way of pursuing their interests regarding civic rights status.[4] Gaius was also aware of the potential for using the imperial cult to achieve his own designs when he ordered that a statue of him be placed in

---

3. See James S. McLaren, "Jews and the Imperial Cult: From Augustus to Domitian," *JSNT* 27 (2005): 257–78.
4. Ibid., 262–66, 269–71.

Jerusalem. He was correct in anticipating there would be protests and resistance. Although it appears Gaius was not fixated on altering the negotiated settlement established by Herod, his action did show how fragile the settlement was and how easily it could be dismantled.

All of these interactions pertain to tangible, explicit expressions of the imperial cult. They relate to visual representations of the cult in the form of statues and existing physical structures recognized as locations for the worship of the sacred. A different approach has recently been argued by Monika Bernett. The notion of the imperial cult being integral to the presence of Rome in general underpins her assessment of the role of the imperial cult in Roman-Jewish relations leading up to the war of 66–70 C.E.[5] Bernett proposes that the imperial cult was a major factor for the Galileans in how they responded to Roman rule, not so much through the cult as an explicit, separate entity, but as part of the general increasing cultural and economic Roman presence in the region.[6] According to Bernett, Galilean involvement in the war can be explained primarily as a reaction to the imperial cult having encroached upon the daily way of life of the locals. Crucial to this line of argument is the notion that there was a Roman presence in Galilee that expanded over time, implicitly and explicitly, and that both the locals and the conveyers of this presence understood it in terms of the imperial cult being at work. As such, Bernett views the imperial cult as a phenomenon that was far more expansive than the construction of temples or the erection of statues. It was manifested in coinage, especially issues that depict the imperial family, the founding and naming of cities in honor of the imperial family, and aspects of civic life like the construction of public buildings and the holding of various public events, such as games. It is a view that represents a maximalist approach to how we categorize evidence for the imperial cult.

The following discussion reexamines the early history of Roman-Galilean relations, with a particular concern to assess the extent of an actual Roman presence in the region, and whether the imperial cult was a factor in those relations.

---

5. Monika Bernett, "Roman Imperial Cult in the Galilee: Structures, Functions, and Dynamics Affiliation," in *Religion, Ethnicity, and Identity in Ancient Galilee: A Region in Transition* (ed. Jürgen Zangenberg, Harold W. Attridge, and Dale B. Martin; WUNT; Tübingen: Mohr Siebeck, 2007), 337–56.

6. In particular, Bernett cites activity associated with the cities of Sepphoris and Tiberias and the minting of coinage by Herod Antipas (ibid., 342–53). For a contrasting view, see the comprehensive analysis of the significance of Herod Antipas's coinage by Morten Hørning Jensen, "Message and Minting: The Coins of Herod Antipas in Their Second Temple Context as a Source for Understanding the Religio-Political and Socio-Economic Dynamics of Early First Century Galilee," in *Religion, Ethnicity, and Identity in Ancient Galilee: A Region in Transition* (ed. Jürgen Zangenberg, Harold W. Attridge, and Dale B. Martin; WUNT; Tübingen: Mohr Siebeck, 2007), 277–313.

It will be undertaken from the perspective that evidence for a Roman presence must be clearly established in the first instance. Once such evidence has been identified a compelling case must also be established to show that the Roman presence and influence was designed to be, or was recognized as being, an expression of the imperial cult negotiated in the local setting of Galilee. Contrary to Bernett's line of argument what follows will put forward the case for seeing a very limited extent of Roman presence and influence in Galilee. In turn, the imperial cult was of minimal concern to the people of Galilee and when many of them decided to join the war of independence in 66 C.E. it was due to a shared affiliation with the Jerusalem temple not to any concern about the encroachment of the imperial cult on life in Galilee.

At the outset there are two important observations about the way Galilee is depicted that need to be stated. They echo Galinsky's call for "caution and nuance" regarding discussion of the role of the imperial cult in terms of avoiding unwarranted assumptions. One is a major shift in the reading of some of the literary material associated with life in Galilee. No longer is it deemed standard to view Galilee as the nurturing ground of radical military opposition to Roman rule. The best-known recent advocate of this approach was Martin Hengel, whose zealot theory proposed the existence of a single unified party dedicated to armed resistance against Roman lordship. Inspired largely by information from Josephus, Hengel argued that the origins of this ideologically driven movement lay in Galilee.[7] Two passages in Josephus have been important to this approach, the reference to the followers of John of Gischala as surpassing all other rebels in their "mischievous ingenuity and audacity" (*B.J.* 4.558), and his description of Galilee: "with this limited area, and although surrounded by such powerful foreign nations, the two Galilees have always resisted any hostile invasion, for the inhabitants are from infancy inured to war, and have at all times been numerous; never did men lack courage nor country-men." (*B.J.* 3.41-42, Thackeray)[8]

With good reason the problems associated with the "zealot theory" have been exposed. Through a close reading of the relevant data, the work of people like Morton Smith and Richard Horsley has drawn attention to the complications of trying to find continuity and uniformity between different people and

---

7. Martin Hengel, *Die Zeloten: Untersuchungen zur Jüdischen Freiheitsbewegung in der Zeit von Herodes I. bis 70 n. Chr.* (AGJU 1; Leiden: Brill, 1961), 56–59. For other examples of depicting Galilee as the home of militant opposition to Rome see Solomon Zeitlin, "Who Were the Galileans? New Light on Josephus' Activities in Galilee," *JQR* 64 (1974): 189–203, and Geza Vermes, *Jesus the Jew: A Historian's Reading of the Gospels* (1973; repr., Philadelphia: Fortress, 1981).

8. The identification of the founder of the Fourth Philosophy as a Galilean (Josephus, *B.J.* 2.118) has been a further important plank in the line of argument.

groups where it simply did not exist.⁹ There has also been a major shift away from viewing Galilee as a particularly bellicose region. Josephus's comments about the inhabitants of Galilee are recognized as being laden with personal interest. Nuance is necessary when trying to establish the viability of drawing any conclusions from the way Galileans are depicted in all three of Josephus's narratives about the historical situation.¹⁰

The second observation is that one significant element of Josephus's account about Galilee has remained intact in scholarship. It is the existence of the Fourth Philosophy with Judas the Galilean as the founder. This aspect of Josephus's account is still widely cited, with the underlying assumption that ideological opposition to Roman rule had its origins in Galilee with this group.¹¹ The confidence with which Josephus's link between ideological opposition to Rome and the Fourth Philosophy continues to be accepted is puzzling, given the detailed critical scrutiny applied to other parts of his narrative. This is not the place to dwell on the matter. It has been argued elsewhere at length as to why we should view the Fourth Philosophy as a convenient construct by Josephus to deflect attention away from what was happening in 66 C.E., when the ideology was given practical expression.¹² By restricting his comments about ideologically motivated armed resistance against Rome to a supposedly distinct new group that had its origins in 6 C.E. in Galilee, Josephus successfully provided a scapegoat that was chronologically and geographically removed from Jerusalem. Instead, the principle of "serving God alone" (*B.J.* 2.118) should be acknowledged as a well-known, long-standing ideology.¹³ What happened in 66 C.E. was a radical articulation of that ideology. The crucial point is that we stop working within the reconstruction Josephus has created. Therefore, like the "zealot theory," the depiction of a Fourth Philosophy founded in 6 C.E. that introduced and then cornered the market in

---

9. Morton Smith, "Zealots and Sicarii, Their Origins and Relation," *HTR* 64 (1971): 1–19; Richard A. Horsley, "The Zealots: Their Origins, Relationships and Importance in the Jewish Revolt," *NovT* 28 (1986): 159–92.

10. Sean Freyne, "The Galileans in the Light of Josephus's *Life*," in *Galilee and Gospel: Collected Essays* (WUNT; Tübingen: Mohr Siebeck, 2000), 27–44.

11. The use of the word ideology is deliberate; it ensures the focus is on a way of thinking about the world and how it should operate.

12. James S. McLaren, "Constructing Judaean History in the Diaspora: Josephus's Accounts of Judas," in *Negotiating Diaspora: Jewish Strategies in the Roman Empire* (ed. John M. G. Barclay; LSTS; London: T&T Clark International, 2004), 90–108. For another approach critiquing Josephus's story of Judas see Israel Ben-Shalom, *The School of Shammai and the Zealots' Struggle Against Rome* (Jerusalem: Yad Ben-Zvi, 1993), 151–71.

13. See David Goodblatt, *Elements of Ancient Jewish Nationalism* (Cambridge: Cambridge University Press, 2006), 71–107.

proclaiming ideological opposition to Roman rule, should cease to hold our attention.

The net effect of discarding these two narrative frameworks, one constructed by scholars contending a particular reading of Josephus, and the other constructed by Josephus, is that we have a blank space regarding the type of narrative in which to place the dynamic of Galilee-Roman relations. Essentially, it is a case of going back to the drawing board, no longer required to see Galilee as the home of militant and ideological opposition to Rome. The only restriction is the need to ensure that due attention is given to the information available via archaeological material and the literary sources. In this space, free of previous narrative frameworks, how are we to explain the involvement of Galileans in the war of 66–70 C.E., and how does that involvement relate to our understanding of the relations between the people of Galilee and Rome, if at all? Is it one in which a new factor, such as the encroachment of the imperial cult that Bernett proposes, lies behind the decision to fight? The discussion of these questions will be undertaken in three sequential stages. First, we need to review the actions of the Galilean people at the beginning of the war, restating the case for Galilean participation in the conflict. Second, we need to review the history of interaction between the Romans and the Galileans. In the third and final section, an explanation for much of the Galilean involvement in the war and, more generally, for how we should understand Galilean interaction with Roman rule will be provided.

Galilean Involvement in the War of 66–70 C.E.

It is evident there was significant support for the war in Galilee. When Vespasian commenced his campaign from Syria to reinstate Roman control of the province, he was not able to simply march directly on Jerusalem. No doubt he was motivated by a desire to take a more cautious approach than the one tried by Cestius the previous year, in order not to suffer the same fate. Equally important for Vespasian in deciding how he to proceed, however, was the fact that he encountered resistance along the way. Strategically, he could not afford to approach Jerusalem without first securing his supply line and, if necessary, his line of retreat.

According to Josephus, the Romans met armed resistance at a number of locations in Galilee; for example, Gabara (*B.J.* 3.132–134), Japha (*B.J.* 3.289–306), Gischala (*B.J.* 4.84–120), Mount Tabor (*B.J.* 4.54–61), Jotapata (*B.J.* 3.110–114, 141–288, 316–339), Tarichaeae (*B.J.* 3.462–502), and Gamla (*B.J.* 4.11–53, 62–83).[14] Furthermore, from the perspective of those who claimed to oversee

---

14. The inclusion of Gamla as part of the discussion on Galilee requires brief comment. Strictly speaking the town was part of another region bordering Galilee, Gaulanitis (Josephus, *B.J.* 3.37). However, Josephus is very clear that Gamla should be included in discussion of Gali-

organizing the resistance against the Romans, Galilee was definitively deemed to be part of the war zone, with Josephus appointed as general of the region.[15] Of course, alongside these examples of armed resistance should be listed locations that decided not to fight, such as Sepphoris, locations that were ambivalent about how to behave, such as Tiberias, and those people who remained loyal to Agrippa II and fought with the Romans against the rebel forces. Even at some of the places where the Romans encountered resistance, it was not a case of everyone approving that course of action.[16] In other words, from what Josephus has described, there was a mixed response to the war by Galileans. We will discuss the significance of this diversity and its implications for understanding the relevance of the imperial cult in the final section. For the moment, our attention focuses on those who decided to oppose the Romans and the need to properly acknowledge the involvement of many Galileans in resisting Vespasian.

Three features of the Galilean involvement in the war warrant brief comment. The first feature is the ardent nature of some of the fighting that took place. The excavations at Jotapata and Gamla bear witness to the serious nature of the fighting in each of these locations. The concentration of various projectiles and the signs of destruction indicate that the Romans encountered resistance and that they were more than willing to suppress it with the use of force.[17] Although not necessarily indicative of the strength and size of the resistance encountered, Roman siege works show that coordinated, purposeful assaults were undertaken to capture the two locations. The second feature is the discovery of bronze revolt coins at Gamla. Danny Syon has established that the coin type is an imitation of the silver coins minted in Jerusalem from late 66 C.E. onwards. The six coins, all locally made from the one cast, were found in the western quarter of Gamla.[18] They are crudely designed, depicting a cup and using paleo-Hebrew and Aramaic script, with the legend "For the redemption of Jerusalem the H[oly]" extending

---

lean responses to Roman rule in 66 C.E. He states that Gamla was part of the territory allocated to him as general (*B.J.* 2.568) and when he describes the situation in Galilee at the start of the revolt in *Vita*, he includes Gamla, listing it alongside Sepphoris, Tiberias, and Gischala (*Vita* 30–61). See also *B.J.* 4.1.

15. Irrespective of the precise nature of the intentions of Josephus and the people who allocated him responsibility for Galilee, the crucial point is that the territory was automatically included as part of the region directly impacted by the decision to go to war (Josephus, *B.J.* 2.562–568).

16. For example, at Gischala (Josephus, *B.J.* 4.84–120) and Tarichaeae (*B.J.* 3.462–502).

17. Mordechai Aviam, "Yodefat/Jotapata: The Archaeology of the First Battle," in *The First Jewish Revolt: Archaeology, History, and Ideology* (ed. Andrea M. Berlin and J. Andrew Overman; London: Routledge, 2002), 121–33, and Danny Syon, "Gamla: City of Refuge," in ibid., 134–53.

18. Danny Syon, "The Coins from Gamla: An Interim Report," *INJ* 12 (1992/93): 34–55, and Syon, "Gamla," 146–49.

over the two sides of the coin. A number of important questions remain unanswered regarding these coins: when the coins were minted; why the coins were minted; and who was responsible for their production?[19] Irrespective of how these questions are to be answered, the presence of these locally made revolt coins at Gamla indicates enthusiasm for the war. Although crude in design and poor in quality, the coins clearly point to a choice being made to align with the war. The third feature is the decision of some Galileans to persist in their support of the war against Rome. Although very critical of them, Josephus describes how a number of Galileans chose to fight on even after Vespasian had subdued resistance in Galilee. John of Gischala and his followers fled to Jerusalem in order to continue the fight against the Romans, where they were active combatants during the siege (*B.J.* 4.121–127; 5.250–254). By implication, regardless of why these people originally took up arms, they believed that once the immediate vicinity of their homes had been reoccupied by the Romans it was still appropriate to carry on the fight in other locations. Although each of these features can be deemed to be isolated to specific locations, in combination they do indicate a high degree of passion and commitment to the war effort for at least some of those who chose to fight the Romans.

From the preceding comments it is clear that Galileans became actively involved in the war against the Romans. How are we to explain this resistance to Rome in Galilee, its spread among towns, villages, and the open countryside, and its persistence in the face of overwhelming odds? Compounding the whole issue is the fact that Josephus describes this war as having commenced in Jerusalem.[20] The people of Galilee could argue that it was not *our* war: the problem related to Jerusalem and the way the governor behaved in the city. It is also not simply a case of people from Jerusalem traveling to Galilee and occupying the territory as a buffer zone in their fight against the Romans, nor a case of conscripting the Galileans to support the war. People who lived in Galilee were proactive in pursuing the war cause and in seeking to organize their resistance against the Romans.[21]

---

19. The dependence on the Jerusalem coins also raises a number of interesting possibilities regarding the interaction between this town and Jerusalem: was it people from Jerusalem who brought coins north which the locals then adapted? Could such coins have being brought north via Josephus and his companions? Alternatively, did people from Gamla bring back from Jerusalem some of the early silver coinage to show their friends and colleagues?

20. Josephus is not entirely clear about when the war commenced. He mentions three events: the dispute at Caesarea Maritima (*B.J.* 2.284–292), the actions of Florus in Jerusalem (*B.J.* 2.293–308), and the cessation of sacrifices offered for the well-being of the emperor and Rome (*B.J.* 2.408–410). Although it is the latter incident that probably marks the beginning of the war, the crucial point here is to note that all the named incidents took place in Judea, not Galilee.

21. For example, some of the inhabitants of Tiberias dismantled the palace before Josephus was able to carry out his instruction (*Vita* 66–69) and John and his followers had prepared

Therefore, an explanation of these examples of open resistance and defiance is necessary.

Evidence of Roman Involvement in Galilee

An obvious starting point for seeking an explanation of the involvement in the war is to apply the principle of cause and effect and to look for a context in the interaction between Rome and Galilee prior to the war. Although much recent scholarship has drawn attention to the issues associated with quantifying the type and level of impact of one society on another, the possible intentions of the Romans and the Galileans, and what label(s) can be used to identify the character of those interactions, these issues will not be discussed here.[22] Instead, the task is one of description and compilation; a search for evidence of the presence of Rome in Galilee, the Roman footprint in the region, and, in particular, the imperial cult. Here we can draw inspiration for what needs to be undertaken from a line in the film *Life of Brian*. At a meeting of some Jews plotting to oppose the Romans, the character played by John Cleese asks: "what have the Romans ever done for us?"[23] For the task at hand we can rephrase the question as, "what have the Romans done *to* us Galileans?" While the question posed by John Cleese was expressed in the context of a number of supposedly positive Roman initiatives, posing the question here leaves us struggling to find much in the brief history of Roman-Galilean relations to explain the enthusiasm for the revolt.

The discussion of evidence for Roman presence in Galilee will be listed in three broad categories: administration, military, and cultural and economic. While such a division into separate categories is somewhat arbitrary and possibly even artificial, it does provide a means by which to probe the nature and extent of Roman involvement in a tangible manner.[24] It is also important to note that each category is a potential avenue for identifying the presence of the imperial

---

the defences at Gischala (*Vita* 45, 189; cf. *B.J.* 2.575). See also the claims of Josephus about other activity undertaken by Justus (*Vita* 341–342).

22. See Milton Moreland, "The Inhabitants of Galilee in the Hellenistic and Early Roman Periods: Probes Into the Archaeological and Literary Evidence," in *Religion, Ethnicity, and Identity in Ancient Galilee: A Region in Transition* (ed. Jürgen Zangenberg, Harold W. Attridge, and Dale B. Martin; WUNT; Tübingen: Mohr Siebeck, 2007), 133–59.

23. Terry Jones, *Life of Brian* (Python [Monty] Pictures Ltd, 1979).

24. For example, it is possible that Roman coinage and religious activity could be evidence of any one or more of the three categories. Another concern with such an approach is the need to avoid assuming that evidence of a Roman presence necessarily means it was a negative one or that it triggered an oppositional response from the Galileans. See the comments of Galinsky, "Cult of the Roman Emperor." The concern here is to ensure we have a clear outline of actual contact over the period under investigation.

cult in Galilee: the search needs to extend beyond trying to find evidence of ritual celebrations or locating physical shrines. The chronological starting point will be 63 B.C.E., the first year of direct Roman interaction with affairs in the Jewish homeland.

Administrative Presence

The key point to note here is the inconsistent nature of the Roman presence. There is no doubt that the people of Galilee could claim frustration by what appeared to be Roman indecision about the way they should be involved in the governing of the region. Although predominantly an indirect presence, through various types of local client rulers, there were occasional experiments with different structures.

A Roman impact on the administration of Galilee was part and parcel of Pompey's intervention in the dispute between Hyrcanus II and Aristobulus II. Even if the intervention was the result of an invitation, Pompey's choice to favor one brother over the other had a definite impact. For the next fifteen to twenty years supporters of the ousted side of the family found support or a sort of refuge, in parts of Galilee. In turn, this resulted in occasional military incursions. The first example of direct intervention in how to structure the administration of the region is undertaken by Gabinus, probably in 57 B.C.E. (Josephus, *B.J.* 1.169–170; *A.J.* 14.190–191). Unfortunately, the precise nature of Gabinus's experiment with the formation of the five *synedrai*, in which Sepphoris was named as the administrative center for Galilee, is not clear.[25] The next significant indication of a Roman presence was the shift to using members of the Herodian family to oversee the governing of the region. This decision impacted on the life of all subsequent generations of Galileans up to the beginning of the war. What varied was the manner in which the Herodian family was employed to administer the region by Rome: governor (Herod [*B.J.* 1.203; *A.J.* 14.158]), king (Herod [*B.J.* 1.282–283; *A.J.* 14.385]), tetrarch (Antipas [*B.J.* 1.668; *A.J.* 17.318]) and king (Agrippa I [*B.J.* 2.215; *A.J.* 18.252], and Agrippa II [*B.J.* 2.252; *A.J.* 20.159]). The Romans made one further change; it was also the most significant one: the introduction of direct Roman rule in 44 C.E. when Agrippa I died (Josephus, *A.J.* 19.360–363). In other words, the first time Roman law and direct Roman taxation became part of daily existence for the people living in Galilee took place approximately one hundred

---

25. Gabinus's primary objective appears to have been a desire to limit the authority of Hyrcanus II, hence the reduced role, oversight only of the temple (Josephus, *B.J.* 1.169–70). These changes appear to have been reversed by Caesar in 47 B.C.E., when he proclaimed Hycranus II as "ethnarch of the Jews" (*A.J.* 14.191). The actions of Gabinus indicate the extent to which he did not understand the importance of the temple within Jewish society.

years after the initial contact.[26] Nero was soon to alter the situation by his decision to cede a prominent portion of Galilee to Agrippa II as king.

It is clear Galileans did not greet these changes to the administration of the region with universal approval. In particular, the decision to favor Hyrcanus II (Josephus, *B.J.* 1.160; *A.J.* 14.82–83, 92–93) and then the appointment of Herod were greeted by opposition and open resistance (*B.J.* 1.208–209, 303, 314–316; 2.56; *A.J.* 14.163–176, 420–433; 15.271–272). However, it is important not to overstate the extent to which most of these administrative changes impacted on the lives of Galileans. These protests may have had as much to do with internal disputes about who should have power, as they had to do with any concern in principle about a change in structure. It was only from 44 C.E. onwards that a Roman administrative presence became a tangible reality throughout the region, and Josephus is alarmingly silent as to whether there was any backlash caused by this major change.

Military Presence

In many ways this category is possibly the most surprising for the notable lack of a presence, especially in the sense of any ongoing Roman involvement. Although Roman troops occasionally traversed Galilee, there are very few examples of Romans undertaking campaigns in Galilee. From what Josephus describes regarding Pompey's route he did not enter Galilee. The first definite instance of Roman troops being in Galilee was when Gabinus pursued and attacked supporters of Antigonus at Mount Tabor (*B.J.* 1.177). Cassius undertook a similar campaign; this time the focus was Aristobulus and his followers (*B.J.* 1.180; *A.J.* 14.120).[27] Later, in his campaigning, Herod fought in Galilee, possible with the aid of Roman troops, in 39 B.C.E. (*B.J.* 1.303–316; *A.J.* 14.413–433). These are all temporary and relatively minor incursions. The target of the military activity was directly affected, but there is no indication that what was undertaken amounted to a campaign in which the local population found itself under any lasting duress.

The next occasion Roman troops were active in Galilee is the most well known one: when Varus marched to the aid of the detachment he placed in Jerusalem to maintain order in the period immediately after Herod's death. As part

---

26. A form of tribute was introduced by Pompey but the details in relation to Galilee are not clear (*B.J.* 1.154; *A.J.* 14.74). See Fabian E. Udoh, *To Caesar What is Caesar's: Tribute, Taxes and Imperial Administration in Early Roman Palestine (63 B.C.E.–70 C.E.)* (BJS 343; Providence, R.I.: Brown Judaic Studies, 2005), 9–30.

27. Josephus mentions Tarichaeae being directly in the firing line, with the town laid waste and people sold into slavery. However, the operation is clearly targeted at the supporters of Aristobulus.

of the effort to restore order, Sepphoris was attacked. Josephus states that the city was burned and the inhabitants sold into slavery (Josephus, *B.J.* 2.68; *A.J.* 17.288–289). Exactly how extensive the destruction was is not clear, in part because evidence of widespread destruction has yet to be found in the excavations. Caution is also warranted from what Josephus describes; Varus did not attack the city with his whole army, but rather sent a small contingent under Gaius to deal with the situation, namely, that Judas and his followers had seized arms from the royal arsenal (Josephus, *B.J.* 2.56; *A.J.* 17.271-272). Irrespective of the extent of destruction, the claims that residents of the city were sold into slavery marks this incident as the first definite instance of Roman involvement that directly affected the local population. In turn, it raises the possibility that news of the action spread through the region and then became part of the remembered experience of what the Romans were willing to do.[28]

The potential psychological impact of ordering the suppression of trouble at Sepphoris is also pertinent to the two other known occasions where a Roman military presence is evident before the war began. Both are linked to the city of Ptolemais, which was located in the hinterland bordering the northwestern part of Galilee. The first occasion is linked with a major incident in 40/41 C.E., when Petronius ordered the troops accompanying him to camp at the city as he tried to negotiate with the Jews about Gaius's order for the erection of his statue in Jerusalem. Although this action was not part of an attempt to establish an explicit, permanent space for the imperial cult in Jerusalem, there is little doubt that it would have roused concerns that the imperial cult was being imposed upon the Jews for those aware of the incident. Although not positioned in Galilee proper, the close proximity of the troops would have been known, especially as the first protest about the order was made by Jews at Ptolemais and then Tiberias was used as the location for discussions between Petronius and the various Jewish delegates (Josephus, *B.J.* 2.192-199; *A.J.* 18.262-263). The other occasion was the decision by Claudius to establish Ptolemais as a military colony in the early 50s C.E. It meant retired soldiers were now encouraged to reside in close proximity to Galilee and that the Romans also had a place of safety that could act as a base from which to launch military activity.[29]

---

28. The fact that Josephus has preserved the story indicates it had become part of the wider shared community story, certainly extending outside of Sepphoris and, presumably, Galilee.

29. Sean Freyne, "The Revolt from a Regional Perspective," in *The First Jewish Revolt: Archaeology, History, and Ideology* (ed. Andrea M. Berlin and J. Andrew Overman; London: Routledge, 2002), 45. He also draws attention to Tacitus's claim that Cumanus was appointed a special envoy over Galilee (Josephus, *A.J.* 12.24). However, on this situation see E. Mary Smallwood, *The Jews Under Roman Rule: From Pompey to Diocletian: A Study in Political Relations* (SJLA 20; Leiden: Brill, 1981), 266-67.

It is important not to overestimate the level of threat associated with these developments regarding Ptolemais and, indeed, regarding Roman military presence in Galilee as a whole. This need for caution is evident from the final action to note, the route used by Cestius in 66 C.E. Although he felt compelled to act with speed once he was informed of the situation in Jerusalem, it is via Ptolemais and the coastal route that Cestius headed to the city (Josephus, *B.J.* 2.500–509). Furthermore, he does not personally go through Galilee.[30] There is no evidence of Roman troops being stationed in Galilee, even when the region was incorporated into the province in 44 C.E. In fact, the first coordinated campaign by Roman troops in Galilee was undertaken by Vespasian. As a result, one of the key elements of the Roman Empire, its army, was not part of the landscape of life in Galilee.[31] Aside from occasional targeted incursions during the middle part of the first century B.C.E., it was only the decision of Varus to make an example of Sepphoris that left any sense of a military footprint.

Cultural and Economic Presence

The possible range of indicators for involvement that fall under this broad category is extensive. At the same time, the notion of what should be labeled as being Roman is also open to debate, which also means that a Roman cultural presence may pervade aspects of daily life not readily visible in either the literary sources or the material remains.[32] As such, it is important to focus on the tangible, explicit indicators of a Roman presence before seeking to plot possible implied indicators. As with the two other categories, the search for evidence of a substantial presence produces limited results.

One of the more obvious signs of a Roman cultural presence is the construction of public structures like theaters, baths, odea, and temples.[33] To date, however, from the numerous excavations in Galilee no such structures built by the Romans before 66 C.E. have been identified. While the construction of buildings requires a significant cost in terms of resources and time, another obvious

---

30. Cestius dispatches Gallus with an unspecified detachment to Galilee (Josephus, *B.J.* 2.510–512). This is a short incursion, concentrated near Sepphoris.

31. On the New Testament references to soldiers (Matt 8:5–13; Luke 7:1–10; Acts 10) see Mark A. Chancey, *Greco-Roman Culture and the Galilee of Jesus* (SNTSMS 134; Cambridge: Cambridge University Press, 2005), 49–56. Although the Herodian client rulers did have troops it is important not to depict them as quasi Romans in another guise: during the war some soldiers from Agrippa II's army fought against the Romans (Josephus, *B.J.* 2.520).

32. For example, see Richard Hingley, *Globalizing Roman Culture: Unity, Diversity and Empire* (London: Routledge, 2005), 91–116, and Chancey, *Greco-Roman Culture*, 9–16.

33. See Daniel Sperber, *The City in Roman Palestine* (New York: Oxford University Press, 1998).

sign of a Roman presence, coinage, has no such complications. Yet even evidence of Roman coinage being in circulation in Galilee prior to the war is sparse, especially when compared to the number of Hasmonean and Herodian coins that have been found. It is clearly not a case of the monetary economy being influenced, let alone dominated, by Roman coinage.[34] In part, the absence of such obvious signs of a cultural and economic presence can be explained by the fact that the territory only came under direct Roman rule very late and that it was on a limited scale. Even more significant in this context, it has been argued that the search should focus on an indirect cultural and economic presence that was disseminated via the Herodian client rulers. In essence, the line of argument is that wherever the Herodian rulers were at work it also meant the presence of Rome.[35] Indeed, the bulk of evidence cited by Bernett for the presence of the imperial cult relates to activities undertaken by the Herodian client rulers.[36]

Of particular importance to the view that the Herodian rulers were the agents of Roman influence is the reference to the rebuilding and expansion of Sepphoris and the founding of Tiberias.[37] The very name of Antipas's new city, Tiberias, clearly evokes the connection he was trying to make between his territory and his Roman overlords. It is also no coincidence that these two cities produced their own coins, long after Antipas had used them to mint his coinage. The development of these two cities clearly resulted in significant change for the dynamic of life in Galilee. However, whether we should necessarily view this change as indicating an expanding Roman cultural impact on Galilee is debatable. Certainly the way the urban landscape of Sepphoris and Tiberias developed in the second century C.E. and beyond explicitly displays signs of Roman influence, in terms of the public structures and private dwellings.[38] In the first century C.E., and certainly before the war began, the situation is quite different. The bulk of our evidence, in terms of the economic and cultural activity, resonates well

---

34. See Marcus Sigismund, "Small Change? Coins and Weights as a Mirror of Ethnic, Religious and Political Identity in First and Second Century C.E. Tiberias," in *Religion, Ethnicity, and Identity in Ancient Galilee: A Region in Transition* (ed. Jürgen Zangenberg, Harold W. Attridge, and Dale B. Martin; WUNT; Tübingen: Mohr Siebeck, 2007), 315–36. There is also a notable paucity of evidence for inscriptions that indicate a Roman presence; see Mark A. Chancey, "The Epigraphic Habit of Hellenistic and Roman Galilee," in *Religion, Ethnicity, and Identity in Ancient Galilee: A Region in Transition* (ed. Jürgen Zangenberg, Harold W. Attridge, and Dale B. Martin; WUNT; Tübingen: Mohr Siebeck, 2007), 83–98.

35. For example, see Richard A. Horsley, "Power Vacuum and Power Struggle in 66-7 C.E.," in *First Jewish Revolt: Archaeology, History, and Ideology* (ed. Andrea M. Berlin and J. Andrew Overman; London: Routledge, 2002), 87–109.

36. Bernett, "Roman Imperial Cult," 342–52.

37. Horsley, "Power Vacuum and Power Struggle," 87–109.

38. See Chancey, *Greco-Roman Culture*, 100–121.

with the area being Jewish. For example, there is a burgeoning local olive oil industry, a local ceramic industry, numerous stone vessels, and plastered stepped pools.[39] Taken as a whole we certainly have a changing economic dynamic, with expanding urban centers being introduced into what had previously been a predominantly rural landscape. It is also clear these cities incorporated features that indicate a Roman presence and influence.[40] At the same time though, the cities display evidence of having a local economy in which most of the indicators of cultural identity were Jewish not Roman, and not a hybrid amalgam. Honoring Rome may have played a part in the actions of the Herodian rulers as they set about the task of developing these cities. There is, however, no suggestion that the local population saw themselves as residents whose allegiance lay with things Roman.

Venturing beyond the two new cities and reviewing what was happening in the region of Galilee as a whole, the situation changes very little. If anything, it is a case of arguing that there is even less evidence of a Roman cultural and economic presence. The complex nature of interpreting a possible Roman impact on the local culture and economy is clearly expressed by Andrea Berlin.[41] At two of the locations where serious fighting took place, Jotapata and Gamla, there is evidence of a Roman cultural presence, in the decor and some of the goods that have been found. However, what stands out from the household wares at both sites is the preference for locally produced goods above imported ones.[42] A limited, restricted indication of a Roman presence outside the two major cities is also evident from coin distributions. At Gamla, Hasmonean coins constitute the overwhelming majority of those found, suggesting the local economy had not been overtaken by a direct Roman presence, nor been subsumed by an indirect

---

39. For example, see David Adan-Bayewitz, *Common Pottery in Roman Galilee: A Study of Local Trade* (Bar-Ilan Studies in Near Eastern Languages and Culture; Ramat-Gan, Israel: Bar-Ilan University Press, 1993); Mordechai Aviam, "Distribution Maps of Archaeological Data from the Galilee: An Attempt to Establish Zones Indicative of Ethnicity and Religious Affiliation," in *Religion, Ethnicity, and Identity in Ancient Galilee: A Region in Transition* (ed. Jürgen Zangenberg, Harold W. Attridge, and Dale B. Martin; WUNT; Tübingen: Mohr Siebeck, 2007), 115–32; Chancey, *Greco-Roman Culture*; Douglas R. Edwards, "Identity and Social Location in Roman Galilean Villages," in *Religion, Ethnicity, and Identity in Ancient Galilee: A Region in Transition* (ed. Jürgen Zangenberg, Harold W. Attridge, and Dale B. Martin; WUNT; Tübingen: Mohr Siebeck, 2007), 357–74; Jonathan L. Reed, *Archaeology and the Galilean Jesus: A Re-Examination of the Evidence* (Harrisburg, Pa.: Trinity Press International, 2000), esp. 23–61.

40. See ibid., 100–138, and Chancey, *Greco-Roman Culture*, 71–99.

41. Andrea M. Berlin, "Romanization and Anti-Romanization in Pre-Revolt Galilee," in *The First Jewish Revolt: Archaeology, History, and Ideology* (ed. Andrea M. Berlin and J. Andrew Overman; London: Routledge, 2002), 57–73.

42. Ibid., 62–67.

influence driven by the Herodian client kingdom.[43] There is simply a lack of evidence to suggest that Galilee was subjected to a sudden wave of Roman cultural and economic influence, let alone a creeping infiltration. If anything, the opposite applies, the material remains suggest an expanding Jewish presence.[44]

Explaining Galilean Responses to the Romans in 66 c.e.

Reviewing the three key areas of possible Roman impact on Galilee shows that the Galileans did have direct experience of being in the sphere of Roman control from 63 b.c.e. onwards. In terms of the imperial cult the evidence is minimal. Aside from Petronius's discussions with Jewish leaders that took place at Tiberias as he tried to negotiate the implementation of Gaius's order, the only other possible evidence for the cult lies in the behavior of the Herodian rulers. They may have viewed the decisions they made regarding the development of cities in the region and the images placed on some coinage as a means of displaying homage and honor to the emperor. There is, however, no reason to suggest that the local inhabitants saw their lives being compromised by encroachment of the imperial cult into Galilee.

Furthermore, there is neither a major one-off action or event nor a sense of a gradual increase in presence that readily explains the willingness of many Galileans to oppose Roman legions in 67 c.e. No doubt Roman decisions about the appropriate administrative system to be used were a source of frustration and, for some Galileans, a reason to protest at certain times. The military presence hung more as a potential threat; it was certainly not a daily fixture in the region. Whatever damage Gaius did to Sepphoris in 4 b.c.e., it is fair to conclude that the action would have been remembered as a negative experience. The cultural and economic impact of Roman control of the region is hard to quantify. The various

---

43. See Danny Syon, "Tyre and Gamla: A Study in the Monetary Inlfluence of Southern Phoenicia on Galilee and the Golan in the Hellenistic and Roman Periods" (Jerusalem: Hebrew University of Jerusalem, 2004), 21 regarding the distribution of coins at Gamla: of the 5,895 identifiable coins, 3,964 were Hasmonean, 928 were Phoenician or autonomous, 610 were Seleucid, and only 304 were Herodian or Roman.

44. Conjecture remains as to the possible motivation of this choice. Berlin, "Romanization and Anti-Romanization," 67–70 argues for much of the choice to be a deliberate rejection of things Roman. Morten Hørning Jensen, "Socio-Economic and Socio-Religious Dynamics in Herod Antipas' Galilee—a Holistic Approach," paper presented at the Annual Meeting of the SBL, New Orleans, 2009, presents a strong case for religious motivation being behind such choices. See also Yoav Arbel, *Ultimate Devotion: The Historical Impact and Archaeological Expression of Intense Religious Movements* (Approaches to Anthropological Archaeology; London: Equinox, 2009). Note also the cautionary comments of Edwards, "Identity and Social Location," 372–73 regarding deciphering the intention of such choices.

physical remains from the period do not suggest the people of Galilee felt overwhelmed by things Roman. Returning to the question posed earlier, "what have the Romans done *to* us Galileans?" the answer is, not very much.[45] Therefore, it is not a case of explaining the involvement of Galileans in the war as a cause and effect dynamic relating to the activities of the Romans in the region and how the Galileans then responded to those activities. By implication, Bennett's proposal that the Galileans were responding to an increasing encroachment of the imperial cult on their way of life lacks credence.[46]

We are compelled to seek another explanation for the behavior of the Galileans in the war. Here, the underlying principle of Bennett's argument provides an important way forward: we should focus attention on the points of contact between Galilee and Judea rather than possible points of difference.[47] Instead of postulating a supposed shared concern about the imperial cult, it is as follows: the people from Galilee who participated in the war did so because they shared with other Jews an ideological commitment to ensuring the temple belonged to God. This provides a straightforward explanation to what happened.[48] When the decision was taken by some of the priests in Jerusalem to cease offering sacrifices for the well-being of the emperor and Rome, it meant those Jews had decided they were no longer willing to negotiate with Rome. This decision was a radical one and represented an innovation. It was a decision that inspired other Jews to become rebels, including numerous Galileans, to take the bold step of putting

---

45. Of course, a minimal direct presence does not necessarily negate a fear factor mentality being influential; that is, concern for what the Romans *might* do to us Galileans. This approach underpins the claim of Josephus that a person from Gamla or Galilee called upon all Jews to oppose Roman rule in 6 C.E. However, it is a highly speculative approach and it does not provide coherence with the overall scope of evidence about life in Galilee in the early Roman period, which displays an affirmation of being Jewish.

46. This absence of a significant Roman presence is especially evident in comparison to what occurred in Judea: the establishment of direct Roman rule much earlier, in 6 C.E., which also meant the introduction of Roman law, taxation (Josephus, *B.J.* 2.117; *A.J.* 17.355, 18.1–2), and, possibly the most important footprint, auxiliary troops being stationed in the province (*B.J.* 5.244; *A.J.* 19.365–366). Although much of the activity was commenced by Herod, evidence of an expanding cultural presence was also clearly on display in the various public structures at Caesarea Maritima. See Peter Richardson, *City and Sanctuary: Religion and Architecture in the Roman Near East* (London: SCM Press, 2002), 104–29.

47. Another approach is to view what happened in 66 C.E. as an internal struggle among Jews as much as it was a war against Rome. As argued by one its key advocates, Richard A. Horsley, what took place was a series of local and regional conflicts; there was no "unifying ideology and no coherent anti-Roman revolt" ("Power Vacuum and Power Struggle," 101). The war was a conflation of urban-rural hostilities and class conflict in individual cities. It is an approach that relies heavily on a reading of Josephus through a prism of modern sociological models and it does not pay sufficient attention to the extensive material remains in Galilee.

48. Bennett, "Roman Imperial Cult," 354–55.

into practice the ideology of "serving God alone" through the use of force. This approach does not require the decision to rebel to be viewed as a response to encroachment or the imposition of things foreign onto the Jewish way of life. Instead, the decision to rebel is a proactive move to protect something fundamental to the Jewish way of life. It was not so much that something Roman was perceived to be taking over, as it was that some Jews, including Galileans, believed Rome failed to recognize that the temple was off limits and that it did not belong to them.[49] The problem related to what took place in the temple in Jerusalem; it was never about anything to do with life in Galilee.

Drawing upon the *Life of Brian* again, if we broaden the question posed earlier and rephrase it as, "what have the Romans done to us *Jews*?" it is evident that the temple stands out as the regular feature of Jewish-Roman relations. There are numerous examples of the Jews being concerned to protect the temple and of Romans not understanding, or not being interested in understanding, that the temple lay outside their sphere of control. The first Roman to intervene directly into Jewish affairs, Pompey, set the tone. After capturing Jerusalem, he entered the holy of holies (Josephus, *B.J.* 1.152–154; *A.J.* 14.71–73). Even allowing for Josephus's depiction of Pompey as "a good Roman" who ordered the immediate purification of the temple, he had set a foreboding precedent. Crassus followed in Pompey's footsteps, extracting money from the temple to help fund his military campaigns (*B.J.* 1.179; *A.J.* 14.105–109).[50] Early in the administration of the province, the governors held the high priest's vestments under guard at the Antonia fortress, much to the displeasure of the Jews (*A.J.* 18.90–95).[51] In 40/41 C.E. Gaius demanded that his statue be erected in Jerusalem (*B.J.* 2.184–203; *A.J.* 18.261–309; Philo, *Legat.* 201–373).[52] Later Cumanus refused to punish Samaritans who had killed one or more pilgrims from Galilee heading to Jerusalem for a festival (*B.J.* 2.232–240; *A.J.* 20.118–124). Whatever the precise intentions were of these Romans, it is understandable that any Jews concerned about the sanctity of the temple would not consider Rome reliable. Whether the Jews were motivated by a perception of possible encroachment by the imperial cult on the functioning

---

49. There is an important clarification required here. The specific issue in 66 C.E. related to the decision of Florus to demand the shortfall in the taxes be paid from the temple treasury (Josephus, *B.J.* 2.293, 405). For the rebels, this was not an issue of the negotiation process breaking down, nor was it a gradual or rapid encroachment by Rome. What Florus had done was to ignore totally that the temple was Jewish, not Roman.

50. Cassius also extracted money but it is not clear if funds were taken from the temple (*B.J.* 1.218–222; *A.J.* 14.271–276). In 4 B.C.E. Sabinus tried to extract funds from the temple as well as other locations (*B.J.* 2.16–19, 39–54; *A.J.* 17.252–268).

51. Note also the unsuccessful attempt by Fadus to reclaim control of the vestments (*A.J.* 20.6–14).

52. Ibid., 348 argues that Galilean involvement in this incident was extensive.

of the temple is unclear. Almost every generation since the advent of a Roman presence in the region, some sort of incident about how one or another Roman did not properly recognize the sanctity of the temple could be cited. However, lack of respect for the temple did not necessarily mean the Romans were interested in converting the temple into a Roman place of worship. The imperial cult was already well represented in the Jewish homeland. Therefore, when Florus demanded in 66 C.E. that the arrears in tax were to be paid out of temple funds, his action could be viewed as simply another part of a larger narrative of Roman behavior and poor decision making. The crucial difference on this occasion was that a sufficient number of Jews with the necessary power decided to take action to control their fate, putting into practice the ideology of "serving God alone" by ensuring that the temple was the property of God. They barred Rome from their public space, ceased the sacrifices offered on behalf of Rome and the emperor, ousted the Roman garrison, and commenced establishing their own new independent state.[53]

There is an important rider associated with this explanation for Galilean involvement in the war, namely, the absence of any direct evidence in the narratives of Josephus to support such a view. Nowhere does Josephus suggest that the rebels were motivated by an ideology that was shared by many other Jews, let alone that some were also willing to put that ideology into practice in the manner done in 66 C.E. As noted at the outset, the reconstruction Josephus provides deliberately strips the rebels of any ideological motivation for their actions and marginalizes them from the wider community. As such, there is no surprise in stating that we are not in a position to enlist Josephus's account in direct support of what is being proposed and that we need to read his narratives outside his reconstruction. Instead, the appeal of the explanation outlined for Galilean involvement in the war is based on the manner in which it coheres with what we know about the situation in general in Galilee before and during the war. It is appropriate to note here two key examples of this coherence. One example relates to the observation that the Galileans were temple observant, in the sense that they regularly participated in the annual pilgrimage festivals. The willingness of Galileans to travel to Jerusalem for the festivals and their evident commitment to the

---

53. The imagery on the coinage is a significant statement of claims: a new state had been proclaimed with a new dating system. See James S. McLaren, "The Coinage of the First Year as a Point of Reference for the Jewish Revolt (60–70 CE)," *Scripta Classica Israelica* 22 (2003): 135–52, and Leo Mildenberg, "Rebel Coinage in the Roman Empire," in *Greece and Rome in Eretz Israel: Collected Essays* (ed. Aryeh Kasher, Gideon Fuks, and Uriel Rappaprot; Jerusalem: Yad Izhak Ben-Zvi: Israel Exploration Society, 1990), 62–74. For the importance of the temple and, more broadly, Jerusalem, see Goodblatt, *Elements*, 167–203, and Martin Goodman, "The Temple in First Century CE Judaism," in *Temple and Worship in Biblical Israel* (ed. John Day; LHBOTS; London: T&T Clark, 2005), 459–68.

temple meant the decision to join the war in order to assert control of the temple and, therefore, to protect it, was a straightforward extension of an existing loyalty.[54] The second example of the coherence is the dominance of material remains with a distinctly Jewish character in Galilee from the early Roman period. It was noted earlier, when considering the possible signs of a Roman cultural and economic presence, that most of the evidence indicates Jewish occupation and that it is largely consistent with the type of finds in Judea. In other words, the residents of the two regions display far more in common in terms of the material culture than is distinct or different between them. The various social, cultural and religious factors impacting material culture choices that were at play in Judea were also at play in Galilee.[55] As such, it is understandable that what took place in Jerusalem was also seen to be of direct relevance for the lives of the people in Galilee.

Explaining Galilean involvement in the war as part of the same overall decision by Jews in general to fight has the additional benefit of providing a straightforward explanation for two supposed anomalies. They are: the fervor and adherent resistance displayed by some Galileans, and the mixed nature of the Galilean response to the war. The fanaticism of the defenders at Gamla, as depicted by Josephus, and the minting of the revolt coins at Gamla indicate a significant commitment and enthusiasm for the war.[56] By viewing the actions of the Galileans as part of the same broad sweep of approaches adopted by the Jewish community as a whole, it means this level of support was not unusual and something that requires special location-specific explanations. It is an enthusiasm which parallels that displayed by the people who minted the silver coinage at the start of the war and those who defended Jerusalem in 70 c.e.: it needs to be placed within a broader context, rather than being explained as an action that had no context. The second supposed anomaly is the fact that Galileans did not respond to the war with one voice. Efforts have been made to explain the diversity of the response by appeal to issues that are distinctive to the region or the specific location.[57] However, by working from the basis that people who supported the war in Galilee did so for the same basic reason as the people in Judea,

---

54. Sean Freyne, "Galilee-Jerusalem Relations According to Josephus' *Life*," in *Galilee and Gospel: Collected Essays* (WUNT; Tübingen: Mohr Siebeck, 2000), 73–85.

55. Along with those works cited in n. 39, also see Yitzhak Magen, *The Stone Vessel Industry in the Second Temple Period: Excavations at Hizma and the Jerusalem Temple Mount* (ed. Levana Tsfania; Judea and Samaria Publications; Jerusalem: Israel Exploration Society, 2002), 148–64; Arbel, *Ultimate Devotion*, 123–40; and Jensen, "Socio-Economic and Socio-Religious Dynamics."

56. The claim of Josephus that people from Tiberias were among the soldiers opposing the Romans at the siege of Jerusalem also indicates this enthusiasm (*Vita* 354).

57. For example, Horsley, "Power Vacuum and Power Struggle."

it is also appropriate to view the range of responses in Galilee as paralleling what happened in Judea. Some people openly supported the war and actively joined the fighting. Some people opposed the war; they did not favor articulating the ideology by rejecting Rome, declaring independence and taking up arms. Josephus writes of the tension and debate that went on in Jerusalem in 66 C.E. at the beginning of the war, which escalated to open fighting among Jews about what course of action should be taken (Josephus, *B.J.* 2.411–48). A similar situation was unfolding at places like Sepphoris and Tiberias. There was public debate about what to do, ranging from taking up arms to oppose the Romans to offering to support Agrippa II and his Roman allies. What differed between a place like Sepphoris and Jerusalem is which side of the debate became the dominant opinion, the former deciding against the war and the latter deciding for the war. What is notable is that both locations used a very similar technique to let other people know of the decision: the minting of coinage.[58]

Conclusion

The dismissal of the "zealot theory" and the associated notion that Galilee was the home of armed opposition to foreign rule caused a complication: how is the Galilean involvement in the war to be explained? Recent approaches, including Bernett's emphasis on the role of the imperial cult, have continued to focus on looking for circumstances in Galilee. Evidence for a Roman presence in Galilee, however, provides little by way of substance. There is a distinct absence of a significant footprint on the physical and social landscape, and of any evidence of a presence that intensified in the years leading up to the war. As such, it follows that there is also a lack of evidence of the imperial cult being a factor in the lives of people who lived in Galilee. Rather than postulate implicit expressions of the connotations associated with imperial cult in the actions of the Herodian rulers we should heed the geographical evidence. The cult was a tangible, explicit feature of the landscape in the region of Caesarea Maritima, Caesarea Philippi, and Sebaste. It was even accommodated in the daily function of the temple cult at Jerusalem. In Galilee, however, there was no such link with the imperial cult. In order to explain what happened in Galilee at the start of the war we need to stop looking for factors distinctive to the region and instead to see what took place there as mirroring the situation in Judea. Furthermore, we need to be open again to viewing the Galilean resistance as ideologically driven, concerned to serve God alone by asserting that the temple was Jewish. This militant ideology, however,

---

58. Regarding the situation in Sepphoris at the start of the war see Eric M. Meyers, "Sepphoris: City of Peace," in Berlin and Overman, *First Jewish Revolt*, 110–20.

needs to be recognized as something that was Jewish, not specific to one group, or specific to one location.

What set 66 C.E. apart was that the ideology ceased to remain a theoretical discussion. The decision to cease offering the sacrifices meant the Jewish community at large now had to make a choice. All Jews residing in the vicinity of Jerusalem had to decide whether they were willing to put that ideology into practice as open resistance to Rome, or whether they thought there was another way to retain the principle that the temple belonged to God, which did not involve fighting Rome. Once news of what happened in Jerusalem spread, the same decisions had to be made elsewhere. In places like Jotapata and Gamla the answer was "we will fight"; at other places, like Sepphoris, after debate the answer was that "we will not fight"; at others again, like Gischala, "we will fight, until confronted." In effect, the focus on explaining Galilean involvement in the war has shown that such a line of investigation is meaningful only when it avoids trying to find region-specific answers, and views what took place in Galilee as mirroring what also took place in Judea.[59]

The final word goes to the Romans, by way of noting their actions in the immediate aftermath of the war. There is no doubt that how Vespasian and Titus acted was strongly influenced by the situation in Rome. At the same time, the fact that Agrippa II remained loyal to Rome throughout the war would also influence how the Romans behaved in Galilee. Even allowing for these factors, a comparison of the practical actions undertaken in Galilee and Judea is significant, especially as both were locations of resistance. Having methodically suppressed all opposition in both locations, in Galilee Rome exacted no further punishment. In Judea, however, they pulled down what was left of the temple, leaving it in ruins, and they stationed a legion in the city, overlooking the Temple Mount. All of these actions suggest the Romans understood the temple was central to the war that commenced in 66 C.E. As a consequence, measures had to be taken to ensure the temple would not be a rallying point for Jews again in the near future, wherever they resided.[60]

---

59. On the situation in Idumea see Allan Appelbaum, "'The Idumaeans' in Josephus' *The Jewish War*," *JSJ* 40, (2009): 1–22, esp. 19, and Freyne, "The Revolt from a Regional Perspective."

60. It is possible the decision to destroy the temple complex at Leontopolis should also be understood as a part of the concern to remove a potential rallying point (Josephus, *B.J.* 7.421). On the Roman response also see James Rives, "Flavian Religious Policy and the Destruction of the Jerusalem Temple," in *Flavius Josephus and Flavian Rome* (ed. J. C. Edmondson, Steve Mason, and J. B. Rives; Oxford: Oxford University Press, 2005), 145–66.

Bibliography

Adan-Bayewitz, David. *Common Pottery in Roman Galilee: A Study of Local Trade*. Bar-Ilan Studies in Near Eastern Languages and Culture. Ramat-Gan, Israel: Bar-Ilan University Press, 1993.

Appelbaum, Allan. "'The Idumaeans' in Josephus' *The Jewish War*." *Journal for the Study of Judaism in the Persian, Hellenistic, and Roman Period* 40 (2009): 1–22.

Arbel, Yoav. *Ultimate Devotion: The Historical Impact and Archaeological Expression of Intense Religious Movements*. Approaches to Anthropological Archaeology. London: Equinox, 2009.

Aviam, Mordechai. "Distribution Maps of Archaeological Data from the Galilee: An Attempt to Establish Zones Indicative of Ethnicity and Religious Affiliation." Pages 115–32 in *Religion, Ethnicity, and Identity in Ancient Galilee: A Region in Transition*. Edited by Jürgen Zangenberg, Harold W. Attridge, and Dale B. Martin. Wissenschaftliche Untersuchungen zum Neuen Testament. Tübingen: Mohr Siebeck, 2007.

―――. "Yodefat/Jotapata: The Archaeology of the First Battle." Pages 121–33 in *The First Jewish Revolt: Archaeology, History, and Ideology*. Edited by Andrea M. Berlin and J. Andrew Overman. London: Routledge, 2002.

Ben-Shalom, Israel. *The School of Shammai and the Zealots' Struggle Against Rome*. Jerusalem: Yad Ben-Zvi, 1993.

Berlin, Andrea M. "Romanization and Anti-Romanization in Pre-Revolt Galilee." Pages 57–73 in *The First Jewish Revolt: Archaeology, History, and Ideology*. Edited by Andrea M. Berlin and J. Andrew Overman. London: Routledge, 2002.

Bernett, Monika. "Roman Imperial Cult in the Galilee: Structures, Functions, and Dynamics Affiliation." Pages 337–56 in *Religion, Ethnicity, and Identity in Ancient Galilee: A Region in Transition*. Edited by Jürgen Zangenberg, Harold W. Attridge, and Dale B. Martin. Wissenschaftliche Untersuchungen zum Neuen Testament. Tübingen: Mohr Siebeck, 2007.

Chancey, Mark A. "The Epigraphic Habit of Hellenistic and Roman Galilee." Pages 83–98 in *Religion, Ethnicity, and Identity in Ancient Galilee: A Region in Transition*. Edited by Jürgen Zangenberg, Harold W. Attridge, and Dale B. Martin. Wissenschaftliche Untersuchungen zum Neuen Testament. Tübingen: Mohr Siebeck, 2007.

―――. *Greco-Roman Culture and the Galilee of Jesus*. Society for New Testament Studies Monograph Series 134. Cambridge: Cambridge University Press, 2005.

Crossan, John Dominic. *God and Empire: Jesus Against Rome, Then and Now*. San Francisco: HarperSanFrancisco, 2007.

Edwards, Douglas R. "Identity and Social Location in Roman Galilean Villages." Pages 357–74 in *Religion, Ethnicity, and Identity in Ancient Galilee: A Region in Transition*. Edited by Jürgen Zangenberg, Harold W. Attridge, and Dale B. Martin. Wissenschaftliche Untersuchungen zum Neuen Testament. Tübingen: Mohr Siebeck, 2007.

Freyne, Sean. "The Galileans in the Light of Josephus's *Life*." Pages 27–44 in *Galilee and Gospel: Collected Essays*. Wissenschaftliche Untersuchungen zum Neuen Testament. Tübingen: Mohr Siebeck, 2000.

―――. "Galilee-Jerusalem Relations According to Josephus' *Life*." Pages 73–85 in *Galilee and Gospel: Collected Essays*. Wissenschaftliche Untersuchungen zum Neuen Testament. Tübingen: Mohr Siebeck, 2000.

⸻. "The Geography of Restoration: Galilee-Jerusalem Relations in Early Jewish and Christian Experience." *New Testament Studies* 47 (2001): 289–311.

⸻. "The Revolt from a Regional Perspective." Pages 43–56 in *The First Jewish Revolt: Archaeology, History, and Ideology*. Edited by Andrea M. Berlin and J. Andrew Overman. London: Routledge, 2002.

Galinsky, Karl. "The Cult of the Roman Emperor: Uniter or Divider?" Paper presented at the Annual Meeting of the SBL, Boston, 2008, and ch. 1 in this volume.

Goodblatt, David. *Elements of Ancient Jewish Nationalism*. Cambridge: Cambridge University Press, 2006.

Goodman, Martin. "The Temple in First Century CE Judaism." *Pages 459–68 in Temple and Worship in Biblical Israel*. Edited by John Day. Library of Hebrew Bible/Old Testament Studies. London: T&T Clark, 2005.

Hengel, Martin. *Die Zeloten: Untersuchungen zur Jüdischen Freiheitsbewegung in der Zeit von Herodes I. bis 70 n. Chr.* Arbeiten zur Geschichte des antiken Judentums und des Urchristentums 1. Leiden: Brill, 1961. Translated by D. M. Smith as *The Zealots. Investigations into the Jewish Freedom Movement in the Period from Herod I until 70 A.D.* (Edinburgh: T&T Clark, 1989).

Hingley, Richard. *Globalizing Roman Culture: Unity, Diversity and Empire*. London: Routledge, 2005.

Horsley, Richard A., ed. *Paul and Empire: Religion and Power in Roman Imperial Society*. Harrisburg, Pa.: Trinity Press International, 1997.

⸻. *Archaeology, History, and Society in Galilee: The Social Context of Jesus and the Rabbis*. Valley Forge Pa.: Trinity Press International, 1996.

⸻. "Power Vacuum and Power Struggle in 66–7 C.E." Pages 87–109 in *The First Jewish Revolt: Archaeology, History, and Ideology*. Edited by Andrea M. Berlin and J. Andrew Overman. London: Routledge, 2002.

⸻. "The Zealots: Their Origins, Relationships and Importance in the Jewish Revolt." *Novum Testamentum* 28 (1986): 159–92.

Jensen, Morten Hørning. "Message and Minting: The Coins of Herod Antipas in Their Second Temple Context as a Source for Understanding the Religio-Political and Socio-Economic Dynamics of Early First Century Galilee." Pages 277–313 in *Religion, Ethnicity, and Identity in Ancient Galilee: A Region in Transition*. Edited by Jürgen Zangenberg, Harold W. Attridge, and Dale B. Martin. Wissenschaftliche Untersuchungen zum Neuen Testament. Tübingen: Mohr Siebeck, 2007.

⸻. "Socio-Economic and Socio-Religious Dynamics in Herod Antipas' Galilee – a Holistic Approach." Paper presented at the Annual Meeting of the SBL. New Orleans, 2009.

Jones, Terry. *Life of Brian*. Python (Monty) Pictures Ltd, 1979.

Josephus. Translated by H. St. J. Thackeray et al. 10 vols. Loeb Classical Library. Cambridge, Mass.: Harvard University Press, 1926–1965.

Magen, Yitzhak. *The Stone Vessel Industry in the Second Temple Period: Excavations at Hizma and the Jerusalem Temple Mount*. Edited by Levana Tsfania. Judea and Samaria Publications. Jerusalem: Israel Exploration Society, 2002.

McLaren, James S. "The Coinage of the First Year as a Point of Reference for the Jewish Revolt (60–70 CE)." *Scripta Classica Israelica* 22 (2003): 135–52.

———. "Constructing Judaean History in the Diaspora: Josephus's Accounts of Judas." Pages 90–108 in *Negotiating Diaspora: Jewish Strategies in the Roman Empire*. Edited by John M. G. Barclay. Library of Second Temple Studies. London: T&T Clark International, 2004.

———. "Jews and the Imperial Cult: From Augustus to Domitian." *Journal of the Study of the New Testament* 27 (2005): 257–78.

Meyers, Eric M. "Sepphoris: City of Peace." Pages 110–20 in *The First Jewish Revolt: Archaeology, History, and Ideology*. Edited by Andrea M. Berlin and J. Andrew Overman. London: Routledge, 2002.

Mildenberg, Leo. "Rebel Coinage in the Roman Empire." Pages 62–74 in *Greece and Rome in Eretz Israel: Collected Essays*. Edited by Aryeh Kasher, Gideon Fuks, and Uriel Rappaprot. Jerusalem: Yad Izhak Ben-Zvi: Israel Exploration Society, 1990.

Moreland, Milton. "The Inhabitants of Galilee in the Hellenistic and Early Roman Periods: Probes Into the Archaeological and Literary Evidence." Pages 133–59 in *Religion, Ethnicity, and Identity in Ancient Galilee: A Region in Transition*. Edited by Jürgen Zangenberg, Harold W. Attridge, and Dale B. Martin. Wissenschaftliche Untersuchungen zum Neuen Testament. Tübingen: Mohr Siebeck, 2007.

Price, S. R. F. *Rituals and Power: The Roman Imperial Cult in Asia Minor*. Cambridge: Cambridge University Press, 1984.

Reed, Jonathan L. *Archaeology and the Galilean Jesus: A Re-Examination of the Evidence*. Harrisburg, Pa.: Trinity Press International, 2000.

Richardson, Peter. *City and Sanctuary: Religion and Architecture in the Roman Near East*. London: SCM Press, 2002.

Rives, James. "Flavian Religious Policy and the Destruction of the Jerusalem Temple." Pages 145–66 in *Flavius Josephus and Flavian Rome*. Edited by J. C. Edmondson, Steve Mason, and J. B. Rives. Oxford: Oxford University Press, 2005.

Sigismund, Marcus. "Small Change? Coins and Weights as a Mirror of Ethnic, Religious and Political Identity in First and Second Century C.E. Tiberias." Pages 315–36 in *Religion, Ethnicity, and Identity in Ancient Galilee: A Region in Transition*. Edited by Jürgen Zangenberg, Harold W. Attridge, and Dale B. Martin. Wissenschaftliche Untersuchungen zum Neuen Testament. Tübingen: Mohr Siebeck, 2007.

Smallwood, E. Mary. *The Jews Under Roman Rule: From Pompey to Diocletian: A Study in Political Relations*. Studies in Judaism in Late Antiquity 20. Leiden: Brill, 1981.

Smith, Morton. "Zealots and Sicarii, Their Origins and Relation." *Harvard Theological Review* 64 (1971): 1–19.

Sperber, Daniel. *The City in Roman Palestine*. New York: Oxford University Press, 1998.

Syon, Danny. "The Coins from Gamla: An Interim Report." *Israel Numismatic Journal* 12 (1992/93): 34–55.

———. "Gamla: City of Refuge." Pages 134–53 in *The First Jewish Revolt: Archaeology, History, and Ideology*. Edited by Andrea M. Berlin and J. Andrew Overman. London: Routledge, 2002.

———. "Tyre and Gamla: A Study in the Monetary Inlfluence of Southern Phoenicia on Galilee and the Golan in the Hellenistic and Roman Periods." Jerusalem: Hebrew University of Jerusalem, 2004.

Udoh, Fabian E. *To Caesar What is Caesar's: Tribute, Taxes and Imperial Administration in Early Roman Palestine (63 B.C.E.–70 C.E.)*. Brown Judaic Studies 343. Providence, R.I.: Brown Judaic Studies, 2005.

Vermes, Geza. *Jesus the Jew: A Historian's Reading of the Gospels.* 1973. Repr. Philadelphia: Fortress, 1981.
Zeitlin, Solomon. "Who Were the Galileans? New Light on Josephus' Activities in Galilee." *Jewish Quarterly Review* 64 (1974): 189–203.

Chapter 10
Roman Imperial Power:
A New Testament Perspective

Warren Carter

I want to thank the organizers of this dialogue, especially Professor Jonathan Reed, for the opportunity to contribute a few reflections. I begin by locating this field of inquiry in the larger context of New Testament scholarship, then take up a couple of issues in Professor Galinsky's very helpful paper, "The Cult of the Roman Emperor: Uniter or Divider?,"[1] and then engage in some analysis of texts from the Jesus movement in Asia.

I note that my title focusing on Roman imperial power is much broader than the topic of Professor Galinsky's paper, which centered on the imperial cult. The cult was of course embedded in and expressive of Roman power but it was not its only expression. I have persevered with the more expansive title recognizing that it is unmanageable in a brief paper but also as a reminder that the emerging New Testament work over the last decade or so on negotiating Roman power has not restricted its attention to the imperial cult, but has focused more broadly on numerous sites of interaction between early Jesus believers and the Roman Empire.[2]

---

1. Karl Galinsky, "The Cult of the Roman Emperor: Uniter or Divider?" paper presented at the Annual Meeting of the SBL, Boston, 2008, and ch. 1 in this volume.

2. For some examples of this work, on Paul, see Richard A. Horsley, ed., *Paul and Empire: Religion and Power in Roman Imperial Society* (Harrisburg, Pa.: Trinity Press International, 1997); Richard A. Horsley, ed., *Paul and Politics: Ekklesia, Israel, Imperium, Interpretation: Essays in Honor of Krister Stendahl* (Harrisburg, Pa.: Trinity Press International, 2000); Richard A. Horsley, ed., *Paul and the Roman Imperial Order* (Harrisburg, Pa.: Trinity Press International, 2004); Peter Oakes, *Philippians: From People to Letter* (SNTSMS.110; Cambridge: Cambridge University Press, 2001); John Dominic Crossan and Jonathan L. Reed, *In Search of Paul: How Jesus's Apostle Opposed Rome's Empire with God's Kingdom* (San Francisco: HarperSanFrancisco, 2004); Neil Elliott, *The Arrogance of Nations: Reading Romans in the Shadow of Empire* (Paul in Critical Contexts; Minneapolis: Fortress Press, 2008); Davina C. Lopez, *Apostle to the Con-*

This recent work evidences some distinct differences from ways in which the interaction between the Jesus movement and the empire has been engaged by New Testament scholarship in the twentieth century. For instance much twentieth-century New Testament scholarship—with some notable exceptions such as Adolf Deissmann[3]—was simply oblivious to the empire, preferring spiritualized and individualized readings of the New Testament that rendered the empire—the empire of Rome that is—invisible or dismissing it with the woefully inappropriate term "background" or defaulting to an unsustainable universal persecution scenario as the only form of interaction. Some work has been and continues to be quite hostile to the notion that the early Christian movement had anything to do with the Roman Empire or that it adopted any role other than that of submission to Roman power as divinely ordained.[4]

More recent imperial-critical work, I think, attests a shift in the way the question of the interaction of Jesus believers with the empire is being engaged. New methods are being employed that draw eclectically not only from historical and classical studies but also from subaltern and postcolonial literatures. While oppositional binaries have been dominant in the first wave of studies, my sense

---

quered: *Reimagining Paul's Mission* (Minneapolis: Fortress, 2008); Christopher D. Stanley, *The Colonized Apostle: Paul Through Postcolonial Eyes* (Paul in Critical Contexts; Minneapolis: Fortress Press, 2011). On Matthew, see Warren Carter, *Matthew and the Margins: A Sociopolitical and Religious Reading* (The Bible & Liberation; Maryknoll, N.Y.: Orbis Books, 2000); Warren Carter, *Matthew and Empire: Initial Explorations* (Harrisburg, Penn.: Trinity Press International, 2001); John Riches and David C. Sim, eds., *The Gospel of Matthew in Its Roman Imperial Context* (JSNTSup 276; London: T&T Clark International, 2005). On Luke, see Steve Walton, "The State They Were in: Luke's View of the Roman Empire," in *Rome in the Bible and the Early Church* (ed. Peter Oakes; Carlisle, England; Grand Rapids, Mich.: Paternoster Press; Baker Academic, 2002), 11–44; Gary Gilbert, "Luke-Acts and Negotiations of Authority and Identity in the Roman World," in *The Multivalence of Biblical Texts and Theological Meanings* (ed. Christine Helmer; SBLSymS 37; Atlanta: Society of Biblical Literature, 2006), 83–104. On John, see Warren Carter, *John and Empire: Initial Explorations* (New York: T&T Clark, 2008).

3. Adolf Deissmann, *Light from the Ancient East: The New Testament Illustrated by Recently Discovered Texts of the Graeco-Roman World* (trans. Lionel R. M. Strachan; London: Hodder & Stoughton, 1910).

4. For a recent example that launches *ad hominem* attacks on scholars who see diverse negotiations, misrepresents their work, and scornfully dismisses political engagement—while failing to recognize that his own insistence on Paul and Luke's (monolithic) submissive ethic is a form of political (dis)engagement, see Seyoon Kim, *Christ and Caesar: The Gospel and the Roman Empire in the Writings of Paul and Luke* (Grand Rapids, Mich.: Eerdmans, 2008). My review: Warren Carter, review of Seyoon Kim, *Christ and Caesar: The Gospel and the Roman Empire in the writings of Paul and Luke*, RBL (2009). Online: http://www.bookreviews.org/bookdetail.asp?TitleId=6957&CodePage=6957,1856,2845. For similar concerns, see Yung Suk Kim, review of Seyoon Kim, *Christ and Caesar: The Gospel and the Roman Empire in the writings of Paul and Luke*, CBQ 71 (July 2009): 648–49.

is that now increasingly there is an emerging recognition of the complexities of interaction and negotiation with the empire, and more sophisticated analysis embracing not just opposition but various dynamics, including claims of superiority, self-protective accommodation, hybridity, reinscribing, and imitation.

This growing edge or shift in terms of the larger context of empire is consonant with many of the issues Professor Galinsky named in his paper on the cult of the Roman emperor, issues underlined by comments from several of the respondents. Professor Galinsky's paper both affirms some of what I think is already happening and identifies areas for further exploration. I appreciate so much this interdisciplinary connection; in my own journey in this work, I have benefitted greatly from the work of classicists and am happy to take this opportunity to express that appreciation.

Among some of Professor Galinsky's emphases are the following: he urges, for example, that the empire or the imperial cult not be reduced "to a single, let alone simple, matrix," that there was no such thing as a monolithic "the imperial cult," it was not "a centrally steered phenomenon." Nor is it adequate to formulate Christian engagement or negotiation of it by employing "a limited and ahistorical binary construct of 'us against them.'" It is also important to recognize, he argues, that the "cult of the emperor often was intertwined with that of other gods"; it was not the dominant overwhelming cult, and not the only cult Christians had to negotiate. Religious pluralism, including the growth of autonomous cults, was part of the cultural mix, and the challenge exists of contextualizing the Jesus movement within this evolving pluralism. He suggests that rather than opposition, competition or a "more perfect version of the same concept" might be an important dimension of the negotiation.[5]

I find this discussion very helpful and want to develop it in relation to several New Testament texts, but before I do so, two other comments. I take the point that imperial cult practices were not monolithic, and Steve Friesen's suggestion of the plural term "imperial cults" might be a helpful linguistic shift.[6] But the point needs to be noted that in some centers associated with the early Jesus movement—such as Antioch on the Orontes in Syria commonly associated with Matthew's gospel—we simply don't have good knowledge of local conditions and observances involving the imperial cult. It is of course possible that there was no observation of imperial cult practices in Antioch. I think, though, that that is unlikely in a provincial capital that was the basis for the governor of Syria (Josephus, *B.J.* 7.54–62), the base at least for some time of three or four legions

---

5. Galinsky, "Cult of the Roman Emperor," 3, 4, 12.
6. Steven J. Friesen, "Normal Religion, or, Words Fail Us: A Response to Karl Galinsky's 'The Cult of the Roman Emperor: Uniter or Divider?,'" paper presented at the Annual Meeting of the SBL, Boston, 2008 (and ch. 2 in this volume), 24.

(Josephus, *B.J.* 2.186; 3.8, 29), and the center with responsibilities for Judea and Galilee. And Josephus includes that vague reference to an elite and highly acculturated Jew by the name of Antiochus, son of a Jewish leader, who having accused other Jews of a plot to burn the city, uses troops under Roman command to compel Jews to join him in sacrificing (*B.J.* 7.46–51). It is not clear whether Antiochus urges sacrifice to city gods or to imperial gods or emperor or to all of the above, though perhaps the involvement of Roman troops might suggest at least an imperial cult connection (Josephus, *B.J.* 7.47–59). And it seems very likely after the fall of Jerusalem and with the visit to Antioch of the victorious Titus and the parade of captives and booty on its way to the Flavian triumph in Rome that nonmandatory civic celebrations of the imperial cult honoring Rome, the empire, and the imperial household abounded in the city in the cluster of typical activities associated with the imperial cult, namely sacrifices, prayers, offerings, processions, games, street parties, and distributions, thereby displaying divinely blessed Roman power.

Of course, "likely" and "typical" are not proof. But if one wants to pursue the question of how Matthew's Gospel might negotiate Roman power, including the imperial cult—as this one has wanted to do—then in the absence of specific local information, one has to engage in a somewhat generic reconstruction or model informed by a cluster of likely and typical imperial cult practices. I claim as a companion in such generic reconstruction none other than Professor Simon Price who in his interesting section on sources for discussing imperial cult observances in Asia identifies nonliterary material, numismatics, and inscriptions from 180 communities. Price also appeals to "the archetypal Greek city" and draws material from North Africa, southern Italy, and mainland Greece[7]—very generic indeed it seems.

The alternative to not resorting to a judicious reconstruction of the generic is to simply not ask the question at all, thereby removing from New Testament discourse consideration of how early Jesus followers negotiated this aspect of Roman power. Not asking the question in my view would be a regrettable loss for a discipline already far too comfortable with the notions that religion and politics have nothing to do with each other and that the New Testament is a religious book that has nothing to do with Roman power—even though its hero ended up on a Roman cross. That is, in the absence of the specific, the generic, the likely, and the typical are what we have to work with.

Moreover, I also take the point that the imperial cult was intertwined with local religious divinities and observances, as well as the point that various reli-

---

7. S. R. F. Price, *Rituals and Power: The Roman Imperial Cult in Asia Minor* (Cambridge: Cambridge University Press, 1984), 5, 20.

gious traditions and groups grew as autonomous entities separate from imperial power. Professor Barbette Spaeth illustrated these factors of religious pluralism, and of the imperial cult's pervasive embeddedness, in her paper on the imperial cult in Corinth.[8] I have noted in my book on *John and Empire* various ways in which imperial power and personnel become aligned with Artemis in the city of Ephesus, as well as with Zeus, Nike, and river gods Marnas and Claseas (associated with the two streams feeding an aqueduct dedicated by the proconsul in 92–93 C.E.).[9] The recognition of such intertwining as well as distancing—that is, a context of religious pluralism and growth of autonomous groups—requiring negotiation by Jesus believers is clear. But it does not mean, I think, that all such expressions were created equal as far as Jesus believers were concerned, that all required the same level or type of negotiation, that all have high profiles or posed the same levels of competition or threat. My hunch is that imperial claims about ordering the world in terms of power over history, the world, nations, deities, and society might be of greater interest for Jesus believers, some of whom at least embraced apocalyptic traditions with their central question, as Ernst Käsemann expressed it, "to whom does the sovereignty of the world belong?"[10] I suspect that the gods Marnas and Claseas associated with a couple of streams posed much less of an issue than the alliance of world-dominating Roma with Artemis.

Professor Galinsky's urging to complexify the analysis of the interactions between Jesus believers and the imperial cult is well stated. To assist in this task Steve Friesen appeals for better theorizing[11] and James Hanges rightly points to postcolonial discourse,[12] already a source for some work by New Testament scholars whether they identify themselves specifically as postcolonial scholars or not. I would add to this eclectic mix the immense value of James Scott's widely used work[13] along with the work of colleagues in classical studies.

---

8. Barbette Stanley Spaeth, "Imperial Cult in Roman Corinth: A Response to Karl Galinsky's 'The Cult of the Roman Emperor: Uniter or Divider?,'" paper presented at the Annual Meeting of the SBL, Boston, 2008, and ch. 6 in this volume.

9. Carter, *John and Empire*, 58–64.

10. Ernst Käsemann, "On the Subject of Primitive Christian Apocalyptic," in *New Testament Questions of Today* (Philadelphia: Fortress, 1969), 135.

11. Friesen, "Normal Religion," 25–26.

12. James Constantine Hanges, "To Complicate Encounters: A Response to Karl Galinsky's 'The Cult of the Roman Emperor: Uniter or Divider?,'" paper presented at the Annual Meeting of the SBL, Boston, 2008, and ch. 3 in this volume.

13. James C. Scott, *Domination and the Arts of Resistance: Hidden Transcripts* (New Haven, Conn.: Yale University Press, 1990). See also Richard A. Horsley, ed., *Hidden Transcripts and the Arts of Resistance: Applying the Work of James C. Scott to Jesus and Paul* (SemeiaSt 48; Atlanta: Society of Biblical Literature, 2004).

Some of the complexity to which Professor Galinsky refers is evident in a consideration of some texts of Jesus followers in Asia.[14] I will say a little about the book of Revelation to demonstrate the claim that Jesus followers did not negotiate the empire and its cult in a monolithic manner.

For example, the rebuking rhetoric of the letters in Revelation chapters 2–3 addressed to the seven congregations in Asia—"I have this against you" (2:4, 14, 20); the calls to repent (2:5, 16, 22; 3:2); various threats of judgment (2:16; 3:3, 16)—indicates that the writer of Revelation has considerable differences with some or many in the congregations over issues of cultural and cultic participation. And tensions and divisions exist within the congregations over the same matters. In 2:6, for example, the writer John commends the Ephesian congregation for hating "the works of the Nicolaitans which I also hate" (2:6) though he goes on to suggest that they have not hated enough. John's rhetoric especially targets a group of characters, "Nicolaitans," "Balaamites," and "Jezebel."[15] It draws these figures together by using their names synonymously (2:6, 14–15) and by linking them with the same activities of "eating idol-food," and "fornication," the latter probably a metaphor for participating in the ways of Gentile cultures, including idolatry[16] (2:14–15, 20; cf. Rev 17:2; 18:3, 9; Ps 106(LXX105):34–39).

John's fight is particularly with the prophetess he pejoratively nicknames "Jezebel." I will set aside the nasty references to the "synagogue of Satan" which nevertheless I think are also in the mix (2:9; 3:9). Her nickname, along with that of the Balaamites, not only links these Jesus believers with idolatry and false prophets but also employs a rhetoric of abuse to present the opponents as divinely condemned for societal interactions and practices contrary to the divine will.

John's condemnation of Jezebel's promotion of cultural and cultic participation is evident in the four identities ascribed to "Jezebel" in 2:20: a woman, prophet, teacher,[17] and deceiver/beguiler who leads "my servants" astray into

---

14. For a fuller statement of this argument, see my "Accommodating 'Jezebel' and Withdrawing John: Negotiating Empire in Revelation Then and Now," *Int* 63 (2009): 32–47.

15. Jezebel, a Phoenician, and her husband King Ahab of Israel are associated with idolatry (1 Kgs 16:31–34; 18:4, 13; 19:1–3; 21:25; 2 Kgs 9:22). Her bloody death is presented as God's will (1 Kgs 21:23–24; 2 Kgs 9:30–37). The link with Balaam seems to have less to do with Balaam's refusal to bless Israel (Num 22–24) but more to do with subsequent traditions expanding Num 25 and his involvement with the god Baal of Peor and the cultural entanglement of Israelite men marrying Midianite women (Philo, *Mos.* 1.292–304; Josephus, *A.J.* 4.126–58).

16. Also Hos 4:10–19; Ezek 16:15, 34.

17. I discuss her identity as "woman" and "deceiver/beguiler" below. Her identity as prophet is disqualified in 3:20 ("she calls herself a prophet") in the context of chapter 1's extensive legitimation for John as prophet speaking a prophecy from God (1:3, 10–13; 4:1; 22:9). Her teaching (2:20) is condemned by association with that of Balaam. In 2:13, the previous use of the verb, "Balaam taught Balak to put a stumbling block before the people of Israel so that they would eat food sacrificed to idols and practice fornication."

"fornication" (idolatry) and eating "food sacrificed to idols." No particular cult is named for these condemned activities though it is reasonable to suggest from the larger contexts of both the document as a whole and the historical contexts of the churches in the cities that are addressed that the imperial cult is at least in the mix. Plenty of evidence attests its celebration in the named cities such as Ephesus and Smyrna. And of course the document itself has Rome especially in sight. The two beasts of chapter 13 are the agents of the dragon, "the Devil and Satan" in 12:9. The empire is presented as being in the power of the devil and embodies that power, a claim made also by Matthew (Matt 4:8–9) and Luke (Luke 4:5–7). The first beast whom the "whole earth" follows and worships (13:3–4) is often interpreted to be Nero. The second beast who promotes both worship and economic activity (13:12, 16) is variously interpreted as provincial governors or imperial priesthoods or, perhaps more likely and inclusively, as local elites who actively promoted and financed imperial cult celebrations in local communities.[18] The judgments come to a head in chapter 18's lament over Babylon's fall that includes its client kings (18:9), merchants and traders (18:11), sea merchants (18:17), entertainers, and artisans (18:22).

"Jezebel," the advocate of so-called fornication/idolatry, is the first of several women figures in Revelation who are presented negatively.[19] More precisely, in chapter 17, for example, Rome is presented as the "great whore" (τῆς πόρνης τῆς μεγάλης; 17:1), a woman (17:4) condemned by God. Shared language (the Greek term "whore" evokes "Jezebel's" activity of "fornication" with the shared *pornē* stem), shared gender, and divine condemnation secure the alliance between "Jezebel" and Babylon/Rome. John opposes them as intermingled cultural entities.

By labeling her a "deceiver" John links her with three other deceivers: the "great dragon ... that ancient serpent who is called the Devil and Satan, the deceiver of the whole earth" (12:9; cf. 20:3, 10); the second beast who "deceives the inhabitants of earth telling them to make an image for the beast..." (13:14; cf. 19:20); and Babylon/Rome itself, whose "merchants were the magnates of the earth, and all nations were deceived by your sorcery" (18:23). She is thereby iden-

---

18. Steven J. Friesen, "The Beast from the Land: Revelation 13:11–18 and Social Setting," in *Reading the Book of Revelation: A Resource for Students* (ed. David L. Barr; SBLRBS 44; Atlanta: Society of Biblical Literature, 2003).

19. For discussion, Barbara R. Rossing, *The Choice Between Two Cities: Whore, Bride, and Empire in the Apocalypse* (Harrisburg, Pa.: Trinity Press International, 1999); Tina Pippin, "The Heroine and the Whore: The *Apocalypse of John* in Feminist Perspective," in *From Every People and Nation: The Book of Revelation in Intercultural Perspective* (ed. David Rhoads; Minneapolis: Fortress, 2005), 127–45; Stephen D. Moore, "Metonymies of Empire: Sexual Humiliation and Gender Masquerade in the Book of Revelation," in *Postcolonial Interventions: Essays in Honor of R. S. Sugirtharajah* (ed. Tat-siong Benny Liew; Sheffield: Sheffield Phoenix Press, 2009), 71–97.

tified with the Devil, the imperial cult and its advocates, and Rome, intertwined with three entities condemned by God.

Clearly we have here, then, evidence for a dispute among Jesus believers over negotiating the Roman world and imperial cult. There is no monolithic position vis-à-vis the empire and imperial cult.

The writer of Revelation—the canonical winner in this dispute—does not dignify Jezebel's position with reports of her rationale or engage her arguments. But it is worth pressing the question: what were her arguments? What was she teaching that advocated the view that Jesus believers could actively participate in imperial society, including in rituals that honor deities and imperial personnel? On what basis might she formulate such arguments? While the text silences her, it is possible to hear something of her voice by drawing on some other Christian writings. Debates about levels and strategies of societal participation were not restricted to Revelation and it was not self-evident to all Jesus followers that cultic involvement was off-limits (as 1 Cor 8–10, Acts 15:20, and 1 Peter 2:14–17 indicate).

One of her arguments might comprise the pragmatic and pastoral argument of self-protective survival. Since most, if not all, members of the congregations were nonelites and most likely knew some degrees of poverty at least for some periods of time,[20] it can be argued that such active participation was necessary for survival. Participation in guilds or associations, in patron-client relationships enabled socioeconomic activity.[21] Cultic activity was intertwined in socioeconomic activity in associations for instance. There were few alternative ways of sustaining a household.

Perhaps as a second argument she argued that John's strategy of distancing from cultic practices had not turned out well in that it had endangered Jesus followers. The strange reference in 2:13 to a martyr, Antipas, names the only actual "martyr" in Revelation. The text offers no explicit reason for his death that happened some time previously ("in the days of"), though it presents it very positively in contrast to the accommodating Nicolaitans. In the context of "Satan's throne" (perhaps a reference to Pergamum's temples of Athena, Zeus, Asclepius, or Augustus and Rome), Antipas had been "my faithful witness," the same title

---

20. Peter Garnsey, *Food and Society in Classical Antiquity* (Cambridge: Cambridge University Press, 1999), ix, argues that "for most people, life was a perpetual struggle for survival."

21. Philip A. Harland, "Honouring the Emperor or Assailing the Beast: Participation in Civic Life Among Associations (Jewish, Christian, and Other) in Asia Minor and the Apocalypse of John," *JSNT* 22 (2000): 99–121; Philip A. Harland, *Associations, Synagogues, and Congregations: Claiming a Place in Ancient Mediterranean Society* (Minneapolis: Fortress, 2003); Richard Bauckham, "The Economic Critique of Rome in Revelation 18," in *The Climax of Prophecy: Studies on the Book of Revelation* (Richard Bauckham; Edinburgh: T&T Clark, 1993), 338–83.

used for Jesus in relation to his death (1:5). Perhaps Antipas had been killed in some sort of confrontation over not honoring local deities and imperial personnel. While honoring was not required, it indicated civic responsibility in ensuring the good will of deities and imperial powers toward the city. A refusal to participate in civic or associational activity could create political and social resentment among those who feared inevitable civic or group reprisals from offended deities or political powers (cf. Acts 19:27). Perhaps experience had taught the leader "Jezebel" that confrontation and retreat were not good strategies and that active participation was more effective.

A third possible argument for active cultural-cultic involvement perhaps consisted of superior theological knowledge. Paul's discussion in 1 Corinthians of eating idol meat indicates that some believers in the Corinthian congregations justified the practice on the basis of their knowing that "no idol in the world really exists" and that "there is no God but one" (1 Cor 8:4). The Paul of Acts 19 is accused—in Ephesus—of teaching "that gods made with hands are not gods," a teaching that could lead equally to conflictual abandonment of the gods (as in Acts 19:21–41) or to active, nonconfrontational, societal participation, as in Corinth, based in the knowledge that they are nothing. The latter seems compatible with Jezebel's views and congregational practices in Rev 2–3. Societal and cultic participation did not compromise faithfulness; pervasive idols, images, and rituals that constituted civic and socioeconomic life held no power, danger, or reality for some followers of Jesus.

There are other possible arguments that "Jezebel" might make. She could appeal to the biblical account of Jeremiah who advised his conquered people to seek the welfare of the city.[22] She could share the claim made by Josephus that Rome was God's chosen agent.[23] Whether these are the sorts of arguments Jezebel made for active cultural and cultic participation is of course masked by Revelation. But they are reasonable guesses.

---

22. There are biblical examples of characters blessed by God who were active participants in, even agents of, imperial power, biblical examples that would sustain a lifestyle of societal participation and accommodation. Jeremiah's exhortation to the exiles in Babylon to "build houses ... plant gardens ... take wives ... [and] seek the welfare of the city ... for in its welfare you will find your welfare" offers an example (Jer 29:4–7). So too does Joseph's active participation and rise to power in Egypt (Gen 37–50).

23. In the aftermath of the destruction of Jerusalem and its temple, both the futility of rebellion and Rome's status as an empire chosen by God had become very clear at least to some such as Josephus (*B.J.* 2.360, 390–391; 5.367–368; 5.378; cf. 5.396, 412). And within the biblical tradition exist various examples of empires used by God to accomplish God's purposes, namely Assyria (Isa 10:5–11), Babylon (Jer 25:1–11), Persia and its leader Cyrus (Isa 44:28; 45:1), and Antiochus Epiphanes (2 Macc 6:12–17). Cultural participation in the benefits of empire ensures the experience of God's blessing.

The suggestion that Jezebel's teaching supports the cultural and cultic participation of Jesus believers in Asia is echoed in 1 Peter. I have previously argued—and there is not space here to rehearse the argument—that 1 Peter commands Asian Jesus believers to "honor the emperor" (1 Pet 2:17), a command that endorses cultic participation (1 Pet 2:11-17).[24] While commentators on 1 Peter regularly supply exceptive clauses to the command to argue that it means cooperate *except for* involvement in the imperial cult, and thereby default in their interpretation to resistance, there is no exceptive clause in 1 Peter and no explicit command, whether directly from "Peter" or in any of the letter's numerous Hebrew Bible citations, to avoid idolatry.[25] The letter's strategy of securing the honor or favor of "the Gentiles" and thereby minimizing conflict and silencing opponents necessitates such cultic involvement (2:12, 15). Stephen Mitchell's study of Anatolia observes an "overwhelming pressure [on Jesus believers] to conform imposed by the institutions of the city and the activities of neighbors."[26] I have also argued in my book *John and Empire* that John's Gospel addresses a context in which Jesus believers were significantly embedded culturally. John's construction of a dualistic cosmos along with various other strategies constructs a "rhetoric of distance" to change these patterns that the author regards as excessive cultural accommodation among Jesus believers.[27]

Yet to identify Jezebel's stance as exclusively "accommodationist" is too simple. Jezebel's position is more complex. If she views involvement with imperial society, including with images and idolatry, as harmless and inconsequential for faithful relationship with God, her "accommodationist" approach is nevertheless based on a profound devaluing or rejection of a fundamental dimension of imperial society. Certainly imperial claims and practices involving the honoring of the gods who sanctioned the empire and the emperors who had presided over it took these practices and images, and the claims they represented, seriously. Her embracing of this practice because idols are nothing empties them of significance, notably reframing their valency. Her so-called accommodationist position is neither simple nor pure, but marked by ambiguity and complexity.

---

24. Warren Carter, "Going All the Way? Honoring the Emperor and Sacrificing Wives and Slaves: 1 Peter 2.13–3.6," in *A Feminist Companion to the Catholic Epistles and Hebrews* (ed. Amy-Jill Levine; Feminist Companion to the New Testament and Early Christian Writings 7; London; New York: T&T Clark, 2004), 14–33.

25. Nor can 1 Pet 4:3 be appealed to with its reference to "wanton" or "lawless" idolatries. The item appears at the end of a list that has condemned *immoderate or excessive behaviors* typical of Gentiles. Sex and wine are not prohibited per se, but only in the excessive expressions of "licentiousness, passions, drunkenness, revels, and carousing."

26. Stephen Mitchell, *The Celts in Anatolia and the Impact of Roman Rule* (vol. 1 of *Anatolia: Land, Men, and Gods in Asia Minor*; Oxford: Clarendon, 1993), 10.

27. Carter, *John and Empire*.

But nor is John's commonly identified "oppositional" position unambiguous. Along with its obvious opposition,[28] we should also note that Revelation negotiates empire and cult by imitating imperial ways, and reinscribing and sanctioning them as the ways of God. The destiny of the nations provides one example. In Augustus's *Res Gestae* there is only one way—the submission of the nations—but there are different paths, namely "spare or destroy." Augustus boasts of waging war "on land and on sea ... throughout the whole world" though "I spared all citizens who asked for forgiveness" (10). This one imperial goal of the submission of the nations can be accomplished by different strategies: "spare or destroy."

The submission of the nations is graphically presented, for example, in terms of dominant masculinity and submissive femininity in the approach to the imperial temple in Aphrodisias. A series of statues personifies the conquered nations as female figures, with statues depicting Claudius violently overcoming the seminaked Britannia and Nero violently overcoming the seminaked Armenia. In Revelation, the final all-encompassing cosmic scenario involves the cosmic Christ who will "strike down the nations, and he will rule them with a rod of iron" (19:15), and at 21:9 the nations led astray by Satan are consumed by fire that "came down from heaven." Yet in the new Jerusalem "the kings of the earth bring their glory into it" (21:24), an image of tributary surrender in accord with 15:4 and a Hebrew Bible tradition of the conversion—read submission—of the nations (Isa 2:1–4; Ezek 16:52–63; Mic 4:1–4). Opposition yes, but also reinscribing, imitation, cosmic elevation, divinizing of imperial ways.

Or again, the heavenly worship scenes of chapters 4–5 disqualify all and any worship of other deities and emperor—the imperial cult—since only God is worthy to receive worship: "you are worthy our Lord and God to receive glory and honor and power for you created all things" (4:11). And in chapter 5 the lamb is also the one worthy of worship "to receive power and wealth and wisdom and might and honor and glory and blessing" (5:11), worship interestingly offered by "every creature in heaven and on earth and under the earth and in the sea." These scenes of totalizing and idealized worship contrast and disqualify any other worship but they are, if David Aune is correct, a projection of Roman imperial court ceremonial.[29] So for example the twenty-four elders prostrate themselves with *proskynēsis*, singing hymns and shouting ascriptions of praise (4:4, 10–11), behaviors well attested from imperial court ceremonial. Augustus (*Res gest. divi Aug.* 10) declares that "my name was included in the Salian hymn," the Salii comprising twelve priests who honored the god Mars (cf. Dio Cassius 51.20.1).

---

28. For John's arguments against active cultural participation, Carter, "Accommodating 'Jezebel,'" 39–45.

29. David E. Aune, "The Influence of Roman Imperial Court Ceremonial on the Apocalypse of John," *BR* 28 (1983): 5–26.

The Senate according to Dio Cassius prostrated itself before the empty throne of Gaius Caligula with hymns and prayers (59.24.5). Tacitus notes that the Augustani shouted ascriptions of praise and divinity to Nero (*Ann.* 14.15). That is, John is deeply indebted to these imperial practices which he imitates and reinscribes even while he opposes them and actively constructs an alternative, a superior alternative, to them.

And then there is the failure of John to translate his verbal protest into a practical program. This failure is especially evident in the vagueness of John's command in 18:4 to his followers in the midst of the fall of Babylon to "come out from her." The language of course turns the sexual image of fornication into an exhortation to cultural withdrawal. But what exactly does he mean by the command to "come out from her?" What precisely does he want his readers to do—culturally, economically? What practices does he want them now to adopt to redefine their cultural interaction in terms of cultural distance? What comprises the boycott for which he calls? The very vagueness of the command is significant. He has much rhetoric, much anger, much passion, much vision, but finally, ultimately, he does not have a specific program. He has, it seems, not taken his own argument seriously enough to elaborate his alternative, to develop specifics, to formulate a program. The rhetorical effect of this lack of an explicit and specific program is by default accommodation.

There is clearly a complex situation of diverse practices and debate among Jesus believers in these cities of Asia over the issue of cultural and cultic participation. Neither John's nor Jezebel's positions are "pure"; both are complex and ambiguous.

New Testament scholars are deeply indebted to classicists such as Professor Galinsky in pursuing this investigation of how early Jesus believers sought to negotiate this embedded and entangled "web of power" we call the imperial cult. I note that classicists regularly observe that our sources for imperial cult practices are invariably elite sources, from those who have the resources and status to monumentalize themselves, or the resources and status to be monumentalized by others.[30] I also note that mostly classicists ignore the New Testament texts, seldom utilizing them as sources for understanding the imperial cult. Perhaps by attending to these New Testament texts as acts of imperial negotiation and as texts emanating from some of the empire's little people as I have done in these brief comments, we—both New Testament scholars and classicists—might be able to glimpse further some of the incredibly complex and diverse ways that nonelites negotiated both the imperial cult and the empire that it celebrated.

---

30. Price, *Rituals and Power*, 6.

Bibliography

Aune, David E. "The Influence of Roman Imperial Court Ceremonial on the Apocalypse of John." *Biblical Research* 28 (1983): 5–26.
Bauckham, Richard. "The Economic Critique of Rome in Revelation 18." Pages 338–83 in *The Climax of Prophecy: Studies on the Book of Revelation*. Richard Bauckham. Edinburgh: T&T Clark, 1993.
Carter, Warren. "Accommodating 'Jezebel' and Withdrawing John: Negotiating Empire in Revelation Then and Now." *Interpretation* 63 (2009): 32–47.
———. "Going All the Way? Honoring the Emperor and Sacrificing Wives and Slaves: 1 Peter 2.13–3.6." Pages 14–33 in *A Feminist Companion to the Catholic Epistles and Hebrews*. Edited by Amy-Jill Levine. Feminist Companion to the New Testament and Early Christian Writings 7. London; New York: T&T Clark, 2004.
———. *John and Empire: Initial Explorations*. New York: T&T Clark, 2008.
———. *Matthew and Empire: Initial Explorations*. Harrisburg, Penn.: Trinity Press International, 2001.
———. *Matthew and the Margins: A Sociopolitical and Religious Reading*. The Bible & Liberation. Maryknoll, N.Y.: Orbis, 2000.
———. Review of Seyoon Kim, *Christ and Caesar: The Gospel and the Roman Empire in the Writings of Paul and Luke*. *Review of Biblical Literature* (2009).
Crossan, John Dominic, and Jonathan L. Reed. *In Search of Paul: How Jesus's Apostle Opposed Rome's Empire with God's Kingdom*. San Francisco: HarperSanFrancisco, 2004.
Deissmann, Adolf. *Light from the Ancient East: The New Testament Illustrated by Recently Discovered Texts of the Graeco-Roman World*. Translated by Lionel R. M. Strachan. London: Hodder & Stoughton, 1910.
Elliott, Neil. *The Arrogance of Nations: Reading Romans in the Shadow of Empire*. Paul in Critical Contexts. Minneapolis: Fortress Press, 2008.
Friesen, Steven J. "The Beast from the Land: Revelation 13:11–18 and Social Setting." Pages 49–64 in *Reading the Book of Revelation: A Resource for Students*. Edited by David L. Barr. Society of Biblical Literature Resources for Biblical Study 44. Atlanta: Society of Biblical Literature, 2003.
———. "Normal Religion, or, Words Fail Us: A Response to Karl Galinsky's 'The Cult of the Roman Emperor: Uniter or Divider?'." Paper presented at the Annual Meeting of the SBL, Boston, 2008, and ch. 2 in this volume.
Galinsky, Karl. "The Cult of the Roman Emperor: Uniter or Divider?" Paper presented at the Annual Meeting of the SBL, Boston, 2008, and ch. 1 in this volume.
Garnsey, Peter. *Food and Society in Classical Antiquity*. Cambridge: Cambridge University Press, 1999.
Gilbert, Gary. "Luke-Acts and Negotiations of Authority and Identity in the Roman World." Pages 83–104 in *The Multivalence of Biblical Texts and Theological Meanings*. Edited by Christine Helmer. Society of Biblical Literature Symposium Series 37. Atlanta: Society of Biblical Literature, 2006.
Hanges, James Constantine. "To Complicate Encounters: A Response to Karl Galinsky's 'The Cult of the Roman Emperor: Uniter or Divider?'." Paper presented at the Annual Meeting of the SBL, Boston, 2008, and ch. 3 in this volume.

Harland, Philip A. *Associations, Synagogues, and Congregations: Claiming a Place in Ancient Mediterranean Society.* Minneapolis: Fortress, 2003.

———. "Honouring the Emperor or Assailing the Beast: Participation in Civic Life Among Associations (Jewish, Christian, and Other) in Asia Minor and the Apocalypse of John." *Journal for the Study of the New Testament* 22 (2000): 99–121.

Horsley, Richard A., ed. *Hidden Transcripts and the Arts of Resistance: Applying the Work of James C. Scott to Jesus and Paul.* Semeia Studies 48. Atlanta: Society of Biblical Literature, 2004.

———, ed. *Paul and Empire: Religion and Power in Roman Imperial Society.* Harrisburg, Pa.: Trinity Press International, 1997.

———, ed. *Paul and Politics: Ekklesia, Israel, Imperium, Interpretation: Essays in Honor of Krister Stendahl.* Harrisburg, Pa.: Trinity Press International, 2000.

———, ed. *Paul and the Roman Imperial Order.* Harrisburg, Pa.: Trinity Press International, 2004.

Käsemann, Ernst. "On the Subject of Primitive Christian Apocalyptic." Pages 108–37 in *New Testament Questions of Today.* Philadelphia: Fortress, 1969.

Kim, Seyoon. *Christ and Caesar: The Gospel and the Roman Empire in the Writings of Paul and Luke.* Grand Rapids, Mich.: Eerdmans, 2008.

Kim, Yung Suk. Review of Seyoon Kim, *Christ and Caesar: The Gospel and the Roman Empire in the Writings of Paul and Luke. Catholic Biblical Quarterly* 71 (2009): 648–49.

Lopez, Davina C. *Apostle to the Conquered: Reimagining Paul's Mission.* Minneapolis: Fortress, 2008.

Mitchell, Stephen. *The Celts in Anatolia & the Impact of Roman Rule.* Vol. 1 of *Anatolia: Land, Men, and Gods in Asia Minor.* Oxford: Clarendon, 1993.

Moore, Stephen D. "Metonymies of Empire: Sexual Humiliation and Gender Masquerade in the Book of Revelation." Pages 71–97 in *Postcolonial Interventions: Essays in Honor of R. S. Sugirtharajah.* Edited by Tat-siong Benny Liew. Sheffield: Sheffield Phoenix, 2009.

Oakes, Peter. *Philippians: From People to Letter.* Society for New Testament Studies Monograph Series 110. Cambridge: Cambridge University Press, 2001.

Pippin, Tina. "The Heroine and the Whore: The *Apocalypse of John* in Feminist Perspective." Pages 127–45 in *From Every People and Nation: The Book of Revelation in Intercultural Perspective.* Edited by David Rhoads. Minneapolis: Fortress, 2005.

Price, S. R. F. *Rituals and Power: The Roman Imperial Cult in Asia Minor.* Cambridge: Cambridge University Press, 1984.

Riches, John, and David C. Sim, eds. *The Gospel of Matthew in Its Roman Imperial Context.* Journal for the Study of the New Testament: Supplement Series 276. London: T&T Clark, 2005.

Rossing, Barbara R. *The Choice Between Two Cities: Whore, Bride, and Empire in the Apocalypse.* Harrisburg, Pa.: Trinity Press International, 1999.

Scott, James C. *Domination and the Arts of Resistance: Hidden Transcripts.* New Haven, Conn.: Yale University Press, 1990.

Spaeth, Barbette Stanley. "Imperial Cult in Roman Corinth: A Response to Karl Galinsky's 'The Cult of the Roman Emperor: Uniter or Divider?'" Paper presented at the Annual Meeting of the SBL, Boston, 2008, and ch. 6 in this volume.

Stanley, Christopher D. *The Colonized Apostle: Paul Through Postcolonial Eyes.* Paul in

Critical Contexts. Minneapolis: Fortress Press, 2011.

Walton, Steve. "The State They Were in: Luke's View of the Roman Empire." Pages 11–44 in *Rome in the Bible and the Early Church*. Edited by Peter Oakes. Carlisle, England; Grand Rapids, Mich.: Paternoster Press; Baker Academic, 2002.

Chapter 11
The Emperor Cult and Christian Iconography

Robin M. Jensen

A 2007 BBC television special, *Art of Eternity: Painting Paradise,* examined the emergence and style of Christian art in late antiquity. In one segment, focused on the different ways Christ was depicted, host Andrew Graham-Dixon visits the Christian catacombs of Rome and points to a painting of Jesus in the guise of the Good Shepherd (fig. 1).

In the next scene, Graham-Dixon alights from his Vespa at the Arch of Constantine and gestures toward the relief that shows the victorious Christian emperor distributing largesse to the city's citizens. Finally, he turns up at the fourth-century imperial mausoleum of Sta. Constanza. Gazing at a mosaic depiction of Christ seated on the orb of the universe and giving the keys of the kingdom to St. Peter (fig. 2), Graham-Dixon comments, "It's as if we are a world away from that image of Christ in the catacombs, where he is depicted as a common shepherd. Now he is shown as a king—robed in divine and regal vestments."[1]

This transition, he further asserts, reflects the impact of the emperor's conversion to Christianity: dividing its adherents into two distinct camps. On one side were those who adhered to a religion that preached personal humility and urged its followers to care for the poor and the meek. Members of the other camp sought a savior who exuded power and majesty.

Such analysis reflects the well-established belief that the themes of "post pacem" Christian art visually manifest a significant shift in the faith's social location and values: from a religion of and for the poor and the meek to an established cult of and for the rich and the mighty. Commentators like our BBC host unquestioningly assume that the motifs that adorned fourth-century Christian monuments were designed for the express purpose of advancing the political or imperialist goals of those who commissioned (and funded) them. In a broader context, this thesis presupposes the continuance of the emperor cult through

---

1. Quoted from *Art of Eternity: Painting Paradise* (United Kingdom: BBC, 2007).

Fig. 1. The Good Shepherd, from the Catacomb of Callixtus, Crypt of Lucina, mid-third century C.E., Rome. *Photo credit: Estelle Brettman, copyright International Catacomb Society.*

and beyond the conversion of the emperor to Christianity, insinuating itself into the very fabric of the faith as it became the official religion of the empire. With reference to Karl Galinsky's opening essay of this volume, a common historical assessment judges the mid-fourth century to be a watershed moment when the church ceased to be anti-imperial or anticolonial and instead became a "collaborator" with "evil empire."[2] No longer countercultural, Christianity entered a kind of "Babylonian captivity" that underwrote and adapted the Roman imperial cult that began during the Augustan era. This captivity arguably continued for another twelve hundred years, through the Byzantine and medieval theories of a divinely sanctioned *imperium*.

Theoretically, as in that BBC special, one of the most visible manifestations of this captivity is in the artworks of the time, in particular those that portray Christ as enthroned, supposedly equating him with the fourth-century Roman emperor and, correspondingly, the human emperor with God. Ergo, Christian art reveals the church's capitulation to the earlier "pagan" imperial cult. Given that

---

2. See Karl Galinsky, "The Cult of the Roman Emperor: Uniter or Divider?" paper presented at the Annual Meeting of the SBL, Boston, 2008 (and ch. 1 in this volume), 2.

Fig. 2. Apse mosaic from the Mausoleum of Sta. Contanza, mid-fourth century C.E., Rome. *Photo credit: Robin M. Jensen (author).*

the artworks in question were monumental buildings or luxury items made for wealthy patrons, one might conclude that the impetus for this starts from the elite classes, if not from the imperial household itself. Of course, given the obvious benefits of imperial patronage, many upper-level church bureaucrats also could have been implicated in a widespread movement to imbue Christian doctrine and liturgy—as well as art—with imperially sanctioned content.

Thus, it might appear that the emperor (or, more likely, his agents) consciously guided an artistic symbolization of divine endorsement (or mutual admiration). Such a program of artistic propaganda served the purposes of a ruler who needed to establish his authority and legitimate his right to rule. Thus, a religion once preoccupied with personal salvation and the pursuit of humanitarian virtues became, in the fourth century, a modified version of the "imperial cult."[3]

In his controversial 1993 book *The Clash of Gods: A Reinterpretation of Early Christian Art*, Thomas Mathews challenges this conventional view of fourth-century art as "a self-confirming system" of "interlocking arguments about imperial

---

3. Perhaps the most well known early proponent of this assessment is André Grabar, *L'empereur dans l'art byzantine* (Strasbourg: Faculté des letters de l'université de Strasbourg, 1936). Other examples are discussed below.

precedents and imperial ideology."[4] In brief, Mathews's monograph attacks the analyses of mid-twentieth-century art historians who initially formulated the theory that fourth-century Christian art was derived from imperial prototypes. Instead he sees a "clash" of images, in which the Christian god supplanted the old Roman pantheon. Mathews claims that Christ was not, therefore, presented in the guise of the emperor, but modeled after the iconography of the traditional Roman gods. As such, he was a competitor with Jupiter or Apollo. Moreover, Mathews argues that Christ's image was not only *not* imperial, but directly challenges—or even opposes—imperial authority. Jesus takes on the attributes of the philosopher-teacher, or even a magician and, through his miracles, "shows himself to be a god of the 'little man,' a genuine 'grass-roots' god."[5] Thus, for Mathews, Jesus is a "caring god" who would walk among his people, being seen by them and offering them comfort, healing, and even magic through his "warm and life-giving hands."[6] In this way Mathews's work both dismisses the so-called imperialist interpretation of the art and replaces it with something that looks more like Graham-Dixon's Good Shepherd figure.

Reviews of Mathews's book were mixed, some very positive, others quite critical. Nevertheless, most generally agree that the question needs to be revisited and that Mathews has started an important discussion.[7] For example, Frederick Norris, an historian of early Christianity, characterizes Mathews's argument as compelling insofar as it "fits a growing perception of the early church's resistance to state control."[8] Art historian Dale Kinney acknowledges that "tendentiousness is a fact of scholarship," but notes the especially "agonistic relationship" of Mathews to previous generations of art historians, whom he wishes to depose, like his Jesus dethrones Jupiter.[9] Peter Brown takes on the larger socio-political context of the debate, asserting that "without a sense of the realities of life lived in a profoundly hierarchical society, claims for the emergence of a new, "grass-roots" god' complete with an appropriate array of sensitive or 'caring' images

---

4. Thomas F. Mathews, *The Clash of Gods: A Reinterpretation of Early Christian Art* (Princeton, N.J.: Princeton University Press, 1993), 16.

5. Ibid., 92.

6. Ibid.

7. In addition to those cited below, see reviews by W. Eugene Kleinbauer, *Spec* 70 (1995): 937–41; Annabel Wharton, *AHR* 100 (1995): 1518–19; W. H. C. Frend, *JEH* 46 (1995): 490–91; and Sister Charles Murray, *JTS* 47 (1996): 703–5.

8. Frederick W. Norris, review of Thomas F. Mathews, *The Clash of Gods: A Reinterpretation of Early Christian Art*, *CH* 64 (1995): 251–52.

9. Dale Kinney, review of Thomas F. Mathews, *The Clash of Gods: A Reinterpretation of Early Christian Art*, *Studies in Iconography* 16 (1994): 327–42.

must forever tremble on the brink of sentimentality."[10] Brown finishes his review, however, with this plea: "Let us hope that the discussion will continue with all the erudition and the intellectual courtesy which a topic of such importance ... deserves to receive."[11]

Despite this call for more discussion, the established view of fourth-century Christian art as thoroughly imperial and supportive of imperial values remains a standard assumption of contemporary art-historical scholarship, while the yearning for the god of the "little man" is generally satisfied by pre-Constantinian exemplars. For example, paralleling the 2007 BBC program, Johannes Deckers, an eminent art historian, recently described the third-century image of Christ as that of a physician or "unassuming philosopher."[12] As such, Deckers observes, "he puts into practice and demonstrates the truth and power of brotherly love and nonviolence." Furthermore, as these works of caretaking are not those of an emperor, according to Deckers, Jesus needs neither nimbus nor scepter, and certainly no gem-studded throne. In the pre-Constantinian era, Deckers insists, it would have "struck the Christian faithful as blasphemous for the emperor to base his authority on Christ after receiving his help in killing his enemies." How, then, he asks, did such an "unprecedented imperialization of the image of Christ and of Christian churches—so contrary to the faith's doctrines and practices of peace and modesty—continue after the reign of Constantine?"[13]

The answer, Deckers concludes, is based on the traditional relationship between the Roman emperors and the gods. So long as the gods granted the emperors their military victories, they gave them divine mandate to rule and a claim to absolute power. Constantine had to suppress the image of Christ as a teacher or peace bringer, since it was "hardly appropriate as a representation of the omnipotent deity to whom a Roman emperor owed his triumphs."[14]

This assessment resonates with other appraisals of fourth-century Christianity as repudiating its original and superior virtues (e.g., egalitarian, pacifist, charity, and justice-seeking principles) while undergoing a nearly wholesale capitulation to the values of the empire, the upper classes, and the court. This narrative of decline and corruption often draws its evidence from the art and architecture of the period, the largest percentage of which comes from Rome and

---

10. Peter Brown, review of Thomas F. Mathews, *The Clash of Gods: A Reinterpretation of Early Christian Art*, *ABull* 77 (1995): 499–502.
11. Ibid., 499–502.
12. Johannes G. Deckers, "Constantine the Great and Early Christian Art," in *Picturing the Bible: The Earliest Christian Art* (ed. Jeffrey Spier; New Haven, Conn.: Yale University Press, 2007), 107.
13. Ibid.
14. Ibid.

its environs. Here, imperially influenced imagery, presumably unthinkable in an earlier era when Christians were targets of persecution, reflects the ideology of the ruling powers and advances their purposes.[15] Such analyses are tinged with a kind of nostalgia for a time when Christianity was a religion of the poor and the marginalized and the faithful were untainted by power politics or colonial aspirations. Whether such a time ever existed is probably beyond the point, since its mythic attraction is so powerful.

Fourth-century Christian (and Roman) art was undoubtedly influenced by imperial iconographic motifs, and its political context and possible significance is undeniable. Furthermore, Jesus is not depicted as enthroned until the era just after Constantine. Yet, I believe that seeing this art as being captive merely to imperial purpose or bearing only political meaning is absurdly reductionistic. I thus wish to suggest a set of slightly different interpretations of the extant objects, offering an alternative perspective on the significance of such borrowing at that time and place, while simultaneously accounting for a multiplicity of meanings that must have varied according to viewer and context. This diversity of meanings is exactly what Mathews wishes to emphasize in his work. The image of an enthroned Jesus is polysemic. It would have projected different messages, some perhaps even somewhat contradictory ones. Such multivalence is clear, as well, in Karl Galinsky's assertion that the imperial cult is better described as a culturally variegated "umbrella phenomenon."[16]

This alternative appraisal also reflects my judgment that many analyses of this iconography are too little cognizant of other iconographic parallels, contemporary church teachings, and the ways that emerging church institutions and their leaders understood their newly evolving relationship to a quasi-secular power structure. In this essay, I wish to consider a group of Roman sarcophagi that are regularly offered as prime examples of imperially determined post-Constantinian Christian monuments, in order to see how consideration of some of these other dynamics might affect their interpretations. These monuments are often grouped under the descriptive category "Passion Sarcophagi," because they include motifs that refer to the narrative of Christ's passion.

Most of these sarcophagi are, today, in the Vatican Museum, having been discovered in one of the ancient cemeteries outside the walls of Rome. They date from the mid- to late fourth century and their consistent and unifying motif is their central image: a cross whose crossbar supports a christogram within a wreath and serves as the perch for two doves (fig. 3).

---

15. This argument is made by Geir Hellemo, *Adventus Domini: Eschatological Thought in 4th-Century Apses and Cateches* (VCSup 5; Leiden: Brill, 1989), xvii.
16. See above, Galinsky, "Cult of the Roman Emperor," 3.

Fig. 3. Passion sarcophagus, ca. 340 C.E., Rome. Now in the Museo Pio Cristiano, Vatican Museums. *Photo credit: Vanni/Art Resource, New York.*

Fig. 4. Sarcophagus with central christogram mounted on a cross, ca. 340–350 C.E., Rome. Now in the Museo Pio Cristiano, Vatican Museums. *Photo credit: Alinari/Art Resource, New York.*

In one instance, an eagle holds the wreath in its beak, his wings spread to create the arch of the heavens (indicated by the busts of the sun and moon, Sol and Luna). Beneath the cross sit two soldiers resting on their shields, presumably the ones posted to keep guard (Matt 27:36).

This symbol identifies these monuments as Passion Sarcophagi, although they often (but not always) include scenes from the Passion Narrative itself. For example, one includes depictions of Simon carrying Christ's cross, Jesus being crowned by a Roman soldier, and Jesus before Pilate (fig. 3) while another features narratives from the Old Testament (Cain and Abel presenting their gifts to God and Job with his wife) along with the arrests of Peter and Paul (fig. 4).

A third shows a procession of apostles bearing wreaths or crowns. The central image here is the same: a wreathed christogram set on top of a cross.

In an article that supplemented the catalogue for New York's Metropolitan Museum of Art 1977–78 exhibition, *The Age of Spirituality,* Beat Brenk characterized these Passion Sarcophagi as having been strongly influenced by Roman triumphal art. According to Brenk, fourth-century theologians provided the impetus for this, as they more and more frequently referred to Christ as a *basileus* ("king"). Thus, Brenk concludes, Christian teaching came to be understood as a *basilikos nomos* ("imperial law").[17] Among the motifs that Brenk saw as most reflecting this imperial influence included the central christogram, Christ's crowning, and the processing apostles carrying their wreaths. He specifically compares the first of these three motifs to the Constantinian *labarum*, a military trophy that symbolically proclaimed one's victory over an enemy: "Because of its outward appearance, the cross presented a certain similarity to the *tropaeum*, the pagan victory sign ... so it was, then, that on the sarcophagi with Passion scenes, the pagan *tropaeum* became combined with the *labarum* and refashioned to form the actual cross, while the *chi rho* was refashioned into a crown of laurels."[18]

Although undoubtedly a Constantinian symbol, the *labarum* as a cross type had been noted by earlier Christians, among them Minucius Felix (ca. 300) who specifically compares Roman military ensigns, standards, and banners to Christian crosses: "Your trophies of victory copy not merely the appearance of a simple cross, but that of a man fastened to it as well."[19] Moreover, the *chi rho* sign most likely predated Constantine. Larry Hurtado has argued that, as early as the second century, Christians often used the monogram as a form of the name of Christ.[20]

This christogram-on-cross motif occupies the central niche of all these sarcophagi. This dominant image, although certainly a reference to Christ's passion, unquestionably bears some likeness to the military standard (*labarum* or *vexillum*) that Constantine carried into battle and then displayed as a trophy in commemoration of his victory. The *labarum*'s design was patterned after a vision Constantine reportedly received prior to his battle with Maxentius at the Milvian Bridge in 312. Recounted in two versions, one by Lactantius and the other by Eusebius, the symbol includes Christ's monogram: the Greek letters *chi* and *rho*.[21] According to Lactantius, Constantine received a divine instruction to place this figure on the shields of his soldiers. Eusebius describes a slightly different object. In this alternate version, Christ appeared to Constantine in a dream and told him to make his standard in the form of a cross. This, Eusebius explains, consisted of a long spear fixed with a transverse bar topped with a wreath encircling the *chi rho* monogram. A richly embroidered banner was suspended from the crossbar displaying portraits of the emperor and his children. Eusebius adds that the emperor

---

17. Beat Brenk, "The Imperial Heritage of Early Christian Art," in *Age of Spirituatlity: A Symposium* (ed. Kurt Weitzmann; New York: Metropolitan Museum of Art, 1977), 43.

18. Ibid.

19. Marcus Minucius Felix, *The Octavius of Marcus Minucius Felix* (trans. G. W. Clarke; ACW 39; New York: Newman Press, 1974), 107.

20. Larry W. Hurtado, *The Earliest Christian Artifacts: Manuscripts and Christian Origins* (Grand Rapids, Mich.: Eerdmans, 2006), 137–39.

21. See Lactantius, *Mort.* 44.5–6; Eusebius, *Vit. Const.* 1.28–31.

Fig. 5. Coin (*nummus*) of Constantine I, 319–320 C.E. *Photo courtesy of the American Numismatic Society.*

used this object constantly as a talisman against enemies and commanded that it be carried at the head of all his armies.[22]

According to Eusebius whenever this symbol appeared in battle, the enemy fled. Seeing its power, the emperor gave orders that the "salutary trophy" should be moved in to help any forces that were particularly hard-pressed. Acting like a "triumphant charm," it inspired, refreshed, and encouraged the combatants. Immediate victory was the result.[23] Whatever actually took place with regard to this sign, Constantine led his troops to victory over Maxentius's army and, based on the appearance of the *chi rho* on subsequent monuments (including coins), it seems likely that Constantine's soldiers carried the Christian monogram or symbol on their military standards or armor.[24]

One especially interesting coin reverse motif (dated to the 320s) shows a military standard similar to the one Eusebius describes. A *chi rho* appears above the crossbar and, below, the banner bears three portrait busts (presumably of Constantine and his two sons). The standard pierces a snake.[25] The legend reads *SPES PUBLICA* (the "public hope"—fig. 5).

Although both image and legend might refer to Constantine's defeat of Licinius in 324 (the victory that allowed him to become sole ruler), it also may refer to supernatural enemies. Its iconographic parallels to a painting, described by Eusebius, that adorned the public entrance to the new imperial residence in Constantinople, are very suggestive. This painting supposedly included a portrait of the emperor and his children beneath the "salutary sign" and above the scene of a dragon, "the secret adversary of the human race" (e.g., Satan), being speared by a lance and cast into the sea.[26]

---

22. Eusebius, *Vit. Const.* 1.31.
23. Eusebius, *Vit. Const.* 2.8; 2.16.
24. On Constantine coinage see the now classic essay of Patrick M. Bruun, "The Christian Signs on the Coins of Constantine," *Arctos* 3 (1962): 5–35, or a more recent treatment by Carlos F. Noreña, "The Communication of the Emperor's Virtues," *JRS* 91 (2001): 146–68.
25. See Patrick M. Bruun, *Constantine and Licinius A.D. 313–337* (ed. C. H. V. Sutherland and R. A. G. Carson; vol. 7 of *The Roman Imperial Coinage*; London: Spink & Son, 1966), 572, no. 19.
26. Eusebius, *Vit. Const.* 3.3. See also Robert Grigg, "Constantine the Great and the Cult Without Images," *Viator* 8 (1977): 1–32. A similar motif appears on certain redware lamps from North Africa, which show Christ spearing a serpent with a long shafted cross-like object.

In the next decades, the christogram appeared on the coins of other Roman emperors. For example, the usurpers Magnentius (350–53) and Decentius (his brother—proclaimed Caesar in late 351) both produced coins with *chi rho* symbols in the 350s. These christogram reverses bear no obvious allusion to military battles or conquests, but their religious purpose is also debatable. Magnentius may not even have been a Christian, but merely borrowed the type because he wished to be associated with key symbols of Constantinian dynasty. Or it may have become simply an important talisman, symbolically associating the ruler with some general divine power or favor. Following the example of Galerius, he did not need to be a Christian himself to benefit from the patronage of the Christian god or from the prayers of Christians for the well-being of the ruler.[27]

Whatever the case, a *chi rho* on a coin reverse probably does not tell us much about any particular emperor's certain intention to align himself with the Christian god. Given the symbol's appearance on helmets, shields, and standards, at this early stage Constantine likely considered Christ as a military patron whose favor brought him victory on the battlefield. It seems reasonable to suppose that other claimants to the purple would have desired the same.

Nevertheless, the christogram also appears in a variety of other contexts in the early to mid-fourth century, most of them lacking any overt associations with Constantine, battle gear, or military trophies. The most common fourth-century contexts for the *chi rho* are, in fact, funeral inscriptions, tomb monuments, and Christian wall paintings (fig. 6).

In many of these examples, the christogram appears with one or two doves, an iconographic parallel to the doves on the crossbars of the Passion Sarcophagi trophies (figs. 3 and 4). In these instances, the dove appears to symbolize peace (in particular the peace of the soul at rest), especially when the words "*in pace*" are included.[28] Altogether, the juxtaposition of Christ's monogram within a laurel wreath, doves, and a funeral epitaph suggests the invocation of the divine name (or presence) over the remains of the faithful departed. The victory is no longer an earthly, but a heavenly and eschatological one. This theme is already present in the Epistle to the Colossians: "God made you alive together with him ... He disarmed the rulers and authorities and made a public example of them,

---

27. They may have striven for this identification even though in revolt against both Constantius. J. P. C. Kent, *The Family of Constantine I (A.D. 337–364)* (ed. C. H. V. Sutherland and R. A. G. Carson; vol. 8 of *The Roman Imperial Coinage*; London: Spink & Son, 1981), 123, no. 34 (30A) and 188, no. 154. On Galerius, see above, Galinsky, "Cult of the Roman Emperor," 14.

28. See Jerome, *Epist.* 69.6, where the dove also represents the Holy Spirit and brings tidings of peace to Noah, Christ (at his baptism), and, when carrying an olive branch, to the whole world.

Fig. 6. Christian funerary epitaph, mid-fourth century C.E., Rome (Basilica of San Lorenzo fuori le mura). *Photo credit: Robin M. Jensen (author).*

triumphing over them in [the cross]" (2:15). Later, the fourth-century poet Prudentius expresses this idea explicitly:

> Dic tropaeum passionis, dic trumphalem crucem,
> Pange vexillum notatis quod refulget frontibus.
>
> Tell of the trophy of the passion, of the triumph of the cross,
> Sing of the shining banner, marked on our foreheads.[29]

In addition to the christogram and the doves, one other crucial detail of this central panel is the pair of sleeping Roman soldiers beneath the cross (cf. fig. 3). These figures also have parallels in Roman imperial military iconography, specifically the depiction of captive peoples, often shown bound and seated beneath the *labarum* on Constantinian coinage (fig. 7).

Here the similarity between the captives' posture—and their position relative to the *labarum*—clearly demonstrates the adaption of a military motif. Yet, the fact that the Roman soldiers are neither bound nor presented as barbarians merits consideration. They are not depicted as the "enemy." One sleeps on his shield, while the other gazes up at the cross. He may be meant to be the Roman centurion who proclaimed, "surely this man was God's son" (Matt 27:54). If this is the case, the image is transformed from a symbol of conquest to a sign of (Roman) conversion.

Brenk notes a second imperial motif in the Passion Sarcophagi: the crowning of Christ. This image appears in only one of the sarcophagi, in a niche just to the left of the central christogram (cf. fig. 3). Here a Roman soldier (in greaves, helmet, short tunic, and *chlamys*) holds a wreath over Christ's head but not one

---

29. Prudentius, *Cath.* 9.84–85, CSEL 61.54, trans. author.

Fig. 7. Coin (*nummus*) of Constantine I, 327–328 C.E.
Photo courtesy of the American Numismatic Society.

made of thorns. Rather, this is a laurel crown that is studded with gems. Thus it no longer alludes to Christ's mockery but is, instead, an emblem of honor. Laurel crowns were awarded to conquering generals and, later, a decoration generally reserved to emperors. In Roman iconography, the goddess Victory usually holds the crown just above the head of a victorious general or emperor. This was a widespread and popular motif dating from even before the time of Augustus, and was an integral part of Roman triumph ceremonies. Sol Invictus, however, commonly does the honors on Constantine's coinage instead of the winged figure of Victory.

Johannes Deckers specifically identifies this particular sarcophagus scene (of the Roman soldier crowning Jesus) as an imperial allusion: "The scene thus recalls the central rite in the elevation of a Roman emperor, in which an officer crowns the successor with a victory wreath in view of his army."[30] Assuredly, the transformation of the crown of thorns into a jeweled wreath is significant. However, modern readers might be confused by the word "crown" (*stephanos*) and visualize the kind of object worn by the kings and queens of Europe. More precise terminology will help. Most pre-Constantinian imperial portraits tend to show the ruler wearing something that would better be called a "diadem" (cf. fig. 5). This, a kind of headband or fillet made of ribbons, decorated with gems or pearls, and tied at the nape of the neck (with dangling ends), was the specific attribute of a sovereign. The crown (*stephanos*) was a wreath or garland of leaves and the insignia of a military conqueror and should not be confused with the royal diadem.[31] Thus the message would have been read as an allusion to victory rather than to enthronement (coronation). Although the Word of God is described as wearing many in Rev 19:12, Jesus is not depicted wearing a diadem in any early Christian visual art.

Wreaths, however, were commonly depicted in late-antique art and accorded to a variety of persons in addition to victorious generals and emperors. Other kinds of victors who earned their laurels included athletes and poets (fig. 8), married couples, Christian apostles and martyrs (fig. 9), and even the newly baptized (fig. 10).

---

30. Deckers, "Constantine the Great," 106.
31. See Dio Cassius 6.21; Pliny the Elder, *Nat.* 22.4–7. See Mathews, *Clash of Gods*, on the different significations of a crown/wreath in antiquity.

Fig. 8. Prizes of the Pancratium, detail from a Roman mosaic of the spectacles from Batten Zamour, mid-fourth century C.E. Now in the Musée Archeologique, Gafsa, Tunisia. *Photo credit: Gilles Mermet/Art Resource, New York.*

The protomartyr Stephen's name (*Stephanos* = "crown") is an allusion to his. The symbol of the (imperishable) crown is frequent in the New Testament as a reward for faithfulness or perseverance in the face of trials and temptations (cf. 1 Cor 9:25, 2 Tim 4:8, James 1:12, 1 Pet 5:4, Rev 2:10 and 3:11). The African writer, Tertullian, dedicated an entire treatise to the case of a Christian soldier rejecting his military crown and his gesture—a symbolic rejection of values of both secular and army culture—won him a heavenly "corona."[32] Cyprian of Carthage, at the end of his treatise *On the Lapsed*, proclaims that the formerly lapsed but newly brave confessor will merit not only God's pardon but also a crown.[33] Prudentius dedicated a cycle of hymns to the martyrs titled *On the Crowns* (*Peristephanon*).

Despite the rich significance of a crown in Christian literature, when it appears in art, historians often interpret the symbol only as indicating military or imperial honors. For example, art historian Otto von Simson argued that the apostles' procession in the baptisteries of Ravenna was a Christianized version of the *aurum coronarium*: a ceremonial presentation of golden wreaths to the victorious general or emperor that demonstrated the homage owed by both citizens

---

32. Tertullian, *Cor.*
33. Cyprian, *Laps.* 36, CCSL 3, 242.

Fig. 9. Dome mosaic, Neonian (Orthodox) Baptistery, Ravenna, ca. mid-fifth century C.E.
Photo credit: Robin M. Jensen (author).

and captives.[34] Yet, in one instance (the so-called Orthodox Baptistery), the apostles process in a circle, meeting one another (fig. 9), while in another they process toward a throne occupied by an empty gem-studded cross rather than to the feet of a divine ruler.

Furthermore, their white robes suggest that iconography is just as likely derived from the imagery of Rev 7 as from a specific court ritual. Similarly, as in the procession of martyrs on sarcophagi or in the sixth-century church of Sant'Apollinare Nuovo, the martyrs carrying their crowns are the victors themselves; having earned their crowns, they will keep them.

Art historians also have noted the parallels to the *aurum coronarium* in the conventional presentation of the three magi presenting gifts to the Christ child

---

34. Otto G. von Simson, *Sacred Fortress: Byzantine Art and Statecraft in Ravenna* (Princeton, N.J.: Princeton University Press, 1987), 99. See also Grabar, *L'empereur dans l'art byzantine*, 54–57.

Fig. 10. Dome mosaic, baptistery of Sta. Restituta, Naples, early fifth century C.E. *Photo credit: Robin M. Jensen (author).*

(fig. 11), especially when the first of the three offers a wreath (to indicate his gift of gold).

According to Johannes Deckers, this composition unquestionably alludes to the imperial ceremony. That the first of the magi frequently offers a wreath rather than gold coins is, to Deckers, a "remarkable detail not mentioned in the text of Matthew." He insists, "a contemporary viewer would have immediately recognized it as an indication that the Christ Child was just as powerful as the divine emperor."[35] Yet, this observation could be read in a completely different way: the

---

35. Deckers, "Constantine the Great," 105; and see also Johannes G. Deckers, "Die Huldigung der Magier in der Kunst der Spätantike," in *Die Heiligen Drei Könige, Darstellung und Verehrung: Katalog zur Ausstellung des Wallraf-Richartz-Museums in der Josef-Haubrich-*

Fig. 11. Sarcophagus with magi and Daniel, mid-fourth century C.E., Rome. Now in the Museo Pio Cristiano, Vatican Museums. *Photo credit: Vanni/Art Resource, New York.*

magi are presenting their gifts to a small boy sitting in his mother's lap, and not to an enthroned emperor. He is supremely powerful, but not in the way anyone expects.[36]

Additionally, Deckers's noticing that the first magus presents his gift of gold in the form of a wreath (rather than coins) is ironically undermined by the fact that for practical reasons, around the end of the second century, the presentation had become an offering of gold coins instead of gold wreaths, and was more associated with taxation than with ritual homage. Although exclusively the right of the emperor, it had as much association with imperial coronations and anniversaries as with military victories.[37]

Nevertheless, the image of eastern-garbed figures presenting gifts to the Christ Child bears some parallels to contemporary secular imagery. One example appears on the base of the Theodosian obelisk, erected in Constantinople's hippodrome around 390, which shows a group of figures dressed in Persian garb presenting round bowls or baskets to the emperor (seated above in the imperial box). The image calls to mind Pacatus's *elogium* for that very emperor who, along with his "companion deity," deserves both private and public reverence.[38] A similar motif appears on the (much later) Justinian-era Barberini ivory. Here the gifts are a wreath, a box piled with small round objects (possibly meant to be coins), and an ivory tusk.

Kunsthalle Köln, 1. Dezember 1982 bis 30. Januar 1983 (ed. Rainer Budde; Cologne: Wallraf-Richartz-Museum, 1982), 20–32. A recent variation of this theory was posited by Beat Brenk, *The Apse, the Images and the Icon: An Historical Perspective of the Apse as a Space for Images* (Spätantike, frühes Christentum, Byzanz. Reihe B: Studien und Perspektiven 26; Weisbaden: Reichert, 2010), 62.

36. Here I agree with Mathews, *Clash of Gods*, 83–88, but not because—as Mathews then argues—because Christ was a super-magician (rather than an emperor).

37. See Georges Depeyrot, "Economy and Society," in *The Cambridge Companion to the Age of Constantine* (ed. Noel Lenski; Cambridge: Cambridge University Press, 2006), 241–42.

38. On this panegyric see above, Galinsky, "Cult of the Roman Emperor," 14.

This raises the ever-elusive question of how an ancient viewer would have understood any particular image. In this instance, it is reasonable to assume that most would have perceived the allusions to court rituals and their underscoring of imperial regime. However, it is also possible that the imagery implied the existence of something ultimately superior to or even subversive of such dominion. That a vulnerable child, born in a humble stable, is worthy of a golden crown (along with other gifts that point to his messianic and priestly roles) is a visual inversion of mere earthly powers. Martyrs are depicted garbed like Roman nobles, even though many of them were lowborn (at least in this world), persecuted by actual earthly governors, and subjected to humiliating and gruesome punishments from which *honestiores* would have been spared. Jesus surely is a type of king (John 18:36) who humiliates secular rulers and authorities by his triumph (Col 2:15), who leads his followers in a triumphal procession (2 Cor 2:14), and is seated on a heavenly throne (Rev 4:2). Here we can see the negotiation that Karl Galinsky describes: an appropriation of imperial art that could only make sense so long as viewers recognized an image's original meaning, but could only succeed so long as that image was transformed and applied to a new purpose or context.

In the end, Christ's victory *tropaion* is like Constantine's, yet crucially different. It is not a weapon wielded in human conflict, but a Christian cross, surmounted by doves, and encircled with a wreath. The cross, originally an instrument for executing criminals, has been transformed into a symbol of triumph. Viewers must have been meant to understand that transformation as a clash of old and new meanings. Before the symbol of earthly victory and political enemies; now the sign of cosmic conquest and the destruction of everyone's enemy: death. This *crux invicta* is the perfect adornment of a Christian tomb. Read in this light, the iconography of the Passion Sarcophagi expresses a deceased person's fervent hope: "Death has been swallowed up in victory. Where, O death, is your victory? Where, O death, is your sting?" (1 Cor 15:54-56).

In conclusion, several themes of Karl Galinsky's essay have resonance with the art of Rome in the fourth century. Galinsky points out the desire of certain modern historians to situate the early Jesus movement with an agenda of social justice and a repudiation of the perceived values of "empire" (oppression, injustice, and colonialism). However, Galinsky asserts the social, ethnic, and geographic diversity of the "emperor cult" in the first century, which makes this subject much more complex and in need of nuance. Galinsky contends that the emperor Augustus's appropriation of certain epithets or phrases of his predecessors and competitors was less oppositional than competitive. In other words, that Augustus intended to define himself along the lines of his models and then do them one better. Finally, Galinsky points out that the fourth-century Christian emperors had no motivation to eliminate the imperial cult because they simply could juxtapose, rather than oppose, it. The same impulse shapes the iconography of Christ that emerges in the fourth century. Mathews may be right that Christ must surpass Jupiter or Apollo, but in this particular art, Christ also becomes the divine ruler. And this transcendent ruler was as present to the little people as to the nobles, as regal and majestic as he was compassionate and caring. The attributes did not need to cancel one another out, and they did not require the demise of the human emperor's cult.

Bibliography

Art of Eternity: Painting Paradise. United Kingdom: BBC, 2007.
Brenk, Beat. *The Apse, the Images and the Icon: An Historical Perspective of the Apse as a Space for Images.* Spätantike, frühes Christentum, Byzanz. Reihe B: Studien und Perspektiven 26. Weisbaden: Reichert, 2010.
———. "The Imperial Heritage of Early Christian Art." Pages 39–52 in *Age of Spirituality: A Symposium.* Edited by Kurt Weitzmann. New York: Metropolitan Museum of Art, 1977.
Brown, Peter. Review of Thomas F. Mathews, *The Clash of Gods: A Reinterpretation of Early Christian Art. The Art Bulletin* 77 (1995): 499–502.
Bruun, Patrick M. "The Christian Signs on the Coins of Constantine." *Arctos* 3 (1962): 5–35.
———. *Constantine and Licinius A.D. 313–337.* Vol. 7 of *The Roman Imperial Coinage.* Edited by C. H. V. Sutherland and R. A. G. Carson. London: Spink & Son, 1966.
Deckers, Johannes G. "Constantine the Great and Early Christian Art." Pages 87–109 in *Picturing the Bible: The Earliest Christian Art.* Edited by Jeffrey Spier. New Haven, Conn.: Yale University Press, 2007.
———. "Die Huldigung der Magier in der Kunst der Spätantike." Pages 20–32 in *Die Heiligen Drei Könige, Darstellung und Verehrung: Katalog zur Ausstellung Des Wallraf-Richartz-Museums in der Josef-Haubrich-Kunsthalle Köln, 1. Dezember 1982 bis 30. Januar 1983.* Edited by Rainer Budde. Cologne: Wallraf-Richartz-Museum, 1982.
Depeyrot, Georges. "Economy and Society." Pages 226–54 in *The Cambridge Companion to the Age of Constantine.* Edited by Noel Lenski. Cambridge: Cambridge University Press, 2006.
Frend, W. H. C. Review of Thomas F. Mathews, *The Clash of Gods: A Reinterpretation of Early Christian Art. Journal of Ecclesiastical History* 46 (1995): 490–91.
Galinsky, Karl. "The Cult of the Roman Emperor: Uniter or Divider?" Paper presented at the Annual Meeting of the SBL, Boston, 2008, and ch. 1 in this volume.
Grabar, André. *L'empereur dans l'art byzantine.* Strasbourg: Faculté des letters de l'université de Strasbourg, 1936.
Grigg, Robert. "Constantine the Great and the Cult Without Images." *Viator* 8 (1977): 1–32.
Hellemo, Geir. *Adventus Domini: Eschatological Thought in 4th-Century Apses and Catecheses.* Supplements to Vigiliae Christianae 5. Leiden: Brill, 1989.
Hurtado, Larry W. *The Earliest Christian Artifacts: Manuscripts and Christian Origins.*

Grand Rapids, Mich.: Eerdmans, 2006.

Kent, J. P. C. *The Family of Constantine I (A.D. 337–364)*. Vol. 8 of *The Roman Imperial Coinage*. Edited by C. H. V. Sutherland and R. A. G. Carson. London: Spink & Son, 1981.

Kinney, Dale. Review of Thomas F. Mathews, *The Clash of Gods: A Reinterpretation of Early Christian Art*. *Studies in Iconography* 16 (1994): 237–42.

Kleinbauer, W. Eugene. Review of Thomas F. Mathews, *The Clash of Gods: A Reinterpretation of Early Christian Art*. *Speculum* 70 (1995): 937–41.

Marcus Minucius Felix. *The Octavius of Marcus Minucius Felix*. Translated by G. W. Clarke. Ancient Christian Writers 39. New York: Newman, 1974.

Mathews, Thomas F. *The Clash of Gods: A Reinterpretation of Early Christian Art*. Princeton, N.J.: Princeton University Press, 1993.

Murray, Sister Charles. Review of Thomas F. Mathews, *The Clash of Gods: A Reinterpretation of Early Christian Art*. *Journal of Theological Studies* 47 (1996): 703–5.

Noreña, Carlos F. "The Communication of the Emperor's Virtues." *Journal of Roman Studies* 91 (2001): 146–68.

Norris, Frederick W. Review of Thomas F. Mathews, *The Clash of Gods: A Reinterpretation of Early Christian Art*. *Church History* 64 (1995): 251–52.

Simson, Otto G. von. *Sacred Fortress: Byzantine Art and Statecraft in Ravenna*. Princeton, N.J.: Princeton University Press, 1987.

Wharton, Annabel. Review of Thomas F. Mathews, *The Clash of Gods: A Reinterpretation of Early Christian Art*. *The American Historical Review* 100 (1995): 1518–19.

Chapter 12
Capitalizing on the Imperial Cult:
Some Jewish Perspectives

L. Michael White

Studies of Roman imperialism and "Romanization" (*scare quotes obligatory*) from a postcolonial perspective are, needless to say, a fixture these days in both classical and New Testament scholarship. All to the good, I'd say, both as a corrective to older notions of a top-down imposition of Roman rule on native populations (as in Mommsen and Haverfield)[1] and as an impetus to seeing various kinds of religious activities—and the cult(s) of the Roman emperor in particular—in a new light. At the same time, it must be said that the spate of "anti-imperial" studies in the New Testament field is fast approaching fad level, and that is where the cautionary efforts of this three-stage program are a welcome improvement. It reminds me a bit of some earlier fads in New Testament scholarship, such as Schmithals et al. finding "Gnosticism" behind every rock in the New Testament. Where have all the gnostics gone? Nor should we be too eager to capitalize simplistically on "anti-imperialist" approaches.

Instead, I want to applaud those recent studies that have highlighted the problematic tendency to frame the discussion in rigidly dualistic terms, so that there is, functionally at least, no middle ground between accommodation (or acceptance) and resistance.[2] Far too often it seems to be an "all or nothing" game. That having been said, however, it is not my intention in this paper to tag any particular studies for criticism or approbation. Rather I want us to step outside

---

1. P. W. M. Freeman, "Mommsen Through to Haverfield: The Origins of Romanization Studies in Late 19th-Cent. Britain," in *Dialogues in Roman Imperialism: Power, Discourse, and Discrepant Experience in the Roman Empire* (ed. D. J. Mattingly; JRASup 23; Providence, R.I.: Journal of Roman Archaeology, 1997), 27–50.

2. D. J. Mattingly, "Africa: A Landscape of Opportunity?" in *Dialogues in Roman Imperialism: Power, Discourse, and Discrepant Experience in the Roman Empire* (ed. D. J. Mattingly; JRASup 23; Portsmouth, R.I.: Journal of Roman Archaeology, 1997), 134–35.

for a moment and look at a "parallel universe" of experience for some guidance in thinking about how the imperial cults and other instruments of "Romanization" really operated at ground level. In this case, I will be focusing on Jewish groups in Greek and Roman cities. My point is that we can find a spectrum of possible impulses and reactions ranging from integration (or acculturation) to resistance. Of course, we can find both extremes as well. On the one side, there is total assimilation, as in the case of Philo's apostate nephew, Tiberius Julius Alexander, who served both as procurator of Judea[3] and later as governor of Egypt. Having massacred fifty thousand Alexandrian Jews, according to Josephus, at the beginning of the Revolt, he later facilitated Vespasian's acclamation as emperor.[4] On the other, and precisely contemporaneous, there is total resistance, as in the blatantly anti-Roman rhetoric of the *War Scroll* from Qumran.

But that is my point: such examples form the extremes, where the apparition of dualism gains sharp relief. In reality, however, both extremes represent a miniscule proportion of actual Jewish experience across a more gradual and variegated spectrum of responses. To sharpen the point, let me say that I sometimes wonder if one extreme—total assimilation, like that of Tiberius Julius Alexander—is effectively forgotten in the current dualizing equation. It must be remembered, then, that Josephus—at least the postwar Josephus—still falls in the middle, somewhere "left" of Philo, perhaps, but well to the "right" of Philo's nephew. He reminds us further that people can move along this spectrum. To lop off the farther extreme, then, basically truncates the full spectrum of possibilities and tilts the balance unnaturally and unrealistically in the direction of "resistance." We would have the same imbalance in reverse if we were to ignore the Essenes and others who did openly resist.

Thus, I would suggest that *most* Jewish communities, at least *most* of the time, hovered in the middle ground between complete assimilation and outright resistance.[5] Sometimes they might slide—*or be pushed*—one way or the other, but that is precisely what they were having to "negotiate" on an ongoing basis. I am reminded how many of the great dicta about cultural dos and don'ts among ancient Jews have been hauled up short when we examine the evidence more carefully. Such is the case of the discovery of the Dura Synagogue and its art. One

---

3. Josephus, *A.J.* 20.100–102.
4. Josephus, *B.J.* 2.487–498; 5.43–46; 6.237–238.
5. I am particularly concerned here with Diaspora communities, but Schwartz makes the same point regarding Jewish Palestine in the Rabbinic period: Seth Schwartz, *Imperialism and Jewish Society, 200 B.C.E. to 640 C.E.* (Jews, Christians, and Muslims from the Ancient to the Modern World; Princeton, N.J.: Princeton University Press, 2001), 176; Seth Schwartz, "The Rabbi in Aphrodite's Bath: Palestinian Society and Jewish Identity in the High Roman Empire," in *Being Greek Under Rome: Cultural Identity, the Second Sophistic, and the Development of Empire* (ed. Simon Goldhill; Cambridge: Cambridge University Press, 2001), 361.

of my other favorites is the story from the Mishnah of Rabbi Gamaliel II traveling to Ptolemais to enjoy the baths of Aphrodite (*Avodah Zarah* 3:4). He seems to have had no problem "negotiating" that complex encounter (double entendre intentional), assuming, that is, that the story is historical.[6] But even if not, what was the story trying to convey to its late second-century Jewish audience? Seth Schwartz says "it *functioned* as accommodation," especially for Jews living in urban contexts.[7]

The operative word in most of the recent studies has been "negotiation," which, as James Hanges reminds us, needs to be more nuanced than just an obstacle course metaphor.[8] It is precisely on this point that I wish to focus my efforts today. For if we are to do what Hanges asked, we need to think carefully what "negotiation" means in economic, political, and social terms. To this end I want to bring the discussion back down to ground by looking at several non-literary reflections of Jewish experience in the local social economy of Roman rule. At the end I will return to some brief, theoretical points.

The Rhetoric of Honors in Jewish Inscriptions

In the bulk of this paper I will focus on several Jewish inscriptions that seem to me to be reflecting the active negotiation process—and generally in congenial terms—for Jews living in Roman and Greco-Roman cities.[9] The difficulty, of course, is that with highly rhetorical literary texts it is easy to read ideas into them, whether as "hidden transcripts" or otherwise. That is not to say that inscriptions are lacking in their own, highly cultivated rhetoric. Rather, it means that we will have to take account of the rules of that rhetoric in its own, scripted

---

6. A further point regarding this negotiation is often overlooked in treatments of this passage because it is typically assumed that Ptolemais (Acco, or modern Acre, just above Haifa) was part of Judea/Palestine in those days. It was *not*. Ptolemais was a Greek city, like Tyre and Sidon, and was administratively part of the Province of Syria. Thus, Gamaliel had to *leave* the Galilee, understood as the Jewish homeland, and *enter* a Greek, and thus Diaspora, city in order for this encounter to occur. Thus, I would suggest that there is another dimension to the "boundary" symbols of the story that are being negotiated. So notice that Schwartz's otherwise excellent study of this passage (see next note) does not address this geographical feature of the story and its boundary/identity symbolism.

7. Ibid., 359 (italics his); cf. Schwartz, *Imperialism and Jewish Society*, 165–74 (the same quotation, with italics, appears on 173).

8. James Constantine Hanges, "To Complicate Encounters: A Response to Karl Galinsky's 'The Cult of the Roman Emperor: Uniter or Divider?,'" paper presented at the Annual Meeting of the SBL, Boston, 2008 (and ch. 3 in this volume), 30.

9. James S. McLaren, "Jews and the Imperial Cult: From Augustus to Domitian," *JSNT* 27 (2005): 257–78 primarily discusses evidence from the Jewish homeland; therefore, this discussion may serve as a useful supplement.

social arenas, and specifically where the language, formulas, and epigraphic conventions place these Jewish "texts" in an openly Roman conversation, usefully characterized by Ramsay MacMullen as "the epigraphic habit."[10]

Akmoneia, Phrygia

We begin with the Jews of Akmoneia, Phrygia and their honors for the benefactor Julia Severa. (app., Inscription 1a.) The date of this inscription is ca. 60–80 c.e. and shows the local Jewish community offering customary benefaction honors for four individuals, three male Jewish leaders and the woman Julia Severa. Although nowhere indicated within this text, it turns out that Julia Severa was not Jewish, and thus her relationship to the Jewish community and the three Jewish leaders named in the inscription becomes a central issue. The plaque reads as follows:

> This edifice, which was erected by Julia Severa, Publius Tyrronius Clados, archisynagogos for life, Lucius son Lucius, archisynagogos, and Popilius Zotikos, archon, have renovated from their own funds and from the common treasury (of the congregation); they have decorated the walls and the ceiling, and they have made the security of the gates and all the rest of the decoration. The congregation (synagogue) honors all these individuals with a gold shield on account of their excellent leadership and their kindly feelings and zeal on behalf of the congregation (synagogue). (*MAMA* 6.264)[11]

As I have argued elsewhere,[12] the situation seems to be that the edifice, whatever it might have been originally, was donated to the Jewish community by Julia Severa, while the three Jewish leaders took responsibility for its renovation as a synagogue, paid for out of their own funds and the community treasury. I argue further, based on the names,[13] that the social context and occasion for the gift

---

10. Ramsey MacMullen, "The Epigraphic Habit in the Roman Empire," *AJP* 103 (1982): 233–34; cf. Walter Ameling, "Die Jüdische Diaspora Kleinasiens und der 'Epigrapic Habit,'" in *Jewish Identity in the Greco-Roman World [Jüdische Identität in der Griechisch-Römischen Welt]* (ed. Jörg Frey, Daniel R. Schwart, and Stephanie Gripentrog; Ancient Judaism and Early Christianity 71; Leiden: Brill, 2007), 255 and 258–62.

11. The Greek and Latin texts for all inscriptions to be discussed in this study are found in the Appendix; all translations are my own. This inscription is on a white marble plaque 49 x 58 cm, 15 cm thick.

12. L. Michael White, *Texts and Monuments for the Christian Domus Ecclesiae in Its Environment* (vol. 2 of *The Social Origins of Christian Architecture*; HTS 42; Valley Forge, Pa.: Trinity Press International, 1997), no. 65.

13. The name of the archisynagogos P. Tyrronius Clados seems to suggest a linkage to Julia's comagistrate of the city, [Publius] Tyrronius Rapo, while the other two Jewish benefactors

of Julia Severa arose from the fact that these Jewish leaders, and perhaps other members of the congregation, were her clients or in some relationship of social dependence. In other words, there were two distinct acts of patronage at work: that of Julia Severa toward her Jewish clients and that of the clients, the synagogue leaders, toward the Jewish congregation. The inscription and the gold shield were presumably set up in the synagogue or on its façade. We should imagine, too, that Julia Severa was the guest of honor at its dedication,[14] comparable perhaps to the benefactor Tation, wife of Strato, who was honored by the Jewish congregation of nearby Phocaea with a *proedrion* in the synagogue.[15]

None of this argument is new, and other scholars have generally granted my reconstruction of the process.[16] Nor is the language of this inscription in any way unusual. While the specific benefactions thus break into two distinct acts, it is worth noting that all four individuals are honored together with a single, unified gesture, even though Julia Severa was not a member of the Jewish congregation. It is the second text from Akmoneia (Inscription 1b) that casts this clearly Jewish text in a new light.

> The gerusia (of Akmoneia) honors Julia Severa, daughter of Gaius, high priestess and agonothetess of the entire house of the gods, the Sebastoi, in gratitude for all her virtuous deeds and benefactions toward it [the gerusia], and (by?) having erected.... (*MAMA* 6.263)

This text now shows that Julia Severa was honored by the Akmoneian council (the *gerousia*) as high priestess and agonothete of the local imperial cult and as civic benefactor, probably also in connection with imperial cult activities.[17] It was

---

also carry Latinized names with other possible connections to members of her social network, e.g., Lucius Servenius Capito and [Publius] Tyrronius Rapo, respectively.

14. Assuming, of course, that the renovation project mentioned was not significantly later than her original gift.

15. *IGR* 4.1327 (*CIJ* 738); cf. White, *Texts and Monuments*, no. 68.

16. Cf. Tessa Rajak and David Noy, "*Archisynagogoi*: Office, Title, and Social Status in the Greco-Jewish Synagogue," in *The Jewish Dialogue with Greece and Rome: Studies in Cultural and Social Interaction* (Tessa Rajak; 1993; repr., AGJU 48; Leiden: Brill, 2001), 418; Tessa Rajak, "The Synagogue in the Greco-Roman City," in *The Jewish Dialogue with Greece and Rome: Studies in Cultural and Social Interaction* (Tessa Rajak; 1999; repr., AGJU 48; Leiden: Brill, 2001), 463–78. Rajak herself, "Synagogue in the Greco-Roman City," 473, offers the further possibility that the archisynagogos P. Tyrronius Clados, who would seem to be a citizen, might *not* be Jewish but a pagan sympathizer. Given his title, it is possible but unlikely. It is just as likely that he was a Jewish freedman who had been enfranchised.

17. *MAMA* 6.265 refers to a festival in honor of the emperor during her tenure as magistrate, which may be the one at which she also served as agonothete (so Buckler and Calder in *MAMA* 6.263, note).

carved on a white marble statue base (63 x 49 cm, and 88 cm high) that likely carried an honorific statue (presumably a *togata*) of her.[18] We may compare the inscription honoring the imperial cult priestess Indelvia Valerilla at Nîmes (Nemausus, Gaul), which mentions this type of honorific statue along with statues honoring the emperor: *Indelviae T(iti) fil(iae) | Valerillae | flaminicae | perpetuae | quae pro eo honore | statuam argenteam cum | basi ex HS L m(ilibus) n(ummum) | in basilica posuit | ob quam munificentiam | ordo sanctissimus | statuam ei ponendam | de publico decrevit | quae honore contenta | inpendium remisit.*[19]

The Akmoneia inscriptions tells us further that Julia Severa served as eponymous city magistrate,[20] and she minted coinage under Nero. The date of these inscriptions might be under Nero or Vespasian. In another study,[21] I showed how this Galatian royal was herself a relative newcomer to Akmoneia. She had married an aspiring Italian equestrian, Lucius Servenius Capito, a colonist from Pisidian Antioch.[22] Their civic functions and benefactions were helping to promote the family toward Roman senatorial status in the person of their son, Lucius Servenius Cornutus.[23] In other words, Julia Severa, like many of her aristocratic peers—as well as her lesser dependents—was also in an active process of negotiating status and identity within the civic framework of imperial rule.

So, my question is this: how should the Jewish community be expected to view her participation in the local imperial cult? And what do the Jewish honors say about their ongoing relations with these local elites and their ties to Rome? If

---

18. In my view it is likely that the final, fragmentary clause (as restored by Buckler and Calder) refers either to her setting up a statue of the emperor or, more likely, to the gerusia's erection of the statue and base honoring her. For the latter sense, I might emend the final word as πο[ιη-] | [σαμένῳ . . .]. *MAMA* 6.266 contains a complete form of the final clause with this sense erecting a statue to honor another benefactor at Akmoneia.

19. R. L. Gordon, "The Veil of Power: Emperors, Sacrificers and Benefactors," in *Pagan Priests* (ed. Mary Beard and John North; London: Duckworth, 1990), 226. The text is *AE* 1982:682. For statues of the emperor erected by an individual civic benefactor but also in the name of the city, compare *IGR* 4.362 and 363 from Pergamum (reign of Caracalla); cf. S. R. F. Price, *Rituals and Power: The Roman Imperial Cult in Asia Minor* (Cambridge: Cambridge University Press, 1984), 253.

20. *MAMA* 6.266 identifies her as a *quinquinial duovir* (δύο πεντατηρικοὺς) along with Tyrronius Rapo.

21. L. Michael White, "Counting the Cost of Nobility: The Social Economy of Roman Pergamon," in *Pergamon: Citadel of the Gods* (ed. Helmut Koester; Harrisburg, Pa.: Trinity Press International, 1998), 351–52.

22. For other discussion of the family see Barbara Levick, *Roman Colonies in Southern Asia Minor* (Oxford: Clarendon, 1967), 105–7, and Helmut Halfmann, *Die Senatoren aus dem östlichen Teil des Imperium Romanum bis zum Ende des 2. Jahrhunderts n. Chr.* (Hypomnemata 58; Göttingen: Vandenhoeck & Ruprecht, 1979), 102–3.

23. Honors for L. Servenius Cornutus at Akmoneia having served as Praefect of Cyprus, see *MAMA* 6.254 and 262.

her career should fall as late as the end of Nero's reign or in the reign of Vespasian, then it raises other issues of how the Akmoneian Jews negotiated these local relationships with the specter of the war in Judea. In this case, we cannot even hint at such a hidden subtext. On the public face of it, these inscriptions leave a very clear impression that there was no resistance at all. If there were dissenting voices we do not hear them. Instead, the Jewish community was actively engaged in brokering its relationship to this local elite to increase and placard its own social status. At the same time, Julia Severa's acts of patronage would have served to increase her prestige locally, by insuring a regular flow of honors and obligations from the city and from her Jewish clients. In turn, as a municipal archon and member of the city council, Julia Severa was similarly obliged to participate in the regular rotation of local and provincial honors offered to the emperor. Thus, this case begins to open up a much more subtle web of relationships that had to be negotiated by Jews and others in the complex calculus of urban life. We shall return to this inscription later in this study.

SARDIS, LYDIA

The case of Akmoneia raises further issues when we consider the participation of Jews in local civic government. Here we may compare the evidence from nearby Sardis, where a number of the members of the Jewish community known from the donor inscriptions also held various civic functions. Sixteen were citizens of Sardis (using the title *Sardianos*),[24] while at least nine of these were also members of the city council or boule (using the title *bouleutes*).[25] (See Inscription 2, the donor inscription of Aurelius Alexandros, dating from the late third century C.E.) Others still were involved in the provincial administration, including a former procurator (*epitropos*),[26] a count (*comes*),[27] and an administrative *Assistant* in the state archives (*boēthos tablariou*), here probably meaning the local "deputy" in the provincial bureaucracy.[28] While these texts date to the late third and fourth centuries, all of these individuals would have been involved in various capacities in the local functions of honoring the emperor, or later, the state. For our purposes, perhaps the most significant might be the nine city councilors. This office was reserved for those of high civic rank; it was open "only to the

---

24. John H. Kroll, "The Greek Inscriptions of the Sardis Synagogue," *HTR* 94 (2001): 5–55, nos. 3, 11, 13, 16/17, 24, [25/26], 27, 30, 31, 32, 33, 37, 41, 43, 66, 67.
25. Ibid., nos. 3, 13, 16/17, 24, 25/26, 31, 34, 37, 67.
26. Ibid., no. 70.
27. Ibid., no. 5. The honorific title was conferred on high provincial officials beginning with Constantine. Here it dates to sometime after 341 C.E.
28. Ibid. 2001, no. 13/14.

wealthier families, with membership, once purchased, being hereditary and held for life."[29] All of these city councilors seem to be Jews, in contrast to the situation at Aphrodisias, where the nine city councilors named are all listed among the "Godfearers."[30] Consequently, citizenship and membership in the boule constituted a significant investment in the social and political structures of the city. As donors to the Sardis synagogue, probably the largest and most opulent known from antiquity, these same individuals were likewise investing in the social and political fortunes of the local Jewish community.

What might have been expected of these Jewish city councilors in relation to local imperial cult functions? What if they received alimentary distributions in conjunction with local and imperial cult celebrations as we find at Ephesus and similarly at relatively tiny Sillyon, Pamphylia?[31] As Simon Price has pointed out, sacrifices *to* the emperor (or his statue) were actually rare.[32] Far more common were sacrifices *for* or *on behalf of* the emperor.[33] Diaspora Jews had a solid precedent, as both Josephus and Philo confirm, because sacrifices to God *on behalf of the emperor* were offered in the temple at Jerusalem twice a day.[34] In fact, this subtle provision seems to have allowed Diaspora Jews to participate more freely in civic functions.[35] It was ratified by legislation of Septimius Severus and Caracalla (ca. 207–211 C.E.), which granted Jews the right "to hold public office but imposed on them (only) such duties as did not offend against their religion (lit. *superstitio*)."[36] The provision was reaffirmed later in the Constantinian period.[37] We shall return to other aspects of the Severan period later. For now, however, we will do well to remember that prayers on behalf of monarchs had already been

---

29. Ibid., 10, citing A. H. M. Jones, *The Greek City from Alexander to Justinian* (Oxford: Clarendon, 1940), 141, 176, 180–93.

30. Joyce Reynolds and Robert Tannenbaum, *Jews and God-Fearers at Aphrodisias: Greek Inscriptions with Commentary: Texts from the Excavations at Aphrodisias Conducted by Kenan T. Erim* (Supplementary Volume 12; Cambridge: Cambridge Philological Society, 1987), 6–7; cf. White, *Texts and Monuments*, no. 64.

31. For the latter see Gordon, "Veil of Power," 228–29.

32. Price, *Rituals and Power*, 216–17.

33. Ibid., 210–13.

34. Applying, of course, to the period before the Revolt. See Josephus, *B.J.* 2.197; Philo, *Legat.* 317. Cf. McLaren, "Jews and the Imperial Cult," 271–73.

35. Tessa Rajak, "Jews, Pagans, and Christians in Late Antique Sardis: Models of Interaction," in *The Jewish Dialogue with Greece and Rome: Studies in Cultural and Social Interaction* (Tessa Rajak; AGJU 48; Leiden: Brill, 2001), 447–62; cf. Price, *Rituals and Power*, 209–10.

36. *Dig.* 50.2.3.3; cf. Margaret Willliams, *The Jews Among the Greeks and Romans: A Diasporan Sourcebook* (Baltimore: Johns Hopkins University Press, 1998), 109 (V.8); Amnon Linder, *The Jews in Roman Imperial Legislation*, in *Jews in Roman Imperial Legislation* (Detroit: Wayne State University Press, 1987), no. 2.

37. *Cod. theod.* 16.8.2, 4; Ibid., 134–35.

a standard mechanism for Jewish participation in Hellenistic Egyptian society going back to the Ptolemaic period (Inscription 3a and b) and continuing into early Roman rule (Inscription 3c). Another inscription (3d) shows that these prayers were reciprocated by royal protection of the synagogues, and that this tradition continued into early Roman times. In many ways, the ability of Jews to conscience both local civic religion and the cult of the emperors, especially in the Greek East, was a direct outgrowth of these earlier Hellenistic customs and conventions. By the time we get to the case of Sardis, the custom had become a genuine *mos maiorum*, having been operative for nearly five hundred years. Even then there were subtle forms of negotiation, as Rajak suggests regarding donations made as "gifts from the *gifts of God*."[38]

BERENIKE, CYRENAIKA

Now let's return to the case of Akmoneia to pick up yet another line of negotiation, namely Jewish honors for local magistrates. In this case we see the context of synagogue structures, both physical and social, integrated to a large degree in the local Roman political organization. Two examples come from the Julio-Claudian period in Berenike, Cyrenaika (Inscriptions 4a and b). The first inscription (4a) shows the Jewish *politeuma* unanimously honoring Decimus Valerius Dionysius for his benefactions in renovating a portion of the local amphitheater that was apparently also used by the Jewish congregation for its meetings.[39]

> In the year [2]3, on the 5th of Phamenoth, in the archonship of Arimmas son of [...], Dorion son of Ptolemaios, Zelaios son of Gnaios, Ariston son of Arax[..]as, Sarapion son of Andromachos, Nikias son of [... (and) ...] son of Simon.
> *Whereas* Decimus Valerius Dionysius son of Gaius, *praepositus* of the [council?] continues to be an honorable and good man in word, in deed, and in purpose, and doing whatever good he is able, whether in public or private matters (dealing rightly) with each of the citizens, and
> *Whereas*, moreover, he has plastered the floor of the amphitheater and painted the walls, it is hereby resolved by the archons of the *politeuma* of the Jews in Berenike to inscribe him in the [...] of a Jew (?), and that he be exempted from all liturgies whatsoever, and moreover to crown him with an olive crown and a wooden nameplate at each synod and new moon.
> *Wherefore*, the archons, having inscribed this resolution on a stele of Parian marble, are to set it up in a conspicuous place in the amphitheater.
> (The vote:) all whites.   (*vac.*)

---

38. Tessa Rajak, "The Gifts of God at Sardis," in *Jews in a Graeco-Roman World* (ed. Martin Goodman; Oxford: Clarendon, 1998), 236–39.

39. On the nature of the building see White, *Texts and Monuments*, no. 63, n. 36 (following Reynolds in *IBerenike* 247).

> Decimus Valerius Dionysius, son of Gaius, both plastered the floor of the amphitheater and painted (it) at his own expense as a gift to the *politeuma* (of the Jews). (*IBerenike* 18)

This is a large marble stele measuring 77 cm in height, ca. 38 cm wide, and 11 cm thick, as preserved. In this case, it is generally assumed that Valerius was Jewish, although it is by no means certain.[40] He was definitely a local magistrate of some sort and almost certainly a Roman citizen.[41] It is possible that he was the civic or provincial magistrate who liaised with the Jewish *politeuma* and sat in their public meetings, whether or not he was Jewish himself.[42] His benefactions earned him some special honorary status within the Jewish community and public recognition in their regular rituals. I would conjecture that, if he was Jewish, the new honorific status included enrolling him among the archons of the Jewish *politeuma*, "at no cost." It is striking here that the financial obligations of the Jewish archons are called "liturgies," using the standard civic-religious terminology. If he was not Jewish, however, it would seem to be enrolling him honorarily in the Jewish *politeuma* itself, with something like "equal status" and "at no cost." In either case, it is his favorable representation and treatment of the Jewish community in civic matters, as well as his direct benefactions, that earn him these honors. Among his benefactions are paving of the floor and paintings (using *zographein*) on the walls, which would seem to refer to figural art.[43]

A second inscription (Inscription 4b) from the same Jewish *politeuma* comes some thirty years later and honors another Roman, this time the provincial prefect for Berenike.

---

40. So Gert von Lüderitz, *Corpus jüdischer Zeugnisse aus der Cyrenaika* (Beihefte zum Tübinger Atlas des Vorderen Orients. Reihe B, Geisteswissenschaften; Wiesbaden: L. Reichert, 1983), 151; G. H. R. Horsley, *New Documents Illustrating Early Christianity: A Review of the Greek Inscriptions and Papyri 4 1979* (North Ryde, Australia: North Ryde Ancient History Documentary Research Centre, Macquarie University, 1987), 203, 209 (no. 111), but see further discussion below.

41. Lüderitz, *Corpus jüdischer*, 151 (following Reynolds); Horsley, *NDIEC* 4, 209.

42. Assuming that πρηπο(σί)της in line 6 is restored correctly. *Praepositus* seems rather clearly to be a Latin loanword; it refers to an official in charge of some specific provincial or civic function. That this reference occurs in the first paragraph of the resolution, which stresses larger civic functions, suggests that he might not be Jewish on comparison with the analogous section of Inscription 4b. The restoration at the beginning of line 7 is more difficult. Although [τῆς συναγ]ωγῆς seems to be a possibility, the stone is too badly damaged to be sure. Lüderitz read only [...]ΩΓΗΣ, with each letter being uncertain. The original editors, J. and G. Roux, had read [....]ΔΑ[...]ΩΓΗΣ, which would make any form of συηαγωγή virtually impossible. On the terms συηαγωγή and ἀρχισυηάγωγος used (sometimes in tandem) of non-Jewish groups, see Rajak and Noy, "*Archisynagogoi*," 428–29.

43. Horsley, *NDIEC* 4, 203–8.

In the year 55, on the 25th of Phaoph, in the assembly on the Feast of Sukkoth, in the archonship of Cleander son of Stratonikos, Euphranor son of Ariston, Sosigenes son of Sosippos, Andromachos son of Andromachos, Marcus Lailios Onasion son of Apollonios, Philonidos son of Hagemon, Autocles son of Zenon, Sonikos son of Theodotoos, and Josephos son of Straton:

Whereas Marcus Tittius, son of Sextus, of the tribe Aimilia, being an honorable and good man, having come into the provincial praefecture for public affairs, he well served as their president both nobly and philanthropically, and in his term ever demonstrating a quiet character, he continues to do so, and not only did he present himself in a not-overbearing manner in these (public matters) but also to those of the citizens who encountered him privately. *and*

Whereas still more for Jews from our *politeuma*, both publicly and in private, serving the presidency beneficially, he did not cease acting worthily of his own nobility, in gratitude for which it is hereby resolved by the archons and the *politeuma* of the Jews in Berenike, to praise him by name and to crown him with an olive crown and wooden nameplate at each synod and new moon.

Wherefore, the archons shall inscribe this decree on a stele of Parian marble and set it up in a conspicuous place in the amphitheater.

(The vote:)   All whites.   (*IBerenike* 17)

This inscription is slightly smaller than the first, measuring 44 x 36 cm, as preserved. It shows the Jewish community honoring the prefect, Marcus Tittius, for unspecified favors granted to them and for generally being a "good guy" in his administration of the provincial diocese. It is also worth noting that at least two of the Jewish archons named in this second inscription seem to be the sons of archons in the earlier inscription,[44] while one of the later archons seems to have been enfranchised as a Roman citizen.[45] A third inscription honoring contributors to a synagogue construction project shows the continuation of this Jewish community another generation later (55/56 C.E.). It opens with a dating formula using full imperial titulature: "*In the second year of the Emperor Nero Claudius Caesar Drusus Germanicus.*"[46] At least two names on this last inscription likely represent members of the same leading families noted in Inscription 4a above. Thus, we have a multigenerational history of the Jewish community

---

44. Ephranor son of Ariston and Andromachus son of Andromachus (lines 3–5).
45. Marcus Lailios Onasion (line 5).
46. In this case, the inscription is a roster of donors from within the Jewish community for a renovation project on the synagogue edifice. The precise nature of the project is not known, but the stele "of Parian marble" seems to have been modeled after the two above. The total of the gifts listed is not large (208 drachmae), and the bulk comes from a few individuals. See Baruch Lifshitz, *Donateurs et fondateurs dans les synagogues juives, répertoire des dédicaces grecques relatives à la construction et à la réfection des synagogues* (Cahiers de la Revue Biblique 7; Paris: J. Gabalda, et Cie, 1967), no. 100; Lüderitz, *Corpus jüdischer*, no. 72; White, *Texts and Monuments*, no. 63b.

and its dealings with local Roman officials and other trappings of Roman provincial administration. These Roman officials were, as already noted, obliged to participate in honoring the emperor and the state. Since part of the "kindly treatment" recognized in both inscriptions includes the Jewish use of a civic arena, the Jewish *politeuma* likely had to make some gestures in this vein as well, at the very least along the lines of prayers on behalf of the emperor. In turn, we see the Jewish *politeuma* decreeing recognition and honors (including prayers?) for Roman magistrates during their regular religious observances.

Finally, we may notice the consistent formulaic nature of these two inscriptions, which emulate formal honors voted in the local city council. In other words, the Jewish *politeuma* not only identifies itself as part of the larger citizenry of Berenike, but also apes local civic structures and modes of address. While the title "archon" is commonplace among Jewish inscriptions, here it has an additional dimension as it shows organizational structure of the Jewish *politeuma* parallel to but enmeshed within that of the city itself.[47] We should also note that both inscriptions were set up on stele of Parian marble, a highly prized commodity, and displayed in a conspicuous public location within the civic amphitheater. Thus, these Jewish inscriptions are meant to do more than just honor officials who have been kindly toward them. Rather, as public displays they are meant to participate in a broader discourse of honors by advertising the elite social networks in which the Jews operated and the status and respect they were afforded.[48] To put it another way, these inscriptions granting honors to provincial officials are in reality claiming and *proclaiming* honors and civic status for the Jews themselves.[49] At the same time, they are meant to oblige the benefactor to further demonstrations of beneficence. In that sense, too, the inscriptions themselves are part of the medium of exchange in a multifaceted brokering of honors. In light of their good relations with the Roman administration, it might be worth noting that there is no epigraphic evidence for the kind of disruption, rioting, and reprisals in Berenike that we find elsewhere in Cyrenaika, and notably at Cyrene, in connection with the "Jewish *tumult*," as the Romans called it, of 115–117 C.E.[50]

---

47. On *politeuma* here as part of the larger Greek city, see Joseph Mélèze Modrzejewski, "How to Be a Jew in Hellenistic Egypt?" in *Diasporas in Antiquity* (ed. Shay J. D. Cohen and Ernest S. Frerichs; BJS 288; Atlanta: Scholars Press, 1993), 78–79 and nos. 36 and 42, arguing against Aryeh Kasher, *The Jews in Hellenistic Egypt* (TSAJ 7; Tübingen: Mohr Siebeck, 1985).

48. See also Tessa Rajak, "Benefactors in the Greco-Jewish Diaspora," in *The Jewish Dialogue with Greece and Rome: Studies in Cultural and Social Interaction* (Tessa Rajak; 1996; repr., AGJU 48; Leiden: Brill, 2001), 375–78; she discusses these two inscriptions on 382–83.

49. Cf. Ameling, "Jüdische Diaspora," 270–72.

50. The term "Jewish tumult" (*tumultu Iudaico*) is found in a number of Hadrianic inscriptions from the ensuing period; the analogous term in the Greek inscriptions is τάραχος (for ταραχή). For the inscriptions from Cyrene, see Lüderitz, *Corpus Jüdischer*, nos. 17–25,

Ostia, Italia.

With that we come to our last case, from my current excavations in the synagogue at Ostia, the port city of ancient Rome (Inscription 5a). It is a building inscription commemorating the gifts of an individual (and his family?) in constructing the local synagogue edifice and its Torah shrine.

> *For the well-being of the Emperor(s).*
> Mindi(u)s Faustus [together with his household]
> built (this building) and made it from his own gifts,
> and he dedicated the ark for the Holy Law.

The Greek inscription on a white marble plaque (54.3 x 37 cm) was found in the 1961 excavations reused as a paver in the opus sectile floor of the later synagogue; however, its Jewishness is clear enough from the terminology used of the Torah shrine emplacement as "the ark for the holy law" (τὴν κ{ε}ιβωτὸν … νόμῳ ἁγίῳ). It most likely dates to the early Severan period and apparently commemorates the initial construction of the main hall of the synagogue as we know it today.[51] It is unfortunate that the name of the original donor has been chiseled off and reinscribed with the name Mindius Faustus, who appears to be a later donor to the synagogue, probably at the time of renovations in the late third or fourth centuries. Its ultimate reuse in paving the floor of the later synagogue is now provisionally dated to the fifth century. Most striking for our purposes is the fact that the inscription opens with a standard Latin *Pro Salute Aug.* formula found very commonly in the Antonine and Severan periods.[52] The broken ending of the first line would have indicated whether it was for one emperor or two, and thus a

---

detailing both the level of destruction there, including its Caesareion or imperial cult temple (No. 17) and the temple of Zeus (No. 22). For discussion and texts related to other locations in Egypt and Cyrenaica see Miriam Pucci Ben Zeev, *Diaspora Judaism in Turmoil, 116/117 CE: Ancient Sources and Modern Insights* (Interdisciplinary Studies in Ancient Culture and Religion 6; Leuven: Peeters, 2005), 167–90; Shim'on Applebaum, *Jews and Greeks in Ancient Cyrene* (SJLA 28; Leiden: Brill, 1979); and Willliams, *The Jews Among the Greeks and Romans*, 135–37 (V.83–88).

51. This dating is based on our recent excavations with chronological confirmation both from ceramics and coins. See n. 50 below. While the dedication of construction would seem to correspond with that of the main hall of the synagogue (Room 14) in terms of date, the connection of the inscription to this building must still be considered circumstantial on archaeological grounds due to the plaque's final disposition.

52. For other examples from Ostia and Rome see White, *Texts and Monuments*, 392 (n. 163).

slightly more precise date.[53] The opening salutary formula is clearly original as it is in the same hand as the remainder of the text in Greek.[54] For sake of comparison, we may note the similarity with another *Pro Salute* inscription that was also found in the hall of assembly of the synagogue, as yet unpublished.[55] The "hand" is similar to that in Inscription 5. The opening lines read as follows:

> For the well-being of the Emperor·s, Caesar Marcus Aurelius Antoninus ·and P. Septimius Geta, and Julia Augusta, mother of our Lord·s, the Emperor·s,. ...[56]

The invocation formula clearly belongs to the period from 211–212 when Caracalla and Septimius Geta were coemperors; the *damnatio memoriae* of Geta dates the secondary treatment of the stone to 212–217. In this case, unfortunately, the precise nature of the dedication is lost due to the fragmentary nature of the plaque. Its findspot suggests that it might belong to the synagogue complex, but it might also be a spoil.

At least two other Jewish inscriptions with similar formulas are known, both from the Severan period. One is from Palestine and uses the equivalent Greek

---

53. The space at the end of the first line would allow for AVG[G] (the typical abbreviation for *Augustorum*), but the stone is broken at that point. The alignment of the right edge of the stone would favor the plural abbreviation. If restored correctly in the plural, as found commonly at Ostia, the joint emperors being honored might be either Marcus Aurelius and Lucius Verus (161–169), Marcus Aurelius and Commodus (176–180), Septimius Severus and Caracalla [and sometimes Geta] (204–211), or Caracalla and Geta (211–212). If correctly restored in the singular, the emperor being honored might be either Marcus Aurelius (169–176), Commodus (180–192), Septimius Severus (193–204), or Caracalla (212–217). Horsley, *NDIEC* 4, 112; David Noy, *Italy (Excluding the City of Rome), Spain and Gaul* (vol. 1 of *Jewish Inscriptions of Western Europe*; Cambridge: Cambridge University Press, 1993), 25, following Chevalier and Guarducci, suggested late-second century for the first hand, while both Horsley and Noy proposed late-third century for the second hand in Lines 6 and 7. A date after 190 and during the Severan period (211–224) is now made more likely by recent finds in the University of Texas excavations of the synagogue: one is a coin of Commodus dating to 190; the other, a second *"Pro Salute"* inscription naming the joint emperors Caracalla and Geta (211–212), to be discussed below. Publication of both items is forthcoming.

54. As shown by the forms of the A/Alpha, the O/Omicron, and the T/Tau between the Latin and Greek portions of the text.

55. This inscription (Ostia Inv. 8981, 8995, 8996, 8998) was found in the excavations of the 1960s but was never published. The findspot, as confirmed by entries in the Ostia archives, was in the main hall of assembly, but its precise disposition or use is not known. The text and discussion will appear in my forthcoming catalogue of inscriptions as part of our reports on the new excavations of the Ostia synagogue.

56. The double brackets indicate erasures on the stone, in this case as *damnatio memoriae* of Geta.

formula, ὑπὲρ σωτηρίας, to honor Septimius Severus; the other, from Pannonia, contains a dedication for Severus Alexander and Julia Mamea.[57]

For the present discussion we shall limit ourselves only to the first inscription (No. 5a) from Ostia. It seems to reflect the conscious efforts of the original donor of the synagogue construction to situate the Jewish community in relation to the local imperial cult by using the standard formula. Precisely why this gesture—perfunctory or otherwise—remains uncertain, but a few conjectures are possible. For one, the other known Jewish inscriptions from Ostia, all funerary plaques, show that they used "Romanized" names, such as Livius Dionysus and Gaius Julius Justus, two members of the local Jewish *gerusia* who were also Roman citizens (Inscription 5b).[58] In both cases, the names suggest that they were freedmen or clients of prominent Ostian families, such as the *A. Livii*. Gaius Julius Justus, whose Jewish name must have been *Tsaddoq*, was probably an imperial freedman himself or from one of the prominent local families descended from imperial freedmen. He was honored for his service to the Jewish community as *gerusiarch* by the gift of a sizeable tomb plot on which he built a typical local "house tomb" adorned with this rather large and elaborate *titulus*. He would thus be a likely candidate for the original donor of our inscription, but, alas, we shall never know for sure. Even Mindius Faustus belongs to a local gens, the *L. Mindii*, who show up frequently in Ostian collegial rosters.[59] All these texts show the members of the Jewish community participating in the full range of patronal activities and other relationships.[60]

A second possible reason for the imperial invocation comes from the location of the synagogue. It was situated alongside the prominent coastal highway that ran from Portus to Antium. Known as the *Via Severiana*, it was built as part of an extraurban expansion project sponsored by Septimius Severus and Caracalla at the beginning of the third century C.E. The area had earlier been the site a large suburban villa of the Flavian period, which was covered over in

---

57. See *CIJ* 2.972 and Noy, ibid., 25.

58. This inscription was discovered at Castel Porziano a few miles south of Ostia, but along the same coastal highway, the Via Severiana, on which the synagogue is situated. The area to the southeast of the synagogue along the coast was dotted by *nekropoleis*, and this text probably came from that region.

59. For discussion of these names and the relevant inscriptions, see White, *Texts and Monuments*, nos. 84–85 and other literature cited there. See also Noy, *Jewish Inscriptions*, nos. 13 and 18.

60. Another inscription with the name Mindius Faustus shows him granting tomb rights for a recently deceased young man (*CIL* 14.845). The name may also be restored on the roster of one of the *collegia* of Ostia (*CIL* 14.4564, column 1.11). Another funerary inscription identifies Plotius Fortunatus as *archisynagogos* who is apparently commemorated a "patron" in the inscription by two clients. Cf. Noy, *Jewish Inscriptions*, no. 14.

this expansion project. Our archaeological evidence suggests that the founding of the synagogue was also part of this urban development at the beginning of the third century.[61] We know too that some of the architectural members used in the synagogue are *spolia*, and this includes the monumental marble columns and Corinthian capitals. They probably came from an earlier temple complex of Domitianic or Trajanic date that was rebuilt by the Severan emperors, and thus made available for reuse.[62] Were they simply purchased off the used column lot? Or were they an imperial gift? Caracalla's favoritism toward Jews is documented elsewhere.[63] This is where I would love to be able to say that the Ostian Jews were both figuratively and literally "*capitalizing* on the imperial cult," but we cannot be sure. Still it is a possibility, although the colonnade seems now to be a secondary installation in the building, perhaps as late as the early fourth century C.E.[64] Even so, the *Pro Salute* formula at the head of our inscription suggests that there were important ties to the local and imperial networks in Ostia that go beyond mere formalities. The Ostia synagogue is probably the next most opulent known from antiquity, after the one at Sardis, and one of the longest surviving. We now also have archaeological evidence for a major renovation project in the synagogue dating to the late fifth century. The edifice continued in operation from its founding in the early Severan period well into the sixth century C.E., at the least.

The Imperial Cult as Political Capital

The small sampling of inscriptions discussed here reflects involvement of local Jews with their non-Jewish neighbors in the civic arena of Roman provincial rule, and clearly includes several forms of interaction with local imperial cult activi-

---

61. The original excavator, M. Floriana Squarciapino (working from 1961 to 1979), dated the building to the mid-first century C.E., based almost entirely on the masonry. Our work has shown that such a narrow date range for this masonry type is not warranted. Furthermore, we have now turned up solid stratigraphic evidence from ceramics and numismatics found under the floors to indicate that the hall of the synagogue was not constructed prior to 190 C.E. A date in the Severan period for the founding of the synagogue hall seems to be most likely.

62. Based on the identification of the capitals by Patrizio Pensabene, *Scavi di Ostia VII: I capitelli* (Rome: Istituto Poligrafico dello Stato, 1973), nos. 232–234.

63. *Inter alia*, see Shaye J. D. Cohen, "'Those Who Say They Are Jews and Are Not': How Do You Know a Jew in Antiquity When You See One?" in *Diasporas in Antiquity* (ed. Shaye J. D. Cohen and Ernest S. Frerichs; BJS 288; Atlanta: Scholars Press, 1993), 21–22.

64. In other words, they probably belong to a subsequent phase of renovation some time after the original construction of the building. It is possible that it was the secondary project sponsored by Mindius Faustus that occasioned the recutting of this inscription. Even so, it does not alter the fact that the columns and capitals as *spolia* might have been a gift, either of local magistrates or a later emperor. That might explain how and why Mindius Faustus was able to justify reuse of the *Pro Salute* inscription to commemorate his own gift.

ties of various sorts. As I said at the outset, they by no means represent the full spectrum of Jewish reactions. On the other hand, they do show a much higher degree of accommodation and, dare we say, *participation* than we might normally assume. Consequently, they are important for keeping our scales in proper balance. As James McLaren has suggested for the homeland evidence, imperial cults did not seem to be much of an issue, especially in the pre-70 period.[65] That having been said, we may now step back and think more generally about the kinds of negotiations going on especially for Diaspora communities, along with the role of patronage/benefaction and reciprocal honorifics in the process.

In this connection, we may compare the inscription for Numerius Popidius Celsinus from Pompeii (Inscription 6).

> N(umerius) Popidius Celsinus, son of N(umerius), rebuilt from its foundations the temple of Isis after it had collapsed from an earthquake. On account of his generosity, the decurions have adlected him at no cost into their own order, even though he was only six years old. (*CIL* 10.846)

This inscription is found over the main entryway into the Iseum at Pompeii, and honors Popidius Celsinus for rebuilding the Isis temple after the earthquake of 62 C.E. The most noteworthy features for our purposes are these: first, that the benefactor is a six-year-old boy, and second, that he is *not* being honored by the "Isis community" itself, at least on the face of it. There is a more complex set of brokered relations at work.

Here is the situation. The father of Popidius Celsinus was a relatively wealthy, aspiring freedman named Numerius Popidius Ampliatus; he and his wife Cornelia Celsa, had made several other donations to the Isis temple.[66] Yet in this case, he gives a major donation for rebuilding the temple in the name of his son rather than his own. Why? The answer is simple.[67] Ampliatus is not merely brokering honors for himself from the Isis temple or its "community." Rather he is brokering a status elevation for his son and by extension for all his posterity. As a freedman, Ampliatus, albeit a citizen, could never enter the ranks of the decurionate (the local equivalent of Senate at Rome). But the son of a freedman could do so. Yet

---

65. McLaren, "Jews and the Imperial Cult," 274–75.
66. *CIL* 10.847–848.
67. For discussion and further context see White, *Texts and Monuments*, 31; L. Michael White, ed., *Social Networks in the Early Christian Environment: Issues and Methods for Social History* (Semeia; Atlanta: Society of Biblical Literature, 1991), 16–18; Willem Jongman, *The Economy and Society of Pompeii* (Dutch Monographs on Ancient History and Archaeology 4; Amsterdam: Gieben, 1988), 261–62.

for a freedman family to make such a jump in only one generation was rare.[68] Consequently, Ampliatus has leveraged his gift for additional honors and status for his son. Next, we notice that the honors here accorded to the son only mention the Isis temple as recipient of the gift. The source of the honors is the *curia* itself, the city council of Pompeii, who "announce" that they have admitted the young Celsinus *into their own ranks* and *at no cost*. This action is analogous to the granting of honors at Berenike with exemption from liturgies, as we saw above (Inscription 4a).

Now, *in reality*, it is most likely that the father Ampliatus is the one who paid for the inscription. *In reality*, it is the Isis temple that affords it a highly conspicuous place to display it along its street front façade. Yet, the inscription shows a third party in this triangular set of social and political relations—at least as it is framed rhetorically—as though it were a proclamation by the decurions honoring the young Celsinus and his family for a benefaction, not to the city itself but to the Isis temple. Needless to say, we must guess that Popidius Ampliatus had connections on the city council, either through the membership of the Isis cult or through his ties to the *gens Popidii*, or both. Of course, the need for urban cleanup and renovation in the aftermath of an earthquake make the unusual gesture by the *curia* more logical, but the point remains that there is a three-way exchange of gifts, status, and honor at work. On one axis, an act of beneficence toward a "foreign" cult is honored by the city council with a grant of decurial status to the son of an aspiring local freedman. Even the temple benefits from the exchange, by placarding its stature as one of the established, publicly supported, cults of the city. Hence these networks of friendship, patronage, and benefaction serve as a brokering system within the urban framework of Roman culture and society. The same holds true, as we shall see, when they are used in connection with local imperial cults. An analogous case comes from Nîmes (in Gaul), where Attia Patercla became perpetual priestess of the emperor, *at no cost*, because of her father's civic benefactions:

Attiae L(uci) fil(iae) Pa|terclae flami|nicae perpet(uae) gra|tuitae decret(o) or|dinis [I(uliensium)] A[p]t(ensium) ob libera/litates [p]atri[s] eius qui | praeter cetera CCC(milia) HS | rei pub(licae) IIIIIIvirorum | reliquit ad ludos se|viral(es)

---

68. Most of the known cases come from members of the local Augustales, which often functioned as a kind of *cursus honorum* for freedmen. These aspiring freedmen typically parlayed their participation in the imperial cult, often combined with civic benefactions, for status elevation. While not an Augustales, Popidius Ampliatus was operating in the same way. On the role of the Augustales, see further discussion below.

in perpet(uum) celebr|andos Daphnion | lib(ertus) l(ocus) d(atus) d(ecreto) d(ecurionum).[69]

What we need to remember is that the role and symbolic function of these patronage and benefaction systems, and even the local imperial cult, was changing in the early empire in part as a reaction to the economic and social "strains," to use Charles Whittaker's term, caused by imperial expansion.[70] Whittaker thus compares the role of civic benefaction as a brokering mechanism to the rise of the Augustales, as a kind of *cursus honorum* for freedmen. He says:

> The same purpose [as the Augustales] was achieved through the adoption and adaptation by Augustus himself in Rome, of Hellenistic euergetism and alimentary schemes. Absorbed into the competitive ethos of the city, such expenditure was not so much for the greater glory of local élites, that is, in defining their superiority within the social system, as to institutionalize the relations of poor and rich and lock them both into the same value system.[71]

Simon Price makes essentially the same point about the local imperial cults.[72] Whittaker goes on to argue that "crude" (his term) assumptions about the imperial cult merely being "imposed to strengthen loyalty" are not helpful. As Tessa Rajak also notes, the large number of Jewish benefactor inscriptions shows them likewise to be locked into the same value system, whether or not they mention imperial cult activities or functionaries explicitly.[73] Participating in local civic networks of patronage and benefaction locks them in nonetheless. What we have, then, is a series of responses, not all of which should properly be called resistance or even "resistant adaptation," as Jane Webster terms it.[74] Richard Gordon calls it the "civic compromise."[75] Both Whittaker and Webster call for some notion of "negotiated syncretism" as the operative dynamic.

---

69. *AE* 1982: 680, Antonine or early Severan period; also discussed by Gordon, "Veil of Power," 225.

70. C. R. Whittaker, "Imperialism and Culture: The Roman Initiative," in *Dialogues in Roman Imperialism: Power, Discourse, and Discrepant Experience in the Roman Empire* (ed. D. J. Mattingly; JRASup 23; Providence, R.I.: Journal of Roman Archaeology, 1977), 147–49.

71. Ibid., 148. See also Gordon, "Veil of Power," 206–11 (on Augustus as benefactor) and 219–31 (on priests and provincial elites).

72. Price, *Rituals and Power*, 132.

73. Rajak, "Benefactors," 388–89.

74. Whitaker, "Imperialism and Culture," 149; J. Webster, "Negotiated Syncretism: Readings on the Development of Romano-Celtic Religion," in Mattingly, *Dialogues in Roman Imperialism*, 175–80.

75. Gordon, "Veil of Power," 202; R. L. Gordon, "Religion in the Roman Empire: The Civic Compromise and Its Limits," in *Pagan Priests* (ed. Mary Beard and John North; London: Duckworth, 1990), 235–55.

My own term of choice might be "negotiated symbiosis," and I suggest this biological terminology precisely for its organic notion of adaptation. It comes closer to the linguistic analogy offered by Webster's term "creolization," developed in analysis of "Romanization" in the western provinces.[76] In the eastern empire, however, we must remember that the prior effects of "Hellenization" for roughly three centuries create a different cultural framework at the base level. When we look at these inscriptions that show Jewish participation in this same system— *through benefactions of their own, through honorific responses to benefactors, by aping Roman administrative models and terminology, and by appropriating a common symbolic rhetoric of honors*—we are watching the negotiation and symbiosis at work, no less for them than the aspiring freedman, Popidius Ampliatus. It shows, moreover, how the system worked up and down the socioeconomic ladder, as we see in the case of Akmoneia, with its three distinct local tiers—four if you count the provincial administration and five if you count the emperor. One did not have to be at the top in order to know and feel the effects of this value system of patronage, for nearly everyone was tied to others both above and below them.[77] The system of patronage and euergetism under the empire had changed markedly from the more dyadic form of patron client relations that predominated in republican Rome. Especially in the provinces, the operation of local elites *and* their social and economic dependents in this brokered system of exchange created what Garnsey and Saller call "the secret of government without bureaucracy."[78] Still we have to be attentive to each local situation and with an eye toward how heterogeneous populations operated with each local version of the "system." On the other hand, whenever we see (or hear) the rhetoric of patronage and friendship modeled on common *topoi* from the Greco-Roman world, we should be attuned to the "Romanized" value system that they inscribed as an implicit template of cultural norms. Let me now turn to this issue.

---

76. Jane Webster, "Creolizing the Roman Provinces," *AJA* 105 (2001): 217–19.

77. This is the main point I try to document in my analysis of patterns of immigration to cities such as Ephesus, and specifically in light of the Jewish inscriptions there; see L. Michael White, *Ephesos Metropolis of Asia: An Interdisciplinary Approach to Its Archaeology, Religion, and Culture* (ed. Helmut Koester; HTS 41; Valley Forge, Pa.: Trinity Press International, 1995), 59–65.

78. Peter Garnsey and Richard Saller, *The Roman Empire: Economy, Society, and Culture* (Berkeley and Los Angeles: University of California Press, 1987), 26; cf. W. S. Hanson, "Forces of Change and Methods of Control," in *Dialogues in Roman Imperialism: Power, Discourse, and Discrepant Experience in the Roman Empire* (ed. D. J. Mattingly; JRASup 23; Portsmouth, R.I.: Journal of Roman Archaeology, 1997), 76–77.

So far I have been talking about benefactions, honors, and related imperial cult activities primarily as the *mode*[79] of exchange in the negotiation process. They also constitute the *medium*[80] of exchange and, more precisely, the capital itself. Here we need to remember Bourdieu's notion of "symbolic capital."[81] A good example from Archaic and Classical Greece, and thus from a distinct cultural matrix, is the practice of "guest friendship," which functions as a medium of exchange both as real *social capital* but also as *symbolic capital*.[82] Hellenistic ideas of friendship and euergetism are dual derivatives that then get rejoined and mapped onto the Roman patronage system in the late Republic and early empire. Thus, patronage/euergetism and its use of the symbolic language of friendship are in reality *social* and *political capital* (especially through social networks) that function as *economic capital* (both through money and in place of it) as well as *symbolic capital* for the Roman Empire.[83] We need only remember that one of the most common epithets applied to Herod the Great on the public face of his benefactor inscriptions is "friend of Rome" (*philorōmaios*) and "friend of Caesar" (*philokaisar* or *philosebastos*).[84] These same epithets were regularly used in asso-

---

79. Meaning "a particular functioning arrangement or condition" (*Merriam-Webster's Collegiate Dictionary*; 10th ed., 1993) that is also "customary" (or legitimated by "custom") within its cultural context, and thus *modal* in a second sense. See also Ameling, "Jüdische Diaspora," 273 and 278–81.

80. *Medium* has two primary denotations as *mean* and *medium-intermediary*, and each one is applicable to the specialized meaning usually applied to the economic sense: "A means of effecting or conveying something," and "a substance regarded as the means of transmission of a force or effect," or "a channel or system of communication, information, or entertainment" (*Merriam-Webster's Collegiate Dictionary*; 10th ed., 1993).

81. Pierre Bourdieu, *Outline of a Theory of Practice* (trans. Richard Nice; Cambridge Studies in Social and Cultural Anthropology; Cambridge: Cambridge University Press, 1977), 178–79; Pierre Bourdieu, *Distinction: A Social Critique of the Judgement of Taste* (trans. Richard Nice; Cambridge, Mass.: Harvard University Press, 1984), 219. On Bourdieu's theory in dealing with the creation and maintenance of ideology, and specifically Roman imperial ideology, see Clifford Ando, *Imperial Ideology and Provincial Loyalty in the Roman Empire* (Berkeley and Los Angeles: University of California Press, 2000), 19–28.

82. Paul Cartledge, "The Economy (Economies) of Ancient Greece," in *The Ancient Economy* (ed. Walter Scheidel and Sitta von Reden; Edinburgh Readings on the Ancient World; New York: Routledge, 2002), 29–30 (with further examples and bibliography cited there).

83. See my discussion of patronage in terms of network analysis in White, *Social Networks*, 16–20 and 34–36. See also Douglas R. Edwards, *Religion and Power: Pagans, Jews, and Christians in the Greek East* (New York: Oxford University Press, 1996), 49–61 for discussion of how the terminology of civic euergetism was projected to the cosmic level.

84. For Herod see *OGIS* 414, 427; *IG* II2 3440; *SEG* 12 (1955) 250 (all from Athens); *IEJ* 20 (1970) 97–98 (from Jerusalem); and *ZPE* 105 (1995) 81–84 (from Ashdod). See also Monika Bernett, "Der Kaiserkult in Judäa unter herodischer und römischer Herrschaft: Zu Herausbildung und Herausforderung neuer Konzepte Jüdischer Herrschaftslegitimation," in *Jewish Identity in the Greco-Roman World [Jüdische Identität in der Griechisch-Römischen Welt]* (ed.

ciation with the imperial cults, and especially in Roman Asia.⁸⁵ It could be used of individuals as well as corporately. A good example is Domitian's founding of the cult of the Flavian Sebastoi at Ephesus, by granting the city the title: νεωκόρος καὶ φιλοσεβάστος δῆμος.⁸⁶

It is this *symbolic capital* that creates the "value system" noted by Whittaker in the earlier quotation. Following Habermas and Bourdieu, Cliff Ando prefers to recognize it for what it is, an *ideology*—one that is both generative and flexible while also serving as a normative structure.

> Bourdieu, too, following Victor Turner, emphasizes the bounded flexibility of ideologies, whatever their names. He insists, therefore, that it is unnecessary to posit individual subjects mindlessly misrecognizing the fact of their subjugation to an arbitrary social order. Rather a *habitus*, or an ideology, is a system of belief that channels rather than stifles creativity: *habitus* is generative. Roman imperial ideology need not, therefore, have been monolithic or even universal; rather, "*official language, particularly the system of concepts by means of which the members of a given group provide themselves with a representation of their social relations (e.g., the lineage model or the vocabulary of honor), sanctions and imposes what it states, tacitly laying down the dividing line between the thinkable and the unthinkable, thereby contributing towards the maintenance of the symbolic order from which it draws its authority.*" The emperors and the governing class at Rome did not have to provide their world with Scripture, but merely with a system of concepts that could shape, and in so doing unite, the cultural scripts of their subjects.⁸⁷

This is what I referred to earlier as the "implicit template of cultural norms" within and to which people conform in creative ways.⁸⁸

A further indicator that it operated more at the symbolic level is suggested by Arjan Zuiderhoek's recent study of the role of benefaction in the material

---

Jörg Frey, Daniel R. Schwart, and Stephanie Gripentrog; Ancient Judaism and Early Christianity 71; Leiden: Brill, 2007), 219–51.

85. For the epithets in epigraphic formulae, see Chryssoula Veligianni, "*Philos* und *philos*-Komposita in den griechischen Inschriften der Kaiserzeit," in *Aspects of Friendship in the Graeco-Roman World: Proceedings of a Conference Held at the Seminar für Alte Geschichte, Heidelberg, on 10–11 June, 2000* (ed. Michael Peachin; JRASup 43; Portsmouth, R.I.: Journal of Roman Archaeology, 2001), 63–80.

86. Variations on the formula may be seen in *IvE* 1a.27, 36; 2.236, 449; 3.621; 4.1385. Cf. Steven J. Friesen, *Twice Neokoros: Ephesus, Asia, and the Cult of the Flavian Imperial Family* (Leiden: Brill, 1993), 29–49.

87. Ando, *Imperial Ideology*, 23 (italics added, to mark Ando's dependence on Bourdieu's terminology and formulations); the quotation is from Bourdieu, *Outline*, 21.

88. See also Gordon, "Veil of Power," 228 and n. 76 (responding to Price).

economics of civic construction projects in Asia Minor.[89] He argues that despite previous assumptions, the gifts of elite benefactors did *not* substantially pay the costs of the enormous building programs that recreated these cities in the first to third centuries c.e. They were mostly financed by city and imperial treasuries.[90] So, why do the epigraphic as well as literary sources so strongly promote the opposite picture? Precisely because it shows the role of this implicit value system, which, as Zuiderhoek argues, provided a "spin-off" effect.[91] We might now call it a legitimation structure that created an economic stimulus effect, which in turn kept the economy pumping.[92]

The Roman system of civic euergetism operated by combining a real gift with a symbolic value both of which secure or "purchase" tangible goods and benefits in terms of social status and civic honors. Political patronage operated as a similar kind of *beneficium* mediated through friendship networks and rhetoric, as shown by the more "personal" forms of correspondence of Pliny with Trajan in Book 10 of his letters.[93] By combining civic euergetism and elements of friendship rhetoric with local imperial cult activities, the symbolic value is now raised to another level by tying the local exchange with something even higher and more symbolically valuable.[94] Or to put it another way, it operates simultaneously as cultural template (value system or ideology), socioeconomic framework (exchange/network system), and medium (the "coinage" system or capital). As a result, it does not require either coercion or mindless submission to invest it with palpable force

---

89. Arjan Zuiderhoek, "The Icing on the Cake: Benefactors, Economics, and Public Buildings in Roman Asia Minor," in *Patterns in the Economy of Roman Asia Minor* (ed. Stephen Mitchell and Constantina Katsari; Swansea: Classical Press of Wales, 2005), 167–86.

90. Ibid., 174; cf. Gordon, "Veil of Power," 229.

91. Zuiderhoek, "Roman Asia Minor," 174–77.

92. In the preceding paragraphs and the next I am trying to respond more or less directly to Steve Friesen's call (Steven J. Friesen, "Normal Religion, or, Words Fail Us: A Response to Karl Galinsky's 'The Cult of the Roman Emperor: Uniter or Divider?," paper presented at the Annual Meeting of the SBL, Boston, 2008 [and ch. 2 in this volume], 25) to become more sophisticated about our theories regarding religion in dealing with these issues.

93. See Carlos F. Noreña, "The Social Economy of Pliny's Correspondence with Trajan," *AJP* 128 (2007): 242–46, with special note of *Ep.* 10.51.1-2 (245) and 10.120 (271). For the background of this development in Roman political patronage see also: Lukas De Blois, "The Political Significance of Friendship in the *Letters* of Pliny the Younger," in *Aspects of Friendship in the Graeco-Roman World: Proceedings of a Conference Held at the Seminar für Alte Geschichte, Heidelberg, on 10–11 June, 2000* (ed. Michael Peachin; JRASup 43; Portsmouth, R.I.: Journal of Roman Archaeology, 2001), 129–34, and John Nichols, "*Hospitium* and Political Friendship in the Late Republic," in *Aspects of Friendship in the Graeco-Roman World: Proceedings of a Conference Held at the Seminar für Alte Geschichte, Heidelberg, on 10–11 June, 2000* (ed. Michael Peachin; JRASup 43; Portsmouth, R.I.: Journal of Roman Archaeology, 2001), 99–108.

94. Gordon, "Veil of Power," 228.

and real power.⁹⁵ We might also take special note of the number of women who were actively involved in these local cults, again similar to the case of Julia Severa at Akmoneia.⁹⁶

Let's take an example that illustrates the inner workings of the imperial cult at the local level and in the precise social matrix in which we began, namely the urban environment of Roman Asia. Here we turn to one of the many imperial cult inscriptions that were publicly displayed in these cities. In this case it is an "open letter," inscribed in the theater, from the emperor Caracalla addressed to Aurelius Julianus, a local benefactor at Philadelphia, Lydia (Inscription 7).

> Antoninus (Caracalla) himself made this monument.
>
> The Emperor Caesar Marcus Aurelius Antoninus Pius Augustus, greatest Parthicus, greatest Britannicus, greatest Germanicus.
>
> To the most honored Aurelius Julianus. Greetings.
>
> Although no reason dictates that Julianus, a Philadelphian, exchange the *philotimia* (honors) from the Sardians for that of (his) fatherland, nevertheless, I gladly to do so for your favor, on account of whom also I have bestowed this very Neokorate on the Philadelphians.
>
> Farewell, Julianus, my most honored and dearest (friend).
>
> Read in the theater in the year 245 (= 213 C.E.), on the 5th of Apellaeus.
>
> (*SIG*³ 883)

The situation is as follows: Aurelius Julianus—whose *praenomen* must have been Marcus, suggesting some sort of connection to the imperial line⁹⁷—was a Philadelphian who had moved to Sardis, where he began to make benefactions to promote his new civic status.⁹⁸ Apparently he offered a bequest for one of the imperial cult festivals, and the favors were accepted by the emperor. Here note that a city could not just set up a local imperial cult facility or celebration. Rather

---

95. See also Ibid., 222–24; Gordon, "Religion in the Roman Empire."
96. A point similarly noted by Gordon, "Veil of Power," 230.
97. This inscription comes roughly a year after the *Constitutio Antoniana*, the "universal" grant of citizenship; however, citizenship and rank are two different measures. The use of Aurelius as a *gens nomen* became common even among Jews and Christians after this imperial measure. In this case the date and the use of the name may suggest a simultaneous enfranchisement as Roman citizen with either equestrian or, less likely in this case, senatorial rank. It would suggest that Julianus had already achieved prominence in Philadelphia or Sardis that was now being recognized at the imperial level. He might also have served in the imperial bureaucracy for the province of Asia. It is also possible that he had some prior direct contact with Caracalla, perhaps on the emperor's eastern campaigns of 208/209 and 211.
98. On the issue of provincial elites moving from their hometowns to the larger and more prominent cities in order to promote their family's social status see White, "Roman Pergamon." As noted above, the family of Julia Severa was doing the same thing.

they had to "apply " to the emperor by offering to honor him in some particular manner or on some special occasion. Usually these honors were in some way enmeshed in local cults or civic celebrations (as in the Salutaris inscripton from Ephesus). The emperor then decided to accept (or decline) the honors, usually with a formal decree. In this case, it would seem that Julianus's prior relationship with Caracalla had been a crucial element in clinching the deal. His personal cachet with the emperor was therefore instrumental. Thus, Sardis had given him public honors in celebration of the imperial grants that would naturally ensue. Julianus, however, then elected to take the imperial grant of a *neokorate* and bestow it in his own name to Philadelphia. Was he approached by his friends from Philadelphia, presumably with offers of more lavish honors? A likely scenario but impossible to prove; however, some sort of behind-the-scenes dickering and negotiation would seem to be indicated.[99]

Next, the Sardians appealed to the emperor claiming that they had been cheated in the deal, and demanding that Julianus be *forced* to accept his proper "honors" (*philotiminai*) from Sardis. Presumably here it means Sardian citizenship and the usual array of honorific titles and displays for benefactors. He, too, would likely get a statue dedicated in his honor, like Julia Severa in Akmnoneia. But if we think about it, the idea of "forcing" someone to accept such honors is odd, at least from our cultural perspective. Yet that is precisely the point here, as the giving and receiving of euergetic honors was part of the valorized exchange system of the Roman world. Of course, the real issue for the Sardians was that they should get the *neokorate* for the local imperial cult. Finally, Caracalla ruled against the Sardians, and the placement of the inscription represents the official pronouncement of the *neokorate* status on Philadelphia through the benefaction of Julianus.

An element worth noting in this case is the wording with which the emperor prefaces his decision: "*Although no reason [or principle] dictates ... nonetheless I do it*" (εἰ καὶ μηδεὶς αἱρεῖ λόγος ... ἀλλ' ὅμως ... τοῦτο ποιῶ). In this case, it is imperial fiat—not past precedent—that allowed Julianus to return to his native city. So it would seem that the Sardians had a legitimate right to expect that his Sardian residency, and their support in offering to "host" the imperial cult, should give them claim both to his benefaction and the imperial *neokorate* that it secured. Although anomalous, this case shows something very basic about the economic exchange system at work in the imperial cult and its attendant forms of civic euergetism. Once again, we see a three-way exchange between Julianus, the city (first

---

99. Whereas Sardis had received its first provincial imperial cult temple in the first century, with two more under Antoninus Pius and Elagbalus, this seems to be the first for Philadelphia, the "second" city of Lydia. Philadelphia had been part of the provincial *koinon* of the imperial cult but did not house its own cult center prior to this time. Thus the stakes were high for both cities. See Price, *Rituals and Power*, 259–60.

Sardis and then Philadelphia), and the emperor. Of course, the big winners in this deal are Julianus and the Philadelphians. They both banked added political and symbolic capital from the *neokorate* itself. But Julianus's stock really soared. First, he had brokered the deal based on his personal influence and then leveraged it with an imperial fiat. Second, he bargained it up as a result of the added local honors he would receive at Philadelphia, further enhanced by the status markers accorded him as "*most honored and dearest friend*" of the emperor. That's symbolic capital—*cachet, juice, clout, leverage,* call it what you will.

To bring this full circle, back where we began, if we were Jews living in Philadelphia and we were in the position to post a plaque saying that "the Jewish congregation honors Aurelius Julianus, who gave us our synagogue edifice," or something along these lines, what kinds of claims would we be making both on his status and our own? At the same time, what kinds of social networks, obligations, and an attendant value system would it lock us into? I would suggest that this is precisely the calculus of benefactions and honors, further enriched by the linkage to the imperial cult, that the Jews of Akmoneia negotiated when they honored Julia Severa and the three Jewish leaders. How did they justify it theologically? Or did they even worry about it? We will never know.

Conclusions

By way of conclusion, I would suggest that when we return to the matter of responses on the part of early Christians to imperial cult activities, we should expect to find the same broad spectrum of possibilities and modes of negotiation seen among Jews living in Greek and Roman cities. On this point, then, I would call attention to the recent studies of the Jewish experience by Seth Schwartz and Mireille Hadas-Lebel. Both are extremely valuable because they attempt to track the issue of Jewish attitudes toward Rome and to Roman (and eventually Christian-Roman) imperialism longitudinally over several centuries. Hadas-Lebel argues that the large arc of those attitudes, at least in the Jewish homeland, shifted from general friendship, to disillusionment (and revolt), to conciliation, and finally to a *modus vivendi* that affirmed respect and loyalty toward the emperor, a view legitimated theologically through rabbinic *halakah*.[100]

Schwartz's revisionist history likewise focuses on the homeland experience and argues that "imperialism"—first Hellenistic, then Roman, and then Christian-Roman—was a determinative factor in shaping and reshaping Jewish life

---

100. For the last see Mireille Hadas-Lebel, *Jerusalem Against Rome* (trans. Robyn Fréchet; Interdisciplinary Studies in Ancient Culture and Religion; Leuven: Peeters, 2006), 284–99. She also discusses lingering hostile attitudes toward Rome (265–283), showing that the spectrum of views persisted through these several phases.

and thought, both by reaction and by acculturation. Yet he argues that the more extreme forms of sectarian resistance, such as that of the Essenes, were ultimately less significant to the overall development than might be supposed.[101] His view of the last phase (350–640 C.E.) is well summarized in an opening paragraph to his chapter (6) on "Christianization."

> [C]hristianization, and what is in social-historical terms its sibling, [namely] the emergence of religion as a discrete category of human experience—religion's *disembedding*—had a direct impact on the Jewish culture of late antiquity because the Jewish communities *appropriated* much from the Christian society around them. That is, quite a lot of the distinctive Jewish culture was, to be vulgar about it, repackaged Christianity. Much more importantly, the dominant form of Jewish social organization and patterns of expenditure in late antiquity, the local community of the synagogue (its chief material manifestation), were constituted by appropriative participation by Jews in the common late antique culture.[102]

Other than the development of "religion" as a "discrete category," I would suggest that something analogous marked the Jewish—and eventually the breakaway Christian—experience of Roman imperialism in the Diaspora through the prior centuries.

Let's close by taking one last example from the Apocalypse of John. I doubt that any of us would argue against the premise that it represents stringent resistance to Roman imperialism. In my view, it may be the lone incontrovertible case within the New Testament writings. In light of Steve Friesen's work, it must be seen as a vehement attack on the Flavian imperial cult in the province of Asia.[103] That having been said, however, we must still recognize that the imperial cult as such is a secondary target. The real opprobrium is for those Jesus followers who were, in the view of the author, consorting with the "great whore of Babylon" in various ways. Here I would pick up David Frankfurter's suggestion[104] that this, too, may be seen as a battle over Jewish identity and self-definition, even among those who followed Jesus. I would suggest, however, contra Frankfurter, that the bone of contention here is with the participation of these so-called Jews in the

---

101. Schwartz, *Imperialism and Jewish Society*, 62–99.
102. Ibid., 179 (italics his).
103. Friesen, *Twice Neokoros* and ibid., *Imperial Cults and the Apocalypse of John: Reading Revelation in the Ruins* (New York: Oxford University Press, 2001).
104. David Frankfurter, "Jews or not? Reconstructing the 'Other' in Rev 2:9 and 3:9," *HTR* 94 (2001): 403–25. He thinks they were Gentile converts in the Pauline tradition who were calling themselves "Jews," while the author of the Apocalypse was claiming a "truer" sense of Jewish identity. My following remarks will suggest how I would modify this picture. I do not, however, endorse Frankfurter's suggestions about dates and other social-relational issues reflected in the work.

local social economy of these Asian cities. At Ephesus and the other cities named in Rev 2-3—which include Philadelphia and Sardis—it was symbolized through the operation of the Flavian imperial cult, the very emperors who had only a few years earlier destroyed Jerusalem and the temple. Friesen has suggested that one of its forms might simply be consumption of sacrificial meat during provincial festivals.[105] In the view of the author of Revelation, at least, that is what made them unfit to be called "Jews," which I would argue remains their dominant self-understanding.

What this means is that, despite the author's rhetoric of *uncompromising* resistance, most people in the wider audience—an audience made up largely of "Jews" of one stripe or another—lived in that broad, negotiated middle ground. To what extent or in what ways any of them, including the woman called "Jezebel" (Rev 2:20-23) at Thyatira, ever worried about such accommodations remains opaque at best. One such expression, precisely in this period as we have seen, is that of the Jews of Akmoneia in honoring Julia Severa. I think we can guess what the author of the Apocalypse would have said about these Akmonean Jews. Thus, while the Apocalypse itself is an all-out attack on accommodation to the imperial cult in Roman Asia, it is also written testimony to its very *opposite*—namely the wide-spread reality of just this kind of accommodation. Perhaps we should call it a "hidden transcript," but on the opposite side. In fact, these other so-called Jews seem to have been following the same sort of stance urged by the author of 1 Peter: τὸν βασιλέα τιμᾶτε (2:13-17) in addressing "the *sojourners of the diaspora* (παρεπιδήμοις διασπορᾶς) in Pontus, Galatia, Cappadocia, Asia, and Bithynia" (1:1). By contrast, the history of reception of the Apocalypse of John suggests that it remained a rather isolated call, a minority voice; it failed to convince many people in Roman Asia of its non-negotiable stance. This perspective also helps to relocate the discussion of the rest of the New Testament, appropriately in my view, to the larger arena and wider spectrum of Jewish negotiations with Roman rule.

---

105. Friesen, *Imperial Cults*, 196. Cf. Rev 2:14, 20 (Pergamum and Thyatira, respectively).

Inscriptions

1. Akmoneia, Phrygia

   a. The Jewish Community Honors Julia Severa as Benefactor. Ca. 60–80 c.e. *MAMA* 6.264 (White 1997²: no. 65; *CIJ* 766)

   Τὸν κατασκευασθέντα οἶκον ὑπὸ
   Ἰουλίας Σεουήρας Π. Τυρρώνιος Κλά-
   δος, ὁ διὰ βίου ἀρχισυνάγωγος καὶ
   Λούκιος Λουκίου ἀρχισυνάγωγος
   5 καὶ Ποπίλιος Ζωτικὸς ἄρχων ἐπεσ-
   κεύασαν ἐκ τῶν ἰδίων καὶ τῶν συν-
   καταθεμένων καὶ ἔγραψαν τοὺς τοίχους καὶ τὴν ὀροφὴν καὶ ἐποίησαν
   τὴν τῶν θυρίδων ἀσφάλειαν καὶ τόν
   10 λ{υ}<οι>πὸν πάντα κόσμον, οὕστινας κα[ὶ]
   ἡ συναγωγὴ ἐτείμησεν ὅπλῳ ἐπιχρύ-
   σῳ διά τε τὴν ἐνάρετον αὐτῶν δ[ι]άθ[ε]-
   σιν καὶ τὴν πρὸς συναγωγὴν εὔνοιάν
   τε καὶ σπουδήν.

   Translation. This edifice, which was erected by Julia Severa, Publius Tyrronius Clados, archisynagogos for life, Lucius son of Lucius, archisynagogos, and Popilius Zotikos, archon, have renovated from their own funds and from the common treasury (of the congregation); they have decorated the walls and the ceiling, and they made the security of the gates and all the rest of the decoration. The congregation (synagogue) honors all these individuals with a gold shield on account of their excellent leadership and their kindly feelings and zeal on behalf of the congregation (synagogue).

   b. The City of Akmoneia Honors Julia Severa as High Priestess of the Imperial Cult and Civic Benefactor. Ca. 60–80 c.e. *MAMA* 6.263

   ἡ γερουσία ἐτεί-
   μησεν
   Ἰουλίαν Γαίου θυ-
   γατέρα Σεουή-
   5 ραν, ἀρχιέρειαν κα[ὶ]
   ἀγωνοθέτιν τοῦ
   σύνπαντος τῶν
   [θ]εῶν Σεβαστῶν
   [οἴ]κου, πάσης ἀρε-
   10 [τ]ῆς χάριν καὶ τῆς
   [εἰ]ς αὐτὴν εὐεργε-
   vac. σί[ας]· *vac.*
   [τὴν ἀνάστασι]ν πο[ιη-]
   [σαμένου . . . .]

   Translation: The gerusia (of Akmoneia) honors Julia Severa, daughter of Gaius, high priestess and agonothetess of the entire house of the gods, the Sebastoi, in gratitude for all her virtuous deeds and benefactions toward it [the gerusia], and (by?) having erected....

---

* All translations are the author's.

Notes: 1. Julia Severa was of Galatian royal ancestry from Ankyra. She served as eponymous magistrate (*quinquennial duovir*) of Akmoneia, along with Tyrronius Rapo, during the reign of Nero. For their civic titles, as δύο πενταετηρικοὺς, see also *MAMA* 6.265. She served as high priestess of the local imperial cult at Akmoneia under Nero and/or Vespasian. Her husband was L. Servenius Capito, an Italian equestrian from the colony of Pisidian Antioch. Their son, L. Servenius Cornutus, who was also honored for his benefactions to Akmoneia, was adlected to the Senate under Nero (or Vespasian). For other relevant documents, see *MAMA* 6.153, 254, 262, 265 and *IGR* 4.654–656; 3.315. For coinage minted during her archonship see *BMC* 9 (Phrygia) 39–42, 48–50. For discussion see White 1997[2]: no. 65 and White 1998 (which deals with her as well as other members of her family in Roman Asia).

2. The final, fragmentary clause might refer either to her setting up a statue of the emperor or to the gerusia's erection of the statue and base honoring her, in which case I might emend the final word as πο[ιη-] | [σαμένῳ ...]. For use of this formula at Akmoneia compare *MAMA* 6.266.

2. Sardis, Lydia

Dedication by a Jewish Benefactor and City Councillor. Late third century c.e. Kroll 2001: no. 3 (White 1997[2]: no. 67b).

Αὐρ(ήλιος) Ἀλέ-
ξ[αν]δρος ὁ
κα[ὶ Ἀνα]τόλι-
ο[ς Σα]ρδ(ιανὸς) Βου-
5   λ(ευτὴς) τ[ὸ τρί]τον
διαχώρημα ἐ-
κέντησεν

Translation: Aurelios Alexandros, also called Anatolios, a citizen of Sardis (and) City Councillor, mosaicked the third bay.

Notes: Of the numerous donors known from the inscriptions of the Sardis Synagogue, no fewer than nine were members of the City Council (see Kroll 2001: nos. 3, 13, 16/17, 24, 25/26, 31, 34, 37, 67). See also Rajak 2001: 447–62; Williams 1998: 173–75.

3. Egypt

    a. Invocations for Ptolemaic Monarchs by the Jewish Community at Nitriai. Ca. 140–116 B.C.E. *CIJ* 1442 (Lifshitz 1967: no. 94; Horbury and Noy 1992: no. 25).

Ὑπὲρ Βασιλέως Πτολεμαίου
καὶ Βασιλίσσης Κλεοπάτρας
τῆς ἀδελφῆς καὶ Βασιλίσσης
Κλεοπάτρας τῆς γυναικὸς
5 Εὐεργετῶν, οἱ ἐν Νιτρίαις
Ἰουδαῖοι τὴν προσευχὴν
καὶ τὰ συνκύροντα.

Translation. On behalf of King Ptolemy and Queen Cleopatra, his sister, and Queen Cleopatra, his wife, (our) Benefactors, the Jews of Nitriai (dedicated) the prayerhall and its appurtenances.

    b. Two Invocations for Ptolemaic Monarchs by Jewish Benefactors at Athribis. Second or first century B.C.E. *CIJ* 1443–1444 (Lifshitz 1967: 95–96; Horbury and Noy 1992: 27–28).

1443
Ὑπὲρ Βασιλέως Πτολεμαίου
καὶ Βασιλίσσης Κλεοπάτρας
Πτολεμαῖος Ἐπικύδου
ὁ ἐπιστάτης τῶν φυλακιτῶν
5 καὶ οἱ ἐν Ἀθρίβει Ἰουδαῖοι
τὴν προσευχὴν
Θεῶι Ὑψίστωι

1444
Ὑπὲρ Βασιλέως Πτολεμαίου
καὶ Βασιλίσσης Κλεοπάτρας
καὶ τῶν τέκνων
Ἑρμίας καὶ Φιλοτέρα ἡ γυνὴ
5 καὶ παιδία τήνδε ἐξέδραν
τῆι προσευχῆ<ι>

Translation. On behalf of King Ptolemy and Queen Cleopatra, Ptolemy son of Epikydos, prefect of police, and the Jews in Athribis (made) the prayerhall to God Most High.

Translation. On behalf of King Ptolemy and Queen Cleopatra and their children, Hermias and Philotera, his wife, and children, (made) the exedra for the prayerhall.

    c. Invocations for Cleopatra VII and Ptolemy XIV by Jewish Benefactors. Alexandria, ca. 37 B.C.E. *CIJ* 1432 (Lifshitz 1967: no. 86; Horbury and Noy 1992: no. 13).

['Υπὲρ] Βασ[ιλίσ-]
[ση]ς καὶ Β[ασι-]
[λ]έως θεῶι [με-]
γάλω[ι] ἐ[πηκό-]
5 ωι Ἄλυπ[ος τὴν]
προσε[υχὴν]
ἐπο(ί)ει
(ἔτους) ιε' Με[χείρ - - -]

Translation. On behalf of the Queen and King, Alypos made this prayer(hall?) to the Great God who hears (our prayers). In the 15th year in the month of Mecheir....

    d. Ptolemaic-Early Roman Bilingual Proclamation Protecting a Synagogue. Ca. 47–31 B.C.E., replacing an earlier inscription of 145–116 B.C.E. *CIJ* 1449 (Horbury and Noy 1992: no. 125; corrected).

Βασιλίσσης καὶ Βασι-
λέως προσταξάντων
ἀντὶ τῆς προανακει-
μένης περὶ τῆς ἀναθέσε-
5 ως τῆς προσευχῆς πλα-
κὸς ἡ ὑπογεγραμμένη
ἐπιγραφήτων (*vac.*)
Βασιλεὺς Πτολεμαῖος Εὐ-
εργέτης τὴν προσευχὴν
10 (*vac.*) ἄσυλον. (*vac.*)
Regina et
Rex iusser(un)t.

Translation. On the orders of the queen and king, in place of the previous plaque about the dedication of the prayerhall let what is written below be inscribed. King Ptolemy Euergetes (proclaimed) the prayerhall inviolate. (Latin). The queen and king so ordered.

4. BERENIKE, CYRENAIKA.

    a. The Jewish Politeuma Honors Decimus Valerius Dionysius as Benefactor. 8–6 B.C.E. *IBerenike* 18 (White 1997[2]: no. 63a; Lüderitz 1983: no. 70)

(ἔτους) [κ]γ'. Φ[αμ]ένωθ ε' ἐπὶ ἀρχόντων Ἀρίμμα τοῦ
[ca. 7]ος Δωρίωνος τοῦ Πτολεμίου

Ζελαίου τοῦ [Γ]ναίου Ἀρίστωνος τοῦ Ἀραξα-
[..]ντος Σαρα[πί]ωνος τοῦ Ἀνδρομάχου Νικία
5 τ[οῦ ca. 9–10]Α[....] τοῦ Σίμωνος. ν ἐπεὶ
   [Δέκι]μος Ο[ὐαλέριος Γ]αίο[υ Διον]ύσιος <u>πρηπο<σί>της</u>   (*my conj.*)
   [.........]ΩΓΗΣ ἀνὴρ καλὸς καὶ ἀγαθὸς ὢν δια-
   τελε[ῖ ? λόγω] καὶ ἔργω καὶ αἱρ[έσει καὶ ποιῶν ἀγαθὸν
   [ὅτι] ἄ[ν] δ[ύνηται καὶ κοι]νᾶι καὶ ἰδίαι ἑκάστωι τῶν
10 π[ο]λίτ[ων] καὶ δ[ὴ καὶ] ἐκονίασεν τοῦ ἀνφιθεάτρου
   τ[ὸ ἔδ]αφος καὶ τοὺ[ς] τοίχους ἐζωγράφησεν
   ἔ[δοξε τοῖς ἄ]ρχουσι καὶ τῶι πολιτεύματι
   τ[ῶν] ἐν Βερινικίδι Ιουδαίων καταγράψαι αὐτὸν εἰς
   τὸ τῶν τ[ca. 6]ΕΥΕΙΣ <u>(Ἰο)υδ(α)ίου</u> καὶ εἶεν ἀλειτούρ-   (*my conj.*)
15 γητο[ν πά]σης [λε]ιτουρ[γί]ας [ὁ]μοίως δὲ καὶ στε-
   φα[νοῦν α]ὐτὸν καθ' ἑκάστην σύνοδον καὶ νουμηνίαν στε[φ]άνωι καὶ λημνίσκωι ὀνομαστὶ
   τὸ [δ]ὲ ψήφισμα τόδε ἀναγράψαντεσ οἱ ἄρχον[τες]
   [εἰ]ς στήλην λίθου Παρίου θέτωσαν εἰς τὸν ἐ[πι-]
20 [σημ]ότατον [τόπ]ον τοῦ ἀμφιθεάτρου.
                   λευκαὶ πᾶσαι
                        vac.
   Δέκ(ι)μος Οὐαλέριος Γαίου Διονύσιος
   τὸ ε[δ]α[φ]ος ἐκονίασεν καὶ τὸ ἀμφι-
   θέατρον καὶ ἐζωγράφησεν τοῖς
25 ἰδίοις δαπανήμασιν ἐπίδομα
                   τῶι πολιτεύματι.

Translation. In the year [2]3, on the 5th of Phamenoth, in the archonship of Arimmas son of […], Dorion son of Ptolemaios, Zelaios son of Gnaios, Ariston son of Arax[..]as, Sarapion son of Andromachos, Nikias son of [… (and) …] son of Simon.

Whereas Decimus Valerius Dionysius son of Gaius, praepositus of the [council?] continues to be an honorable and good man in word, in deed, and in purpose, and doing whatever good he is able, whether in public or private matters (dealing rightly) with each of the citizens, and

Whereas, moreover, he has plastered the floor of the amphitheater and painted the walls, it is hereby resolved by the archons of the politeuma of the Jews in Berenike to inscribe him in the […] of a Jew (?), and that he be exempted from all liturgies whatsoever, and moreover to crown him with an olive crown and a wooden nameplate at each synod and new moon.

Wherefore, the archons, having inscribed this resolution on a stele of Parian marble, are to set it up in a conspicuous place in the amphitheater.

          (The vote:)   all whites.   (*vac.*)

Decimus Valerius Dionysius, son of Gaius, both plastered the floor of the amphitheater and painted (it) at his own expense as a gift to the politeuma (of the Jews).

b. The Jewish Politeuma Honors the Provincial Praefect Marcus Tittius. 24/25 C.E. *IBerenike* 17 (Lüderitz 1983, no. 71).

['Έ]τους νε' Φαῶφ κε' ἐπὶ συλλόγου τῆς σκηνο-
πηγίας ἐπὶ ἀρχόντων Κλεάνδρου τοῦ
Στρατονίκου Εὐφράνορος τοῦ Ἀρίστωνος
Σωσιγένους τοῦ Σωσίππου Ἀνδρομάχου
5 τοῦ Ἀνδρομάχου Μάρκου Λαιλίου Ὀνασί-
ωνος τοῦ Ἀπολλωνίου Φιλωνίδου τοῦ Ἁγή-
μονος Αὐτοκλέους τοῦ Ζήνωνος Σωνί-
κου τοῦ Θεοδότου Ἰωσήπου τοῦ Στράτωνος

ἐπεὶ Μᾶρκος Τίττιος Σέξτου υἱὸς Αἰμιλία
10 ἀνὴρ καλὸς καὶ ἀγαθὸς παραγενηθεὶς εἰς
τὴν ἐπαρχείαν ἐπὶ δημοσίων πραγμάτων τήν
τε προστασίαν αὐτῶν ἐποιήσατο φιλανθρώ-
πως καὶ καλῶς ἔν τε τῇ ἀναστροφῇ ἡσύχιον
ἦθος ἐνδ(ε)ικνύμενος ἀεὶ διατελῶν τυγχάνει
15 οὐ μόνον δὲ ἐν τούτοις ἀβαρῆ ἑαυτὸν παρέσ-
χηται ἀλλὰ καὶ τοῖς κατ' ἰδίαν ἐντυγχάνουσι
τῶν πολιτῶν ἔτι δὲ καὶ τοῖς ἐκ τοῦ πολιτεύ-
ματος ἡμῶν Ἰουδαίοις καὶ κοινῇ καὶ κατ' ἰδίαν
εὔχρηστον προστασίαν ποιούμενος οὐ δια-
20 λείπει τῆς ἰδίας καλοκἀγαθίας ἄξια πράσσων
ὧν χάριν ἔδοξε τοῖς ἄρχουσι καὶ τῶι πολιτεύματι τῶν ἐν Βερενίκῃ Ἰουδαίων ἐπαινέσαι τε αὐτὸν καὶ σεφανοῦν ὀνομαστὶ καθ' ἑκάστην
σύνοδον καὶ νουμηνίαν στεφάνωι ἐλαίνωι καὶ
25 λημνίσκωι τοὺς δὲ ἄρχοντας ἀαγράψαι τὸ
ψήφισμα εἰς στήλην λίθου παρίου καὶ θεῖναι εἰς
τὸν ἐπισημότατον τόπον τοῦ ἀμφιθεάτρου
        Λευ- καὶ   πᾶ- σαι

Translation. In the year 55, on the 25th of Phaoph, in the assembly on the Feast of Sukkoth, in the archonship of Cleander son of Stratonikos, Euphranor son of Ariston, Sosigenes son of Sosippos, Andromachos son of Andromachos, Marcus Lailios Onasion son of Apollonios, Philonidos son of Hagemon, Autocles son of Zenon, Sonikos son of Theodotos, and Josephos son of Straton:

Whereas Marcus Tittius, son of Sextus, of the tribe Aimilia, being an honorable and good man, having come into the provincial praefecture for public affairs, he well served as their president both nobly and philanthropically, and in his term ever demonstrating a quiet character, he continues to do so, and not only did he present himself in a not-overbearing manner in these (public matters) but also to those of the citizens who encountered him privately. *And*

Whereas still more for Jews from our politeuma, both publicly and in private, serving the presidency beneficially, he did not cease acting worthily of his own nobility, in gratitude for which it is hereby resolved by the archons and the politeuma of the Jews in Berenike, to praise him by name and to crown him with an olive crown and wooden nameplate at each synod and new moon.

Wherefore, the archons shall inscribe this decree on a stele of Parian marble and set it up in a conspicuous place in the amphitheater.

           (The vote:)   All whites.

5. OSTIA, ITALIA.

    a.   Pro Salute Dedication of Synagogue Construction by a Benefactor. Ca. 190–225 C.E..; later reinscribed. Ostia Inv. 8978 (White 1997²: no. 84; Noy 1993: no. 13).

```
    PRO SALVTE AVG[-]                        Pro Salute Aug(usti or -ustorum)
    ΟΙΚΟΔΟΜΗCΕΝ ΚΕ ΑΙΠΟ                      οἰκοδόμησεν κ(αὶ) ἐπο<ί> -
    ΗCΕΝ ΕΚ ΤωΝ ΑΥΤΟΥ ΔΟ                     ησεν ἐκ τῶν αὐτοῦ δο-
    ΜΑΤωΝ ΚΑΙ ΤΗΝ ΚΕΙΒωΤΟΝ                   μάτων καὶ τὴν κ{ε}ιβωτὸν
5   ΑΝΕΘΗΚΕΝ ΝΟΜω ΑΓΙω                    5  ἀνέθηκεν νόμῳ ἁγίῳ
    ⟦(ΜΙΝΔΙC ΦΑΥCΤΟC Μ)⟧Ε                    ⟦( Μίνδι<ο>ς Φαῦστος μ)⟧ε-
    ]ΝΙΔΙωΝ[                                 ⟦([τὰ τῶ]ν ἰδιῶγ)⟧
```

Translation: **For the well-being of the Emperor(s).** <u>Mindi(u)s Faustos</u> [together with his household] built (this building) and made it from his own gifts, and he dedicated the ark for the Holy Law.

Notes: 1. The name *Mindius Faustus* is clearly secondary, reinscribed in a second hand after the earlier donor's name had been chiseled off. The *L. Mindii* were a common gentilicium in Ostian onomastics. See White 1997² 393 (n. 165) for epigraphic examples.

2. The Latin salutary formula *Pro Salute Aug(usti)* is especially prominent in the Antonine and Severan periods. For other examples from Ostia and Rome see White 1997² 392 (n. 163). The space at the end of the first line would allow for AVG[G] (the typical abbreviation for Augustorum), but the stone is broken at that point. The alignment of the right edge of the stone would favor the plural abbreviation. If restored correctly in the plural, as found commonly at Ostia, the

joint emperors being honored might be either Marcus Aurelius and Lucius Verus (161–169), Marcus Aurelius and Commodus (176–180), Septimius Severus and Caracalla [and sometimes Geta] (204–211), or Caracalla and Geta (211–212). If correctly restored in the singular, the emperor being honored might be either Marcus Aurelius (169–176), Commodus (180–192), Septimius Severus (193–204), or Caracalla (212–217). Horsely (*NDIEC* 4:112) and Noy (1993:25), following Chevalier and Guarducci, suggested a late second century C.E.. for the first hand, while both Horsley and Noy proposed late third century for the second hand in Lines 6 and 7. A date after 190 C.E. and during the Severan period (211–224) is now made more likely by recent finds in the UT excavations of the Synagogue: one is a coin of Commodus dating to 190; the other, a second "Pro Salute" inscription naming the joint emperors Caracalla and Geta (211–212 C.E.). Publication of both items is forthcoming.

b. Funerary Titulus of C. Julius Justus, Jewish gerusiarch from Ostia. Ca. late second–early third century *CIJ* 533 (White 1997[2]: no. 85; Noy 1993: no. 18).

```
   [Universitas or Collegium?] Iudeorum
   [in col(onia) Ost(iensis) commor]antium qui compara-
   [verunt ex conlat]ione locum C. Iulio Iusto
   [gerusiarchae ad m]unimentum struendum
5  [donavit rogantib]us Livio Dionisio patre et
   [... patro?]no gerusiarche et Antonio
   [..... dia b]iu anno ipsorum consent(iente) ge[r]-
   [us(iae) C. Iulius Iu]stus gerusiarches fecit sibi
   [et coniugi] suae lib(ertis) lib(ertabusque) posteriorisque eorum
10 [in fro]nte p(edes) XVIII, in agro p(edes) XVII.
```

Translation: The Community (? Collegium or Synagogue) of the Jews dwelling in the colony of Ostia, who from the collection acquired a place (or plot) for C(aius) Julius Justus, gerusiarch, so that he might construct a monument, have (hereby) donated it to him at the request of Livius Dionysius, father and patron (of the collegium?), gerusiarch, and of Antonius [? archon?] for life, in the year of their office, by consent of the gerusia. C. Julius Justus, gerusiarch, made (this monument) for himself and his wife, together with their freedmen and freedwomen and their descendants, in width, 18 feet; depth, 17 feet.

Notes: This inscription was discovered at Castel Porziano a few miles south of Ostia, but along the same coastal highway, the Via Severiana, on which the Ostia synagogue is situated. The area to the southeast of the synagogue along the coast was dotted by *nekropoleis*, and this funerary titulus probably came from that region. Unfortunately, it cannot be more directly tied to the synagogue itself.

6. POMPEII, ITALIA.

Decurial Honors for N. Popidius Celsinus, "Civic" Benefactor. Ca. 62 C.E. *CIL* 10.846.

N(umerivs) · Popidivs · N(umerii) · f(ilivs)· Celsinvs
   aedem Isidis terrae motv conlapsam
a fvndamento p(ecvnia) s(va) restitvit. Hvnc decvriones ob liberalitem
   cvm esset annorvm sex ordini svo gratis adlegervnt.

Translation: Numerius Popidius Celsinus, son of Numerius [Popidius Ampliatus], rebuilt from its foundations the temple of Isis after it had collapsed from an earthquake. On account of his generosity, the decurions [of Pompeii] have adlected him at no cost into their own order, even though he was only six years old.

7. PHILADELPHIA, LYDIA.

A Decree of the Emperor Caracalla Granting an Imperial Cult (neokoria) in Response to a Local Benefactor. 213 C.E. *SIG*³ 883, *IGR* 4.1619 (White 1998: 358).

Ἀντωνεῖνός σ᾽ ἔκτιζε.
Αὐτοκράτωρ | Καῖσαρ Μάρκος | Αὐρήλιος Ἀντωνεῖ|νος Εὐσεβὴς Σεβασ|τὸς Παρθικὸς μέγισ|τος Βρεταννικὸς μέγ|ιστος Γερμανικὸς | μέγιστος Αὐρηλίῳ |Ἰο[υλιανῶ]ι τῷ τιμι | ωτάτωι χαίρειν.
εἰ καὶ μηδεὶς αἱρεῖ | λόγος τὸν Φιλαδελ|φέα Ἰουλιανὸν ἀπὸ τῶν Σαρδιανῶν| εἰς τὴν τῆς πατρί|δος μεταθεῖναι φι | λοτειμίαν, ἀλλ᾽ ὅμως | σὴν χάριν ἡδέως | τοῦτο ποιῶ, δι᾽ ὃν καὶ | τὴν νεωκορίαν αὐ|τὴν τοῖς Φιλαδελ|φεῦσ[ιν δὲ]δωκα. | ἔρρωσο Ἰουλι[ανὲ] | τιμιώτατέ μοι καὶ φίλ|τατε.
ἀνεγνώσθη ἐν τῷ | θεάτρῳ ἔτους σμε΄, μη|νὸς Ἀπελλαίου ε΄.

Translation: Antoninus (Caracalla) himself made this monument.
The Emperor Caesar Marcus Aurelius Antoninus Pius Augustus, greatest Parthicus, greatest Britannicus, greatest Germanicus.   To the most honored Aurelius Julianus. Greetings.
Although no reasons dictates that Julianus, a Philadelphian, exchange the *philotimia* (honors) from the Sardians for that of (his) fatherland, neverthe-

less, I gladly to do so for your favor, on account of whom also I have bestowed this very Neokorate on the Philadelphians.
Farewell, Julianus, my most honored and dearest (friend).
Read in the theater in the year 245 (= 213 C.E.), on the 5th of Apellaeus.

BIBLIOGRAPHY

Ameling, Walter. "Die Jüdische Diaspora Kleinasiens und der 'Epigrapic Habit." Pages 253–84 in *Jewish Identity in the Greco-Roman World [Jüdische Identität in der Griechisch-Römischen Welt]*. Edited by Jörg Frey, Daniel R. Schwart, and Stephanie Gripentrog. Ancient Judaism and Early Christianity 71. Leiden: Brill, 2007.

Ando, Clifford. *Imperial Ideology and Provincial Loyalty in the Roman Empire*. Berkeley and Los Angeles: University of California Press, 2000.

Applebaum, Shim'on. *Jews and Greeks in Ancient Cyrene*. Studies in Judaism in Late Antiquity 28. Leiden: Brill, 1979.

Beard, Mary, and John North. *Pagan Priests*. London: Duckworth, 1990.

Bernett, Monika. "Der Kaiserkult in Judäa unter herodischer und römischer Herrschaft: Zu Herausbildung und Herausforderung neuer Konzepte Jüdischer Herrschaftslegitimation." Pages 205–51 in *Jewish Identity in the Greco-Roman World [Jüdische Identität in der Griechisch-Römischen Welt]*. Edited by Jörg Frey, Daniel R. Schwart, and Stephanie Gripentrog. Ancient Judaism and Early Christianity 71. Leiden: Brill, 2007.

Bourdieu, Pierre. *Distinction: A Social Critique of the Judgement of Taste*. Translated by Richard Nice. Cambridge, Mass.: Harvard University Press, 1984.

———. *Outline of a Theory of Practice*. Translated by Richard Nice. Cambridge Studies in Social and Cultural Anthropology. Cambridge: Cambridge University Press, 1977.

Cartledge, Paul. "The Economy (Economies) of Ancient Greece." Pages 11–32 in *The Ancient Economy*. Edited by Walter Scheidel and Sitta von Reden. Edinburgh Readings on the Ancient World. New York: Routledge, 2002.

Cohen, Shaye J. D. "'Those Who Say They Are Jews and Are Not': How Do You Know a Jew in Antiquity When You See One?" Pages 1–45 in *Diasporas in Antiquity*. Edited by Shaye J. D. Cohen and Ernest S. Frerichs. Brown Judaic Studies 288. Atlanta: Scholars Press, 1993.

———, and Ernest S. Frerichs, eds. *Diasporas in Antiquity*. Brown Judaic Studies 288. Atlanta: Scholars Press, 1993.

De Blois, Lukas. "The Political Significance of Friendship in the *Letters* of Pliny the Younger." Pages 129–34. In *Aspects of Friendship in the Graeco-Roman World: Proceedings of a Conference Held at the Seminar für Alte Geschichte, Heidelberg, on 10–11 June, 2000*. Edited by Michael Peachin. Journal of Roman Archaeology. Supplementary Series 43. Portsmouth, R.I.: Journal of Roman Archaeology, 2001.

Edwards, Douglas R. *Religion and Power: Pagans, Jews, and Christians in the Greek East*. New York: Oxford University Press, 1996.

Frankfurter, David. "Jews or not? Reconstructing the 'Other' in Rev 2:9 and 3:9." *Harvard Theological Review* 94 (2001): 403–25.

Freeman, P. W. M. "Mommsen Through to Haverfield: The Origins of Romanization Studies in Late 19th-Cent. Britain." Pages 27–50 in *Dialogues in Roman Imperialism:*

Power, Discourse, and Discrepant Experience in the Roman Empire. Edited by D. J. Mattingly. Journal of Roman Archaeology Supplementary Series 23. Providence, R.I.: Journal of Roman Archaeology, 1997.
Frey, Jean-Baptiste, ed. *Corpus of Jewish Inscriptions [Corpus Inscrptionum Judaicarum]: Jewish Inscriptions from the Third Century B.C. to the Seventh Century A.D.* New York: Ktav, 1975.
Frey, Jörg, Daniel R. Schwart, and Stephanie Gripentrog, eds. *Jewish Identity in the Greco-Roman World [Jüdische Identität in der Griechisch-Römischen Welt].* Ancient Judaism and Early Christianity 71. Leiden: Brill, 2007.
Friesen, Steven J. *Imperial Cults and the Apocalypse of John: Reading Revelation in the Ruins.* New York: Oxford University Press, 2001.
———. "Normal Religion, or, Words Fail Us: A Response to Karl Galinsky's 'The Cult of the Roman Emperor: Uniter or Divider?.'" Paper presented at the Annual Meeting of the SBL, Boston, 2008, and ch. 2 in this volume.
———. *Twice Neokoros: Ephesus, Asia, and the Cult of the Flavian Imperial Family.* Leiden: Brill, 1993.
Garnsey, Peter, and Richard Saller. *The Roman Empire: Economy, Society, and Culture.* Berkeley and Los Angeles: University of California Press, 1987.
Goldhill, Simon, ed. *Being Greek Under Rome: Cultural Identity, the Second Sophistic, and the Development of Empire.* Cambridge: Cambridge University Press, 2001.
Goodman, Martin, ed. *Jews in a Graeco-Roman World.* Oxford: Oxford University Press, 1998.
Gordon, R. L. "Religion in the Roman Empire: The Civic Compromise and Its Limits." Pages 235–55 in *Pagan Priests.* Edited by Mary Beard and John North. London: Duckworth, 1990.
———. "The Veil of Power: Emperors, Sacrificers and Benefactors." Pages 199–231 in *Pagan Priests.* Edited by Mary Beard and John North. London: Duckworth, 1990.
Hadas-Lebel, Mireille. *Jerusalem Against Rome.* Translated by Robyn Fréchet. Interdisciplinary Studies in Ancient Culture and Religion. Leuven: Peeters, 2006.
Halfmann, Helmut. *Die Senatoren aus dem östlichen Teil des Imperium Romanum bis zum Ende des 2. Jahrhunderts n. Chr.* Hypomnemata 58. Göttingen: Vandenhoeck und Ruprecht, 1979.
Hanges, James Constantine. "To Complicate Encounters: A Response to Karl Galinsky's 'The Cult of the Roman Emperor: Uniter or Divider?.'" Paper presented at the Annual Meeting of the SBL, Boston, 2008, and ch. 3 in this volume.
Hanson, W. S. "Forces of Change and Methods of Control." Pages 67–80 in *Dialogues in Roman Imperialism: Power, Discourse, and Discrepant Experience in the Roman Empire.* Edited by D. J. Mattingly. Journal of Roman Archaeology Supplementary Series 23. Portsmouth, R.I.: Journal of Roman Archaeology, 1997.
Horsley, G. H. R. *New Documents Illustrating Early Christianity: A Review of the Greek Inscriptions and Papyri 4 1979.* North Ryde, Australia: North Ryde Ancient History Documentary Research Centre, Macquarie University, 1987.
Jones, A. H. M. *The Greek City from Alexander to Justinian.* Oxford: Clarendon, 1940.
Jongman, Willem. *The Economy and Society of Pompeii.* Dutch Monographs on Ancient History and Archaeology 4. Amsterdam: Gieben, 1988.
Kasher, Aryeh. *The Jews in Hellenistic Egypt.* Texte und Studien zum antiken Judentum 7. Tübingen: Mohr Siebeck, 1985.

Kroll, John H. "The Greek Inscriptions of the Sardis Synagogue." *Harvard Theological Review* 94 (2001): 5–55.
Levick, Barbara. *Roman Colonies in Southern Asia Minor*. Oxford: Clarendon, 1967.
Lifshitz, Baruch. *Donateurs et fondateurs dans les synagogues juives, répertoire des dédicaces grecques relatives à la construction et à la réfection des synagogues*. Cahiers de la Revue Biblique 7. Paris: J. Gabalda, et Cie, 1967.
Linder, Amnon. *The Jews in Roman Imperial Legislation*. In *Jews in Roman Imperial Legislation*. Detroit: Wayne State University Press, 1987.
Lüderitz, Gert von. *Corpus jüdischer Zeugnisse aus der Cyrenaika*. Beihefte zum Tübinger Atlas des Vorderen Orients. Reihe B, Geisteswissenschaften. Wiesbaden: L. Reichert, 1983.
MacMullen, Ramsey. "The Epigraphic Habit in the Roman Empire." *American Journal of Philology* 103 (1982): 233–46.
Mattingly, D. J., ed. *Dialogues in Roman Imperialism: Power, Discourse, and Discrepant Experience in the Roman Empire*. Journal of Roman Archaeology Supplementary Series 23. Portsmouth, R.I.: Journal of Roman Archaeology, 1997.
———. "Africa: A Landscape of Opportunity?" Pages 117–39 in *Dialogues in Roman Imperialism: Power, Discourse, and Discrepant Experience in the Roman Empire*. Edited by D. J. Mattingly. Journal of Roman Archaeology Supplementary Series 23. Portsmouth, R.I.: Journal of Roman Archaeology, 1997.
McLaren, James S. "Jews and the Imperial Cult: From Augustus to Domitian." *Journal of the Study of the New Testament* 27 (2005): 257–78.
Modrzejewski, Joseph Mélèze. "How to Be a Jew in Hellenistic Egypt?" Pages 65–92 in *Diasporas in Antiquity*. Edited by Shay J. D. Cohen and Ernest S. Frerichs. Brown Judaic Studies 288. Atlanta: Scholars Press, 1993.
Nichols, John. "*Hospitium* and Political Friendship in the Late Republic." Pages 99–108 in *Aspects of Friendship in the Graeco-Roman World: Proceedings of a Conference Held at the Seminar Für Alte Geschichte, Heidelberg, on 10–11 June, 2000*. Edited by Michael Peachin. Journal of Roman Archaeology Supplementary Series 43. Portsmouth, R.I.: Journal of Roman Archaeology, 2001.
Noreña, Carlos F. "The Social Economy of Pliny's Correspondence with Trajan." *American Journal of Philology* 128 (2007): 239–77.
Noy, David. *Italy (Excluding the City of Rome), Spain and Gaul*. Vol. 1 of *Jewish Inscriptions of Western Europe*. Cambridge: Cambridge University Press, 1993.
Peachin, Michael, ed. *Aspects of Friendship in the Graeco-Roman World: Proceedings of a Conference Held at the Seminar Für Alte Geschichte, Heidelberg, on 10–11 June, 2000*. Journal of Roman Archaeology Supplementary Series 43. Portsmouth, R.I.: Journal of Roman Archaeology, 2001.
Pensabene, Patrizio. *Scavi di Ostia VII: I capitelli*. Rome: Istituto Poligrafico dello Stato, 1973.
Price, S. R. F. *Rituals and Power: The Roman Imperial Cult in Asia Minor*. Cambridge: Cambridge University Press, 1984.
Pucci Ben Zeev, Miriam. *Diaspora Judaism in Turmoil, 116/117 CE: Ancient Sources and Modern Insights*. Interdisciplinary Studies in Ancient Culture and Religion. Leuven: Peeters, 2005.
Rajak, Tessa. "Benefactors in the Greco-Jewish Diaspora." Pages 373–91 in *The Jewish Dialogue with Greece and Rome: Studies in Cultural and Social Interaction*. Tessa Rajak.

1996. Repr. Arbeiten zur Geschichte des antiken Judentums und des Urchristentums 48. Leiden: Brill, 2001.

———. "The Gifts of God at Sardis." Pages 229–40 in *Jews in a Graeco-Roman World*. Edited by Martin Goodman. Oxford: Clarendon, 1998.

———. *The Jewish Dialogue with Greece and Rome: Studies in Cultural and Social Interaction*. Arbeiten zur Geschichte des antiken Judentums und des Urchristentums 48. Leiden: Brill, 2001.

———. "Jews, Pagans, and Christians in Late Antique Sardis: Models of Interaction." Pages 447–62 in *The Jewish Dialogue with Greece and Rome: Studies in Cultural and Social Interaction*. Tessa Rajak. Arbeiten zur Geschichte des antiken Judentums und des Urchristentums 48. Leiden: Brill, 2001.

———. "The Synagogue in the Greco-Roman City." Pages 463–78 in *The Jewish Dialogue with Greece and Rome: Studies in Cultural and Social Interaction*. Tessa Rajak. 1999. Repr. Arbeiten zur Geschichte des antiken Judentums und des Urchristentums 48. Leiden: Brill, 2001.

Rajak, Tessa, and David Noy. "*Archisynagogoi*: Office, Title, and Social Status in the Greco-Jewish Synagogue." Pages 393–430 in *The Jewish Dialogue with Greece and Rome: Studies in Cultural and Social Interaction*. Tessa Rajak. 1993. Repr. Arbeiten zur Geschichte des antiken Judentums und des Urchristentums 48. Leiden: Brill, 2001.

Reynolds, Joyce, and Robert Tannenbaum. *Jews and God-Fearers at Aphrodisias: Greek Inscriptions with Commentary: Texts from the Excavations at Aphrodisias Conducted by Kenan T. Erim*. Supplementary Vol. 12. Cambridge: Cambridge Philological Society, 1987.

Scheidel, Walter, and Sitta von Reden, eds. *The Ancient Economy*. Edinburgh Readings on the Ancient World. New York: Routledge, 2002.

Schwartz, Seth. *Imperialism and Jewish Society, 200 B.C.E. to 640 C.E.* Jews, Christians, and Muslims from the Ancient to the Modern World. Princeton, N.J.: Princeton University Press, 2001.

———. "The Rabbi in Aphrodite's Bath: Palestinian Society and Jewish Identity in the High Roman Empire." Pages 335–61 in *Being Greek Under Rome: Cultural Identity, the Second Sophistic, and the Development of Empire*. Edited by Simon Goldhill. Cambridge: Cambridge University Press, 2001.

Veligianni, Chryssoula. "*Philos* und *philos*-Komposita in den griechischen Inschriften der Kaiserzeit." Pages 63–80 in *Aspects of Friendship in the Graeco-Roman World: Proceedings of a Conference Held at the Seminar für Alte Geschichte, Heidelberg, on 10–11 June, 2000*. Edited by Michael Peachin. Journal of Roman Archaeology Supplementary Series 43. Portsmouth, R.I.: Journal of Roman Archaeology, 2001.

Webster, Jane. "Creolizing the Roman Provinces." Journal of Roman Archaeology Supplementary Series 23, 105 (2001): 209–25.

———. "Negotiated Syncretism: Readings on the Development of Romano-Celtic Religion." Pages 165–84 in *Dialogues in Roman Imperialism: Power, Discourse, and Discrepant Experience in the Roman Empire*. Edited by D. J. Mattingly. Journal of Roman Archaeology Supplementary Series. 23. Providence, R.I.: Journal of Roman Archaeology, 1997.

White, L. Michael. "Counting the Cost of Nobility: The Social Economy of Roman Pergamon." Pages 331–71 in *Pergamon: Citadel of the Gods*. Edited by Helmut Koester. Harrisburg, Pa.: Trinity Press International, 1998.

———. *Ephesos Metropolis of Asia: An Interdisciplinary Approach to Its Archaeology, Religion, and Culture*. Edited by Helmut Koester. Harvard Theological Studies 41. Valley Forge, Pa.: Trinity Press International, 1995.

———. *Texts and Monuments for the Christian Domus Ecclesiae in Its Environment*. Vol. 2 of *The Social Origins of Christian Architecture*. Harvard Theological Studies 42. Valley Forge, Pa.: Trinity Press International, 1997.

———, ed. *Social Networks in the Early Christian Environment: Issues and Methods for Social History*. Semeia. Atlanta: Society of Biblical Literature, 1991.

Whittaker, C. R. "Imperialism and Culture: The Roman Initiative." Pages 143–63 in *Dialogues in Roman Imperialism: Power, Discourse, and Discrepant Experience in the Roman Empire*. Edited by D. J. Mattingly. Journal of Roman Archaeology Supplementary Series 23. Providence, R.I.: Journal of Roman Archaeology, 1997.

Willliams, Margaret. *The Jews Among the Greeks and Romans: A Diasporan Sourcebook*. Baltimore: Johns Hopkins University Press, 1998.

Woolf, Greg. *Becoming Roman: The Origins of Provincial Civilization in Gaul*. Cambridge: Cambridge University Press, 1998.

Zuiderhoek, Arjan. "The Icing on the Cake: Benefactors, Economics, and Public Buildings in Roman Asia Minor." Pages 167–86 in *Patterns in the Economy of Roman Asia Minor*. Edited by Stephen Mitchell and Constantina Katsari. Swansea: Classical Press of Wales, 2005.

CHAPTER 13
IN THE SHADOW (OR NOT) OF THE IMPERIAL CULT:
A COOPERATIVE AGENDA

Karl Galinsky

The purpose of this paper is to outline where we stand with our dialogue project on early Christianity and its imperial Roman *Sitz im Leben* with a focus on the so-called imperial cult.[1] The impulse came from several interdisciplinary National Endowment for the Humanities seminars I directed on Roman religion and, more specifically, from its very activist members on both sides of an ever-diminishing fence, that is, scholars of both religious studies and classicists. I want to thank, especially, Jonathan Reed and Barbette Spaeth for all the time they have put into organizing this dialogue, and my colleagues Michael White and Steve Friesen, who have helped me in more ways than I can recount.

We are not at the end; this is only a beginning. In Boston in 2008, I chose the micro route to discuss some specific details of the imperial cult. This time, my approach is more macro, to identify and comment on some major themes that are important for our current and future agenda.

First, the very fact of the contextualization of the New Testament with its Roman setting at the time. It is a totally positive and overdue development that this is happening now and with infinitely greater force than Adolf Deissmann's *Licht vom Osten*.[2] The reason such initiatives stopped was not the emergence of the other Adolf. One of the main culprits is disciplinary compartmentalization. Being based in Germany a great deal over the next few years I can attest again that the merely physical obstacle course from one departmental library to the next is a handicap for the interdisciplinary researcher, even if it contributes to physical

---

1. Cf., once more, the formulation of Mary Beard, John North, and Simon Price, *Religions of Rome*. Vol. 1: *A History* (Cambridge: Cambridge University Press, 1998), 348: "There is no such thing as '*the* imperial cult.'"
2. Adolf Deissmann, *Licht vom Osten: Das Neue Testament und die neuentdeckten Texte der hellenistisch-römischen Welt* (4th ed.; 1908; repr., Tübingen: Mohr, 1923).

-215-

fitness (there are exceptions). More pertinent, the result of disciplinary separation and lack of cross-training has been that New Testament scholars often very much do their own thing when it comes to working with evidence from Greco-Roman history. Conversely, most classicists will simply stay away from New Testament scholarship—who needs it for teaching the Bible as literature, if that? In that case, there are, by default, no methodological issues whereas in the former, there are, because of the plethora of recent and ongoing publications. By necessity, therefore, I will concentrate on them—at least there is plenty to discuss.

Let me begin with the good news, the *euangelion*. What I have found refreshing is that these approaches are stated openly and clearly. I will give three major examples that are representative of the spectrum in the sense that they illustrate different methods in order to arrive at the same result, the posited anti-imperialism of first-century Christianity (more about that notion later). One approach is to work back from present manifestations of empire. A high-profile example is Richard Horsley's *Jesus and Empire: The Kingdom of God and the New World Disorder* (2003). It starts with a discussion of American identity, moves on to Rome's role as single superpower and, in the end, to a lengthy treatment of "Christian Empire" and "American Empire"—the parallels between the undesirable and oppressive empires of America and Rome are a leitmotif. In that context, the true character of the Jesus movement is constructed as a struggle for social justice, hence the appeal of the New Testament to the *campesinos* in Central America. Hal Taussig, in his prologue to the 2004 Union Theological Seminary conference on "New Testament and Roman Empire: Shifting Paradigms for Interpretation," is just as forthright: "Convened at a time where empire had reemerged as one of the most dangerous and frightening phenomena of our time, the conference addressed directly the ways the New Testament"—liberated at last from centuries of imperial cooptation—"can help shape ways of resisting and negotiating the realities of arrogant power today."[3]

In so many words, the objective is not, unlike a favorite news channel, to be fair and balanced, but to pursue an openly stated *Tendenz*. The lens is clear, but the resulting view can only be blinkered.

Regarding my second methodological example, Warren Carter can speak for himself and does just that in an excellent paper in this collection. I cited his caveats about an all too monolithic anti-imperial interpretation of the New Testament in my earlier paper, but there is one methodological issue taken up by him on which I want to comment. I am referring to his review of Seyoon Kim's

---

3. Brigitte Kahl, Davina C. Lopez, and Hal Taussig, eds., "The New Testament and Roman Empire: Shifting Paradigms for Interpretation," *USQR* 59 (2005): 1.

Christ and Caesar (2008), which I take is not one of his favorite books.[4] A preliminary sidebar: he labels it as anti-anti-imperial, and back we are in the wonderful world of academic dichotomizing that Wendy Doniger, among others, has critiqued with her usual articulation and wit. She usefully quotes Thomas Laqueur's comment on the tendency to impose a "sense of opposition onto a world of continuous shades of difference and similarity."[5] That is a very apt characterization of the world of the Roman Empire and early Christianity. There was a broad spectrum of interactions, by no means limited to anti and pro. Similarly, those of us who don't buy into the construction of early Christianity as a single-minded anti-imperial movement are not *ipso facto* singing *laudes imperii*. Instead, we are seeking to do justice—and that is an aspect of justice, too—to the many faces, and facets, both of the Roman Empire and the various, and varied, Christian communities. It is a task we need to pursue and that, in fact, is what a small but increasing number of New Testament scholars are doing.

Back to method. One of Warren's heuristic instruments is postcolonial theory. A flashpoint comes with Paul, Rom 13:1-7, Paul's admonition to be subservient to worldly rulers. Now, as I said in my earlier paper, citing Neill Elliott, even if we do not take it as expressing "a univocally positive attitude toward 'the governing authorities'" it does show that for Paul, too, there existed contingencies.[6] By contrast and in terms of postcolonial interpretive strategies, Paul's statement can be construed as self-protective mimicry, cooption, or coding. The result, if not the aim, is to elide any discrepancies, contradictions, and variations of point of view in Paul's oeuvre in order to make him and his message uniform. But what compelling, intrinsic reason is there for us to do that? By his own explicit admission, he prided himself on being all things to all people (1 Cor 9:19-23). As for the method, it is good to be in Europe at the moment where such theories often begin and, conversely, end earlier than they do in American academe (a reason may be that theories don't have tenure, but their proponents do). I simply want to advert to the recent article by the very well credentialed French Africanist Jean-François Bayart, "En finir avec les études postcoloniales,"[7] that critically addresses itself to methodological weaknesses like prioritizing discourse and representation over solid empirical research.

---

4. Warren Carter, review of Seyoon Kim, *Christ and Caesar: The Gospel and the Roman Empire in the writings of Paul and Luke*, Review of Biblical Literature (2009). Online: http://www.bookreviews.org/bookdetail.asp?TitleId=6957&CodePage=6957,1856,2845

5. Wendy Doniger, *The Implied Spider: Politics and Theology in Myth* (American Lectures on the History of Religions 16; New York: Columbia University Press, 1998), 148.

6. See the extensive commentary by Robert Jewett, David Roy Kotansky, and Eldon Jay Epp, *Romans: A Commentary* (Hermeneia; Minneapolis: Fortress Press, 2007), 780-803.

7. Jean-François Bayart, "En finir avec les études postcoloniales," *Le débat* 154 (March-April 2009): 119-40.

Again, I am not advocating that we close the doors on this, but make such methodological issues part of our ongoing discussion, though certainly not without continuing empirical work on the ground.[8] Due to my current Max Planck project on history and memory, I am somewhat familiar with the debate, on both sides of the Atlantic, about *Gedächtnisgeschichte*, the related "memory industry," and some of its roots, especially on the American side, in postcolonial theory. One trenchant criticism of such manifestations—and I am not referring to the works of Jan and Aleida Assman, which are in a different category altogether—is that they are "a therapeutic alternative to historical discourse."[9] I have to admit that I find this an apt characterization of outcomes such as Taussig's already cited introduction to the Union Theological Seminary conference and several papers given there; they are notable, just like some writings on memory, for their elegiac and auratic tones, if not their admitted emotionalism. Now, this is not historical scholarship, but I understand the impulse: Seyoon Kim's book, too, ends with an epilogue on "Some Implications for Today."[10] Transfer from academe to pastoral care is not something professional historians at research universities, like myself, have to deal with. Still, desired outcomes for pastoral messages should not impinge on historical research.

My third and last methodological example does, in fact, exhibit a noteworthy amount of historical research, though, as we will see, it is incomplete. A good representative is Justin Hardin's recent monograph on *Galatians and the Imperial Cult*. Here, evidence is industriously gathered from historical sources, archaeology, and numismatics that pertains to the province of Galatia and especially some of its major cities like Pisidian Antioch in the Julio-Claudian period. No doubt, the Roman imprint is noticeable or, as Hardin puts it with a nice evocative touch, "from this brief sketch we can conclude that Pisidian Antioch drank freely from the fountains of Rome."[11] This effort to establish the contemporary setting is not an end in itself, but serves as support for the hypothesis that the troubles referred to in Gal 6:12–13 may involve lack of obeisance to the imperial cult. And I want to stress that Hardin is very careful with such hypotheses in contrast to other New Testament scholars who have been a great deal more absolute on the basis of a far slimmer command of the Roman evidence. Here, too, is progress.

---

8. As exemplified by Ramsey MacMullen, *The Second Church: Popular Christianity, A.D. 200–400* (WGRWSup 1; Atlanta: Society of Biblical Literature, 2009).

9. Kerwin Lee Klein, "On the Emergence of Memory in Historical Discourse," *Representations* 69, Special Issue: Grounds for Remembering (Winter 2000): 145.

10. Seyoon Kim, *Christ and Caesar: The Gospel and the Roman Empire in the Writings of Paul and Luke* (Grand Rapids, Mich.: Eerdmans, 2008), 200–203.

11. Justin K. Hardin, *Galatians and the Imperial Cult: A Critical Analysis of the First-Century Social Context of Paul's Letter* (WUNT 2/237; Tübingen: Mohr Siebeck, 2008), 63.

Let me use this, in the spirit of our program unit, as an opportunity for dialogue and tell you what an ancient historian (not a reference to my age) would do differently here.

There is good attention to detailed, on-the-ground evidence here in one particular region. This agrees well with the general development of scholarship on the Roman Empire in the past three decades or so. The underlying recognition is that we are dealing with individual circumstances, social and political, and, in terms of tradition, in individual places. You can see this, too, in Warren Carter's book on the Gospel of John[12] that addresses itself to the specific situation in Ephesus; similarly, Stephan Witetschek's massive first volume on early Christianity in Ephesus.[13] One size clearly does not fit all. But here Hardin, like many other New Testament scholars writing about the Roman empire, makes up for that deficit by going wholesale rather than retail by resorting to totalizing terms like "imperial ideology" and equally sweeping generalizations such as "the imperial cult was the fastest growing religion of the first century.... Imperial ideology wrapped its fingers around the very fabric of society, so that life itself revolved around the emperor and the divine family."[14]

These are, of course, exactly some of the issues we need to make part of our continuing discussion. The view that is held here is Rome-centric and has, as I mentioned earlier, been abandoned in our discipline for quite some time.[15] All one needs to do is look at the cutting-edge scholarship on Romanization.[16] Also, what is meant by ideology? Is the New Testament ideological, too? How so? "Propaganda" has now generally been discarded, and "ideology" has crept in to fill some of that void, but it needs definition. And it is curious, but by no means untypical, that the one book—and it is a good book (precisely because it leaves plenty of room for disagreement)—that revives this notion even in its title, Cliff

---

12. Warren Carter, *John and Empire: Initial Explorations* (New York: T&T Clark, 2008).
13. Stephan Witetschek, *Ephesische Enthüllungen 1: Frühe Christen in einer antiken Grossstadt: zugleich ein Beitrag zur frage nach den Kontexten der Johannesapokalypse* (Biblical Tools and Studies 6; Leuven: Peeters, 2008).
14. Hardin, *Galatians*, 23.
15. Cf. the discussions by Simon R. F. Price, "Response," in *Paul and the Roman Imperial Order* (ed. Richard A. Horsley; Harrisburg, Pa.: Trinity Press International, 2004), 175–83, and Louise Revell, *Roman Imperialism and Local Identities* (Cambridge: Cambridge University Press, 2009).
16. Paradigms are Greg Woolf, "Becoming Roman, Staying Greek: Culture, Identity, and the Civilizing Process in the Roman East," *PCPhS* 40 (1994): 116–43, Greg Woolf, *Becoming Roman: The Origins of Provincial Civilization in Gaul* (Cambridge: Cambridge University Press, 1998), and Simon Keay and Nicola Terrenato, eds., *Italy and the West: Comparative Issues in Romanization* (Oxford: Oxbow, 2001).

Ando's *Imperial Ideology and Provincial Loyalty in the Roman Empire*,[17] is not cited by Hardin. Nor, for that matter, are Susan Alcock's several nuanced analyses of Greece and the east at that time,[18] and so on. Life was far richer and more varied in all these places than to "revolve around the emperor";[19] at the other end of the spectrum from the *Gleichschaltung*, ideological and other, that is posited here is this view by a Roman historian, in response to the argument that the amphitheater, like the imperial cult, was a means of social control: "It is hard to imagine a state less pervasively prevalent than that of the Romans of the principate. Outside the capital itself, the Roman Empire was a libertarian's dream."[20] Contributing to that assertion is the Romans' general practice of leaving native systems of jurisdiction alone, so long as they were not flagrantly contravening generally accepted norms, reserving only the administration of capital punishment for themselves.[21] So here is another topic for future investigation: in Galatia and other venues of Paul, who exactly are the authorities that are pressing demands? Or are throwing Paul in jail, only to release him, time and again? What do we really know about these authorities and their reasons?

The big elephant that fills the room that is otherwise empty of probative evidence is, of course, the imperial cult. It is a matter of definition whether to label it as "the fastest growing *religion* in the first century" (italics mine). For the lay public, that kind of terminology puts it on the same level as the evangelical movement in our days, and that is simply the wrong matrix. It is more accurate to say that it was one of the fastest growing *civic activities* in the first century. As for the fastest growing *religion* at the time, we need to look at Isis who, as I outlined in my earlier paper, is not just an escapist cult, but often the more touchy-feely companion to that of the Roman emperor—here is another suggestion for a future program. A principal problem, however, is the unwarranted projection of the use the imperial cult as a litmus test for loyalty or whatever from later times into the first century. That evidence simply is not there. Nor is it an issue in Acts or, as

---

17. Clifford Ando, *Imperial Ideology and Provincial Loyalty in the Roman Empire* (Berkeley and Los Angeles: University of California Press, 2000).

18. E.g., Susan E. Alcock, ed., *The Early Roman Empire in the East* (Oxbow Monograph 95; Oxford: Oxbow Books, 1997), and Susan Alcock, "The Reconfiguration of Memory in the Eastern Roman Empire," Susan Alcock, in *Empires: Perspectives from Archaeology and History* (ed. Susan E. Alcock, *et al.*; Cambridge: Cambridge University Press, 2001), 323–50.

19. A point well made and illustrated most recently by Revell, *Roman Imperialism*. The issues are far more varied and less monolithic. One major example is identity: it is fluid and "becomes more of a position within a range of possibilities (or discourse) rather than a fixed set of givens" (8).

20. J. E. Lendon, "Review: Gladiators," *CJ* 95 (2000): 402–3.

21. See, e.g., John Crook, *Law and Life of Rome: 90 B.C. – A.D. 212* (Aspects of Greek and Roman Life; Ithaca, N.Y.: Cornell University Press, 1984), esp. 39–40.

James McLaren[22] has pointed out, in the relations of Jews and Romans during that period. Now, it is not that absence of evidence should always be used in a rigid fashion. At Antioch on the Orontes, for example, as Warren Carter points out in his paper, there is no extant evidence of a temple of the imperial cult, but it would be unreasonable to conclude that this means there was none. In the case of hypothesizing the use of the imperial cult as a persecutorial tool the situation is different as we find only sparse, if any, attestation of it in the first century in contrast to later times.

There is no reason to pursue such dead ends when there are far more promising starting points for gauging the possible role of that cult for Paul and the early Christian communities, and these are the kind of issues I want to outline in this last part of my paper. A good example is the following characterization by James Rives in his recent book *Religion in the Roman Empire*: "These ambiguous and varied expressions of the emperor's religious role actually increased his importance for the religious integration of the empire, since they allowed him to be accommodated within a tremendous range of different traditions. Even Judaeans and Christians, although rejecting any implication that the emperor was himself a god, granted his unique status in relation to the divine."[23] Rives then goes on to point out the continuance of the cult in Christian times and I can refer to my discussion of that topic in my previous paper. Rather, it is the combination of local adaptation and integrative overall framework that strikes me as a perfect model for Paul's own work. There is, at least so far as I can see, considerable consensus in Pauline studies that "each letter is a piece of ad hoc correspondence with a particular community in a distinctive local situation."[24] *Mutatis mutandis*, the same applies to the imperial cult. Now, when it comes to the other part of the equation, the unifying element, one answer on the Pauline side, as we all know, has been to posit his "anti-imperial" message. I would argue, once more, that this is overshooting the target. It seems to me that part of this search for unity, in addition to other factors, is a reaction to the recent highlighting—take some of Bart Ehrman's best-selling books[25]—of the welter of contradictions and divergences in the New Testament. Understandably, there is a desire to come up with some kind of e pluribus unum.

---

22. James S. McLaren, "Jews and the Imperial Cult: From Augustus to Domitian," *JSNT* 27 (2005): 257–78.

23. James B. Rives, *Religion in the Roman Empire* (Blackwell Ancient Religions; Malden, Mass.: Blackwell, 2007), 155.

24. Price, "Response," 175.

25. Most recently, Bart D. Ehrman, *Jesus, Interrupted: Revealing the Hidden Contradictions in the Bible (and Why We Don't Know About Them)* (New York: HarperCollins, 2009).

This brings us back to the underlying reasons and impulses for our cooperative dialogue. Indeed, it is absolutely crucial to study, at last, the many aspects of the embeddedness of Paul, the Gospels, and the early Jesus communities in their cosmopolitan Roman environment and their engagement with it. It is a political environment, but not in a narrow, totalizing way that has provoked an equally narrow and totalizing "anti-imperial" response. Instead, that environment, call it *politeuma* (a term used by Paul; Phil 3:20), was an amalgam of local structures of power, traditions, social customs, and the Roman framework. Paul, for one, engages with it over a broad range of social and religious values.[26] Unsurprisingly, he and the evangelists use the language of that political environment not in the least because it is understood by their audiences. The range and intent of such parallelisms, as I pointed out in my previous paper, again cannot be interpreted narrowly and one-sidedly. There are polemics, but far from exclusively so. The label "anti-imperial" may be convenient, but it is too heavy-handed and imprecise. We have sharper instruments these days just for determining the Romans' diverse notions of *imperium*, notably John Richardson's study *The Language of Empire*.[27]

Instead of "anti-imperialism," therefore, the unifying message can be defined better in terms of "surpassing" or "superiority." Consider the various passages discussed in connection with my earlier paper, such as Paul's citing "peace and security" (1 Thess 5:3) and resonances of the terminology one finds, though by no means uniformly, in inscriptions pertaining to the imperial cult. The emperor is a guarantor of peace, provider of material blessings, savior, and so on. Paul's message is not *anti*-imperial, but *supra*imperial: the emperor and the dispensations of empire go only so far. They are surpassed, in a far more perfect way, by God and the kingdom of heaven.

There are two related factors that enlarge this basic latitude for accommodation. One is strong apocalyptic expectations: soon enough the imperfections of the present time, the *ponēros aiōn* of Gal 1:4, will be over—and that obviates the need for being an active enemy of the Roman order. Another factor is the concept we see in Rom 13, 1 Peter, and *1 Clement*, among others, that the worldly rulers derive their authority only from their superior in heaven who is, well, superior. The author of *1 Clement*, probably a member of a community of Christians in Rome in the 90s C.E., articulates this in a prayer to God by saying that "you, Lord, have given [emperors] the power of sovereignty through *your* majestic and inexpressible might, so that we, acknowledging the glory and honor which *you* have given them, may be subject to them ...; grant them, Lord, health, peace, harmony,

---

26. Cf. the excellent remarks by Price, "Response," 183.

27. John Richardson, *The Language of Empire: Rome and the Idea of Empire from the Third Century BC to the Second Century AD* (Cambridge: Cambridge University Press, 2008).

and stability" (61.1).²⁸ At the same time, and illustrating the variety of accommodations and negotiations, the author defines the role of these Christians as "sojourners" in Rome; the Greek verb (*paroikein*) connotes "living alongside the others," but not really with them. That concept is defined specifically and succinctly in a brief and elegant defense of Christianity, the *Epistle of Mathetes to Diognetus* (5.5): "[Christians] inhabit their own cities, but as foreigners; they participate in everything as citizens, but endure everything as aliens." The date is approximately 200 C.E. and, again, this is of course not reflective of the attitude of *all* Christians.²⁹

The range of possible interactions, then, was as wide and diverse as the local communities of the Roman Empire on the one hand and the Christian communities on the other; for good reason, just to mention this briefly, there is a lot of emphasis in current German scholarship, too, on early Christianities (plural) and their local character.³⁰ Similarly, these scholars maintain, correctly, that there was no imperial religion, *Reichsreligion*, until Christianity was declared as such.³¹ Paradoxically, then, the view of the imperial cult in these terms is a retro projection of a later *Christian* phenomenon onto the imperial cult especially of the first two centuries.

In sum, we still have so much to do and learn from one another. The subject is incredibly rich and I think we have made a good start with articulating more nuanced approaches—a characteristic of all our papers—than be content with stark antinomies. It was probably inevitable that after centuries of the depoliticization of the New Testament the pendulum had to swing way to the other side at first. My concluding analogy, therefore, is with what I am sure is one of your all-time favorite movies, Mel Gibson's *The Passion of the Christ*. I use it regularly in a course I teach on Greece and Rome in film.³² Here is the point of contact, one that Gibson is very clear about on his website. For centuries, most depictions of the passion, especially in art—and he didn't look at Central and Latin America, where that is quite different—were almost literally whitewashed: maybe a drop of blood here and a scratch there, with the body of Christ remaining miraculously inviolate, ready for the resurrection. Now as you know, Gibson made up for that deficit with a vengeance, leaving nothing of Jesus's ordeal to the viewer's imagina-

---

28. Translation from Michael W. Holmes, ed., *The Apostolic Fathers: Greek Texts and English Translations* (Grand Rapids, Mich.: Baker, 1999); italics mine. Cf. Rives, *Religion*, 156.
29. As Rives (ibid.), 130 notes, " at the same time as he asserts the separation of Christians from the larger communities in which they lived, he also implies participation."
30. An excellent example is Christoph Auffarth, "Die frühen Christentümer als lokale Religion," *ZAC* 7 (2003): 14–26.
31. See now Hubert Cancik and Jörg Rüpke, *Die Religion des Imperium Romanum: Koine und Konfrontationen* (Tübingen: Mohr Siebeck, 2009).
32. http://www.utexas.edu/courses/ancientfilmCC304.

tion. It was his deliberate response to extreme neglect. *Mutatis mutandis* again, the same is true of the treatment of the issues that are our concern. But it is clear that we are at a more advanced stage now, not in the least because of dialogues like this one, and we will emerge in better shape, I trust, than the protagonist did throughout that movie.

BIBLIOGRAPHY

Alcock, Susan E., ed. *The Early Roman Empire in the East.* Oxbow Monograph 95. Oxford: Oxbow Books, 1997.

———. "The Reconfiguration of Memory in the Eastern Roman Empire." Susan Alcock. Pages 323–50 in *Empires: Perspectives from Archaeology and History.* Edited by Susan E. Alcock, Terence N. D'Altroy, Kathleen D. Morrison, and Carla M. Sinopoli. Cambridge: Cambridge University Press, 2001.

Ando, Clifford. *Imperial Ideology and Provincial Loyalty in the Roman Empire.* Berkeley and Los Angeles: University of California Press, 2000.

Auffarth, Christoph. "Die frühen Christentümer als lokale religion." *Zeitschrift für antikes Christentum* 7 (2003): 14–26.

Bayart, Jean-François. "En finir avec les études postcoloniales." *Le débat* 154 (March-April 2009): 119–40.

Beard, Mary, John North, and Simon Price. *Religions of Rome.* Vol. 1: *A History.* Cambridge: Cambridge University Press, 1998.

Cancik, Hubert, and Jörg Rüpke. *Die Religion des Imperium Romanum: Koine und Konfrontationen.* Tübingen: Mohr Siebeck, 2009.

Carter, Warren. *John and Empire: Initial Explorations.* New York: T&T Clark, 2008.

———. Review of Seyoon Kim, *Christ and Caesar: The Gospel and the Roman Empire in the writings of Paul and Luke. Review of Biblical Literature* (2009).

Crook, John. *Law and Life of Rome: 90 B.C. – A.D. 212. Aspects of Greek and Roman Life.* Ithaca, N.Y.: Cornell University Press, 1984.

Deissmann, Adolf. *Licht vom Osten: Das Neue Testament und die neuentdeckten Texte der hellenistisch-römischen Welt.* 4th ed. 1908. Repr. Tübingen: Mohr, 1923.

Doniger, Wendy. *The Implied Spider: Politics and Theology in Myth.* American Lectures on the History of Religions 16. New York: Columbia University Press, 1998.

Ehrman, Bart D. *Jesus, Interrupted: Revealing the Hidden Contradictions in the Bible (and Why We Don't Know About Them).* New York: HarperCollins, 2009.

Hardin, Justin K. *Galatians and the Imperial Cult: A Critical Analysis of the First-Century Social Context of Paul's Letter.* Wissenschaftliche Untersuchungen zum neuen Testament. Series 2.237. Tübingen: Mohr Siebeck, 2008.

Holmes, Michael W., ed. *The Apostolic Fathers: Greek Texts and English Translations.* Grand Rapids, Mich.: Baker, 1999.

Horsley, Richard A. *Jesus and Empire: The Kingdom of God and the New World Disorder.* Philadelphia: Augsburg Fortress, 2003.

Jewett, Robert, David Roy Kotansky, and Eldon Jay Epp. *Romans: A Commentary.* Hermeneia: A Critical and Historical Commentary on the Bible. Minneapolis: Fortress Press, 2007.

Kahl, Brigitte, Davina C. Lopez, and Hal Taussig, eds. *The New Testament and Roman*

Empire: Shifting Paradigms for Interpretaton. Union Seminary Quarterly Review 59.3–4 (2005).
Keay, Simon, and Nicola Terrenato, eds. *Italy and the West: Comparative Issues in Romanization*. Oxford: Oxbow, 2001.
Kim, Seyoon. *Christ and Caesar: The Gospel and the Roman Empire in the Writings of Paul and Luke*. Grand Rapids, Mich.: Eerdmans, 2008.
Klein, Kerwin Lee. "On the Emergence of Memory in Historical Discourse." *Representations* 69, Special Issue: Grounds for Remembering (Winter 2000): 127–50.
Lendon, J. E. "Review: Gladiators." *Classical Journal* 95 (2000): 399–406.
MacMullen, Ramsey. *The Second Church: Popular Christianity, A.D. 200–400*. Writings from the Greco-Roman World Supplement Series 1. Atlanta: Society of Biblical Literature, 2009.
McLaren, James S. "Jews and the Imperial Cult: From Augustus to Domitian." *Journal of the Study of the New Testament* 27 (2005): 257–78.
Peppard, Michael. *The Son of God in the Roman World: Divine Sonship in Its Social and Political Context*. New York: Oxford University Press, 2011.
Price, Simon R. F. "Response." Pages 175–83 in *Paul and the Roman Imperial Order*. Edited by Richard A. Horsley. Harrisburg, Pa.: Trinity Press International, 2004.
Revell, Louise. *Roman Imperialism and Local Identities*. Cambridge: Cambridge University Press, 2009.
Richardson, John. *The Language of Empire: Rome and the Idea of Empire from the Third Century BC to the Second Century AD*. Cambridge: Cambridge University Press, 2008.
Rives, James B. *Religion in the Roman Empire*. Blackwell Ancient Religions. Malden, Mass.: Blackwell, 2007.
Witetschek, Stephan. *Ephesische Enthüllungen 1: Frühe Christen in einer antiken Grossstadt: zugleich ein Beitrag zur Frage nach den Kontexten der Johannesapokalypse*. Biblical Tools and Studies 6. Leuven: Peeters, 2008.
Woolf, Greg. "Becoming Roman, Staying Greek: Culture, Identity, and the Civilizing Process in the Roman East." *Proceedings of the Cambridge Philological Society* 40 (1994): 116–43.
———. *Becoming Roman: The Origins of Provincial Civilization in Gaul*. Cambridge: Cambridge University Press, 1998.
———. "Inventing Empire in Ancient Rome." Pages 311–22 in *Empires: Perspectives from Archaeology and History*. Edited by Susan E. Alcock, Terence N. D'Altroy, Kathleen D. Morrison, and Carla M. Sinopoli. Cambridge: Cambridge University Press, 2001.

CHAPTER 14
RESPONSE TO KARL GALINSKY, "IN THE SHADOW (OR
NOT) OF THE IMPERIAL CULT: A COOPERATIVE AGENDA"

H. Gregory Snyder

Listening to these papers and thinking about the possibilities for future work, I'm reminded of what an important and useful experiment it is that we are all participating in, with this interdisciplinary project on Rome and Religion. And so I too thank Jonathan Reed for organizing the panel, Eric Orlin and Barbette Spaeth for all the hard work they've sunk into the Society for Ancient Mediterranean Religions, and finally to Karl Galinsky, who is in a real sense the godfather of this enterprise.

Karl's comments on disciplinary compartmentalization and the necessity for cross-training are certainly apposite. It has too often been the case that New Testament scholars have treated the Greco-Roman world as background, an approach we might call a Gladys Knight and the Pips approach to the ancient world, with a special emphasis on Gladys Knight at the expense of the Pips. One cannot blame New Testament scholars for focusing on their area of particular interest, but the division into foreground and background threatens to introduce certain distortions. When approaching the subject matter this way, it's hard to avoid privileging the foreground at the expense of the background, and this might lead a person to confuse an area of emphasis with an area of importance—to assume that the things one happens to be interested in at present were more important, more momentous at the time than they really were. It took a long time before early Christianity even got to the stage of being a Pip, let alone Gladys Knight.

In my own case, it has been illuminating to approach early Christianity as a smallish eastern cult group alongside Mithraism and Isis devotion in the context of a class on religions of the Roman Empire. I suppose it might be equally illuminating for a scholar of classics to teach a course on early Christianity, and not simply in a Bible-as-literature course. Along those lines, we might also discuss the ways in which insights from religious studies might be of profit to colleagues in classics.

The narrow focus on the New Testament and an instrumental approach to background—that is, letting the foreground determine what elements of background are given weight or even seen—not only imports distortions and exaggerations but also leaves important things out of account. It's rather like looking at the world through a colander: the field of vision is narrow and spotty. Only the things that happen to fall around the chosen sight lines are visible. Looking at the ancient world with a broader set of interests promises to mitigate both problems.

I'm intrigued with the analogy Karl makes between the imperial cult and the dynamics of Paul's work in different Mediterranean cities, namely, that it can be understood in terms of local manifestations and ad hoc situations, but with some overall integrative center. This strikes me as a very fruitful way to think about imperial cult practices. Karl goes on to suggest that when it comes to Paul, New Testament scholars have found an "integrative center" in Paul's anti-imperial message, partly in reaction to the "welter of contradictions and divergences in the New Testament";[1] and here, there are a few items upon which I would like to comment.

My experience with the field of Pauline theology has taught me that no one has come up yet with a widely acclaimed statement of just what the center of Pauline theology is, and along with Karl, I would seriously doubt whether a deliberate anti-imperial animus should be proposed.

It would be useful, I think, when talking about the allegedly anti-imperial nature of Paul's gospel, to make a distinction between a gospel that is anti-imperial by design and one that is incidentally anti-imperial; that is, given its nature and manifestations, it will at various times and places find itself in competition with imperial ideology. However, that is not its sole or chief purpose. I'm reminded of an anecdote about dialectical materialism that goes back to G. K. Chesterton. Chesterton remarked that it was the error of dialectical materialism to assume that because people always wore shoes when they walked around that the only reason they walked around was to buy shoes. Likewise in this particular example: certain aspects of Paul's message about the God of Israel and his messianic agent Jesus would certainly have found themselves running against the grain of imperial ideology; however, that was not its purpose but rather an incidental result, not a central motivation.

One cannot disagree either, when Karl states that, "desired outcomes for pastoral messages should not impinge on historical research."[2] Still, the field of biblical studies finds itself in a unique position at just this point. Most New

---

1. Karl Galinsky, "The Cult of the Roman Emperor: Uniter or Divider?" paper presented at the Annual Meeting of the SBL, Boston, 2008 (and ch. 1 in this volume), 221.

2. Karl Galinsky, "In the Shadow (or Not) of the Imperial Cult: A Cooperative Agenda,"

Testament scholars remain aware that this collection of pamphlets they study is read as sacred scripture by hundreds of millions of people around the globe, very often in the service of what most academics would consider to be retrograde social and cultural agendas. Can they afford to adopt a purely antiquarian stance in this regard? Scholars stand within, not apart from cultural dynamics and their discipline is not isolated from that conversation, nor should it be. It is entirely appropriate in my view, indeed necessary, for New Testament scholars to bring their expertise to bear on these debates, which are larger and more important than simply "pastoral messages." They cannot ignore the fact that there are seventy million *Left Behind* books in circulation, nor should they. If modern American culture used Ovid in the way it uses the New Testament, then classicists would be leading the charge against superficial misappropriation of the texts they study.

Of course, even if the impulse to find anti-imperial messages in Paul is stimulated in part by current political debates, we need not let the tail wag the dog by allowing "desired outcomes ... to impinge on historical research." I, at least, am so old-fashioned as to believe that a degree of objectivity can be attained when it comes to scientific and even humanistic research. In fact, the whole Society for Ancient Mediterranean Religion experiment is an exercise in ensuring precisely this result and that is why it is so valuable. But I do not think that dog and tail can finally be completely separated. Some, at least, of the questions that biblical scholars ask and the areas they explore will reflect and respond to the pull of modern cultural forces. It would be naïve and simply wrong to think we can step outside these fields of force or to pretend that the questions we bring to the study are not influenced by them.

Finally, to take up Karl's question of whether or not we should call the imperial cult "the fastest growing religion in the first century,"[3] as does Justin Hardin. Karl is right to say that deploying the term in this unqualified way will indeed invite misunderstandings of the imperial cult among the *populi*, who have certain ideas about religion as involving creeds and belief, and even among scholars who have the misfortune not to be connected with these enlightened discussions we're all having. I wonder, however, whether "civic activity" taken by itself may understate the case, simply because most modern people have such a low view of what "civic" entails. The imperial cult obviously has many of the features of a religion: certain ritual practices, cultic personnel, and sites that are much the same as temples erected to the gods. And if it's so much like a religious activity (in modern parlance), why not call it a religious activity and then pursue the

---

paper presented at the Annual Meeting of the SBL, New Orleans, 2009 (and ch. 13 in this volume), 218.

3. Galinsky, "In the Shadow (or Not)," 219.

necessary qualifications? If we were to operate for the nonce with Bruce Lincoln's definition of religion,[4] then the imperial cult seems to qualify at least as far as practices, community (at least partially), and institutional structure. It seems to fail, however, when it comes to setting up a discourse of transcendence.

Or is it rather Lincoln's definition that fails when applied to the ancient world? Must we invoke the notion of transcendence? My hunch is that this element of Lincoln's definition owes a good deal to monotheistic presuppositions and to post-Cartesian metaphysics. For the ancient world, this should probably be revised. It's helpful to realize that the gods for the Romans are not transcendental beings in terms of modern metaphysics. They're more like a kind of personified, hypostasized form of electricity: something invisible, powerful, something that must be handled carefully, but something that is with and among us, something generally beneficial in its effects (the comparison to electricity is Jerzy Linder-sky's). And if one conceives of divine beings in this way, then it's not too far to go to place the emperor on the same spectrum: the emperor is invisible in the sense that he is not present. The approach to him must be carefully handled, but the emperor and the governing structure for which he stands, was also experienced by many people as beneficial, a means by which it was possible to advance one's fortunes. Describing this nexus of activities and allegiances with the adjective "civic" falls short of the ancient reality, in my view. Grander allegiances are at work. If one wanted to go this route, we'd need a more robust notion of civic activities. In any event, with the proper qualifications, I believe we can keep the term "religion" when speaking of the imperial cult, though the term "civic" should surely enter into the explanations that would inevitably follow.

Warren Carter's paper[5] also ably raises many issues of interest to those of us here today. Hearing his account of Revelation, I was again reminded that we're reading something by an extreme individual, someone approaching Rome rather like an apologist for the Taliban would approach America, along with its allies and collaborators. The people he's excoriating, and the figure he dubs "Jezebel," are probably involved in quite modest accommodations with Roman society.

Here too, it is difficult to dispute the general thesis of the paper: that Christians did not negotiate Roman imperial power in a monolithic way. Professor Carter lists several reasons why Christians might have countenanced involvement in the imperial cult, namely that:

---

4. Bruce Lincoln, *Holy Terrors: Thinking About Religion After September 11* (2nd ed.; Chicago: University of Chicago Press, 2006), 5–8. Summarized in Jeffrey Brodd, "Religion, Roman Religion, Emperor Worship," paper presented at the International Meeting of the SBL, Rome, 2009 (as "Defying Religion") (and ch. 4 in this volume), 44–45.

5. Warren Carter, "Roman Imperial Power: A Perspective from the New Testament," paper presented at the Annual Meeting of the SBL, New Orleans, 2009, and ch. 10 in this volume.

1) it was necessary for economic survival
2) resistance had turned out badly
3) they were able to participate in a detached, even ironic fashion, based on superior theological knowledge of the sort that Paul ascribes to his audience in 1 Cor 8—that "no idol in the world exists, and that there is no God but one." Carter is right, I think, to say that this way of accommodating is itself a kind of resistance, an opting out.

He goes on to discuss the ways in which the book of Revelation reinscribes Roman imperial ideology, for example, with the *proskynēsis* of the twenty-four elders. He then looks to texts such as Augustus's *Res Gestae*—where Augustus claimed to have obtained control of all affairs by universal consent (§34)—and episodes in Dio Cassius that would ground Revelation's view of things in terms of actual practice. But I can't help but wonder if this still gives too much credit to the fevered conceptions of the writer of Revelation, and that we, by using this as a lens or a mirror where things are reinscribed, don't get swept up in his exaggerations and his overly bifurcating them-versus-us way of looking at Roman imperial power. While it is true that Augustus claimed to have established "control of all affairs," I suspect we should read this as an idealizing piece of imperial propaganda. Or perhaps we should downgrade the claims about "control of all affairs" and take a little more seriously the statement about "universal consent": rather than a system of top down enforcement, the great majority of the inhabitants of the Roman Empire were in fact consenting in various ways with Roman society and receiving benefits as a result.

In fact, this notion of consent goes some distance toward explaining the befuddlement of Pliny when he encounters Christians in Bithynia. He seems to be genuinely surprised and puzzled that the people he's interrogating withhold their consent, or their willing and voluntary acquiescence to the terms of Roman society. Why would someone do such a thing? What could explain this sort of obdurate stubbornness? He just can't figure it out. Had he been imposing Roman colonial power in a brute-force, top-down way, the reaction would not be so puzzling. The degree to which he's flummoxed is the degree to which this consent was considered utterly natural and taken for granted.

There is a wealth of material in Michael White's paper,[6] all of it admirable, though time constraints upon this response allow for only a brief interaction with its content and claims. Mike does a very sophisticated job of tracing the sinews and ligaments of patronage that would have linked people together, and the term "negotiated symbiosis" is a great help when thinking about how this all works.

---

6. L. Michael White, "Capitalizing on the Imperial Cult: Some Jewish Perspectives," paper presented at the Annual Meeting of the SBL, New Orleans, 2009, and ch. 12 in this volume.

This kind of study truly helps us to imagine how things operated among the streets and *fora* of ancient cities.

The inscriptional evidence provides a fundamentally important alternative to the idealizations present in literary sources (see pp. 174–75 on the "great dicta"). Of course, the inscriptions too have their own rhetoric and their own tendencies towards idealization. This came to mind upon reading Mike's claim:

> Thus, these Jewish inscriptions are meant to do more than just honor officials who have been kindly toward them. Rather, as public displays they are meant to participate in a broader discourse of honors by advertising the elite social networks in which the Jews operated and the status and respect they were afforded. To put it another way, these inscriptions granting honors to provincial officials are in reality claiming and *proclaiming* honors and civic status for the Jews themselves.[7]

I found myself wondering whether an inscription like this was evidence that the Jews *did* in fact operate in these elite social networks or whether, by putting up such an inscription, they were *aspiring* to these sorts of interactions, though not exactly enjoying them in full measure. Putting up an inscription such as this certainly makes a play for such honors, but might it fall somewhat short of the reality? Perhaps. We might say, "the elite social networks in which the Jews aspired to operate and the status and respect they would like to be afforded."

I'll end, if I may, with an observation based on a personal experience. On p. 178, Mike asks how the Jewish community in Akmoneia (Phrygia) would have viewed a benefaction from Julia Severa, who we know to have been a "high priestess and agonothetess of the entire house of the gods, the Sebastoi." How shall we imagine the position in which this action placed the local Jewish community? It raised for me a memory that was helpful in understanding how Roman power might have been conceived. Many years ago, I was involved in running a soup kitchen in New York City, along with a Roman Catholic group deeply inspired by the writings of Dorothy Day and Peter Maurin. We prided ourselves on our ideological purity and our principled stand against the various social and political forces that produced the hundreds of homeless and hungry people we served every week. The thing was run on a shoestring budget, and we were constantly scrambling for food donated from local markets.

Then one day, we received a grant for $5,000 from the Philip Morris Foundation. This placed us in a dilemma: here was the promise of a sizeable gift and yet it came from the sort of capitalist, multinational enterprise that we believed to be part of the problem, and moreover, one that made its money on the backs

---

7. Ibid., 184.

and the bodies of the people that stood in lines outside our doors. It seemed to us that by taking this money, we forfeited our moral high ground: by accepting such a gift, our ideological purity was tarnished. But what was most important, our ideological purity or the welfare of those we served? There was, in the language of the Acts of the Apostles, "no small debate" about the matter, and in the end, we followed the time-honored tradition of taking the money.

I wonder if the Jews of Akmoneia and other cities around the Mediterranean may have found themselves in a similar situation. Some resistant groups might have envisioned Roman imperial power as we imagined the capitalist enterprise and talked about it in totalizing ways that made it look more monolithic, more nefarious, more centrally steered than it really was. In fact, my guess is that the great majority of Jews were more integrated into the conventional social and political structures of their day than we were in ours. We do hear from one who was not: the author of the book of Revelation. John the Elder criticizes certain people in Smyrna "who say they are Jews but are not" (2:9). I would suggest, however, that his influence has been outsized, given its canonical status—a special case of the foreground-background distortion mentioned earlier in this response. By way of closure, I refer us back to a statement early in Mike's paper: "both extremes [total resistance, total assimilation] represent a miniscule proportion of actual Jewish experience across a more gradual and variegated spectrum of responses."[8] It is necessary to mark the extremes in order to see the full spectrum of possibilities but we would err by taking this extreme view as representative of anything but a small—but nevertheless real—minority. As Mike observes, the Jewish residents of Akmoneia do not seem to be overly preoccupied with the Roman response to the Jewish revolt in Judaea. The writer of Revelation, on the other hand, can see nothing else.

BIBLIOGRAPHY

Brodd, Jeffrey. "Religion, Roman Religion, Emperor Worship." Paper presented at the International Meeting of the SBL, Rome, 2009 (as "Defying Religion"), and ch. 4 in this volume.
Carter, Warren. "Roman Imperial Power: A Perspective from the New Testament." Paper presented at the Annual Meeting of the SBL, New Orleans, 2009, and ch. 10 in this volume.
Galinsky, Karl. "The Cult of the Roman Emperor: Uniter or Divider?" Paper presented at the Annual Meeting of the SBL, Boston, 2008, and ch. 1 in this volume.
Lincoln, Bruce. *Holy Terrors: Thinking About Religion After September 11*. 2nd ed. Chicago: University of Chicago Press, 2006.

---

8. Ibid., 174.

White, L. Michael. "Capitalizing on the Imperial Cult: Some Jewish Perspectives." Paper presented at the Annual Meeting of the SBL, New Orleans, 2009, and ch. 12 in this volume.

CHAPTER 15
RESPONSE TO GALINSKY, WHITE, AND CARTER

Nancy Evans

All things are in flux. Disciplinary divisions long seemed firm—philology on this side, history over there; archaeology in this room, classics in that one (Latinists and Hellenists each occupying opposite corners), and religious studies in a different building altogether. But now traditional divisions give way and folks who barely knew each other before find themselves working closely together. I come to this meeting today as a Hellenist who travels throughout these disciplines and has had the delightful experience of witnessing several interdisciplinary groups of scholars get to know each other. So I would first like to thank Professor Jonathan Reed who has played a pivotal role in gathering these groups to work with Professor Karl Galinsky. With his expertise in the Roman Empire and his interests in religion and material culture, Professor Galinsky has been the ideal scholar to address the Society for Ancient Mediterranean Religions and the three Society of Biblical Literature program units that are co-sponsoring this panel. Professor Galinksy's ongoing work on Rome and memory enriches our conversations, and encourages us to travel to some fine cities along the way. The food and culture of Rome and New Orleans are second to none, in the modern world, at least.

In his papers given in Boston and New Orleans Professor Galinsky has moved us even further away from a Rome-centric point of view. Roman authority was not entirely a top-down phenomenon, but it provided an overall framework within which local communities could adapt their own traditions and social customs.[1] As Professor Galinsky has just shown, Paul and the Gospel writers were deeply embedded in their political and social environments—they were engaged with the *politeuma* in active and even creative ways that did not single-mindedly oppose Roman power. Viewing their embeddedness from this perspective we can appreciate how early Christians both made use of common cultural and social

---

1. Karl Galinsky, "The Cult of the Roman Emperor: Uniter or Divider?" paper presented at the Annual Meeting of the SBL, Boston, 2008 (and ch. 1 in this volume), 7.

patterns, and even improved upon them by positioning themselves—or better, positioning their leaders and their god—as superior. While the empire and its worldly rulers are limited, the kingdom of God is not, at least not in the ways that mattered to the early followers of Jesus.[2] This was a point I made in my paper on the Rome panel at the International Meeting of the SBL (2009) when I discussed Paul's speech to the Athenians on the Areopagus as recorded in Acts 17. Among the many idols and altars Paul is said to have seen in Athens he focused on an altar to "the unknown God." As Paul reportedly explained to his Greek audience, the Athenians had unknowingly been worshiping the God of Jesus, the true "Lord of heaven and earth" (Acts 17:24). In this episode Paul (like the Romans themselves) constructed the Athenian past so that the past predicted the new order. And when this Paul in Acts looked to the stones of Athens—the monuments, temples, and altars—he claimed that he was perfecting the local traditions. For the author of Acts Athenian polytheism and traditional piety anticipated the redemption possible in Christ, and this new mode of piety as reportedly preached by Paul was clearly superior. The Acropolis and Areopagus were, to quote Professor Galinsky, "surpassed, in a far more perfect way, by God and the kingdom of heaven."[3]

At our present session, Warren Carter and Michael White have added their voices to our cooperative dialogue, and provided additional evidence that we can use as we try to understand the cultural dynamics of the eastern Mediterranean in the first century. By making judicious use of postcolonial theory, Professor Carter examines some early Christian responses to the exercise of Roman power. The imperial cults (deliberate use of the plural, with a nod to Steve Friesen's Boston paper) operated in pluralistic environments that intertwined the cults of the emperor with the cults of traditional local deities. I find compelling Professor Carter's observation that all such expressions of religious pluralism were not created equal as far as the Jesus believers were concerned.[4] Negotiating imperial power meant something very different to a group that early on was grounded in apocalyptic traditions. This becomes especially evident in Professor Carter's extensive discussion of the Apocalypse of John. His analysis of the figure Jezebel in Revelation reveals the outlines of the disputes that were emerging within congregations in west Asia—further evidence for how Jesus believers did not negotiate empire in a monolithic manner, but rather developed different

---

2. Karl Galinsky, "In the Shadow (or not) of the Imperial Cult: A Cooperative Agenda," paper presented at the Annual Meeting of the SBL, New Orleans, 2009 (and ch. 13 in this volume), 222.
3. Ibid.
4. Warren Carter, "Roman Imperial Power: A New Testament Perspective," paper presented at the Annual Meeting of the SBL, New Orleans, 2009 (and ch. 10 in this volume), 141.

strategies for participating in imperial society. The dynamics of the seven west Asian congregations could perhaps be further analyzed in light of what Professor Galinsky calls the "amalgam" of local structures and Roman framework. Indeed Professor Carter points to evidence that some Christian leaders possibly viewed involvement with imperial society as harmless, and even endorsed cultic participation.[5] In Carter's reading Revelation is not an oppositional text. Rather he observes that the writer John himself was not only embedded in the imperial practices—he even constructed a "superior alternative" to them.[6] Here Professor Carter is very much in line with Professor Galinsky's assessment of Paul, namely that the Pauline message was not *anti*-imperial but *supra*imperial.[7]

Michael White's detailed analysis of Jewish inscriptions from the eastern Mediterranean provides further insight into the wide variety of responses to Roman power. Bringing material evidence to the table complements the work of Professors Galinsky and Carter, especially since the cities represented include communities in west Asia, where the seven congregations analyzed by Professor Carter were located, and Egypt, the traditional home of Isis, whose cult was an important companion for the emperors.[8] These inscriptions can tell us how real Jews handled the ambiguities of being simultaneously Jewish and Roman by keeping to the middle ground between complete assimilation and outright resistance.[9] Professor White argues that this negotiation, with all its ramifications in the economic, political, and social spheres, reveals a "higher degree of accommodation" than we might expect.[10] This makes Jews similar to Greeks in some ways, a similarity that becomes even more pronounced when Professor White discusses shifts in the patronage system that occurred during the early empire. When Augustus brought traditional Hellenistic systems of civic sacrifice, liturgies, and benefaction to Rome, the agonistic ethos of ancient communal life touched even more people, regardless of social class and ethnic background.[11] This echoes two of Professor Galinsky's points—one, when he observes that imperial cult was "one

---

5. Ibid., 144–46.
6. Ibid., 148.
7. Galinsky, "In the Shadow (or Not)," 222.
8. Ibid., 220.
9. L. Michael White, "Capitalizing on the Imperial Cult: Some Jewish Perspectives," paper presented at the Annual Meeting of the SBL, New Orleans, 2009 (and ch. 12 in this volume), esp. 174.
10. Ibid., 189.
11. Ibid., 191, C. R. Whittaker, "Imperialism and Culture: The Roman Initiative," in *Dialogues in Roman Imperialism: Power, Discourse, and Discrepant Experience in the Roman Empire* (ed. D. J. Mattingly; JRASup 23; Providence, R.I.: Journal of Roman Archaeology, 1997), 143–63.

of the fastest growing civic activities" in the first century;[12] and two, that a Jew like Paul engaged with his community by using political language that was very clearly understood by his audience.[13] But Jewish communities throughout the eastern Mediterranean differed from the Greeks in a significant way: when Jews participated in these urban social networks they did so by creating a symbiotic and almost parallel universe that mimicked Roman administrative models and appropriated the common and ancient rhetoric of honors.[14] Their "negotiated symbiosis" was *not* rhetorically framed as superior, and this I find very telling.

As a Hellenist listening to this conversation I see several places where the discipline of classics could make valuable contributions. But before I discuss these, I would like to agree with my fellow respondent Greg Snyder who noted that classicists may well have something to learn from our colleagues in religious studies. Having taught early Christianity, Second Temple Judaism, and early Rabbinic Judaism from within a classics department for many years, I can say that paying attention to religious studies methodologies has definitely changed the way I teach traditional Roman and Greek religions, and changed it for the better. As for how classics could likewise contribute to the study of early Christianity, work being done by classicists like Susan Alcock and Simon Price will continue to deepen our understanding of the complex nature of first-century Greek culture under Roman rule. I think that new work that seeks to better understand sacrificial systems would also be beneficial. The interdisciplinary conference on sacrifice at Boston University last year was a good start. We need new comparative studies of sacrifice—Israelite, Greek, Jewish, republican Roman—all traditions that fed into the imperial cults *and* early Christianity. We need cross-cultural and longitudinal analyses that pay attention to the social and class identities of those who participated in civic sacrificial festivals around the eastern Mediterranean. Related to this is one final area that has perhaps been on my mind the most during these past months. It was mentioned in passing by Michael White.[15] When discussing notions surrounding Jewish and Greek resistance and adaptation to imperial cult—negotiated syncretism, creolization, and Romanization—Professor White reminds us that long before the residents of the eastern empire learned to negotiate Romanization, they had felt the effects of three centuries of Hellenization and learned to adapt to that, too. As he says, this creates "a different cultural framework at the base level," an older framework that any subsequent Roman framework had to build upon and adapt to itself. At some level Romans may have found this preexisting condition called Hellenization con-

---

12. Galinsky, "In the Shadow (or Not)," 220.
13. Ibid., 222.
14. L. Michael White, "Capitalizing on the Imperial Cult," esp. 191–192.
15. Ibid.,192.

founding and foreign—even while they tried to emulate it. This older Hellenistic framework will undoubtedly prove to be complex, multifarious, and once again very local—since ancient customs were, if nothing else, a very local phenomenon. But if the breadth of the combined expertise in this room today can be matched by our willingness to listen across disciplinary boundaries—if we can do this, I am sure we can continue to make good progress.

BIBLIOGRAPHY

Carter, Warren. "Roman Imperial Power: A New Testament Perspective." Paper presented at the Annual Meeting of the SBL, New Orleans, 2009, and ch. 10 in this volume.
Galinsky, Karl. "The Cult of the Roman Emperor: Uniter or Divider?" Paper presented at the Annual Meeting of the SBL, Boston, 2008, and ch. 1 in this volume.
———. "In the Shadow (or not) of the Imperial Cult: A Cooperative Agenda." Paper presented at the Annual Meeting of the SBL, New Orleans, 2009, and ch. 13 in this volume.
Whittaker, C. R. "Imperialism and Culture: The Roman Initiative." Pages 143–63 in *Dialogues in Roman Imperialism: Power, Discourse, and Discrepant Experience in the Roman Empire*. Edited by D. J. Mattingly. Journal of Roman Archaeology Supplementary Series 23. Providence, R.I.: Journal of Roman Archaeology, 1997.
White, L. Michael. "Capitalizing on the Imperial Cult: Some Jewish Perspectives." Paper presented at the Annual Meeting of the SBL, New Orleans, 2009, and ch. 12 in this volume.

List of Contributors

Jeffrey Brodd
Professor of Humanities & Religious Studies
California State University, Sacramento
Sacramento, California

Warren Carter
Professor of New Testament
Brite Divinity School at Texas Christian University
Fort Worth, Texas

Nancy Evans
Associate Professor of Classics
Wheaton College
Norton, Massachusetts

Steven J. Friesen
Louise Farmer Boyer Chair in Biblical Studies
Professor of Religious Studies
The University of Texas at Austin
Austin, Texas

Karl Galinsky
Floyd Cailloux Centennial Professor of Classics
The University of Texas at Austin
Austin, Texas

James Constantine Hanges
Professor of Comparative Religion
Miami University
Oxford, Ohio

Robin M. Jensen
Luce Chancellor's Professor of the History of Christian Art and Worship
Vanderbilt University
Nashville, Tennessee

James S. McLaren
Associate Dean of Faculty of Theology and Philosophy (Research)
Associate Professor and Reader, Faculty of Theology and Philosophy
Australian Catholic University
Fitzroy, Victoria

Eric M. Orlin
Professor of Classics
University of Puget Sound
Tacoma, Washington

Jonathan L. Reed
Dean of the College of Arts and Sciences
Professor of Religion
University of La Verne
La Verne, California

Daniel N. Schowalter
Professor of Classics and Religion
Carthage College
Kenosha, Wisconsin

Barbette Stanley Spaeth
Associate Professor of Classical Studies
College of William and Mary
Williamsburg, Virginia

H. Gregory Snyder
Professor of Religion
Davidson College
Davidson, North Carolina

L. Michael White
Ronald Nelson Smith Chair in Classics and Religious Studies
Director, Institute for the Study of Antiquity & Christian Origins
Professor of Classics and Religious Studies
The University of Texas at Austin
Austin, Texas

Subject Index

Acco (modern Acre), 175n6
Acrocorinth, 63, 75, 77
Acropolis, Athenian
   Antony and, 93
   Augustus and, 95
   Christianity and, 236
   emperors' abuse of, 88
   honors on, 90n27, 91, 92
   religious pluralism and, 4
   wartime damages to, 84, 86
Acropolis, at Pergamum, 92n36, 101–2
Aesculapius, 4, 56, 63
Agrippa, Marcus 89
Agrippa I, 120
Agrippa II, 120, 121, 132
Akmoneia, Phrygia, 176–79, 192, 201–2, 232, 233
Alcock, Susan, 220
Alexander the Great, 85, 87, 92
Amazonomachy, 85
Ampliatus, 189–90
Ando, Clifford, 194, 219–20
Antigonis, 87n16, 92n36
Antigonos, 87, 88, 92n36, 121
anti-imperialism, of first-century Christianity, 216, 217, 222–23, 228, 229
Antinous, 6
Antioch, 139–40, 218, 221
Antiochus, 90n27, 140
Antipas (Herod), 120, 124
Antipas (martyr), 144–45

Antony, 86, 88, 91, 93
Aphrodisias, 4, 147, 180
Aphrodite, 63, 75, 174
Apocalypse, the, 142–46, 199–200, 231, 236–37
Apollo Clarius, 4
Apollo Patroos, temple of, 89n24
appropriation, 10–12, 13, 14, 93, 169, 199
Ara Pacis, 89n26
Archaic Temple, 63
archon, 179, 182–83, 184
Areopagus, 94, 236
Ares, 89, 91
Aristobulus II, 120, 121
Aristogeiton, 91
Artemision, 5
Art of Eternity: Painting Paradise, 153
Asad, Talal, 44
Ascanius, 55
Asclepius, 4, 5, 63, 144
Athenagoras, 5–6
Athena Parthenos, 84n3, 88n19, 92
Athens
   Christianity and imperial cult in, 93–96, 236
   establishment of imperial cult in, 86–91
   freedom narrative in, 91–93
   history of, 84–86
   introduction to imperial cult in, 83

Attalids, 85, 92–93
Attalos of Pergamum, 91, 92
Attia Patercla, 190–91
Augustales, 8–9, 67, 70, 72, 190n68, 191
Augustan Culture (Galinsky), 36
Augusteum, 5
Augustus
    appropriation of, 11–12
    Athenian imperial cult and, 88–89
    authority of, 231
    broadened civic participation under, 8–10
    celebrations for, in Pergamum, 106–7
    honors to, 5
    Parthians and, 93
    provincial cults established under, 3
    resistance to, 95
    Roman religion under, 51–58
    statue of, from Julian Basilica, 68
    submission of nations and, 147
Aurelius Julianus, 196–98, 209–10
aurum coronarium, 165–67

Bacchanalia, 52
Bakchai (Euripides), 31, 40
Balch, David, 8
Basil, 17
Bayart, Jean-François, 217
Beard, Mary, 36–37, 38
Bendlin, Andreas, 56
benefaction, 189–98, 231–33. *See also* capitalization on imperial cult
Berenike, Cyrenaika, 181–84, 204–7
Berger, Peter, 41
Bernett, Monika, 113, 127
Bhabha, Homi, 30, 32
Bookidis, Nancy, 75
boule, 103, 179–80

Bourdieu, Pierre, 193
Bowersock, Glen, 16
Brenk, Beat, 159–60
Brown, Peter, 156–57
Brutus, 11, 12, 86, 92
Burrell, Barbara, 102–3, 104–5, 107
Bush, George W., 24–25

Caesareion, 185n50
calendars, of Roman festivals, 53–54, 56
Caligula, 3, 16
Camillus, 50–51
capitalization on imperial cult
    conclusions on, 198–200
    discussion on, 188–98
    introduction to, 173–75
    depicted through honors in Jewish inscriptions, 175–88, 201–10
Capitolia, 54
Capitoline Hill, 50, 53, 54
Capitoline Triad, 54
Capitolium, 5
Caracalla, 180, 186–88, 196–97, 208–10
Carter, Warren, 4, 6–7, 13, 216–17, 219, 230–31, 236–37
Cassius, 12, 86, 92, 121, 128n50
Cenchreae, 13
Central Temple (of Sanctuary of Demeter and Kore, Acrocorinth), 75, 76, 77
Ceres, Liber, and Libera, Santuary of, 63, 65n5, 75, 76, 77
Cestius, 116, 123
Chara, 75, 77
Chesterton, G. K., 228
chi rho, 160–62
Christ and Caesar (Kim), 216–17, 218

Christ child, presentation of gifts to, 167–69
Christian art and iconography
  christogram and chi rho in, 158–63
  conclusions on, 169–70
  crowns in, 163–69
  introduction to, 153–58
Christianity
  anti-imperialism of first-century, 216, 217, 222–23, 228, 229
  Athenian imperial cult and, 93–96
  engagement with imperial cult, 10–17, 111–12, 140–42, 221–23, 230–31, 235–37
  and honors to emperor, 100
  and missing information on imperial cult, 139–40
  religious pluralism and, 7–8
  Roman imperial power and, 6–7, 137–39, 142–48
Christianization, 199
christogram, 158–63
Christology, 16
Chua, Amy, 2–3
Church Fathers, 14–15
citizenship, rank and, 196n97
civic activity, imperial cult as, 220, 229–30
civic benefaction, 189–98. *See also* capitalization on imperial cult
civic cults, 6–7
civic participation
  in Athens, 8–9
  under Augustus, 8–10
  civic benefaction and, 189–98
  of Jews in Akmoneia, Phrygia, 176–79, 201–2
  of Jews in Berenike, Cyrenaika, 181–84, 204–7
  of Jews in Egypt, 203–4
  of Jews in Ostia, Italia, 185–88, 207–9
  of Jews in Sardis, Lydia, 179–81, 202
Clarian Apollo, 63
Claseas, 141
The Clash of Gods: A Reinterpretation of Early Christian Art (Mathews), 155–56
Claudius, 16, 57, 68, 90n27, 122, 147
Cleisthenes, 87n15
Cleopatra VII, 75–76, 203
coins and coinage
  under Augustus, 9–10
  bronze revolt, at Gamla, 117–18, 130
  Christian symbols on, 161–62
  of Constantine, 164
  Corinthian, 67, 71, 72, 73, 76
  in Galilee, 124, 125
  imperial cult manifested in, 113
  under Trajan, 107, 108
Collins, Adela, 15
Commodus, 5, 186n53, 208
compartmentalization, disciplinary, 215–16, 227
consent, 231
Constantine, 157, 160–62
Constitutio Antoniana, 196n97
consumption, of imperial cults, 24–25
Copi, Irving, 41
Corinth, imperial cult in
  colony of, 67, 76–77
  conclusions on, 76–78
  cultural-cultic involvement in, 145
  embeddedness of, 63–71
  introduction to, 61–63
  women's role in, 71–76
Cornelia Celsa, 189
Crassus, 128

crown, in Christian art, 163–67
Cumanus, 122n29, 128
curia, 190
Cyprian of Carthage, 165
Decentius, 162
Decimus Valerius Dionysius, 181–82, 204–7
Deckers, Johannes, 157, 164, 167–68
decurion, 189, 190, 209
decurionate, 189–90, 209
dei Penates, 55–56, 57
Demeter and Kore, Sanctuary of, 63, 65n5, 75, 76, 77
Demetrieia festival, 90
Demetrius Poliorcetes, 84, 87–88, 90–91, 92
Dendera, 75
diadem, 164
dialectical materialism, 228
Diana Pacilucifera Augusta, 67n15
Diaspora, 26, 174n5, 175n6, 180, 189, 199
dikaiosynē, 12–13
Dio Cassius, 3, 106–7, 148, 231
Dionysus, 8, 84, 87, 90n27, 93n39. *See also* "new Dionysus," Antony as
disciplinary compartmentalization, 215–16, 227
divae, divi, and *divus*, 15, 39, 68, 71
Domitian, 194
Doniger, Wendy, 217
do ut des, 40–41
doves, in Christian art, 162
Drusus Caesar, 89n26

early Republic, 50–51
East, Greek, 6–7, 75, 83, 181
east, the, 3, 4, 8, 10, 15, 111
Egypt, honorific inscriptions in, 203–4
ekklēsia, 13

Eleusis, 75
Elliott, Neill, 217
Elsner, Jás, 27, 29
"En finir avec les études postcoloniales" (Bayart), 217
euergetism, 189–98, 231–33. *See also* capitalization on imperial cult
Eumenes, 91, 92n36
Eusebius, 160–61
expansion, imperial, 191, 198–99
expiations, performed outside Rome, 51–52

"family resemblance" theory, 39
Faustina the Elder, 71, 75
Faustina the Younger, 71, 74
festivals, 53–54, 56, 87n14, 88n20, 90, 105–6
First Peter, 146
First Jewish Revolt, 113, 116–19, 126–32
Flavian Sebastoi, 194
Florus, 118n20, 128n49, 129
Forum, Roman, 53, 66–71
Forum of Ardea, 51–52
Forum of Augustus, 89, 93
Forum of Corinth, 62, 63
Fourth Philosophy, 114n8, 115–16
Frankenberry, Nancy, 44
Frankfurter, David, 199
"friend of Caesar," 193–94
"friend of Rome," 193–94
friendship, euergetism and, 193–95
Friesen, Steve, 4, 38, 102–3, 108

Gabinus, 120, 121
Gaius Caesar, 69, 89, 112–13, 122, 126, 128
Gaius Julius Justus, 187
Gaius Julius Spartiaticus, 78

Galatians and the Imperial Cult (Hardin), 218–20
Galerius, 14, 162
Galilee, Roman presence in
  administrative, 120–21
  conclusions on, 131–32
  cultural and economic, 123–26
  evidence of, 119–20
  First Jewish Revolt and, 116–19
  Galilean responses to, 126–31
  introduction to, 111–16
  military, 121–23
Galinsky, Karl
  on definition of religion, 36
  on religion, 42
Gamaliel II, Rabbi, 175
Gamla, 116–17n14, 117–18, 125–26, 130
Garnsey, Peter, 192
Geertz, Clifford, 43–44
Genius, 57, 67, 77n33
Georgi, Dieter, 12
Gerasa, 75
Germanicus, 16
gerusia, 177, 178n18, 187, 201–2
Gibson, Mel, 223–24
Gigantomachy, 85
Gnosticism, 173
Godfearers, 180
godhead, 15–17
God of Israel, 228
Golden Shield, 12
Good Shepherd, 153, 154, 156
Gordon, Richard, 191
gorgoneia, 92n36
Gospels, the, 2, 15, 222, 235. *See also* John, Gospel of; Matthew, Gospel of
Gradel, Ittai, 45–46
Graham-Dixon, Andrew, 153
Granicus, 92

Greek East, 6–7, 75, 83, 181
"guest friendship," 193

Hadas-Lebel, Mireille, 198
Hadrian, 68, 69, 77, 84, 86, 90
Hanges, James, 175
Hannibal, 51–52
Hardin, Justin, 218–20, 229
Harmodius, 91
Hengel, Martin, 114
Hera Lacinia, 52
Herodian rulers, 120, 124, 126
Herod Agrippa I, 120
Herod Agrippa II, 120, 121, 132
Herod Antipas, 120, 124
Herod the Great, 112, 120, 121, 193
honestiores, 169
Horace, 11
Horsley, Richard, 29, 31–32, 127n47, 216
Hurtado, Larry, 160
Hyrcanus II, 120, 121

identity, 28–30
"ideology," 219
idolatry, 142–43, 145–46
idol meat, 145, 200
imperial cult(s)
  attributes of, 3–7
  Christian engagement with, 10–17
  defining, 46
  growth of, 219, 220–21, 229
  impact of, 8–10
  as plural phenomenon, 24, 83, 99–100, 139
  renewed interest in, 1
  as utopian religion, 57
imperial expansion, 191, 198–99
Imperial Ideology and Provincial Loyalty in the Roman Empire (Ando), 219–20

Indelvia Valerilla, 178
inscriptions, Jewish
    in Akmoneia, Phrygia, 176–79,
        201–2
    in Berenike, Cyrenaika, 181–84,
        204–7
    and capitalization on imperial
        cult, 188–98
    in Egypt, 203–4
    Evans on, 237
    in Ostia, Italia, 185–88, 207–9
    in Philadelphia, Lydia, 209–10
    in Pompeii, 209
    in Sardis, Lydia, 179–81, 202
    Snyder on, 232
interpretation, of imperial cults, 25–26
Irni, Spain, 55, 57
Iseum at Pompeii, 189–90
Isis, 13, 75–76, 189–90, 220, 237
Iuppiter Pantheus Augustus, 4

Jerusalem temple, 127–30, 132
Jesus movement. See Christianity
Jewish experience under Roman rule.
    See also First Jewish Revolt
    in Akmoneia, Phrygia, 176–79,
        201–2
    in Berenike, Cyrenaika, 181–84,
        204–7
    and capitalization on imperial
        cult, 188–98
    conclusions on, 198–200
    in Egypt, 203–4
    Evans on, 237–38
    in Galilee, 127–30
    and integration of imperial cult,
        112–13
    introduction to, 173–76
    in Ostia, Italia, 185–88, 207–9
    in Philadelphia, Lydia, 209–10
    in Pompeii, 209

    in Sardis, Lydia, 179–81, 202
    Snyder on, 231–33
    "Jewish tumult," 184n50
    "Jezebel," 142–48
John, Gospel of, 4, 146–48
John of Gischala, 114, 118
Josephus, 114–18, 122, 129, 174
Jotapata, 116, 117, 125, 132
Judaism. See Jewish experience under
    Roman rule
Judas the Galilean, 115, 122
Julia Augusta, 75
Julia Mamea, 187
Julian Basilica, 66, 68, 69, 70
Julia Severa, 9, 176–79, 201–2, 232
Julius Caesar, 76, 107
Julius Justus, 187, 208
Jupiter, 50, 54, 156
Jupiter Optimus Maximus, 52, 86n9
Jupiter Tonans, 53

Käsemann, Ernst, 141
Kerameikos, 86
Kim, Seyoon, 216–17, 218
kingdom of heaven, 222, 236
Kinney, Dale, 156
Kitagawa, J. M., 6
Klose, Dietrich, 103, 106
Koester, Helmut, 12

labarum, 160, 163
Lachares, 88
Lactantius, 160
Laqueur, Thomas, 217
Lares Augusti, 66
Larson, Gerald, 45
late Republic, 52–54, 57, 193
laurel crowns, 164
Lavinium, 55–56
Left Behind, 229
Lévi-Strauss, Claude, 33, 40

Licinius, 161
Lincoln, Bruce, 44–45, 230
Livia, 75, 76
Livius Dionysus, 187, 208
Livy, 50, 51, 53
locality, 30–31, 33
locative religion, Roman religion as, 49–56
Long Rectangular Building (in Corinth), 77n33
Lucius Caesar, 70
Lucius Servenius Cornutus, 178, 202
Lucius Serventus Capito, 177n13, 178, 202
Lucius Verus, 186n53, 208
ludi Romani, 53
Lupercalia, 50, 53
Lysander, 87n11

MacMullen, Ramsay, 176
Maecenas, 3
magi, present gifts to Christ child, 167–69
Magnentius, 162
Marcus Aurelius, 5, 68, 186n53, 208, 209
Marcus Tittius, 183, 206–7
Marnas, 141
Mars Ultor, 52–53, 89
Mater Augusti, 71
Mater Caesaris, 71
Mathews, Thomas, 155–56
Matthew, Gospel of, 139, 140
Maxentius, 160–61
"memory industry," 218
middle Republic, 50–51
migration, 30–31
Millar, Fergus, 6
Mindius Faustus, 185, 187, 188n64, 207–9
Minucius Felix, 160

Mishnah, 33, 175
Mitchell, Stephen, 146
Mithridates of Pontos, 85–86
Momigliano, Arnoldo, 15
municipal cults, 5–6, 8–9

nations, submission of, 147
negotiation. *See also* Jewish experience under Roman rule
  Christian art and, 169
  of Christians, 139, 141, 148, 223, 231
  Galinsky on, 4, 6–8, 10, 14–15
  Herod the Great and, 112
  and identity construction, 29–30
  of Jews, 175, 192, 237
  and resistance, 31–32
Nemausus, Gaul (Nîmes), 178, 190–91
neocorate temples, 102–4, 106, 107–8
neokorate, 197–98
Neotera, 75–76
Nero, 77, 93, 121, 143
"new Dionysus," Antony as, 88, 91
New Historicism, 1
New Testament studies
  and interaction between Christianity and imperial cult, 140–42
  and missing information on imperial cult, 139–40
  Roman imperial power and, 137–39, 142–48
  study of imperial cult and, 1–3, 215–24, 227–29
Nîmes (Nemausus, Gaul), 178, 190–91
Nohlen, Klaus, 101
normal religion, imperial cults as, 23–26
Norris, Frederick, 156
North, John, 7–8, 36–37, 38
Numerius Popidius Ampliatus, 189–90, 209

Numerius Popidius Celsinus, 189–90

Obama, Barack, 24–25
Octavia, Temple of, 66, 76
Octavian, 88. *See also* Augustus
Odeion (Athenian), 89
Odes (Horace), 11
Ostia, Italia, 185–88, 207–9

Pacatus, 14, 168
Palatine Hill, 50, 53
Palestine, 174n5, 175n6, 186–87
Paniyiri Festival, 105n15
Parthians, 93
passion, the, 158, 160
Passion Narrative, 158, 159
The Passion of the Christ, 223–24
Passion Sarcophagi, 158–68
patronage, 189–98, 231–33. *See also* capitalization on imperial cult
Paul (Apostle)
   appropriation and, 10–11
   and consumption of idol meat, 145
   engagement with imperial cult, 221–22, 238
   Hanges on, 31–32
   postcolonial theory and, 217
   in Thessalonica, 8
   views on empire, 2, 12–15, 228–29, 237
   visit to Athens, 93–95, 236
Pausanias, 66, 76
Penates, 55–56
Penner, Hans, 41, 44
Pergamum and Pergamenes, 4, 9, 92n36, 100–108
Persephone, 75
Persian Empire, 84–85, 92–93
Petronius, 122, 126
Pharsalus, 86

Philadelphia, Lydia, 196–98, 209–10
Philip Morris Foundation, 232–33
Philip V of Macedon, 85, 90–91
Phocaea, 177
pietas, 12
Pinakotheke, 85n4
Pliny the Younger, 100, 231
Plotina, 75
pluralism, 7–8, 49, 66, 139, 140–41, 236
pomerium, 50
Pompeii, 189–90, 209
Pompey, 86, 120, 121, 128
pontifex maximus, 53
Poole, Fitz John Porter, 38–39, 41
Popidius Ampliatus, 189–90
Popidius Celsinus, 189–90
Popilius Zotikos, 176
postcolonial theory, 27–33, 217–18, 236
praefecture, 183, 206–7
praepositus, 182n42
prayers, on behalf of monarchs, 180–81
prefect, 182–83, 203
Price, Simon
   on Christianity and imperial cult, 17
   on definition of religion, 36–37
   on embeddedness of imperial cult, 6
   on negotiation, 4
   and reconstruction of imperial cult practices, 140
   on sacrifices to emperor, 180
   theory of, 25
prodigies, occurring outside Rome, 51–52
proedrion, 177
Propylaia, 85n4

Pro Salute Aug. formula, 185–86, 188, 207
provincial coinage, 9–10
provincial cults, 3
Prudentius, 163, 165
Ptolemaia festival, 90
Ptolemais, 122–23, 175n6
Publius Tyrronius Clados, 176
Publius Tyrronius Rapo, 176n13
Purcell, Nicholas, 107

Quadratus, 102–4, 105

Rabbinic Judaism, 238
Rajak, Tessa, 181, 191
rank, citizenship and, 196n97
Regia, 53
religion
    defining, 35–45
    Lincoln's definition of, 230
    as local phenomenon, 28–31, 33
    locative, 49–56
    politics and, 41
    separation of politics and, 23–24
    theories about character of, 25–26
Religions of Rome (Beard et al.), 36–37
religious pluralism, 7–8, 49, 66, 139, 140–41, 236
Republic, late, 52–54, 57, 193
republican Rome, 192
resemblance theory, 39
Res Gestae, 11–12
resistance. *See also* First Jewish Revolt
    in Athens, 95
    of Christians, 6–7, 15, 30–32, 199–200, 231
    of Jews, 173–74
    patronage and, 191
    responses to imperial cults, 24–25
Revelation, book of, 142–46, 199–200, 231, 236–37

ritual
    importance of place to, 50–52, 54–56
    myth and, 33
Rives, James, 221
Roma and Augustus temple, 106–8
Romaia festival, 88n20, 90
Roman Empire
    absence of information on, 139–40
    appropriation and resistance to, 12, 14–15
    coinage in, 9
    conclusions on, 148
    and interaction between Christianity and imperial cult, 140–42
    introduction to, 137–39
    New Testament evidence of, 142–48
    New Testament studies and, 2–4
    religious life in, 7
Roman religion
    defining, 45–46
    as locative religion, 49–53
    as utopian religion, 53–55
Roman Republic, 53
Roman Senate, 13–14, 51, 148
Roman Senate and People, 13
Rome, republican, 192

Sabina, 75
sacrifice, 87n14, 108, 180, 238
Said, Edward, 40
Salii, 147
Saller, Richard, 192
Sanctuary of Demeter and Kore/Ceres, Liber, Libera, 63, 65n5, 75, 76, 77
Sant'Apollinare Nuovo, 166
Sarapis, 9, 30, 65
sarcophagi (Passion Sarcophagi), 158–68

252 ROME AND RELIGION

Sardis, Lydia, 179–81, 202
Schwartz, Seth, 175, 198–99
Sebastophants, 9
Second Temple Judaism, 238
Senate, Roman, 13–14, 51, 148
senatus consultum, 103–4, 106
Sepphoris, 122, 123, 124–25, 131
Septimius Geta, 186, 208
Septimius Severus, 180, 186n53, 187, 208
Severus Alexander, 187
Sibylline Books, 52–53
Sillyon, Pamphylia, 180
Simson, Otto von, 165–66
"situational incongruity," 33
Smith, Jonathan Z., 33, 37, 38, 39n14, 49–50
Snyder, Greg, 238
Society for Ancient Mediterranean Religions, 27, 227, 229, 235
Society of Biblical Literature, 27, 35, 235
Solomon's Temple, 127–30, 132
"son of god," 6, 17
Soteira, 6, 71
sōtēr, 6, 10, 39
South Stoa, 86n8
Spiro, Melford, 37, 41–42, 45
Squarciapino, M. Floriana, 188n61
Sta. Constanza, 153
Stephen, 165
Stoa Basileos, 86
Stoa of Attalos, 85n6
Stoa of Eumenes, 85n6
Stoa of Zeus Eleutherios, 85n4, 93
Stoa Poikile (Painted Stoa), 85n4
Stroud, Ron, 75
submission of nations, 147
Sulla, 85–86, 88n20
Sullivan, Lawrence, 40
"superhuman beings," 42

Sylleia festival, 88n20, 90
symbolic capital, 193–98
synedrai, 120
Syon, Danny, 117

Tarichaeae, 121n27
Tation, 177
Taussig, Hal, 216, 218
temenos, 102
Temple E, 66, 76
temple of Jerusalem, 127–30, 132
"Temple of Octavia," 66, 76
Terminus, 54
Tertullian, 14–15, 165
theater, in Corinth, 67, 73
Theodosian obelisk, 168
Theoi Sebastoi, 4–5
theos, 16
tholos, 4, 86n8, 88, 95
Thuburbo Maius, 5
Tiberias, 117, 122, 124–25, 131
Tiberius, 3, 5, 16
Tiberius Julius Alexander, 174
titulus, 187, 208–9
Titus, 57, 132, 140
Trajan, 8, 67–68, 74, 86, 100–108
Trajaneum, 100–103, 106–8
transcendence, 50, 230
tropaeum, 160
Tutela, 67

utopian religion, 8, 49, 50, 53–58

Valerius Dionysius, 181–82, 204–7
Valerius Maximus, 55
Varus, 121–22, 123
Veii, 50
Venus, 63
Vergil, 2, 11
Vespasian, 57, 68, 77, 116–18, 123, 132, 174

Vesta, 53, 57
Via Severiana, 187
vir clarrisimus, 104
von Simson, Otto, 165–66

Wallace-Hadrill, Andrew, 10, 54
War Scroll, 174
Webster, Jane, 191
Weisser, Bernhardt, 104, 108
west, the, 3, 8, 10, 95
White, Michael, 231–32, 236, 237–38
Whittaker, Charles, 191
Williams, Charles, 65n5
Witetschek, Stephan, 219

Wittgenstein, Ludwig, 39
women, role of, in imperial cult, 71–76
wreaths, 164, 167

Xerxes, 84, 91

Yonan, Edward, 41

zealot theory, 114–15, 131
Zeus Megistos Sarapis, 4
Zeus Philios, 104–5
Zeus Philios and Trajan temple (the Trajaneum), 100–103, 106–8
Zuiderhoek, Arjan, 194–95

Index of Ancient Sources

Inscriptions

CIG (Corpus inscriptionum graecarum)
435	75
III,4716c	75

CIJ (Corpus inscriptionum judaicarum)
533	208
738	177
766	201
1432	203
1442	203
1443	203
1444	203
1449	204
2.972	187

CIL (Corpus inscriptionum latinarum)
2.2004	4
2.2008	4
10.846	189, 209
10.847–848	189
14.845	187
14.4564	187

IG (Inscriptiones graecae)
I^3 136	31
I^3 383	31
II^2 1076	71
II^2 1283	31
II^2 1361	31
II^2 1938	90
II^2 3173	88
II^2 3257	89
II^2 3272	90
II^2 3276	90
II^2 3277	93
II^2 3440	193
III 899	75
XI^4 1299	30

IGR (Inscriptiones graecae ad res romanas pertinentes)
3.315	202
4.18	5
4.39	9
4.362	178
4.363	178
4.39b.15	16
4.654–656	202
4.1327	177
4.1619	209

IvE (Die Inscriften von Ephesos)
1a.27	194
1a.36	194
2.213	5
2.236	194
2.449	194
3.621	194
3.719	5
4.1385	194

IvP (Die Inschriften von Pergamon)		16.8.4	180
II 269	103		
		Cyprian, *Laps.* 36	165
MAMA (Monumenta Asiae Minoris Antiqua)		*Dig.* 50.2.3.3	180
6.153	202		
6.254	178, 202	Dio Cassius, *Historia Romana*	231
6.262	178, 202	6.21	164
6.263	177, 201	50.5.3	76
6.264	176, 201	50.25.3	76
6.265	177, 202	51.20.1	147
6.266	178, 202	51.20.6-9	106
		52.35	3
OGIS (Orientis graeci inscriptiones selectae)		54.7.2-3	95
		59.24.5	148
414	193		
427	193	Duris (of Samos), Frg. 26.71	87
456	9		
456.45	16	*Epistle of Mathetes to Diognetus* 5.5	223
SIG³ (Sylloge inscriptionum graecarum)			
883	196, 209	Eusebius, *Vit. Const.*	
		1.28-31	160
GREEK, ROMAN, JEWISH, AN EARLY CHRISTIAN WRITINGS		1.31	161
		2.8	161
		2.16	161
Appian, *Mith.* 30-41	85	3.3	161
Apuleius, *Metam.* 11.8	13	*1 Clement* 61.1	222-23
Arrian, *Anab.*		Herodotus, *Hist.*	
1.16	92	5.55	91
3.16.8	91	6.109	91
		6.121	91
Athenaeus, *Deipn.* 9.405	88	7.139	84
Athenagoras, *Leg.* 30.1-2	5-6	Horace, *Carm.* 3.30.13-14	11
Avodah Zarah 3:4	175	Jerome, *Epist.* 69.6	162
Cod. theod.			
16.8.2	180		

INDEX OF ANCIENT SOURCES 257

Josephus		1.180	121
A.J.		1.218–222	128
4.126–158	142	1.203	120
12.24	122	1.208–209	121
14.71–73	128	1.282–283	120
14.74	121	1.303	121
14.82–83	121	1.303–316	121
14.105–109	128	1.314–316	121
14.120	121	1.668	120
14.158	120	2.16–19	128
14.163–176	121	2.39–54	128
14.190–191	120	2.56	121, 122
14.191	120	2.68	122
14.271–276	128	2.117	127
14.385	120	2.118	114, 115
14.413–433	121	2.184	128
14.420–433	121	2.186	140
15.171–172	121	2.192–199	122
17.252–268	128	2.197	180
17.271–272	122	2.215	120
17.288–289	122	2.232–240	128
17.318	120	2.252	120
17.355	127	2.293	128
18.1–2	127	2.360	145
18.90–95	128	2.390–391	145
18.252	120	2.405	128
18.261–309	128	2.411–448	131
18.262–263	122	2.487–498	174
19.360–363	120	2.500–509	123
19.365–366	127	2.510–512	123
20.6–14	128	2.520	123
20.100–102	174	2.562–568	117
20.118–124	128	2.568	117
20.159	120	2.284–292	118
B.J.		2.293–308	118
1.152–154	128	2.408–410	118
1.154	121	2.575	119
1.160	121	3.8	140
1.169–170	120	3.29	140
1.177	121	3.37	116
1.179	128	3.41–42	114

Josephus, *B.J.* (cont'd.)		Lex Irnitana 26	57
3.110–114	116		
3.132–134	116	Livy, *Ab urbe condita libri*	
3.141–288	116	5.52	50-51
3.289–306	116	22.1	52
3.316–339	116	31.23–26	85
3.462–502	116, 117	34.54	50
4.1	117	40.37	52
4.11–53	116	44.4–8	90
4.121–127	118		
4.54–61	116	Pacatus, *Panegyrici Latini*	
4.62–83	116	XII[2].6.4	14, 168
4.84–120	116, 117		
4.558	114	Pausanias, *Descr.*	
5.43–46	174	1.25.7	88
5.244	127	1.29.16	88
5.250–254	118	2.2.3	65
5.367–368	145	2.2.4	65
5.378	145	2.3.1	76
5.396	145	2.3.5	77
5.412	145	2.4.6	65
6.237–238	174		
7.46–51	140	Philo	
7.47–59	140	*Legat.*	
7.54–62	139	201–373	128
7.421	132	317	180
Vita		*Mos.* 1, 2	
30–61	117	1.292–304	142
45	119		
66–69	118	Plato, *Resp.*	
189	118	5.475d	94
341–342	119		
354	130	Pliny the Elder, *Nat.*	
		22.4–7	164
Justin, *1 Apol.* 29.4	6	36.6.45	86
Lactantius, *Mort.*		Pliny the Younger, *Ep.*	231
34	14	10.17a	100
44.5–6	160	10.51.1–2	195
		10.96–97	8, 100
		10.120	195

INDEX OF ANCIENT SOURCES 259

| Plutarch | | Vergil, *Georgics* 3 | 11 |

Plutarch
Ant.
34 93
54.6 76
60 88
Demetr.
12 87
23–26 88
Sull.
12–14 85
13.2–3 86
14.3–4 86

Prudentius, *Cath.* 9.84–85 163

Res gest. divi Aug.
1 11
10 147
34 231

Strabo, *Geog.* 10.3.16 31

Suetonius, *Aug.*
52 107
91.2 53

Tacitus, *Ann.* 14.15 148

Tertullian, *Apol.*
36.2 15
39.20–21 14

Tertullian, *Cor.* 165

Thucydides, *Historiae*
1.20 91
6.54–59 91

Valerius Maximus, *Factorum ac dictorum memorabilium libri IX*
1.8.7 55

Vergil, *Georgics* 3 11

BIBLICAL TEXTS
(INCLUDING APOCRYPHA)

Gen 37–50 145

Num 22–24 142

1 Kgs
16:31–34 142
18:4 142
18:13 142
19:1–3 142
21:23–24 142
21:25 142

2 Kgs
9:22 142
9:30–37 142

Ps 106:34–39 142

Isa
2:1–4 147
10:5–11 145
44:28 145
45:1 145

Jer
25:1–11 145
29:4–7 145

Ezek
16:15 142
16:34 142
16:52–63 147

Hos 4:10–19 142

Mic 4:1–4 147

Hab	13	9:25	165
		15:54–56	169
2 Macc 6:12–17	145		
		2 Cor	
Matt	13	2:14	169
4:8–9	143	4:4	16
8:5–13	123		
27:36	159	Gal	
27:54	163	1:4	2, 222
		2	12
Luke		6:12–13	218
4:5–7	143		
7:1–10	123	Phil	
		2:6	15
John	4, 7, 13, 146	2:6–11	16
18:36	169	3:20	222
Acts		Col 2:15	162–63, 169
10	123		
15:20	144	1 Thess 5:3	12, 222
17:7–9	8		
17:15–34	94	2 Tim 4:8	165
17:16	94		
17:19–20	94	Jas 1:12	165
17:23	94		
17:24	95, 236	1 Peter	222
17:29	94	1:1	200
19	5, 145	2:11–17	146
19:21–41	145	2:12	146
19:27	145	2:13–15	15
		2:13–17	200
Rom		2:14–17	144
1:17	13	2:15	146
13	222	2:17	15, 146
13:1–7	14, 217	4:3	146
		5:4	165
1 Cor			
8	231	Rev	199
8–10	144	1:3	142
8:4	145	1:5	145
9:19–23	217	1:10–13	142

2–3	142, 145, 200	7	166
2:4	142, 169	12:9	143
2:5	142	13:3–4	143
2:6	142	13:12	143
2:9	142	13:14	143
2:10	165	13:16	143
2:13	142, 144	15:4	147
2:14	142, 200	17:1	143
2:14–15	142	17:2	142
2:16	142	17:4	143
2:19	233	18:3	142
2:20	142, 200	18:4	148
2:20–23	200	18:9	142, 143
2:22	142	18:11	143
3:2	142	18:17	143
3:3	142	18:22	143
3:9	142	18:23	143
3:11	165	19:12	164
3:20	142	19:15	147
4–5	147	19:20	143
4:1	142	20:3	143
4:4	147	20:10	143
4:10–11	147	21:9	147
4:11	147	21:24	147
5:11	147	22:9	142

www.ingramcontent.com/pod-product-compliance
Lightning Source LLC
Chambersburg PA
CBHW021822300426
44114CB00009BA/279